When we can make our schedules work, my editor and I will have our meetings over drinks. One of the best things about these meetings is that they're very positive. The downside is that, the next morning, I don't remember much of what we went over.

This is my natural hair.

What about it?

HARUICHI FURUDATE began his manga career when he was 25 years old with the one-shot *Ousama Kid* (King Kid), which won an honorable mention for the 14th Jump Treasure Newcomer Manga Prize. His first series, *Kiben Gakuha, Yotsuya Sensei no Kaidan* (Philosophy School, Yotsuya Sensei's Ghost Stories), was serialized in *Weekly Shonen Jump* in 2010. In 2012, he began serializing *Haikyu!!* in *Weekly Shonen Jump*, where it became his most popular work to date.

HAIKYU!!

VOLUME 17
SHONEN JUMP Manga Edition

Story and Art by
HARUICHI FURUDATE

Translation ■ **ADRIENNE BECK**
Touch-Up Art & Lettering ■ **ERIKA TERRIQUEZ**
Design ■ **JULIAN [JR] ROBINSON**
Editor ■ **MARLENE FIRST**

First published in Japan in 2012 by SHUEISHA Inc., Tokyo.
English translation rights arranged by SHUEISHA Inc.

Printed in the U.S.A.

Published by VIZ Media, LLC
P.O. Box 77010
San Francisco, CA 94107

10 9 8 7 6 5 4 3 2 1
First printing, November 2017

SHONENJUMP MANGA

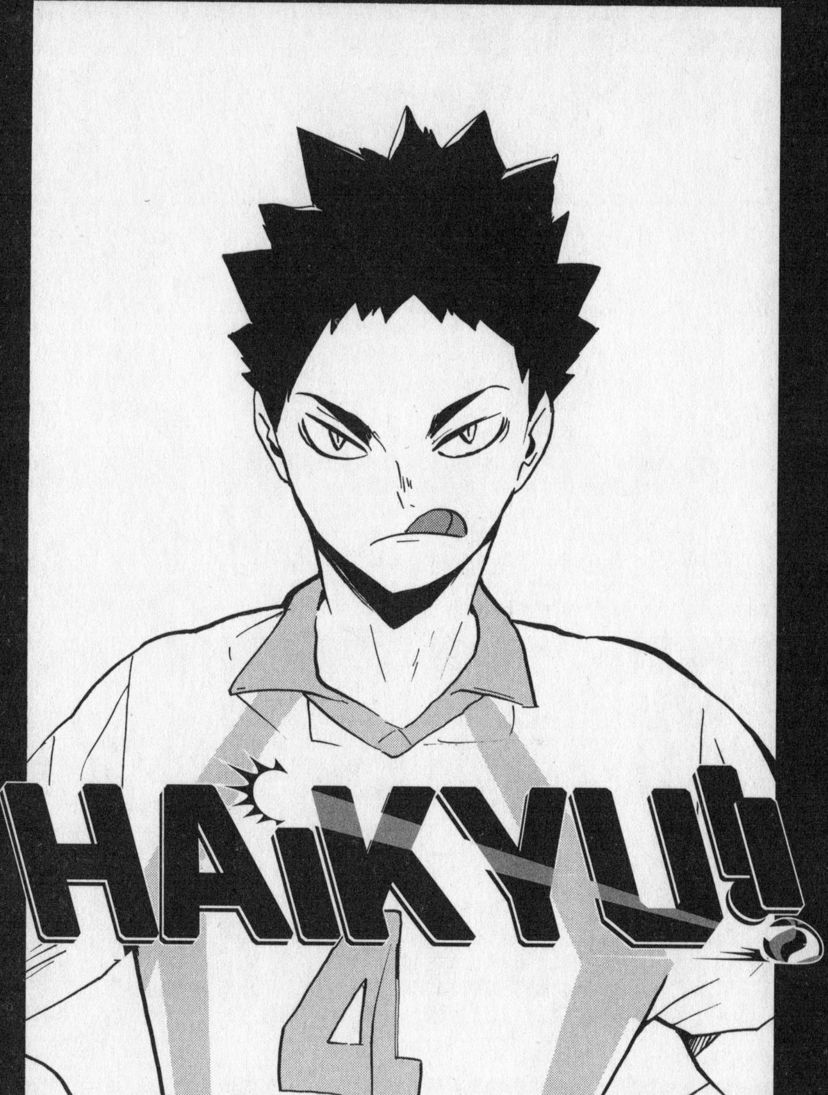

HAIKYU!!

HARUICHI FURUDATE

TALENT AND INSTINCT 17

Karasuno High School Volleyball Club

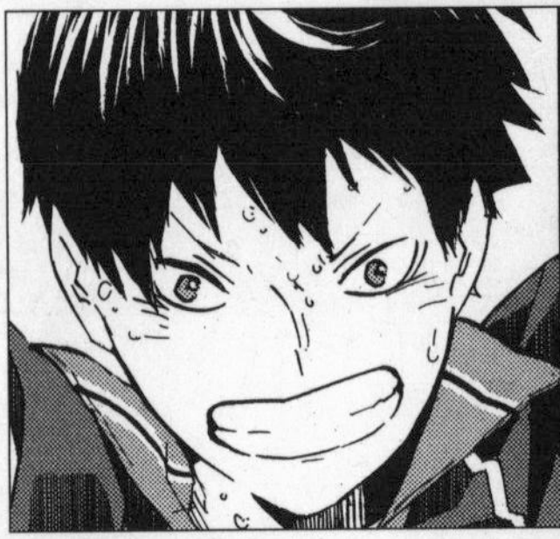
TOBIO KAGEYAMA

1ST YEAR / SETTER
His instincts and athletic talent are so good that he's like a "king" who rules the court. Demanding and egocentric.

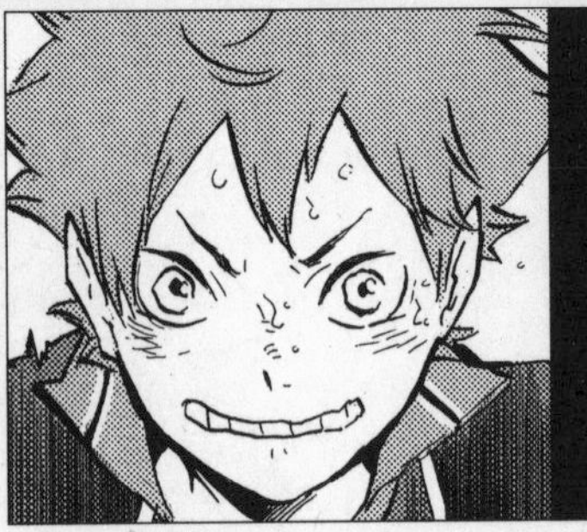
SHOYO HINATA

1ST YEAR / MIDDLE BLOCKER
Even though he doesn't have the best body type for volleyball, he is super athletic. Gets nervous easily.

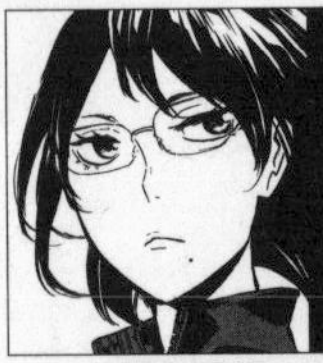
KIYOKO SHIMIZU

3RD YEAR
MANAGER

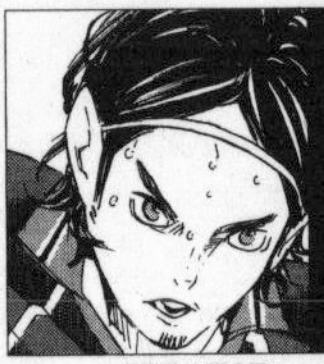
ASAHI AZUMANE

3RD YEAR
WING SPIKER

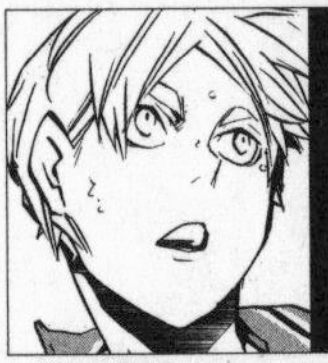
KOUSHI SUGAWARA

3RD YEAR (VICE CAPTAIN)
SETTER

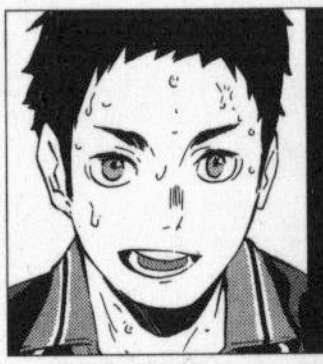
DAICHI SAWAMURA

3RD YEAR (CAPTAIN)
WING SPIKER

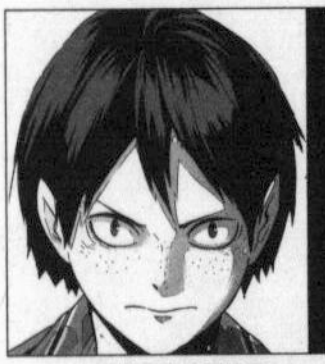
TADASHI YAMAGUCHI

1ST YEAR
MIDDLE BLOCKER

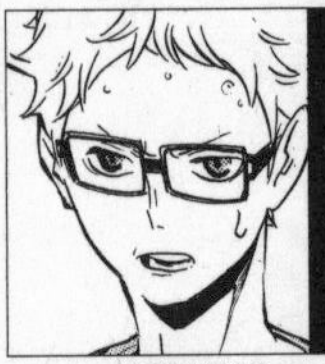
KEI TSUKISHIMA

1ST YEAR
MIDDLE BLOCKER

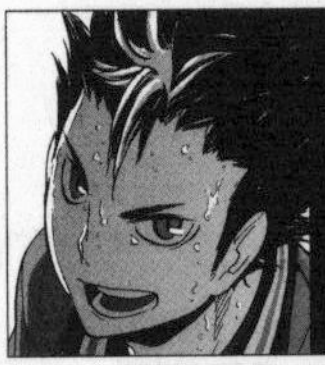
YU NISHINOYA

2ND YEAR
LIBERO

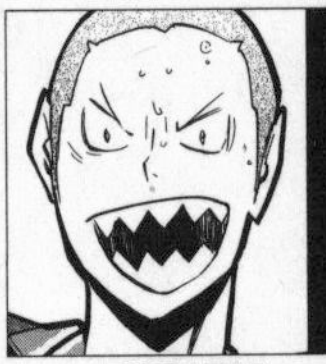
RYUNOSUKE TANAKA

2ND YEAR
WING SPIKER

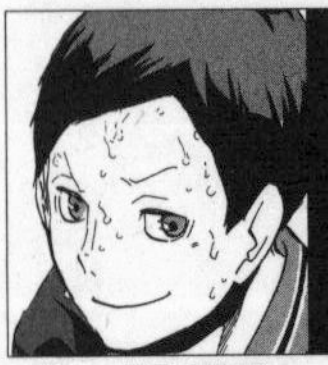
CHIKARA ENNOSHITA

2ND YEAR
WING SPIKER

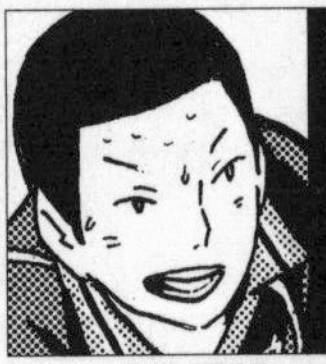
KAZUHITO NARITA

2ND YEAR
MIDDLE BLOCKER

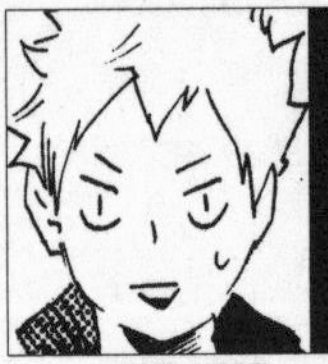
HISASHI KINOSHITA

2ND YEAR
WING SPIKER

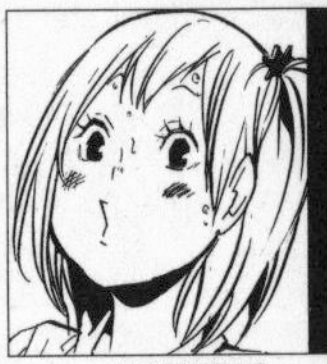
HITOKA YACHI

1ST YEAR
MANAGER

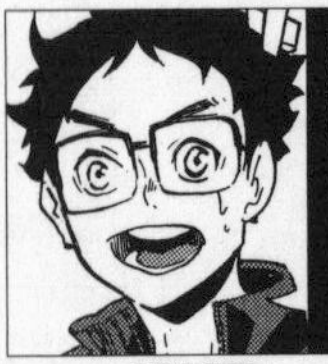
ITTETSU TAKEDA

ADVISER

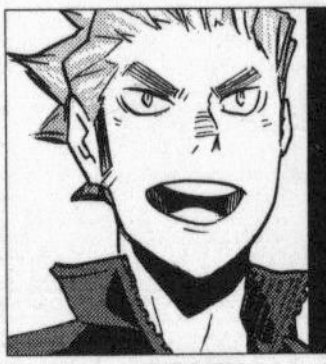
KEISHIN UKAI

COACH

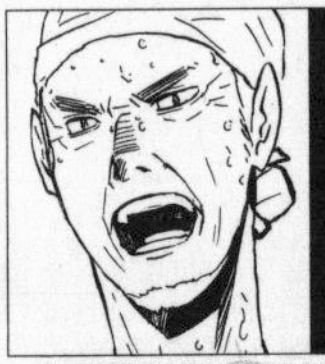
IKKEI UKAI

FORMER HEAD COACH

CHARACTERS

MIYAGI PREFECTURE SPRING TOURNAMENT QUALIFIER TOURNAMENT ARC

Aoba Johsai Volleyball Club

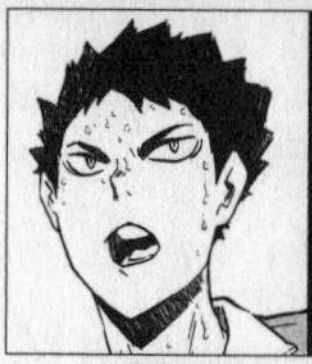
HAJIME IWAIZUMI
3RD YEAR
WING SPIKER

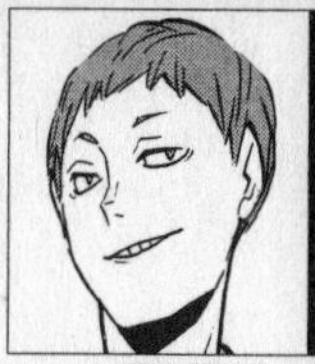
TAKAHIRO HANAMAKI
3RD YEAR
WING SPIKER

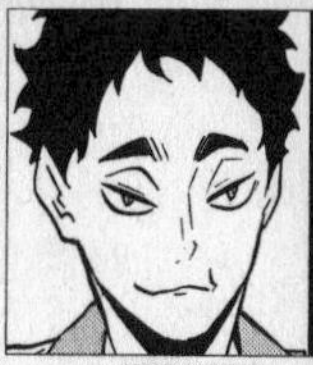
ISSEI MATSUKAWA
3RD YEAR
MIDDLE BLOCKER

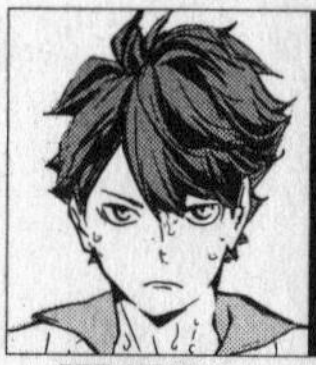
TOHRU OIKAWA
3RD YEAR (CAPTAIN)
SETTER

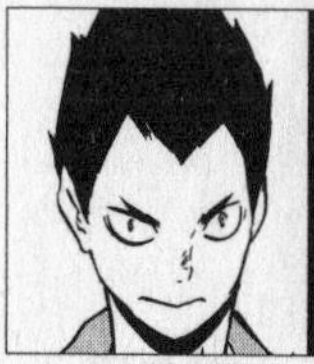
YUTARO KINDAICHI
1ST YEAR
MIDDLE BLOCKER

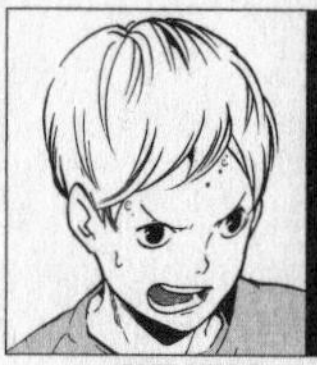
SHIGERU YAHABA
2ND YEAR
SETTER

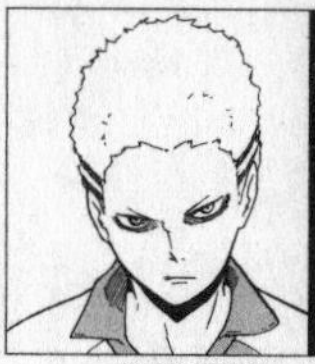
KENTARO KYOTANI
2ND YEAR
WING SPIKER

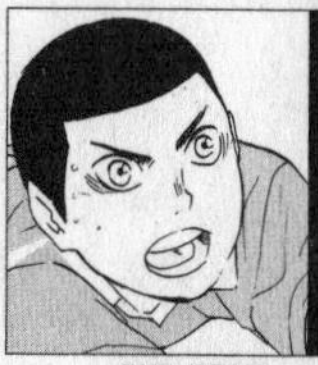
SHINJI WATARI
2ND YEAR
LIBERO

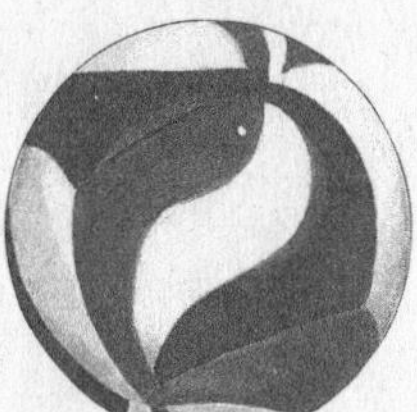

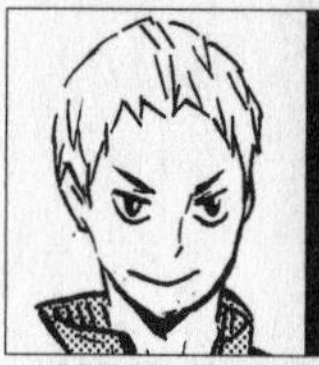
SADAYUKI MIZOGUCHI
ASSISTANT COACH

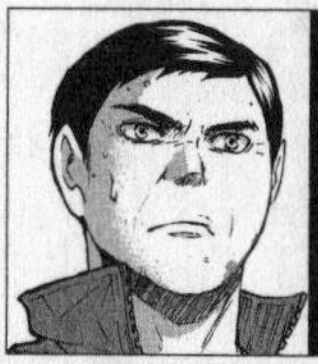
NOBUTERU IRIHATA
HEAD COACH

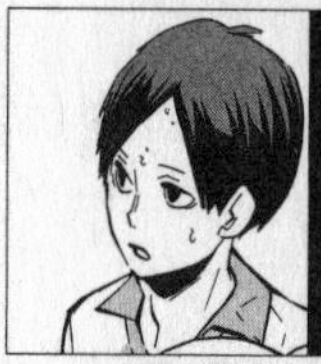
AKIRA KUNIMI
1ST YEAR
WING SPIKER

Ever since he saw the legendary player known as "the Little Giant" compete at the national volleyball finals, Shoyo Hinata has been aiming to be the best volleyball player ever! He decides to join the volleyball club at his middle school and gets to play in an official tournament during his third year. His team is crushed by a team led by volleyball prodigy Tobio Kageyama, also known as "the King of the Court." Swearing revenge on Kageyama, Hinata graduates middle school and enters Karasuno High School, the school where the Little Giant played. However, upon joining the club, he finds out that Kageyama is there too! The two of them bicker constantly, but they bring out the best in each other's talents and become a powerful combo. Having learned new skills from their summer training camp, the team heads into the spring tourney armed with new weapons. Advancing to the semifinals, Karasuno faces its archnemesis, Aoba Johsai! Karasuno takes the first set, but despite Yamaguchi's spectacular performance as a pinch server, Aoba Johsai still snatches the second set. The final set goes back and forth, but it's Aoba Johsai that reaches game point first...!

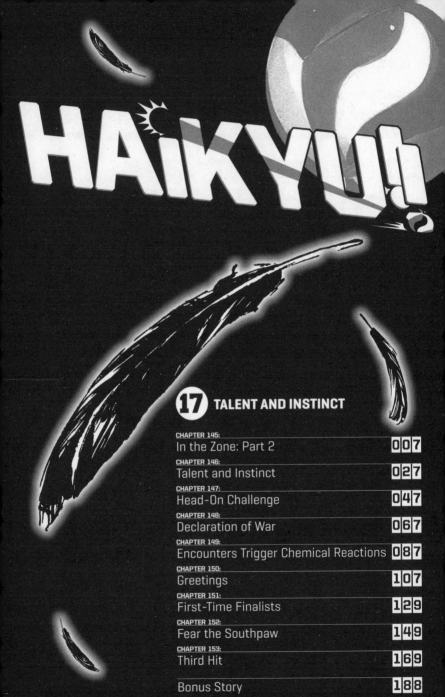

HAIKYU!!

17 TALENT AND INSTINCT

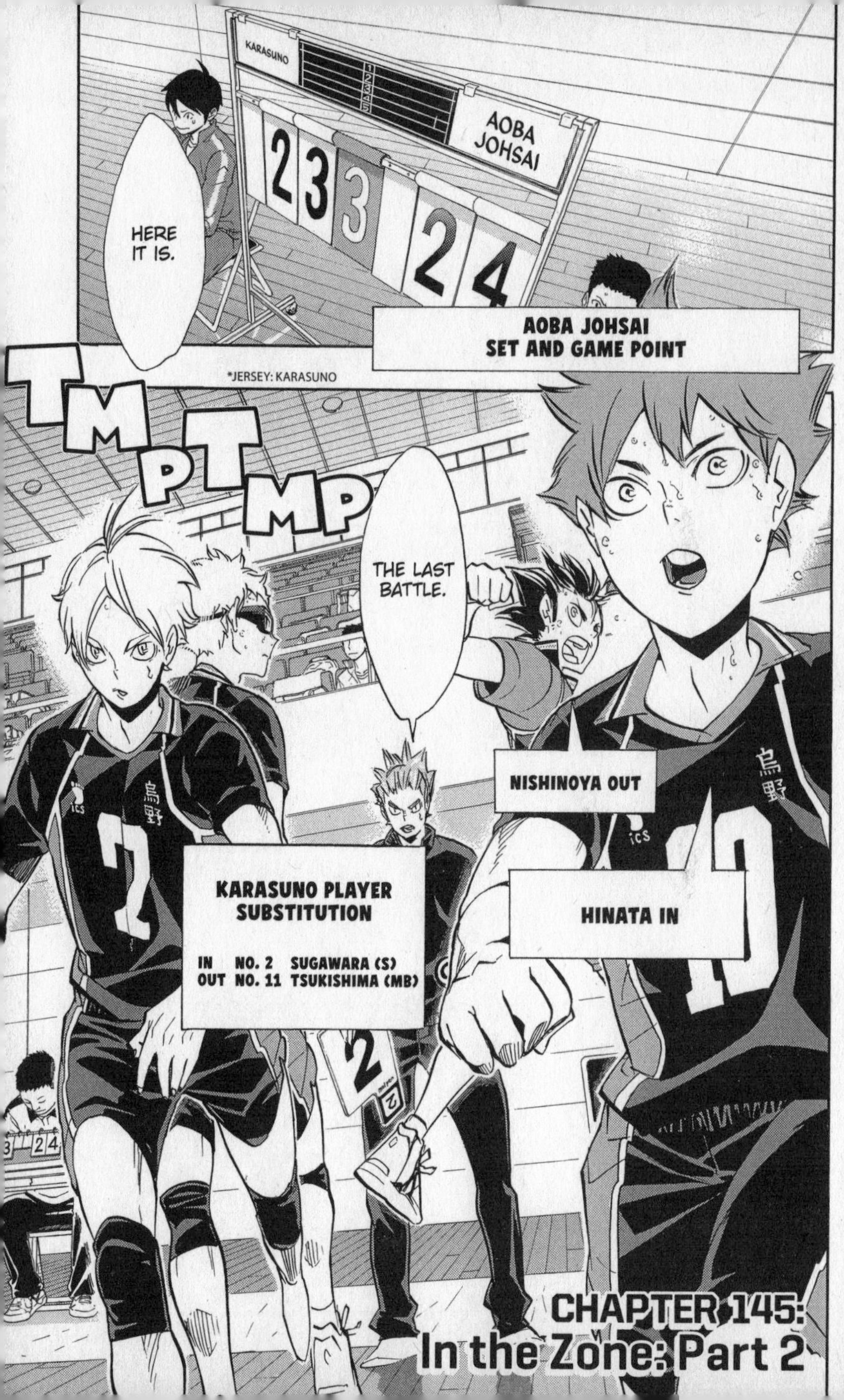
KARASUNO
AOBA JOHSAI
23
24
HERE IT IS.
AOBA JOHSAI SET AND GAME POINT
*JERSEY: KARASUNO
NISHINOYA OUT
HINATA IN
THE LAST BATTLE.
KARASUNO PLAYER SUBSTITUTION
IN NO. 2 SUGAWARA (S)
OUT NO. 11 TSUKISHIMA (MB)
TMP TMP
CHAPTER 145:
In the Zone: Part 2

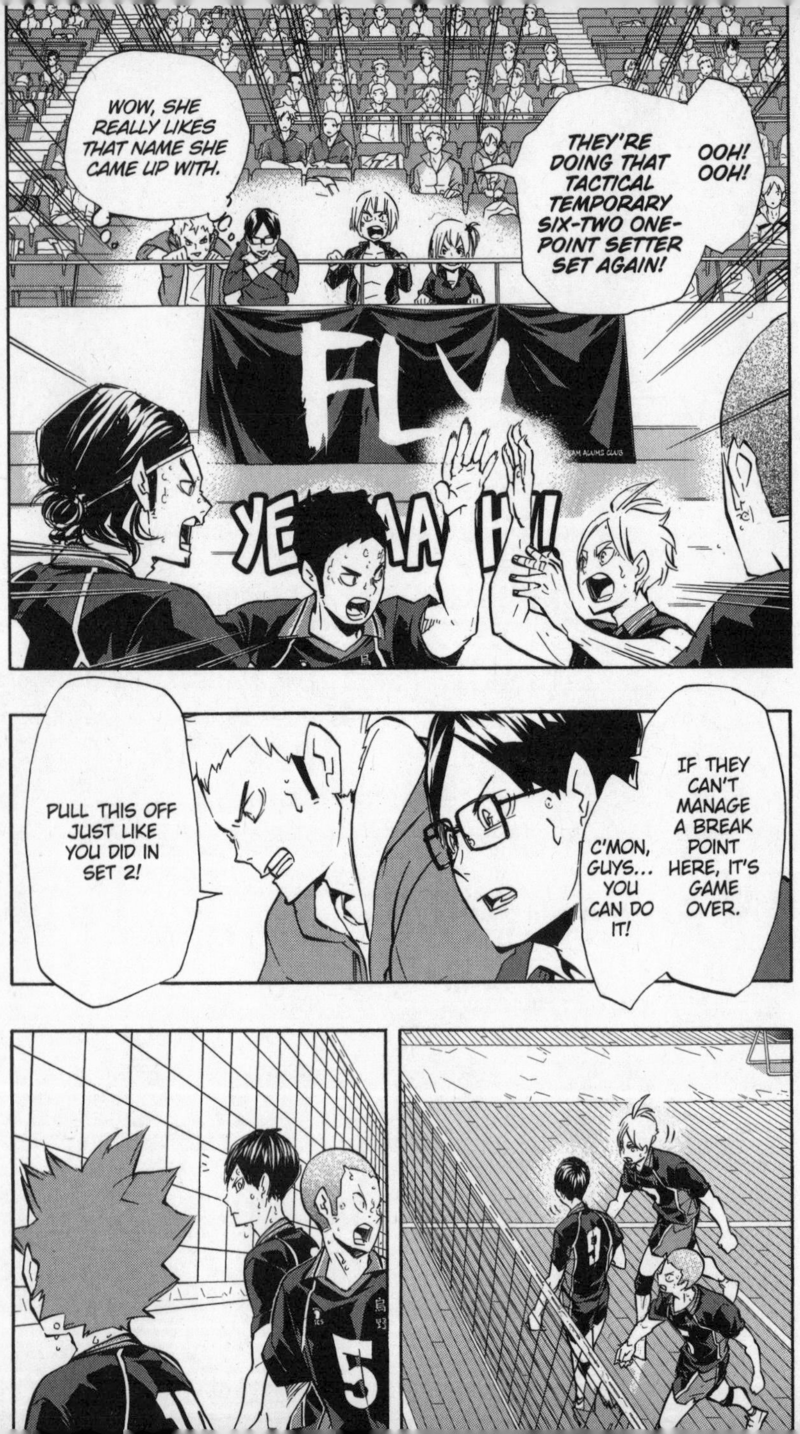
OOH! OOH!
THEY'RE DOING THAT TACTICAL TEMPORARY SIX-TWO ONE-POINT SETTER SET AGAIN!
WOW, SHE REALLY LIKES THAT NAME SHE CAME UP WITH.
FLY
IF THEY CAN'T MANAGE A BREAK POINT HERE, IT'S GAME OVER.
C'MON, GUYS... YOU CAN DO IT!
PULL THIS OFF JUST LIKE YOU DID IN SET 2!

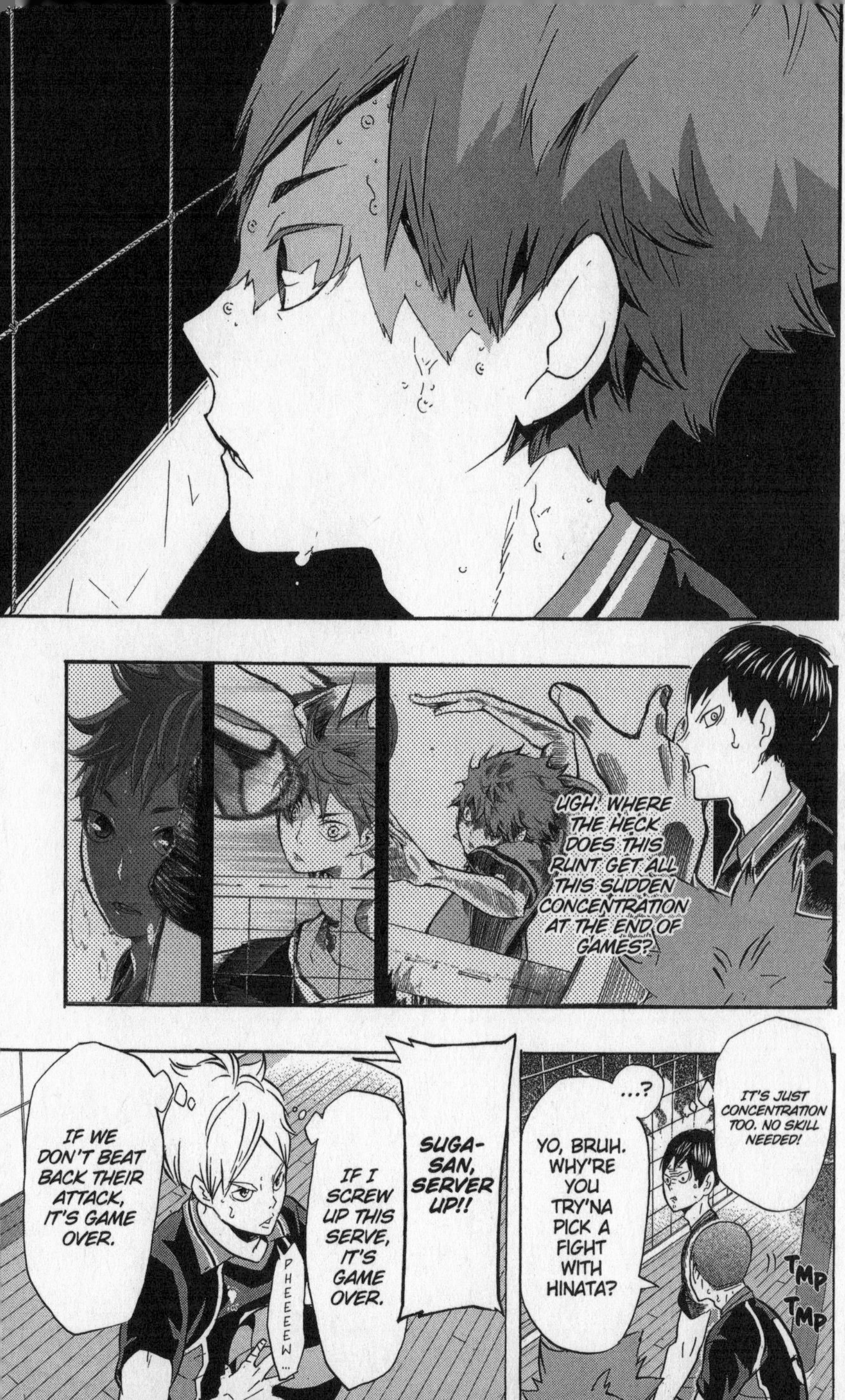
UGH. WHERE THE HECK DOES THIS RUNT GET ALL THIS SUDDEN CONCENTRATION AT THE END OF GAMES?
IT'S JUST CONCENTRATION TOO. NO SKILL NEEDED!
...?
YO, BRUH. WHY'RE YOU TRY'NA PICK A FIGHT WITH HINATA?
TMP TMP
SUGA-SAN, SERVER UP!!
IF I SCREW UP THIS SERVE, IT'S GAME OVER.
PHEEEEW...
IF WE DON'T BEAT BACK THEIR ATTACK, IT'S GAME OVER.

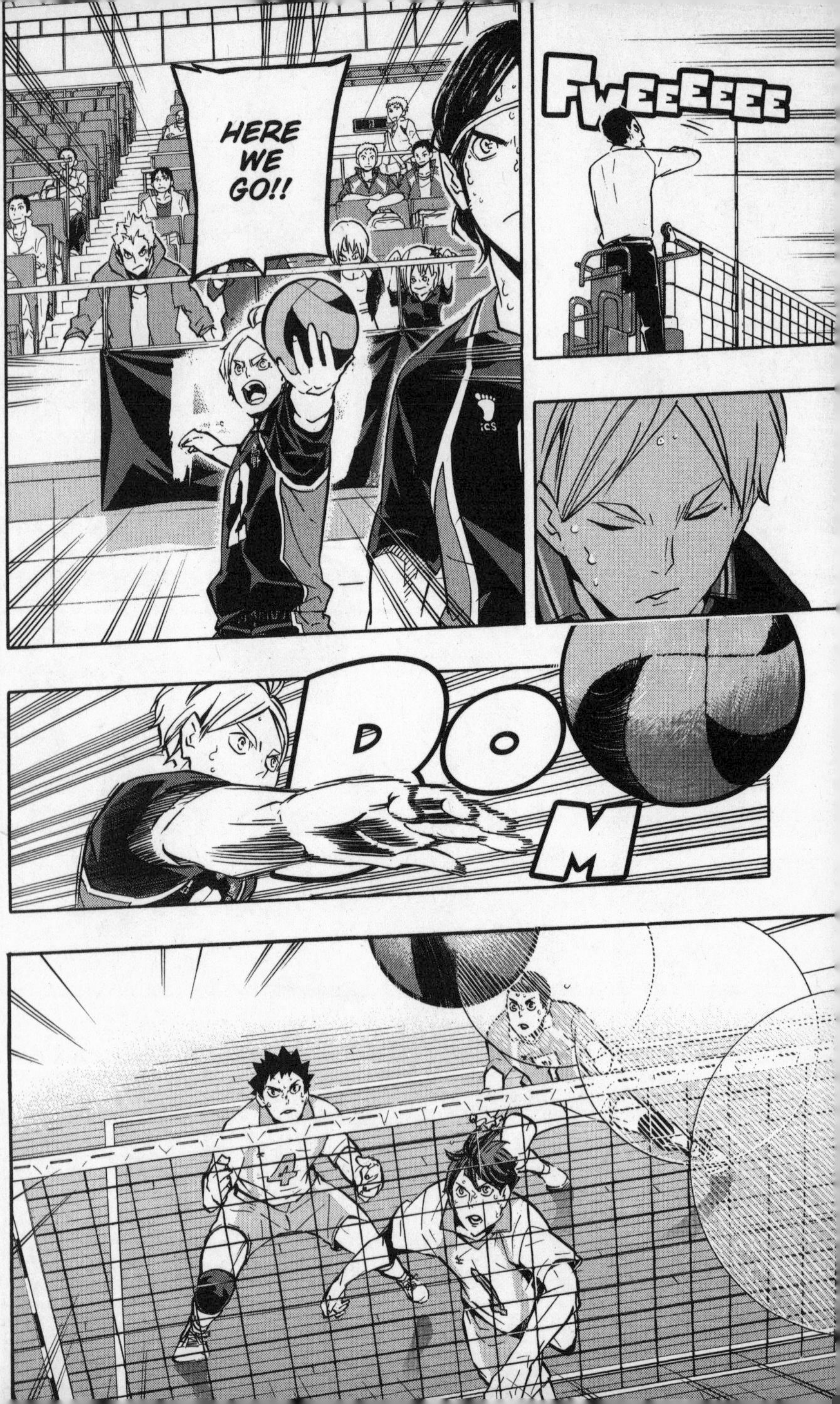
FWEEEEEE
HERE WE GO!!
DOOM

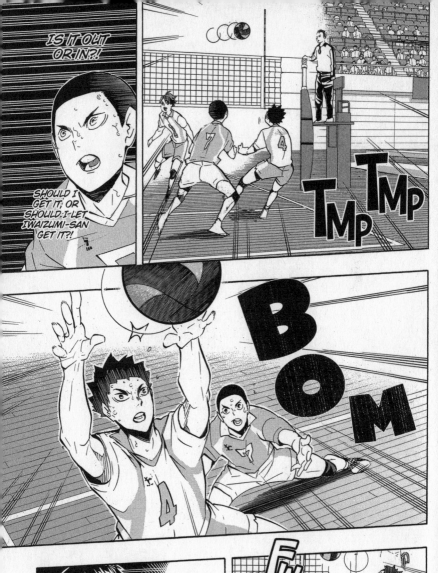

IS IT OUT OR IN?!

SHOULD I GET IT, OR SHOULD I LET IWAIZUMI-SAN GET IT?!

TMP TMP TMP

BOM

DAMMIT, THEY BUMPED IT! BUT THEIR ACE IS OUT OF POSITION!

FWLF

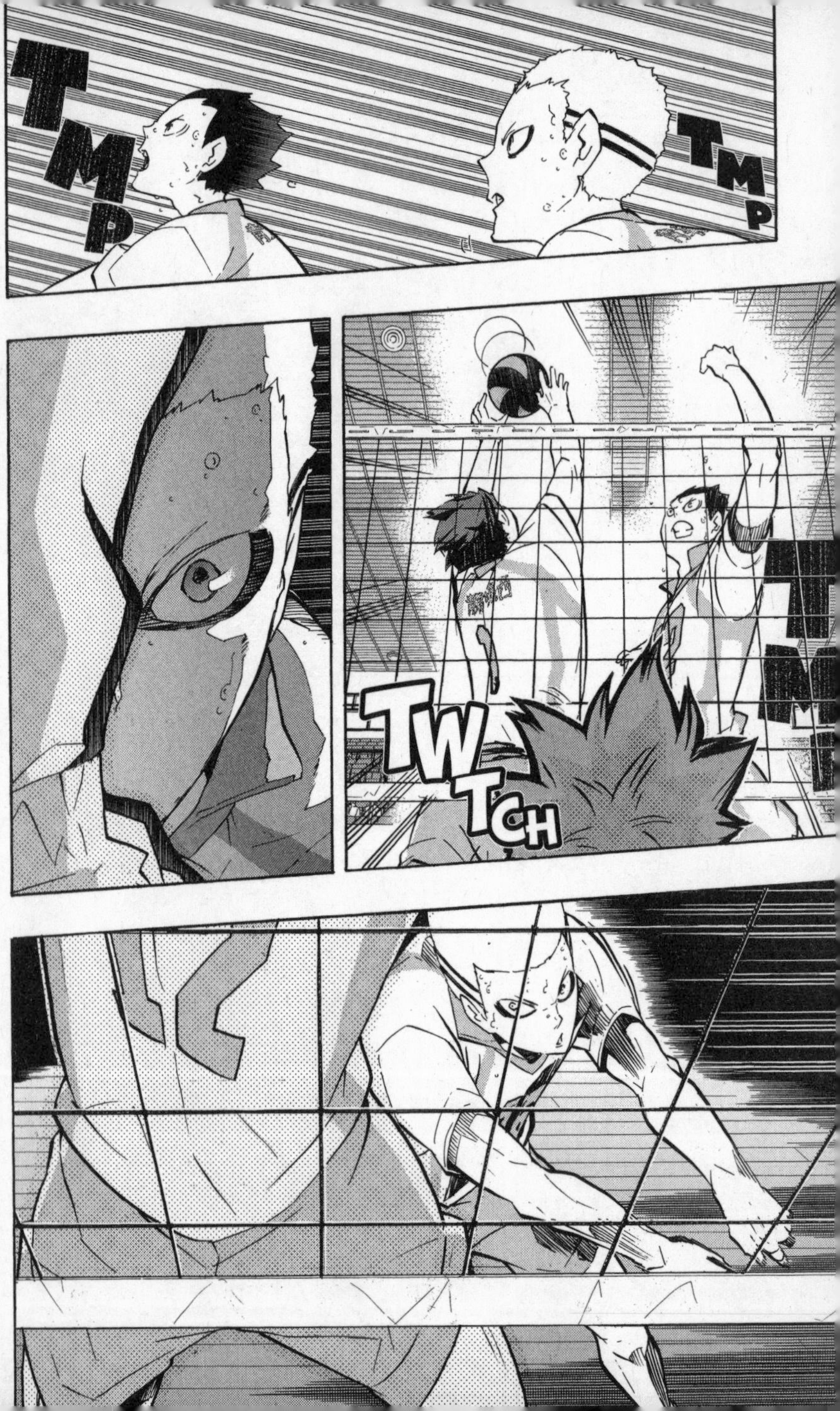
TMP
TMP
TWITCH

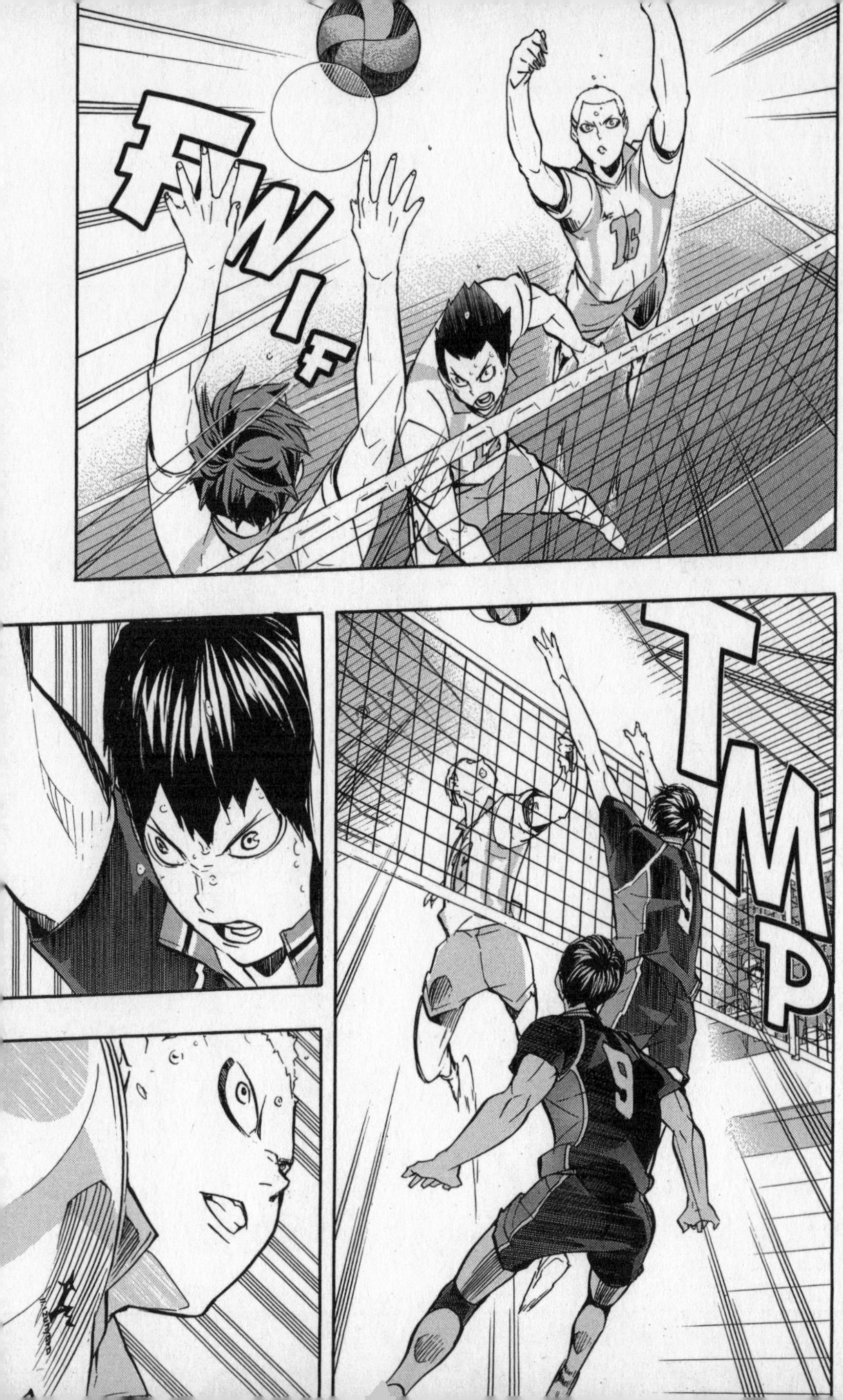
FWIF
TMP

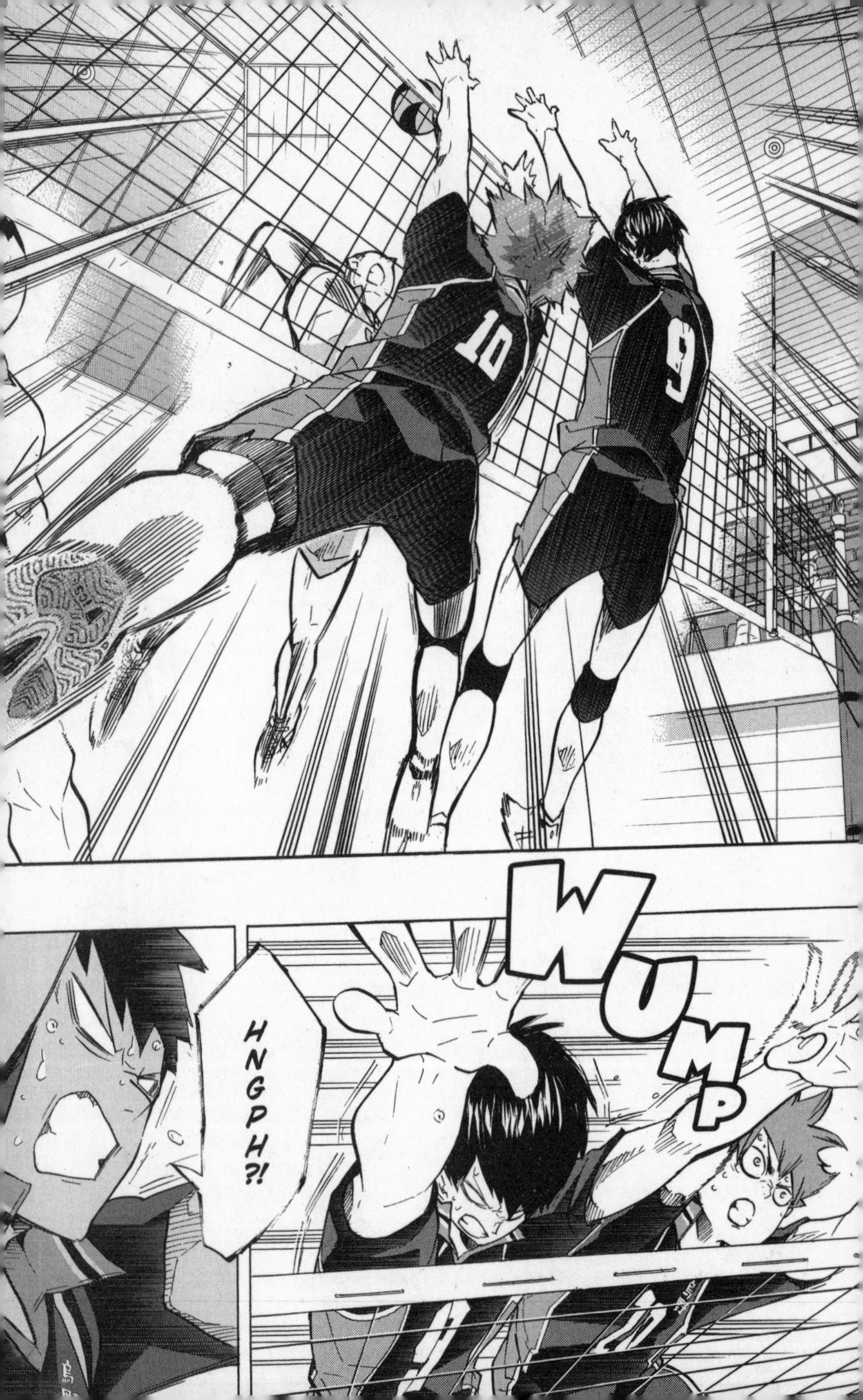
WUMP
HNGPH?!

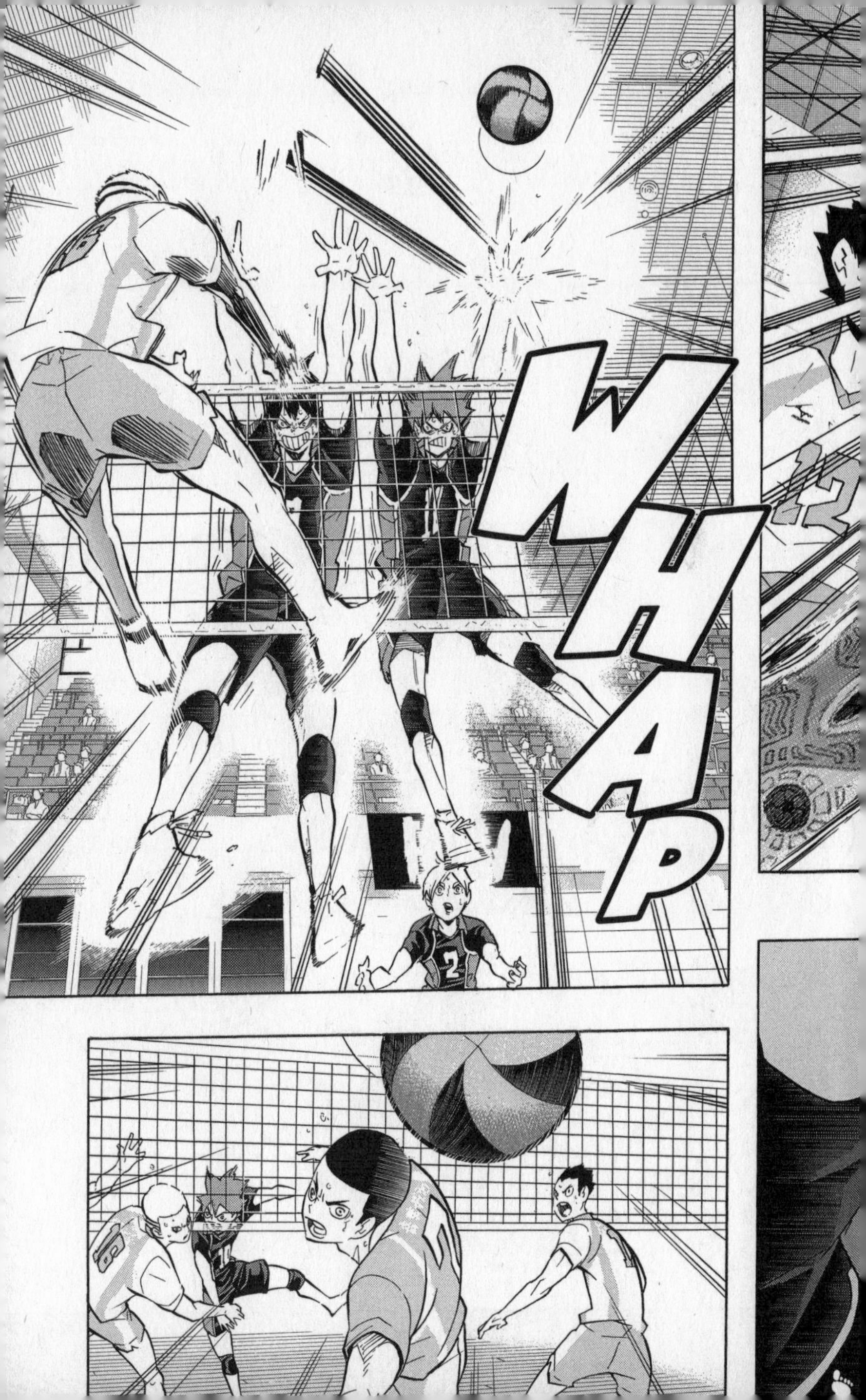
WHAP

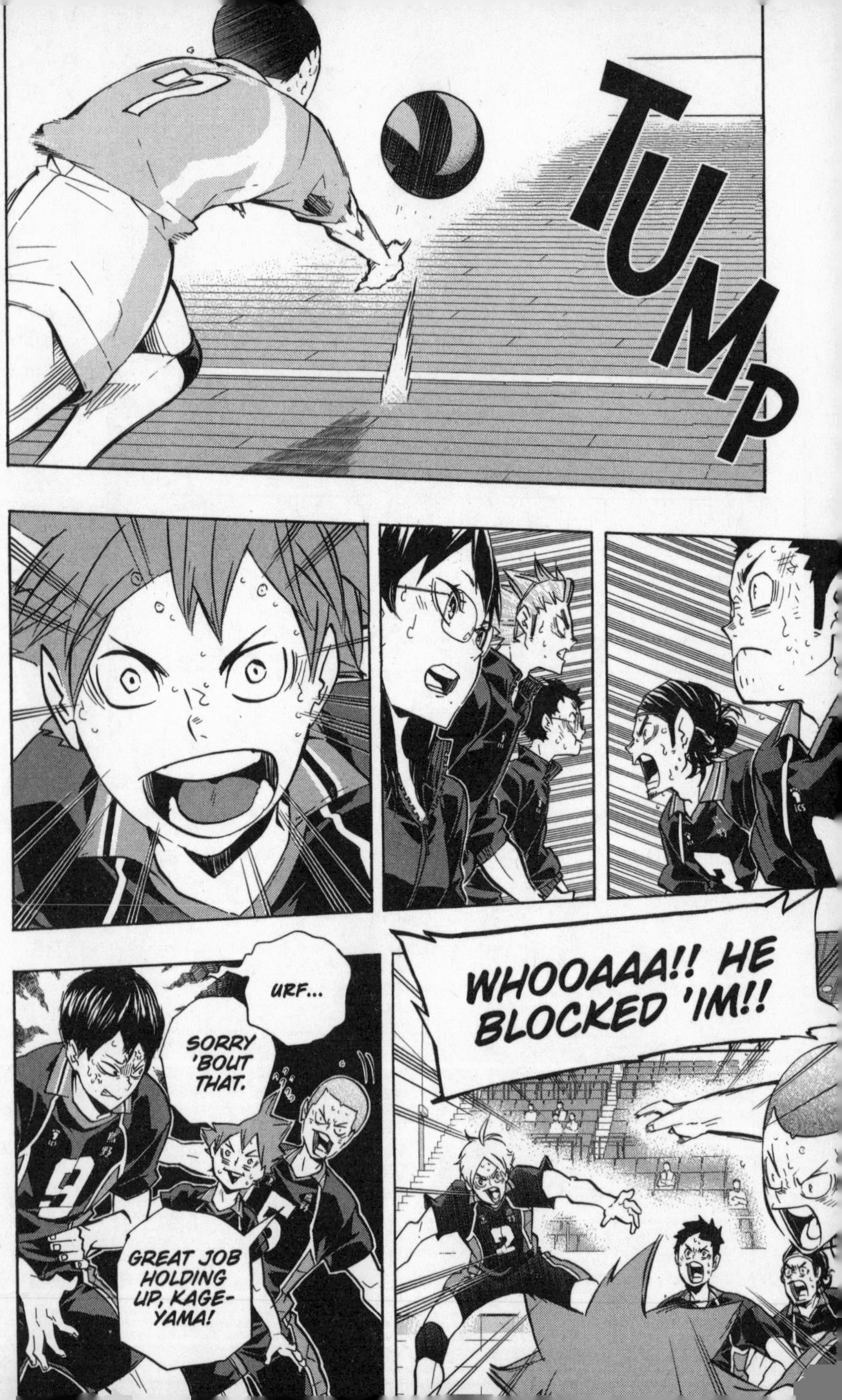
TUMP
WHOOAAA!! HE BLOCKED 'IM!!
URF...
SORRY 'BOUT THAT.
GREAT JOB HOLDING UP, KAGE-YAMA!

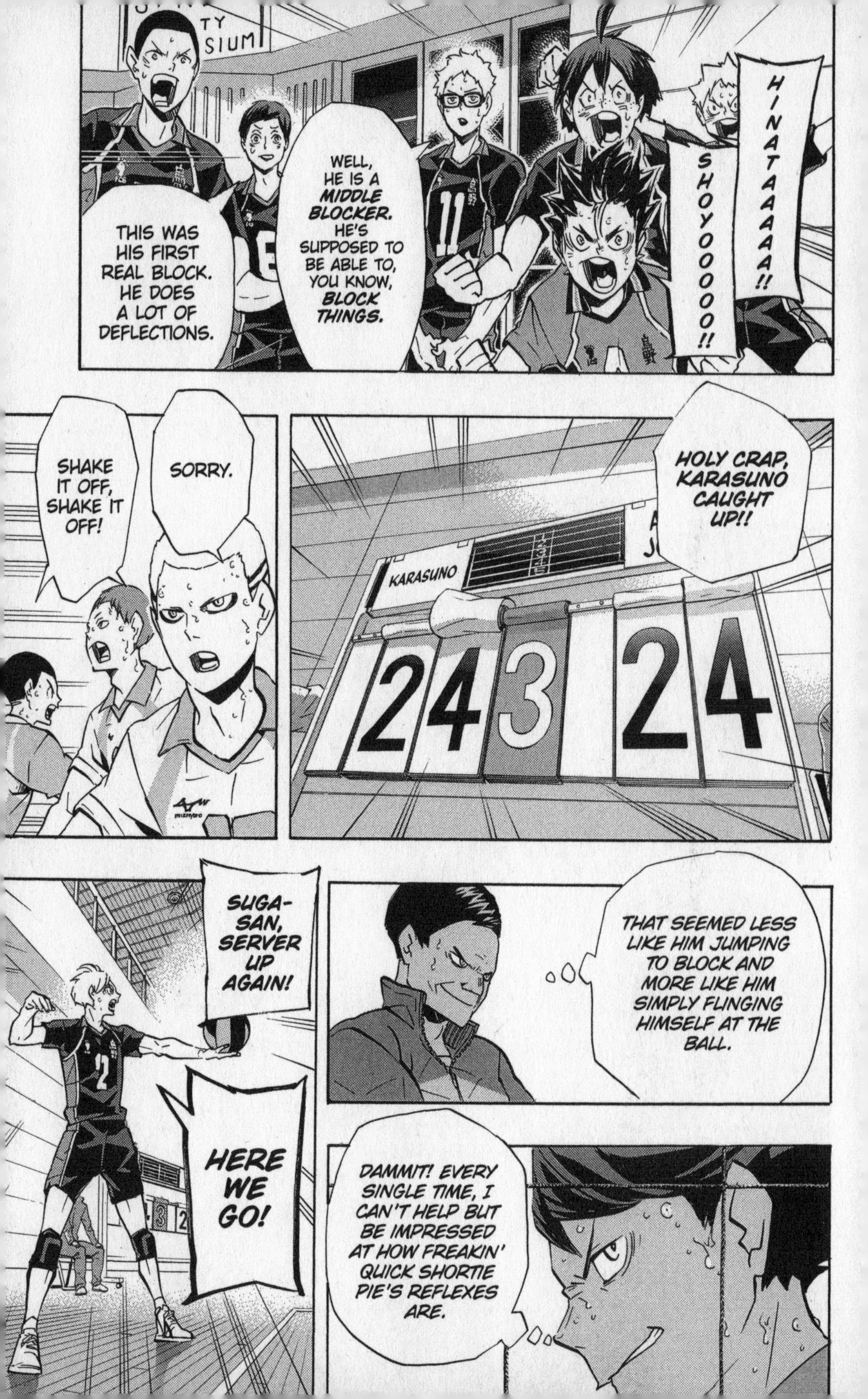
HINATAAAAA!!
SHOYOOOOOO!!
WELL, HE IS A MIDDLE BLOCKER. HE'S SUPPOSED TO BE ABLE TO, YOU KNOW, BLOCK THINGS.
THIS WAS HIS FIRST REAL BLOCK. HE DOES A LOT OF DEFLECTIONS.
HOLY CRAP, KARASUNO CAUGHT UP!!
KARASUNO
24
3
24
SORRY.
SHAKE IT OFF, SHAKE IT OFF!
THAT SEEMED LESS LIKE HIM JUMPING TO BLOCK AND MORE LIKE HIM SIMPLY FLINGING HIMSELF AT THE BALL.
DAMMIT! EVERY SINGLE TIME, I CAN'T HELP BUT BE IMPRESSED AT HOW FREAKIN' QUICK SHORTIE PIE'S REFLEXES ARE.
SUGA-SAN, SERVER UP AGAIN!
HERE WE GO!

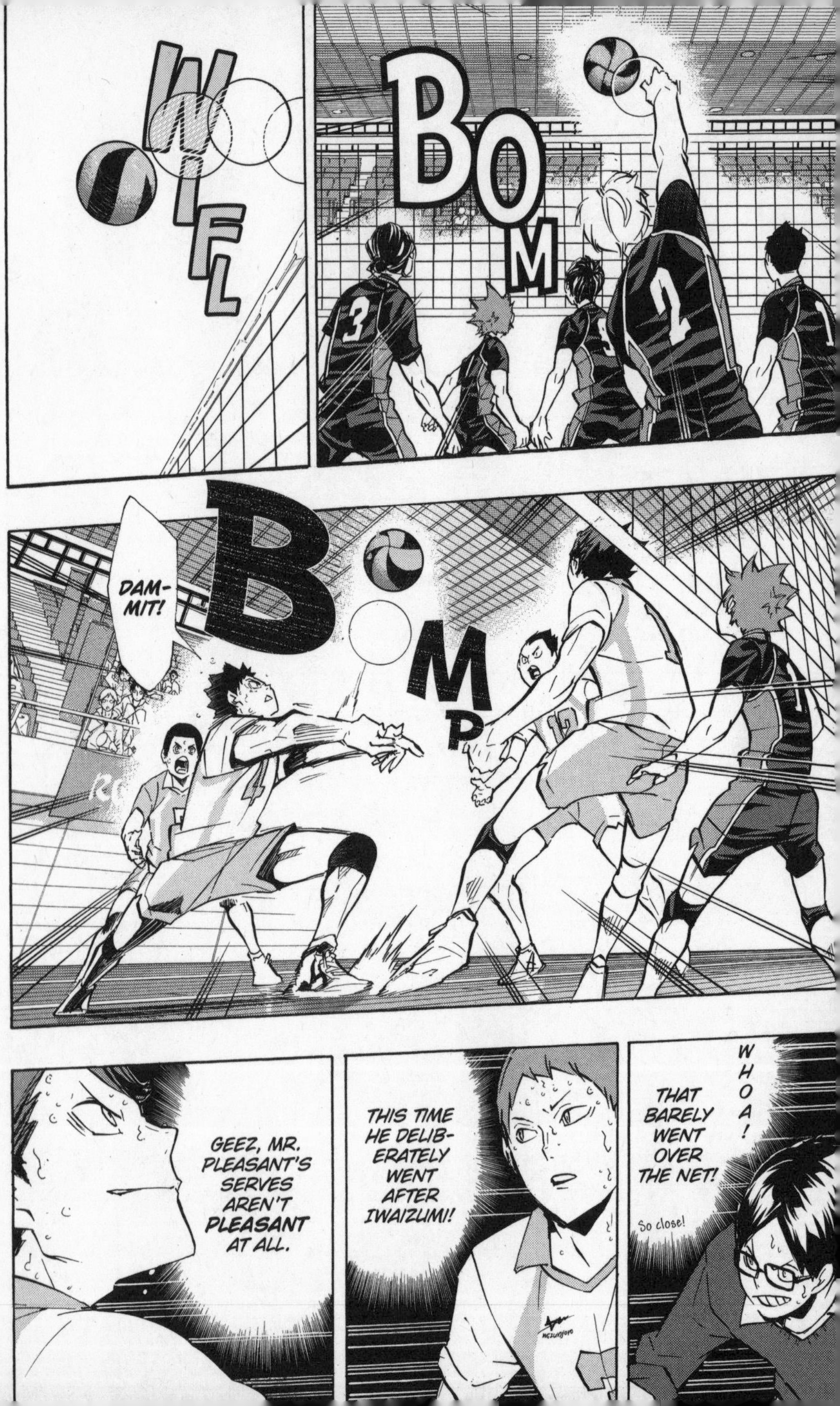
BOOM
WIFL
DAM-MIT!
BOMP
WHOA!
THAT BARELY WENT OVER THE NET!
So close!
THIS TIME HE DELIB-ERATELY WENT AFTER IWAIZUMI!
GEEZ, MR. PLEASANT'S SERVES AREN'T PLEASANT AT ALL.

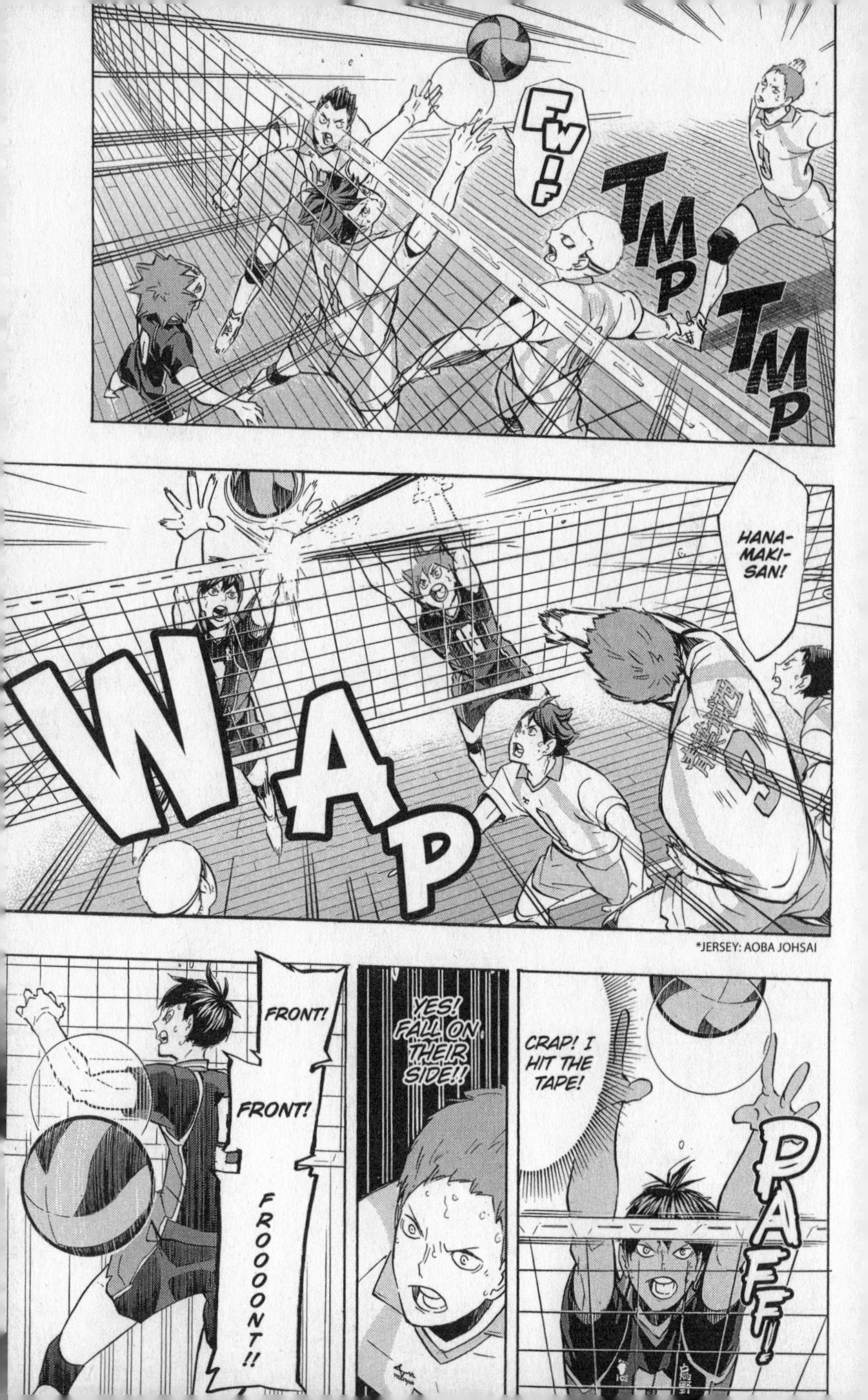
FWIF
TMP
TMP
HANA-MAKI-SAN!
WAP
CRAP! I HIT THE TAPE!
PAFF!
YES! FALL ON THEIR SIDE!!
FRONT!
FRONT!
FROOOOONT!!

*JERSEY: AOBA JOHSAI

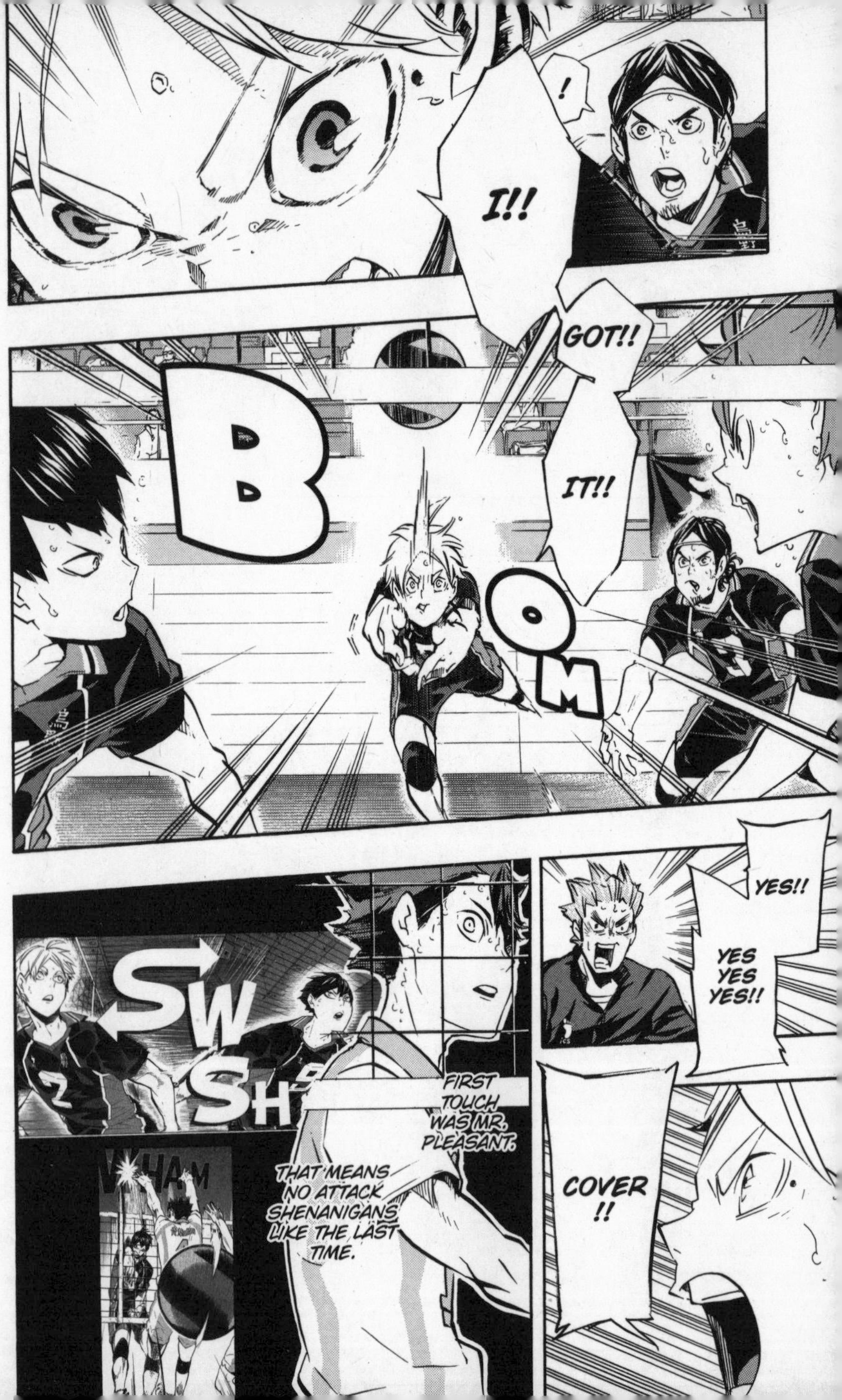
!
I!!
GOT!!
IT!!
BOOM
YES!!
YES YES YES!!
COVER !!
FIRST TOUCH WAS MR. PLEASANT.
THAT MEANS NO ATTACK SHENANIGANS LIKE THE LAST TIME.
SWSH
WHAM

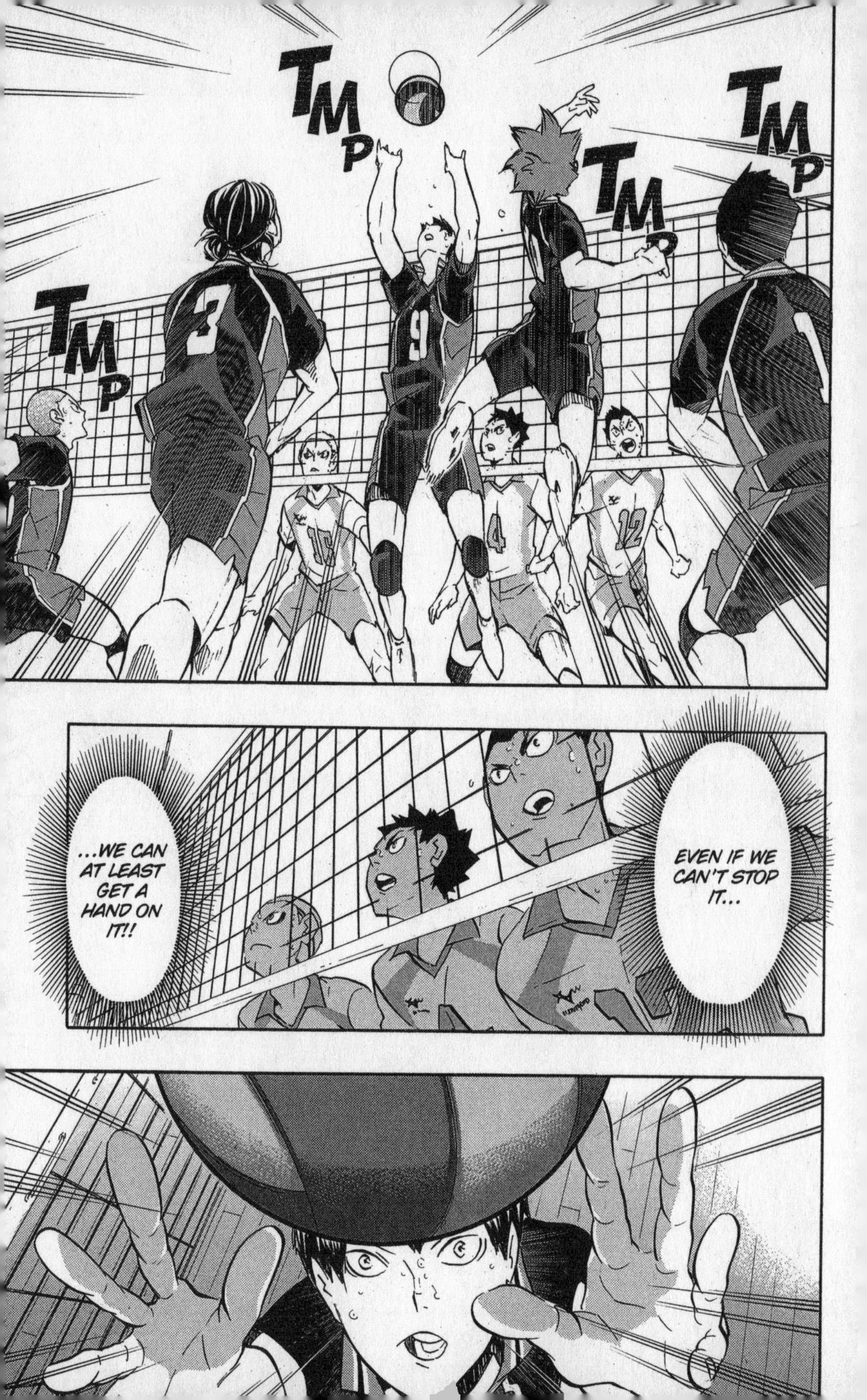
TMP
TMP
TMP
TMP
EVEN IF WE CAN'T STOP IT...
...WE CAN AT LEAST GET A HAND ON IT!!

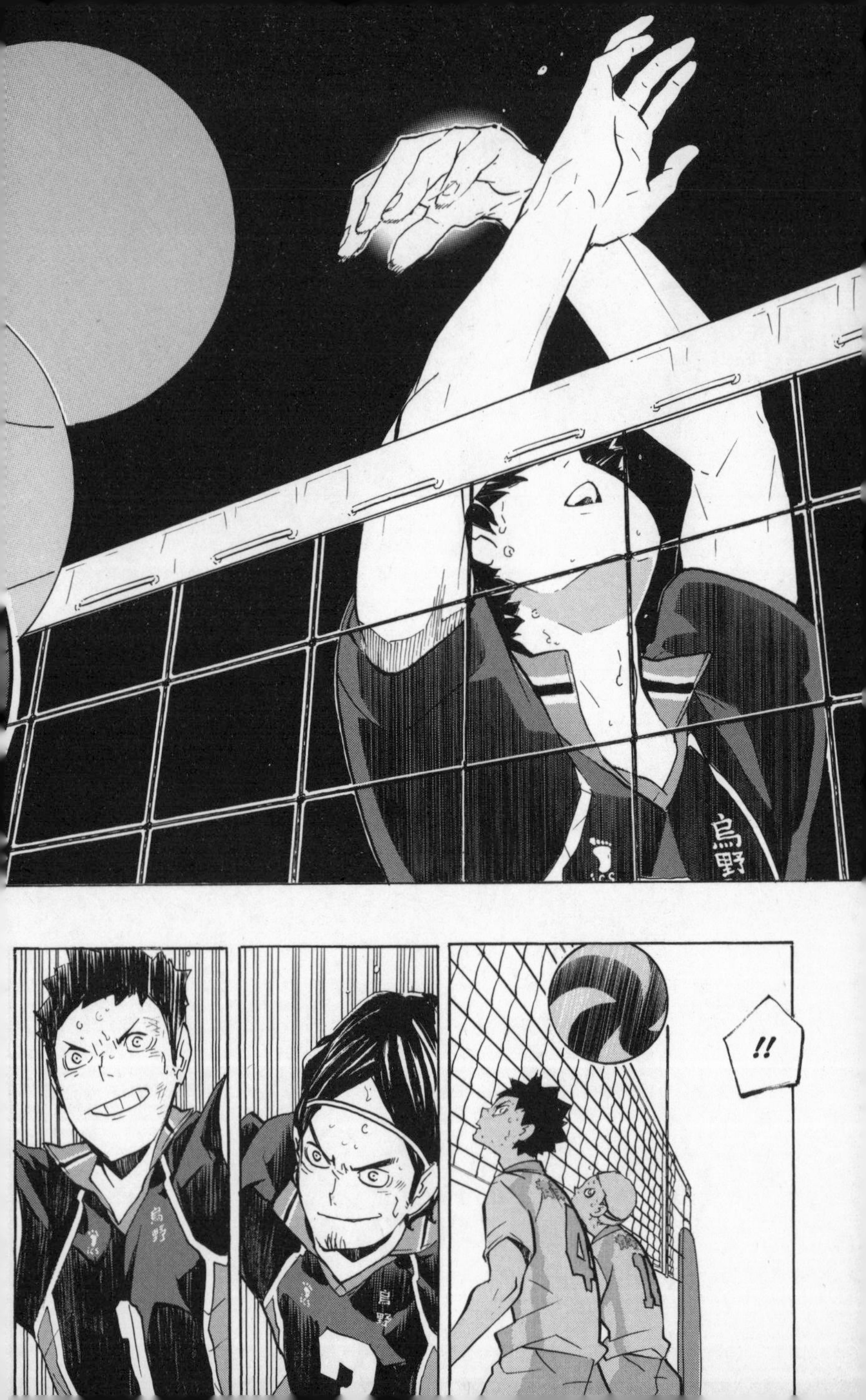
!!

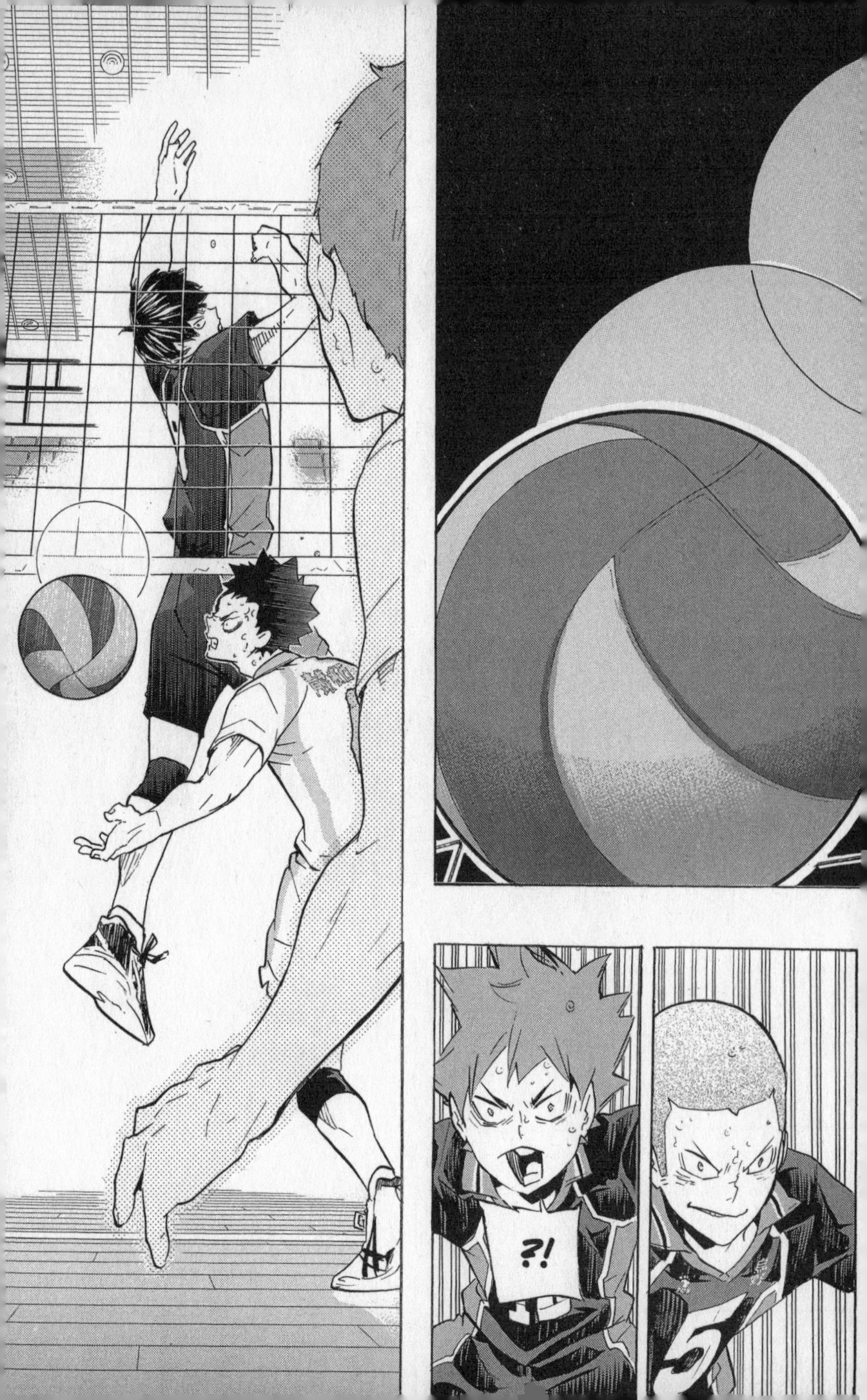
?!

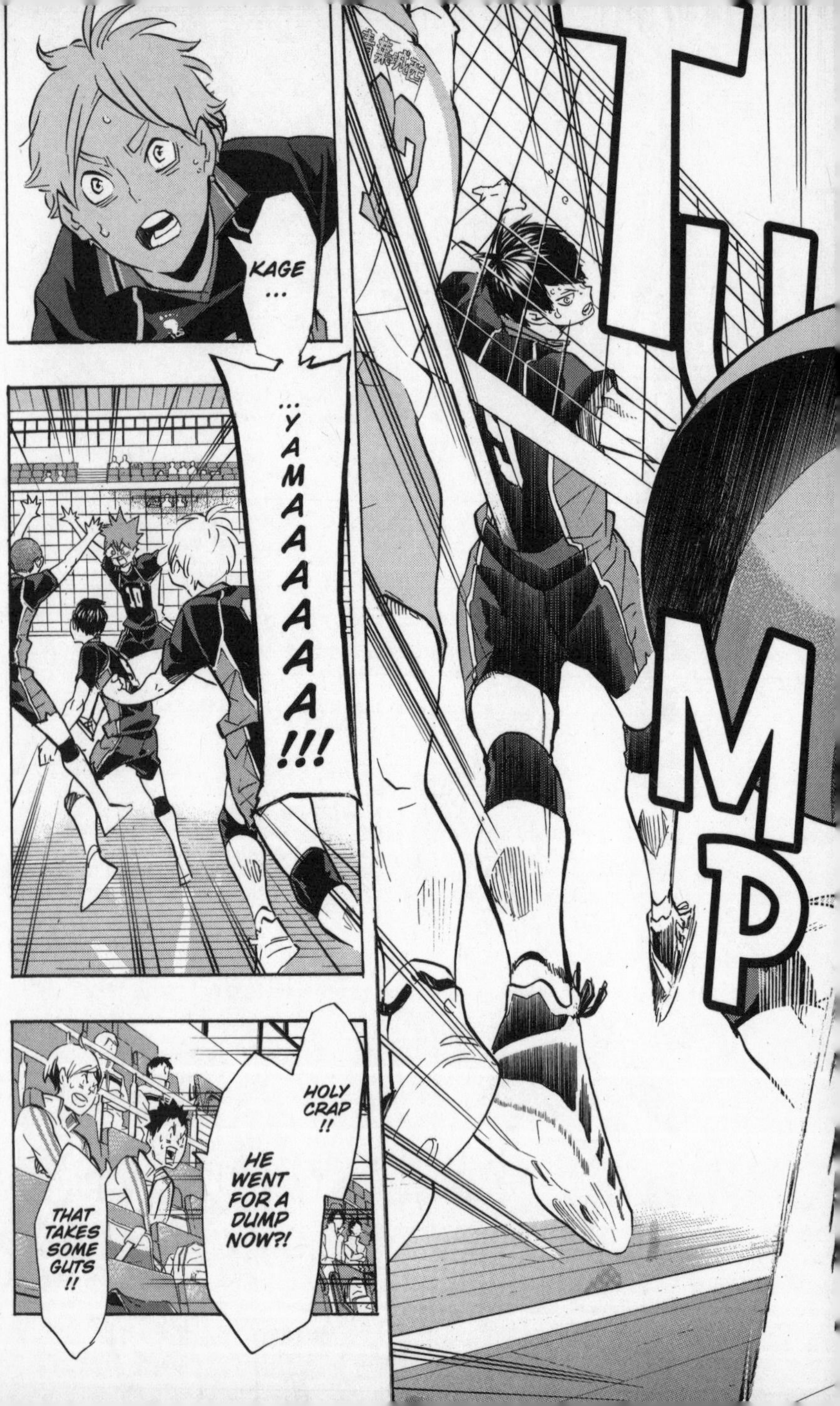
THUMP
KAGE ...
...YAMAAAAAAAAAA!!!
HOLY CRAP!!
HE WENT FOR A DUMP NOW?!
THAT TAKES SOME GUTS!!

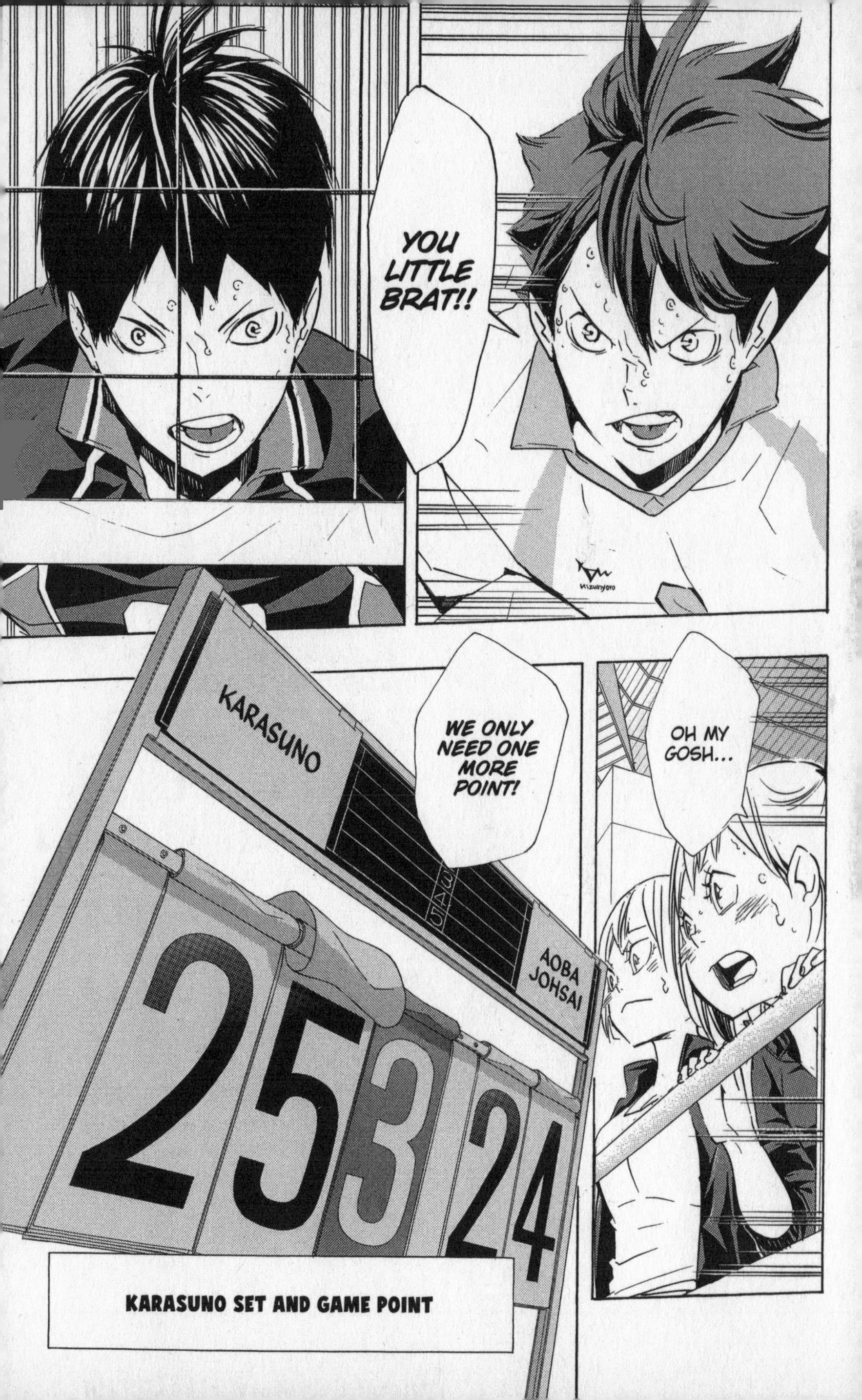
YOU LITTLE BRAT!!
OH MY GOSH...
WE ONLY NEED ONE MORE POINT!
KARASUNO
AOBA JOHSAI
25
3
24
KARASUNO SET AND GAME POINT

GAH! THAT "MR. PLEASANT" GUY ISN'T PLEASANT AT ALL! WHO'S THE IDIOT WHO NAMED HIM "MR. PLEASANT" ANYWAY? I'M THAT IDIOT!

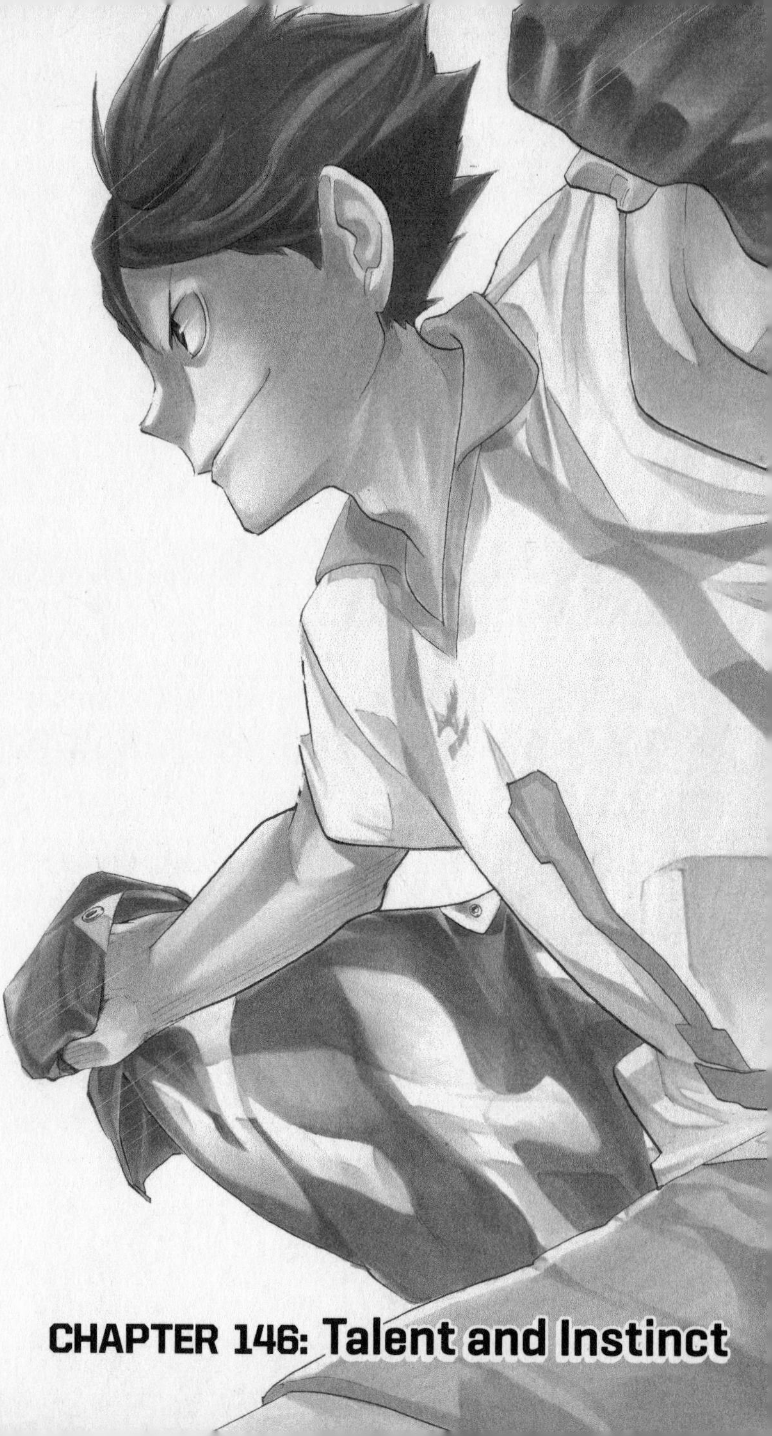

CHAPTER 146: Talent and Instinct

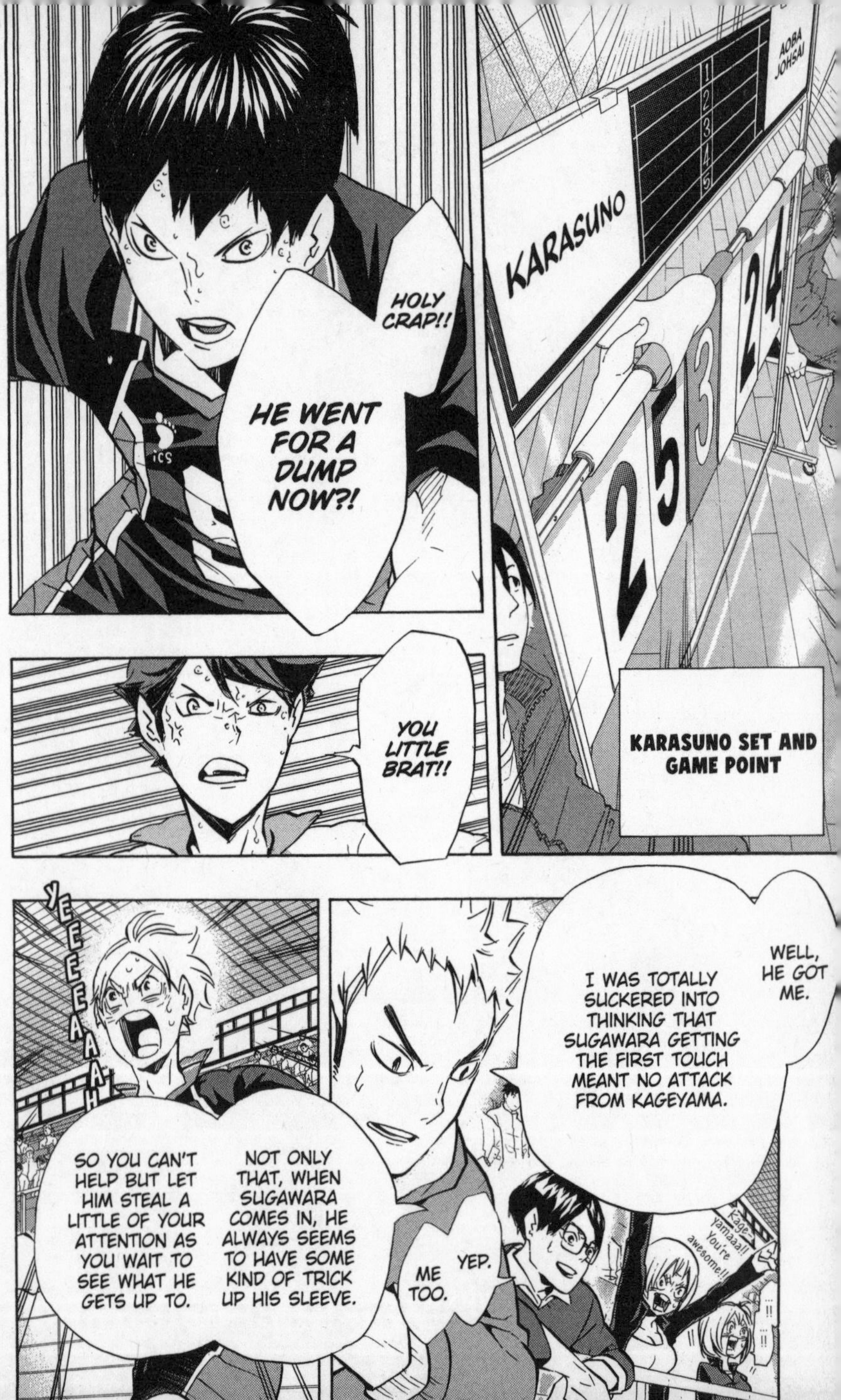
AOBA JOHSAI
KARASUNO
25
3
24
KARASUNO SET AND GAME POINT
HOLY CRAP!!
HE WENT FOR A DUMP NOW?!
YOU LITTLE BRAT!!
WELL, HE GOT ME.
I WAS TOTALLY SUCKERED INTO THINKING THAT SUGAWARA GETTING THE FIRST TOUCH MEANT NO ATTACK FROM KAGEYAMA.
YEP.
ME TOO.
Kage-yamaaa!! You're awesome!!
!!
...!!
YEEEEAAAAH
NOT ONLY THAT, WHEN SUGAWARA COMES IN, HE ALWAYS SEEMS TO HAVE SOME KIND OF TRICK UP HIS SLEEVE.
SO YOU CAN'T HELP BUT LET HIM STEAL A LITTLE OF YOUR ATTENTION AS YOU WAIT TO SEE WHAT HE GETS UP TO.

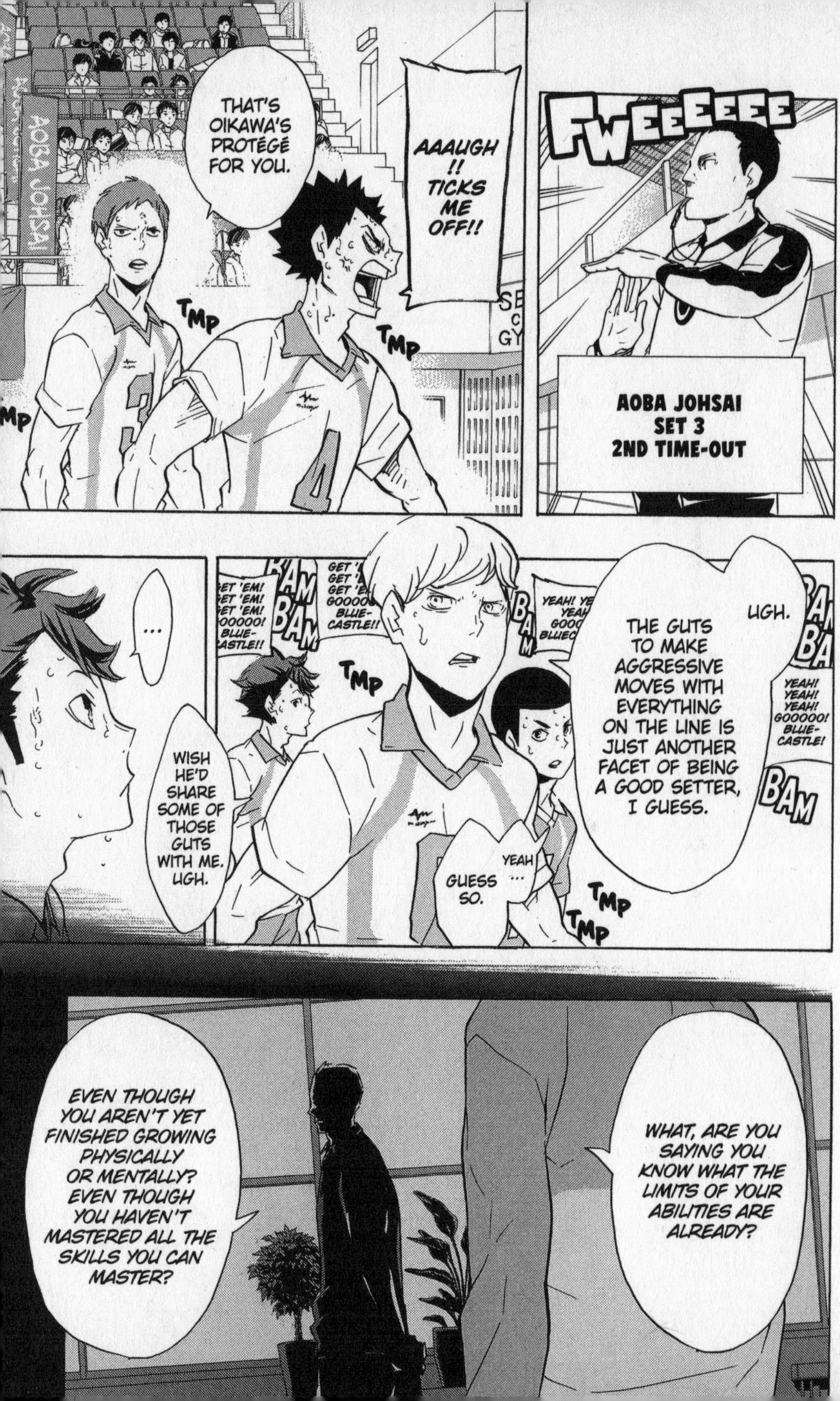
FWEEEEEE
AOBA JOHSAI SET 3 2ND TIME-OUT
AAAUGH!! TICKS ME OFF!!
THAT'S OIKAWA'S PROTÉGÉ FOR YOU.
TMP
TMP
MP
BAM
BAM BA
YEAH! YEAH! YEAH! GOOOOO! BLUE-CASTLE!
BAM
UGH.
THE GUTS TO MAKE AGGRESSIVE MOVES WITH EVERYTHING ON THE LINE IS JUST ANOTHER FACET OF BEING A GOOD SETTER, I GUESS.
YEAH! YEAH! GOOO BLUEC
BAM
GET 'EM! GET 'EM! GET 'EM! GOOOOO! BLUE-CASTLE!!
BAM BAM
GET 'EM! GET 'EM! GET 'EM! GOOOOO! BLUE-CASTLE!!
TMP
YEAH...
GUESS SO.
TMP
TMP
...
WISH HE'D SHARE SOME OF THOSE GUTS WITH ME. UGH.
WHAT, ARE YOU SAYING YOU KNOW WHAT THE LIMITS OF YOUR ABILITIES ARE ALREADY?
EVEN THOUGH YOU AREN'T YET FINISHED GROWING PHYSICALLY OR MENTALLY? EVEN THOUGH YOU HAVEN'T MASTERED ALL THE SKILLS YOU CAN MASTER?

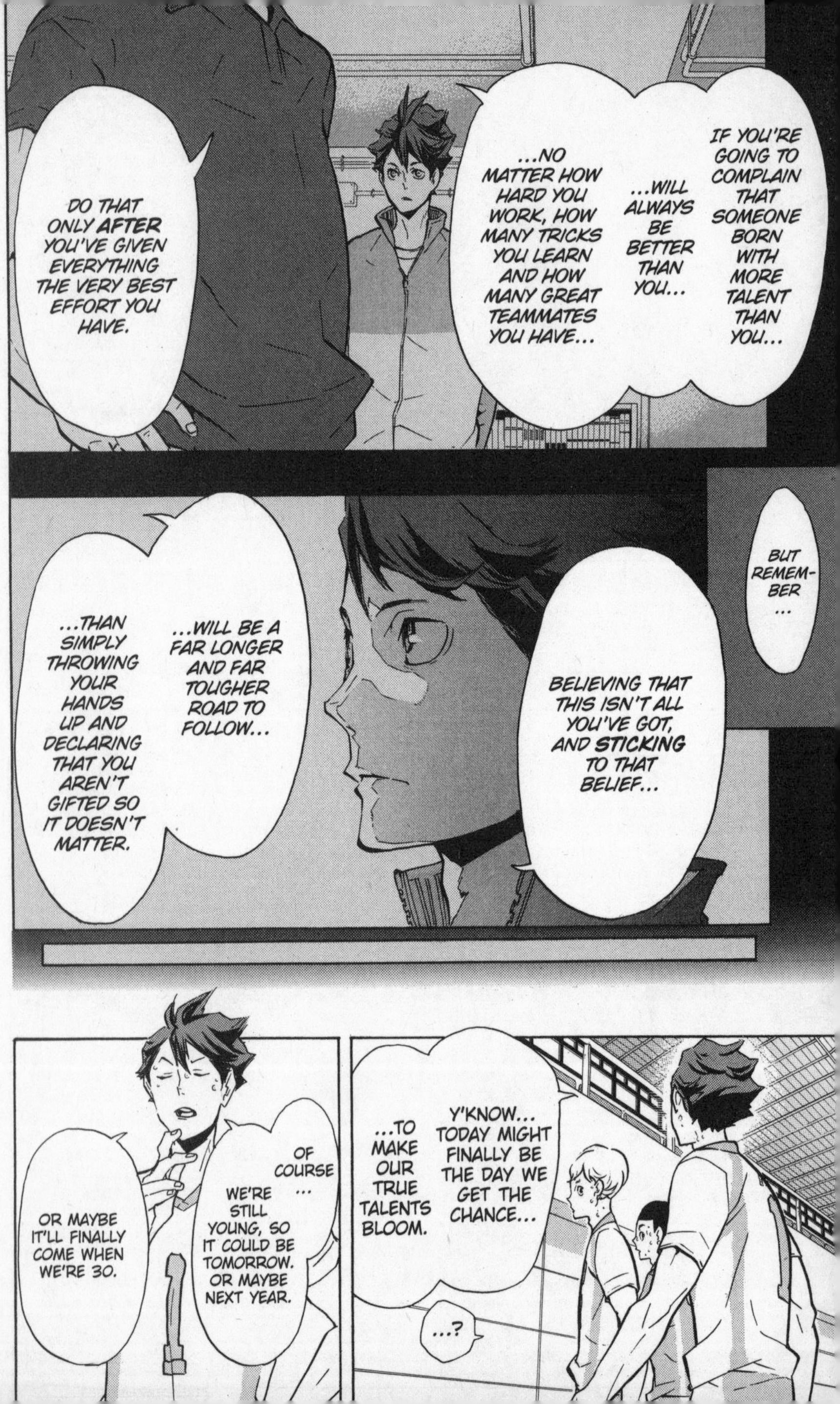
IF YOU'RE GOING TO COMPLAIN THAT SOMEONE BORN WITH MORE TALENT THAN YOU...
...WILL ALWAYS BE BETTER THAN YOU...
...NO MATTER HOW HARD YOU WORK, HOW MANY TRICKS YOU LEARN AND HOW MANY GREAT TEAMMATES YOU HAVE...
DO THAT ONLY **AFTER** YOU'VE GIVEN EVERYTHING THE VERY BEST EFFORT YOU HAVE.
BUT REMEMBER...
BELIEVING THAT THIS ISN'T ALL YOU'VE GOT, AND **STICKING** TO THAT BELIEF...
...WILL BE A FAR LONGER AND FAR TOUGHER ROAD TO FOLLOW...
...THAN SIMPLY THROWING YOUR HANDS UP AND DECLARING THAT YOU AREN'T GIFTED SO IT DOESN'T MATTER.
Y'KNOW... TODAY MIGHT FINALLY BE THE DAY WE GET THE CHANCE...
...TO MAKE OUR TRUE TALENTS BLOOM.
...?
OF COURSE...
WE'RE STILL YOUNG, SO IT COULD BE TOMORROW. OR MAYBE NEXT YEAR.
OR MAYBE IT'LL FINALLY COME WHEN WE'RE 30.

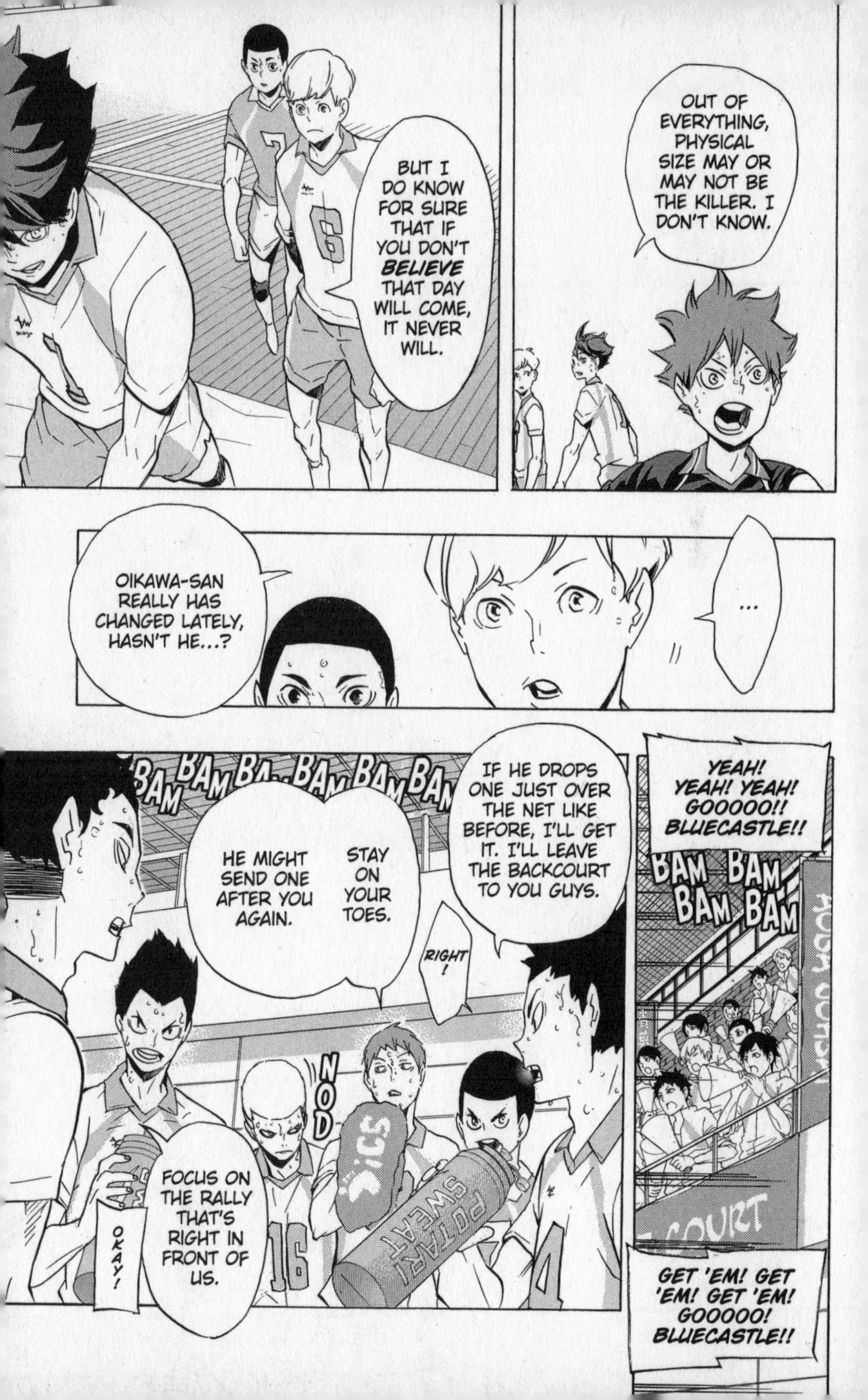
OUT OF EVERYTHING, PHYSICAL SIZE MAY OR MAY NOT BE THE KILLER. I DON'T KNOW.
BUT I DO KNOW FOR SURE THAT IF YOU DON'T ***BELIEVE*** THAT DAY WILL COME, IT NEVER WILL.
...
OIKAWA-SAN REALLY HAS CHANGED LATELY, HASN'T HE...?
YEAH! YEAH! YEAH! GOOOOO!! BLUECASTLE!!
BAM BAM BAM BAM
GET 'EM! GET 'EM! GET 'EM! GOOOOO! BLUECASTLE!!
IF HE DROPS ONE JUST OVER THE NET LIKE BEFORE, I'LL GET IT. I'LL LEAVE THE BACKCOURT TO YOU GUYS.
BAM BAM BA.. BAM BAM BAM
STAY ON YOUR TOES.
HE MIGHT SEND ONE AFTER YOU AGAIN.
RIGHT!
NOD
FOCUS ON THE RALLY THAT'S RIGHT IN FRONT OF US.
OKAY!

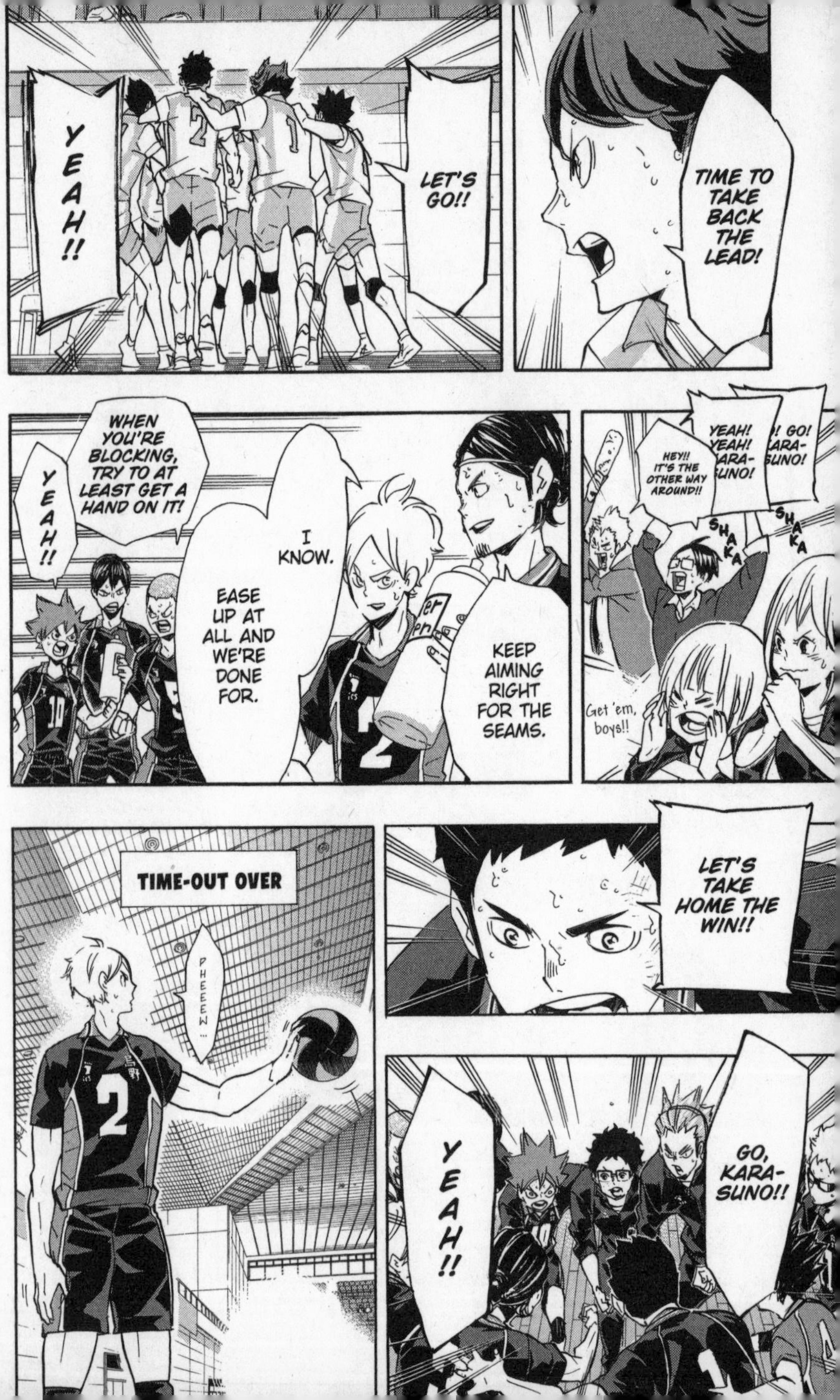

TIME TO TAKE BACK THE LEAD!
LET'S GO!!
YEAH!!
O! GO! KARA-SUNO!
YEAH! YEAH! KARA-SUNO!
HEY!! IT'S THE OTHER WAY AROUND!!
SHAKA
SHAKA
Get 'em, boys!!
KEEP AIMING RIGHT FOR THE SEAMS.
I KNOW.
EASE UP AT ALL AND WE'RE DONE FOR.
WHEN YOU'RE BLOCKING, TRY TO AT LEAST GET A HAND ON IT!
YEAH!!
LET'S TAKE HOME THE WIN!!
GO, KARA-SUNO!!
YEAH!!
TIME-OUT OVER
PHEEEEW...

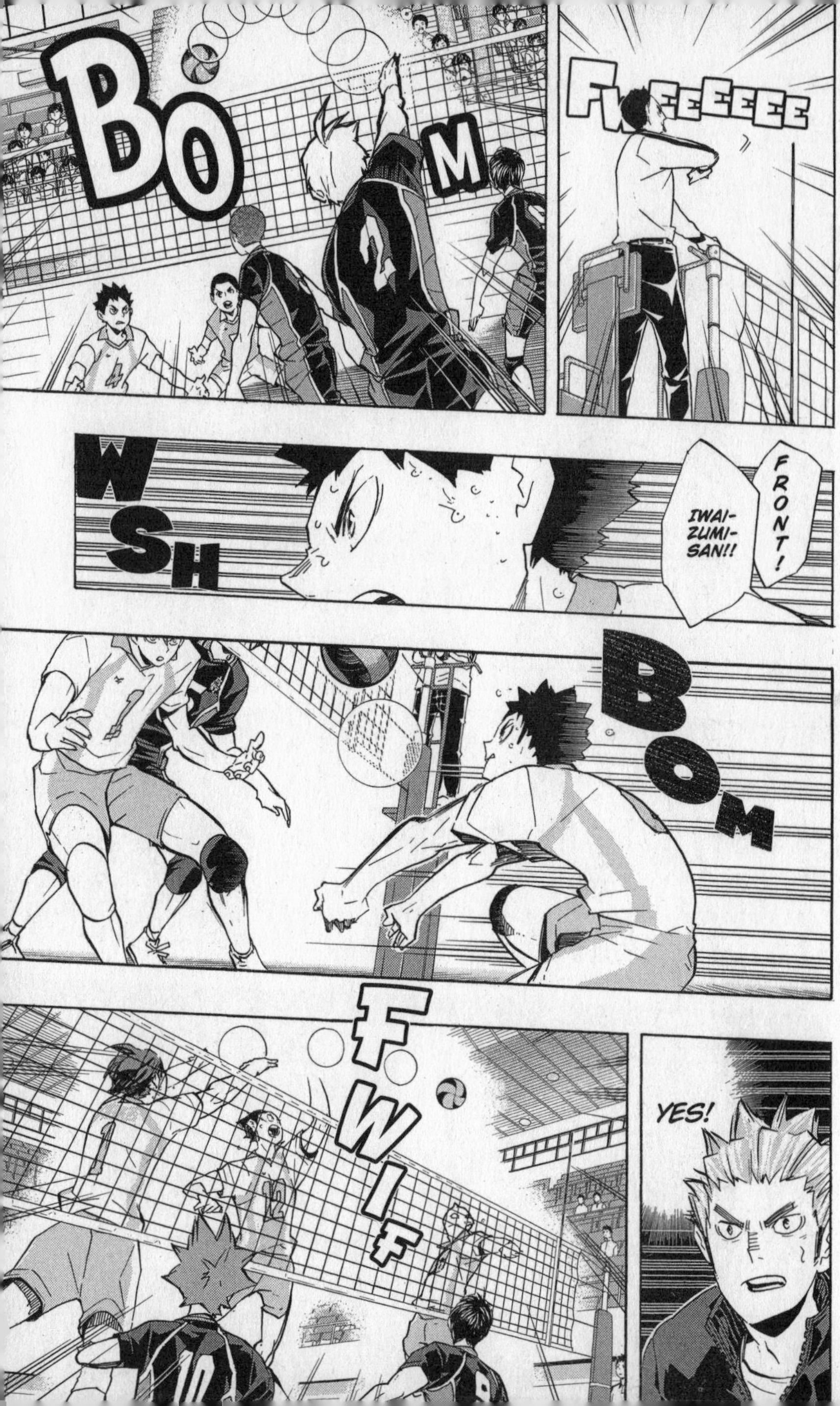
FWEEEEEE
BOOM
FRONT!
IWAI-ZUMI-SAN!!
WSH
BOOM
YES!
FWIF

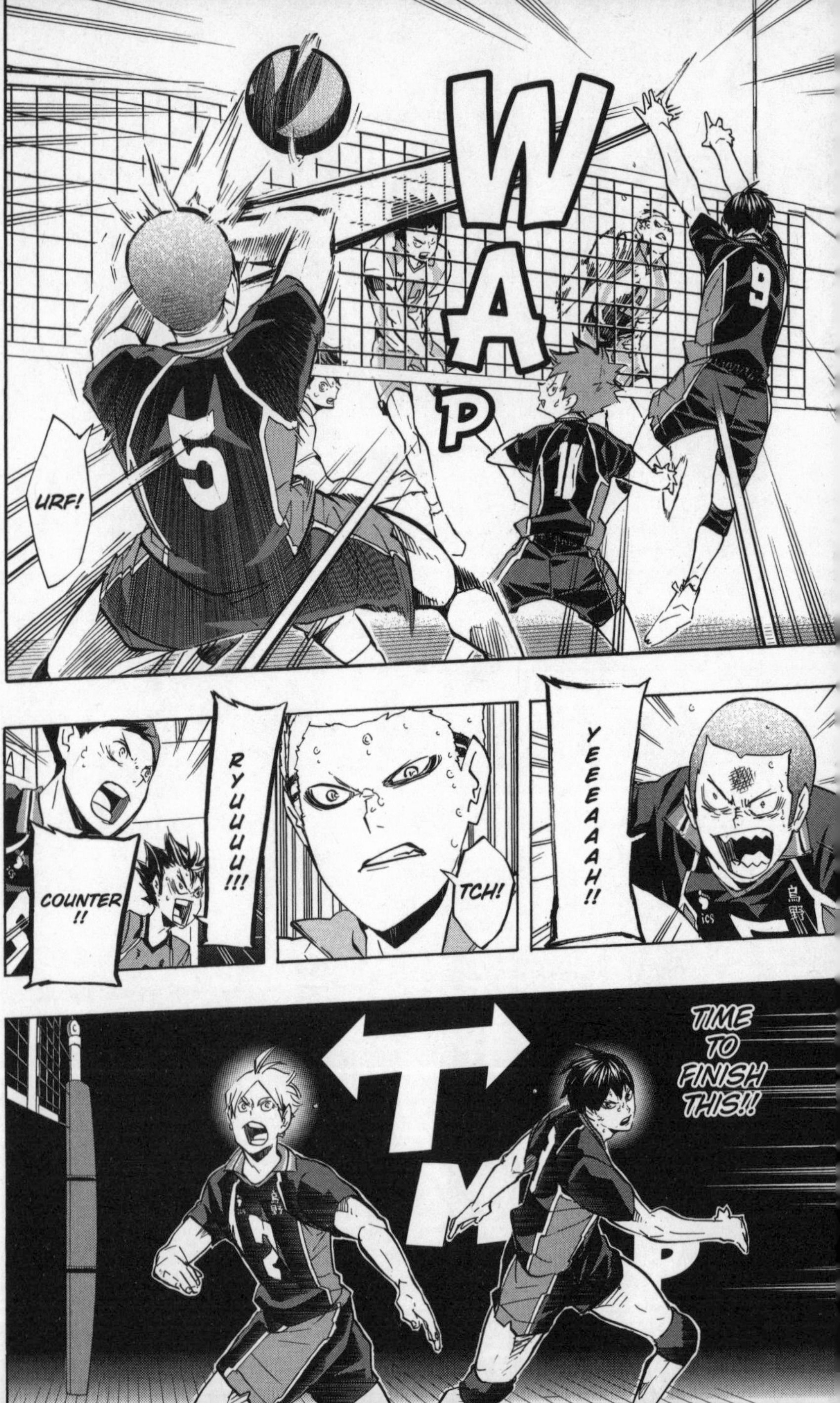
WAP
URF!
YEEEAAAH!!
TCH!
RYUUUUU!!!
COUNTER!!
TIME TO FINISH THIS!!
TMP

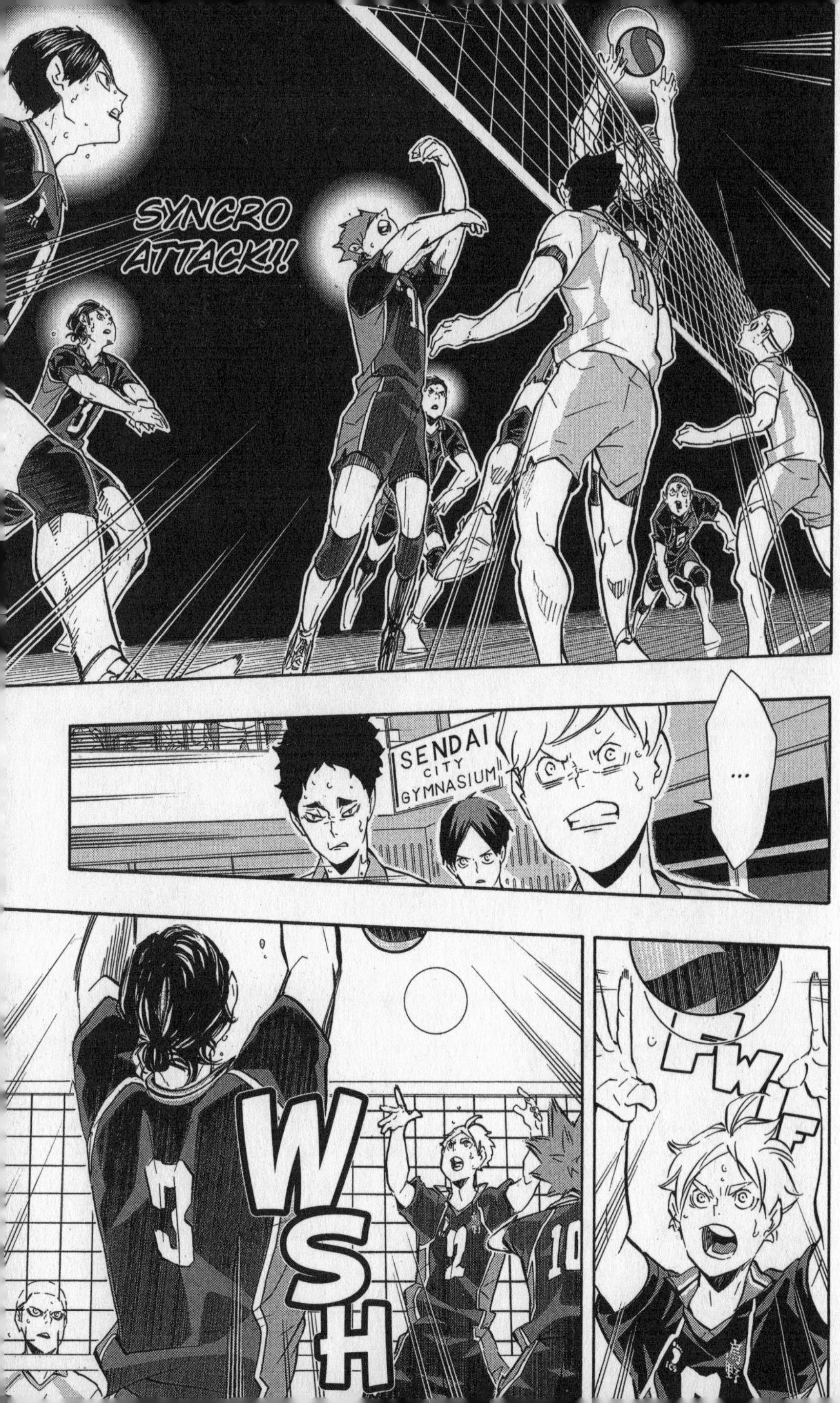
SYNCRO ATTACK!!
SENDAI CITY GYMNASIUM
...
PWFF
WSH

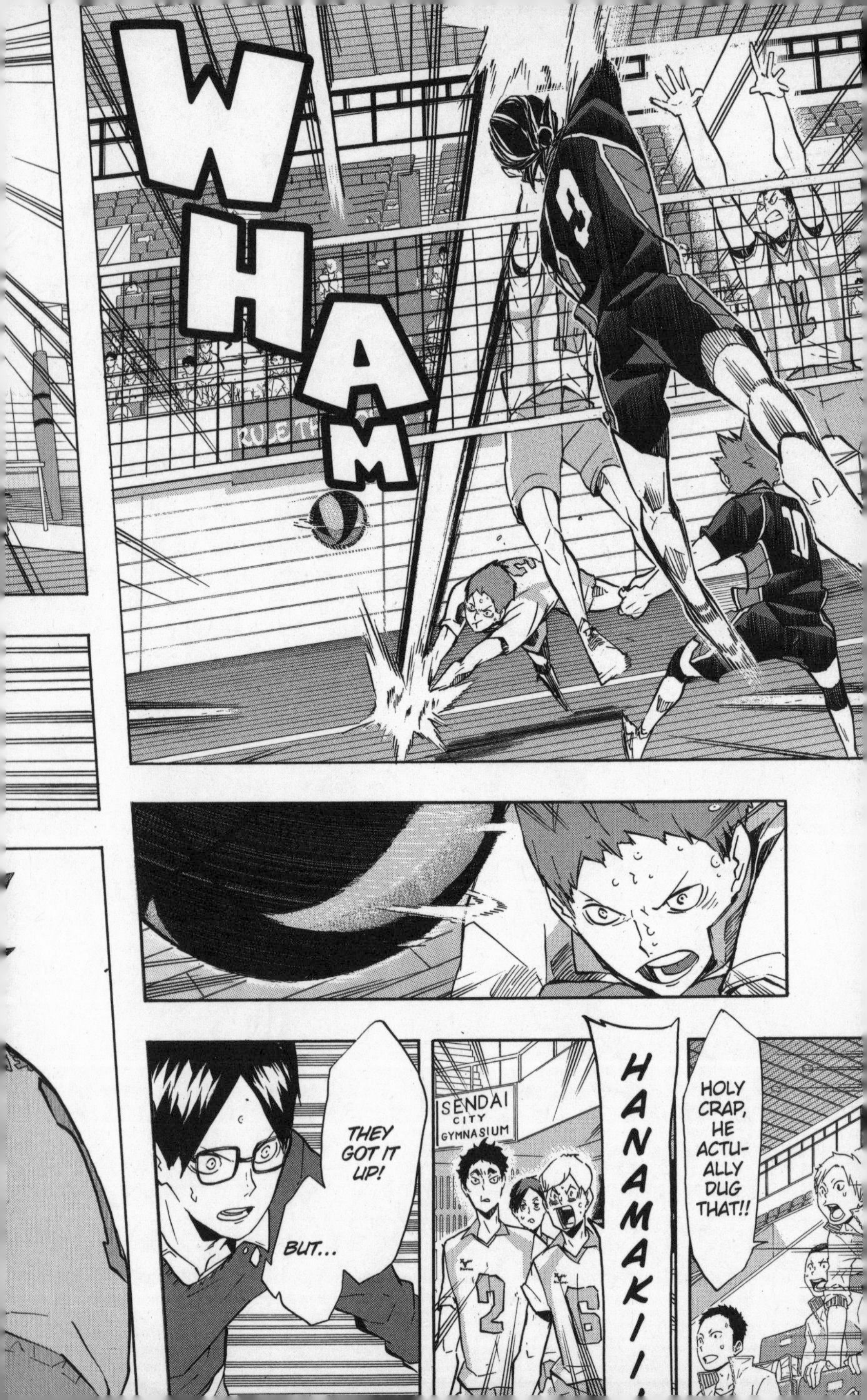
WHAM
RULE TH
HOLY CRAP, HE ACTU-ALLY DUG THAT!!
HANAMAKI!!
SENDAI CITY GYMNASIUM
THEY GOT IT UP!
BUT...

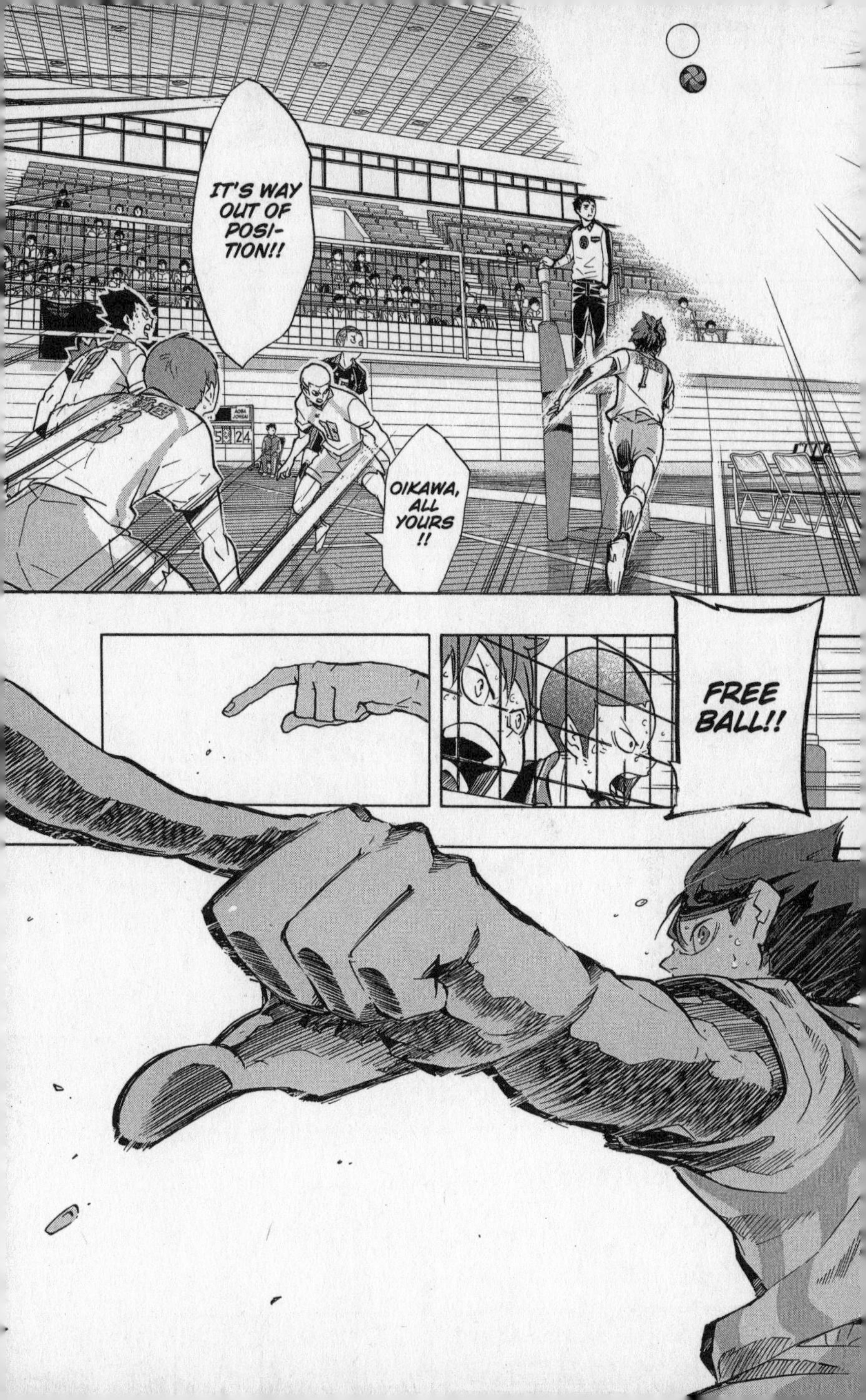
IT'S WAY OUT OF POSI-TION!!
OIKAWA, ALL YOURS !!
FREE BALL!!

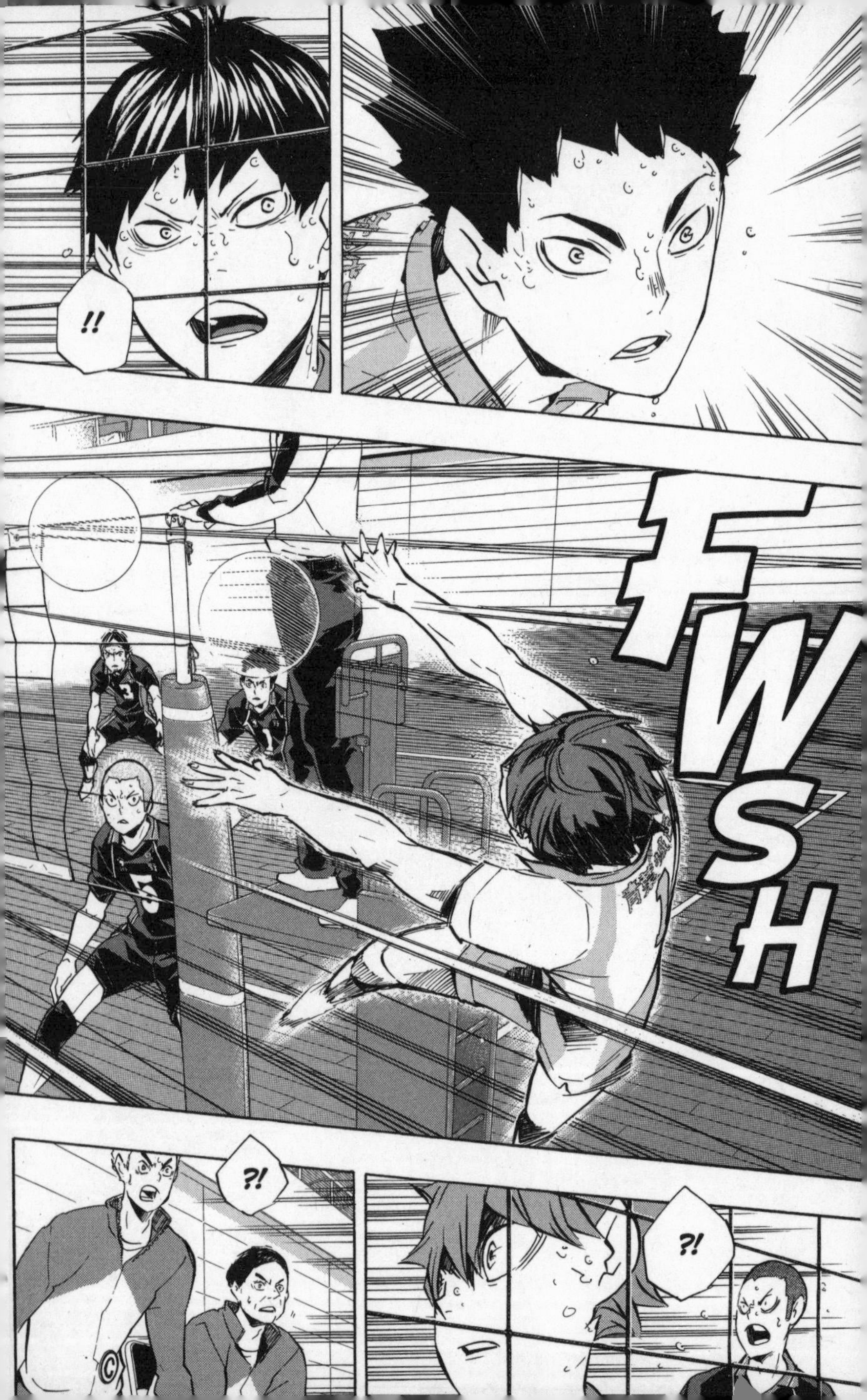
!!
FWSH
?!
?!

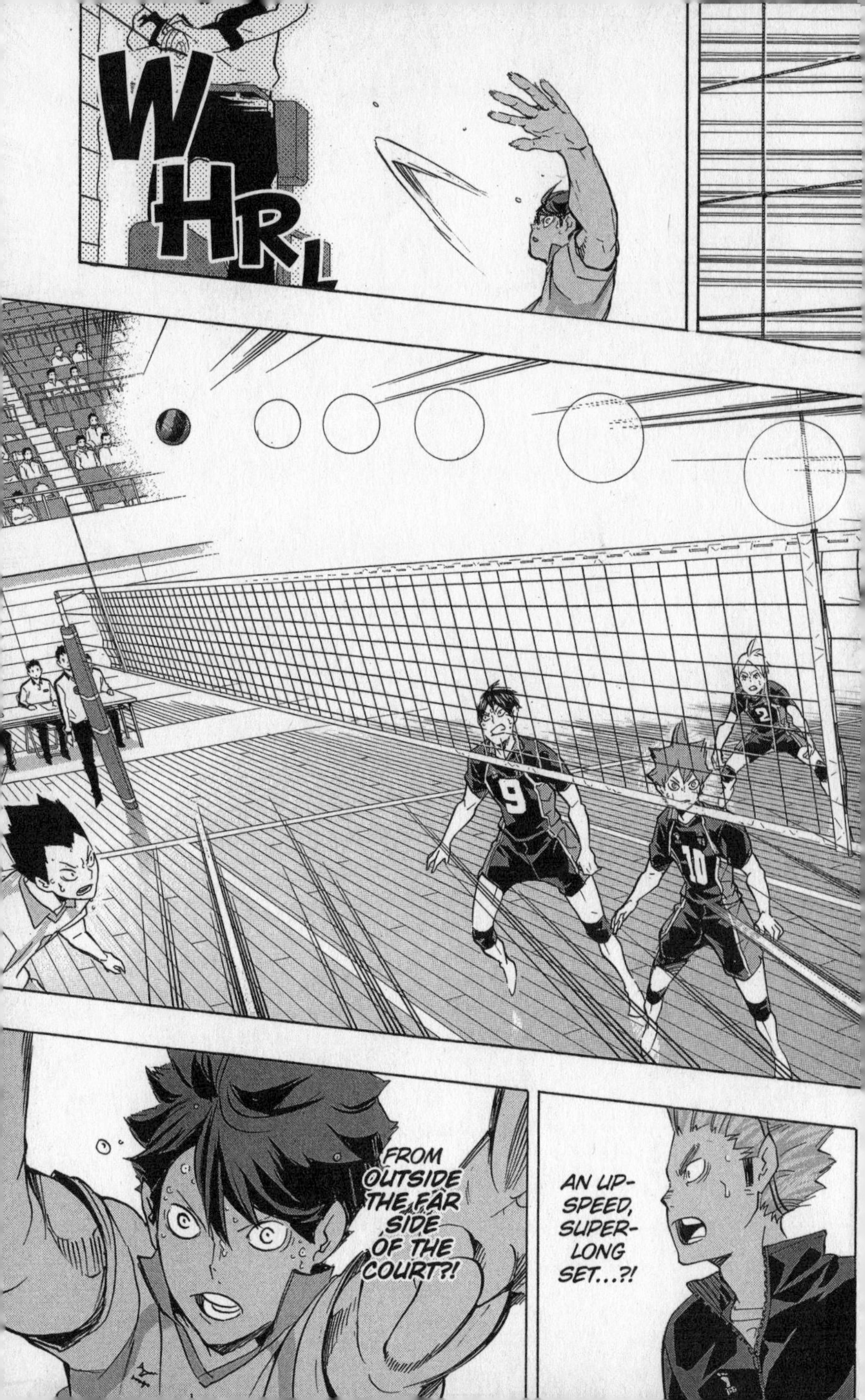
WHRL
AN UP-SPEED, SUPER-LONG SET...?!
FROM OUTSIDE THE FAR SIDE OF THE COURT?!

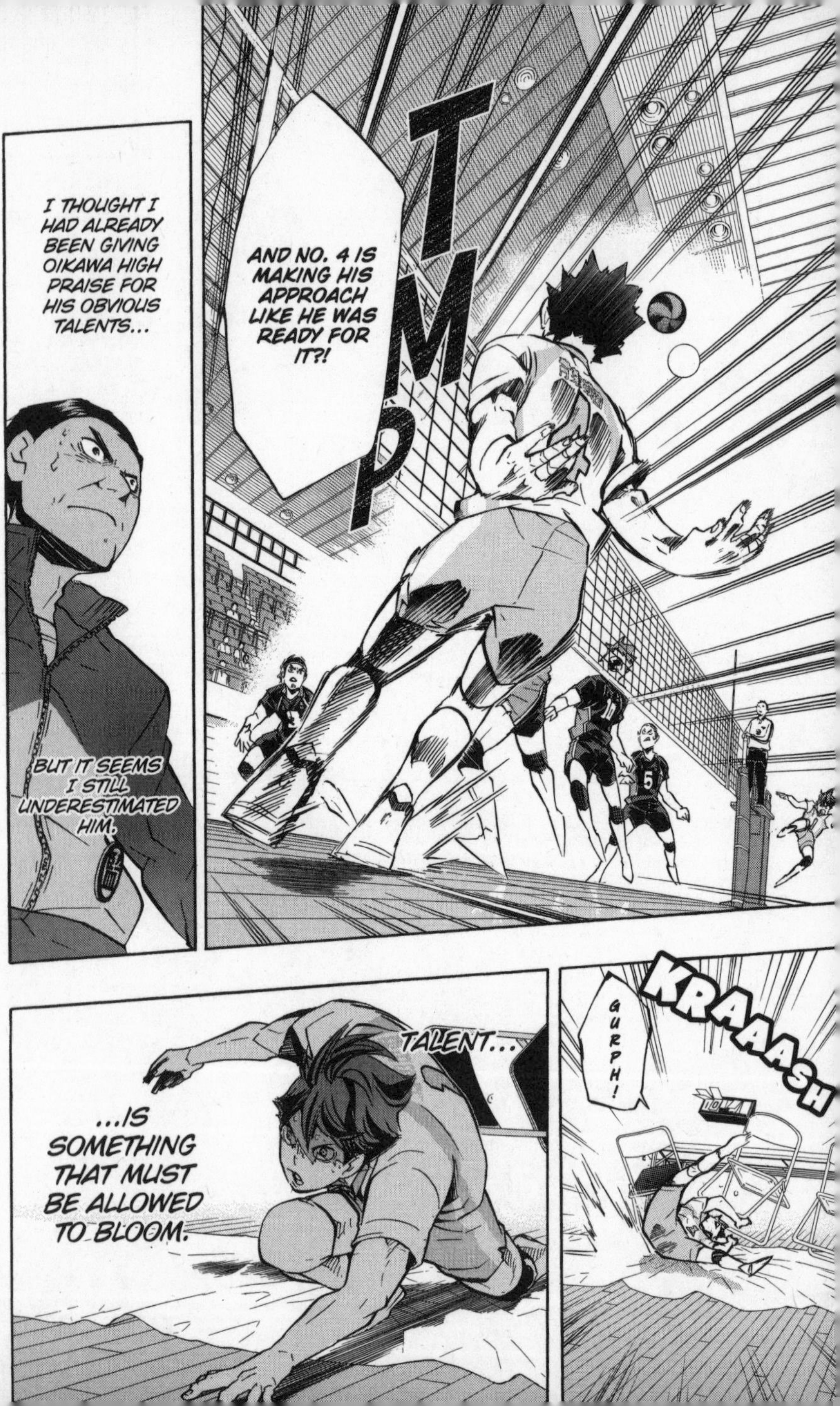
TMP
AND NO. 4 IS MAKING HIS APPROACH LIKE HE WAS READY FOR IT?!
I THOUGHT I HAD ALREADY BEEN GIVING OIKAWA HIGH PRAISE FOR HIS OBVIOUS TALENTS...
BUT IT SEEMS I STILL UNDERESTIMATED HIM.
KRAAASH
GURPH!
TALENT...
...IS SOMETHING THAT MUST BE ALLOWED TO BLOOM.

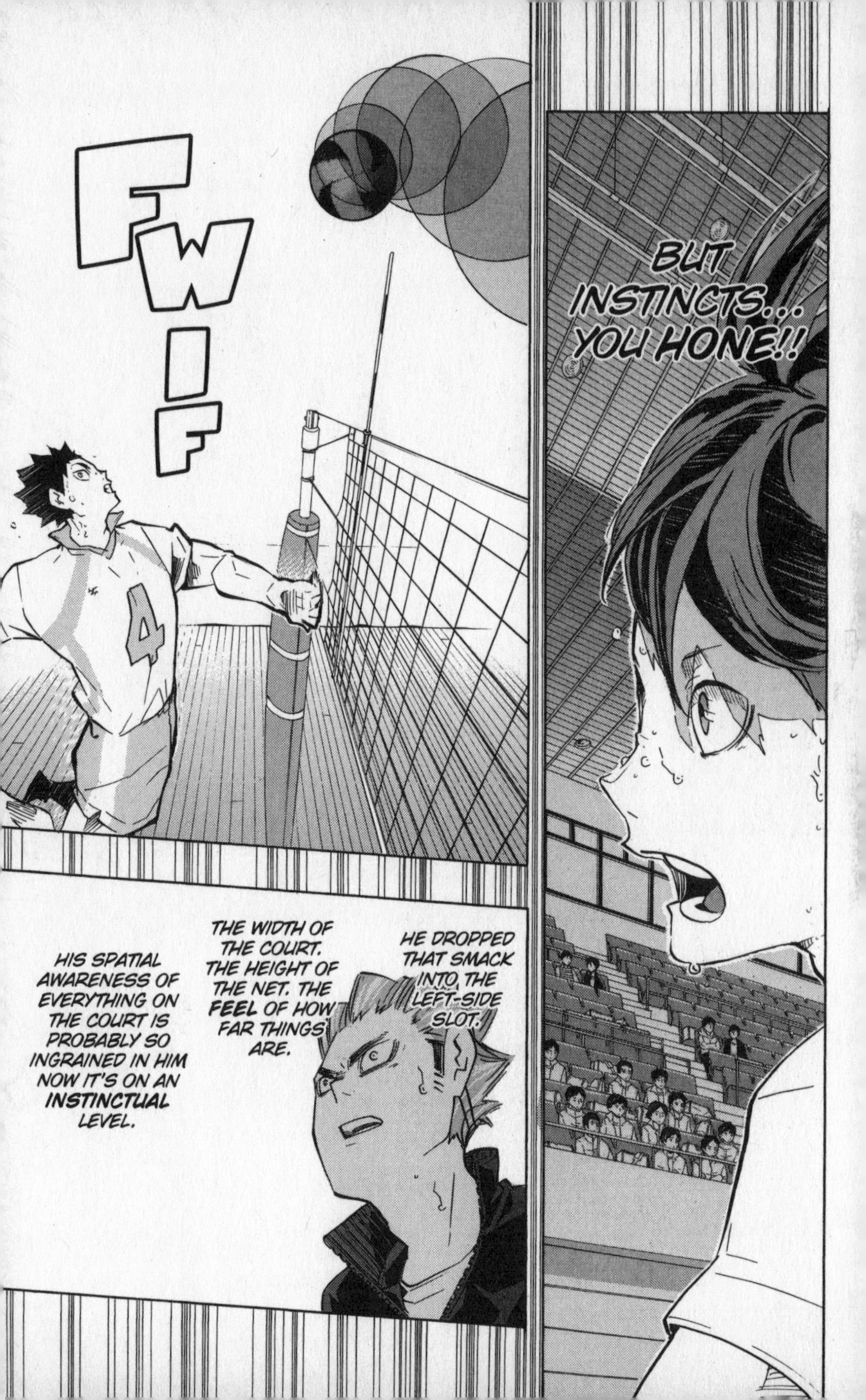
BUT INSTINCTS... YOU HONE!!
FWIF
HE DROPPED THAT SMACK INTO THE LEFT-SIDE SLOT.
THE WIDTH OF THE COURT. THE HEIGHT OF THE NET. THE FEEL OF HOW FAR THINGS ARE.
HIS SPATIAL AWARENESS OF EVERYTHING ON THE COURT IS PROBABLY SO INGRAINED IN HIM NOW IT'S ON AN INSTINCTUAL LEVEL.

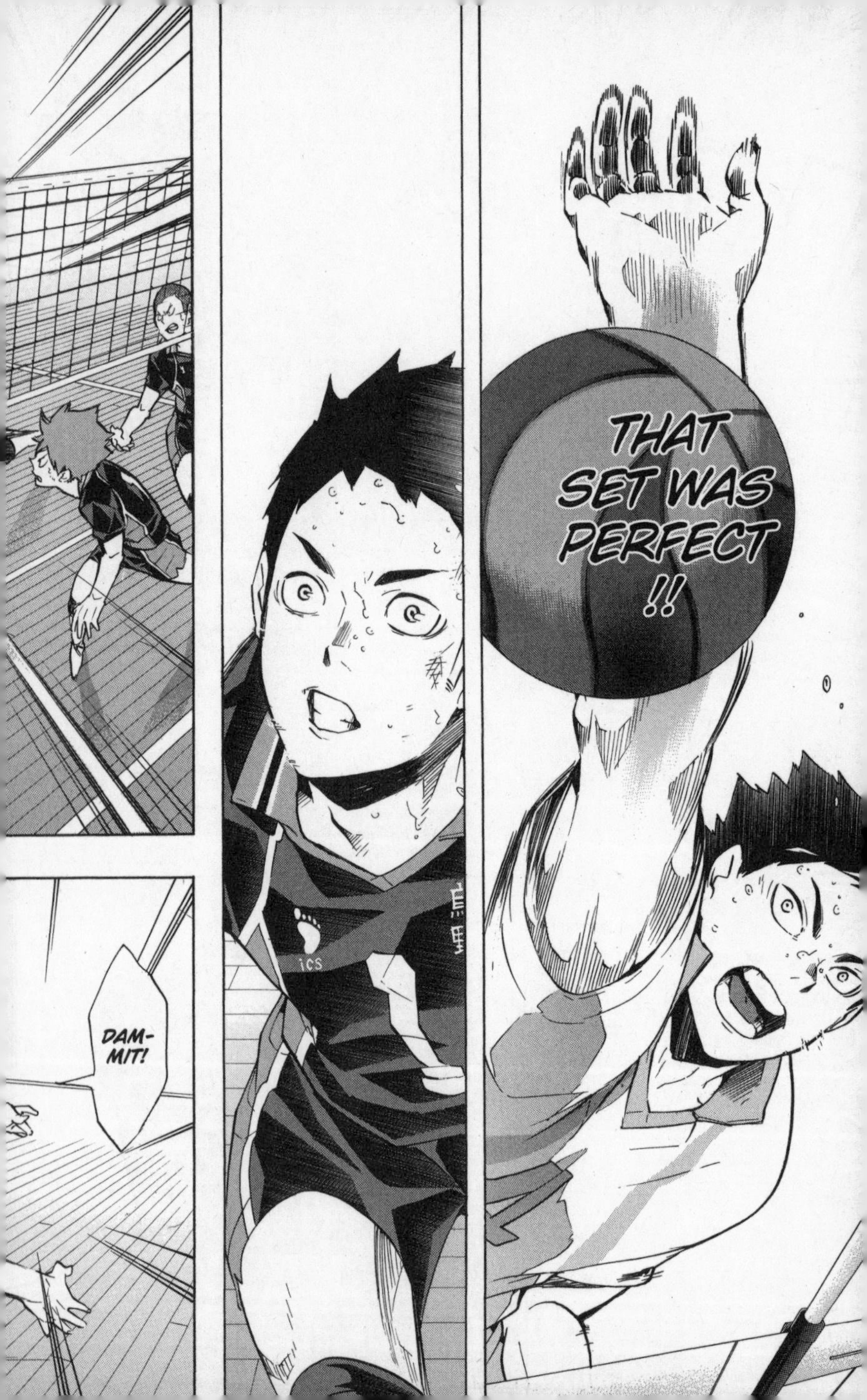
THAT SET WAS PERFECT!!
DAM-MIT!

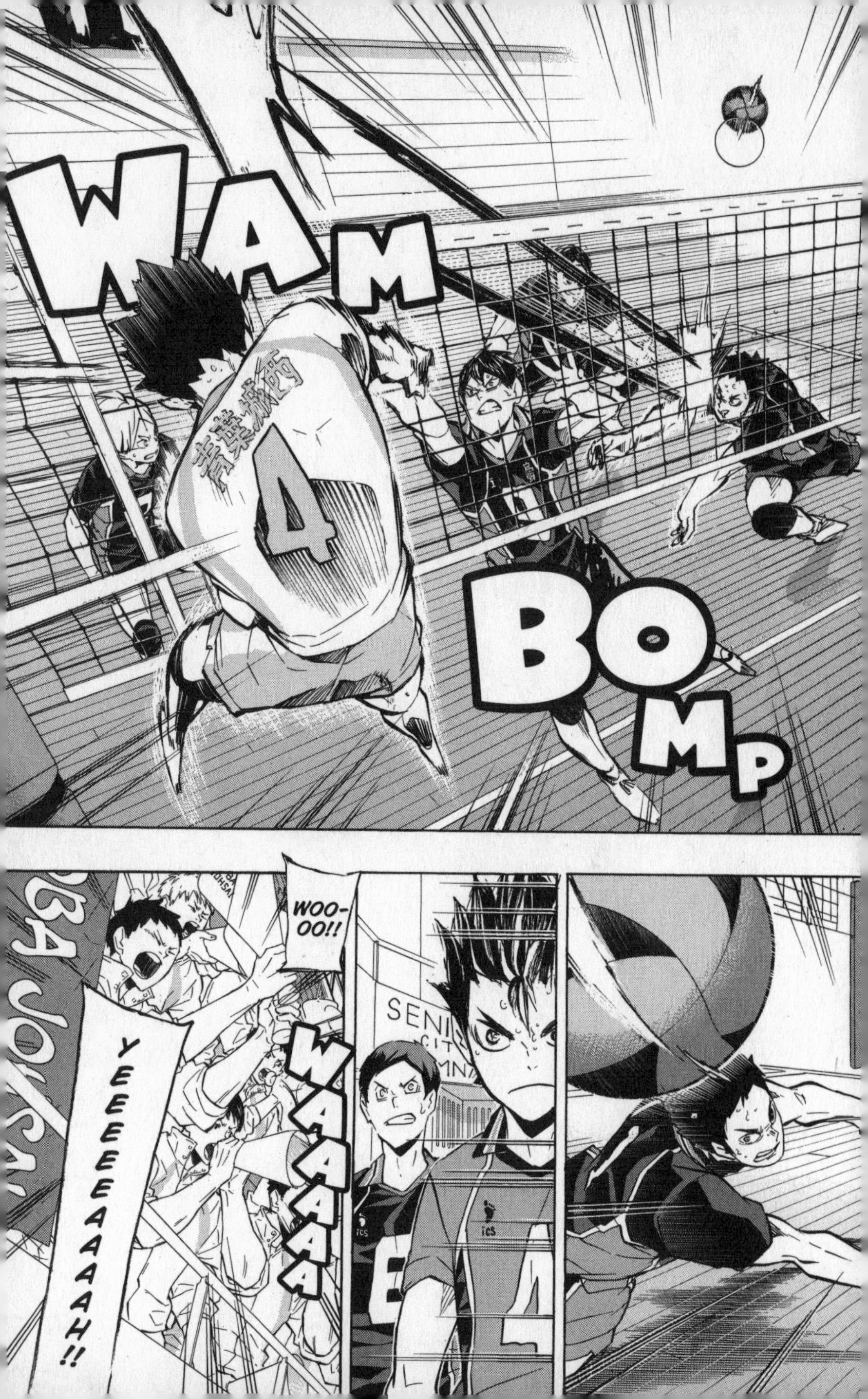
WAM
BOMP
WOO-OO!!
WAAAAAA
YEEEEEEAAAAAH!!

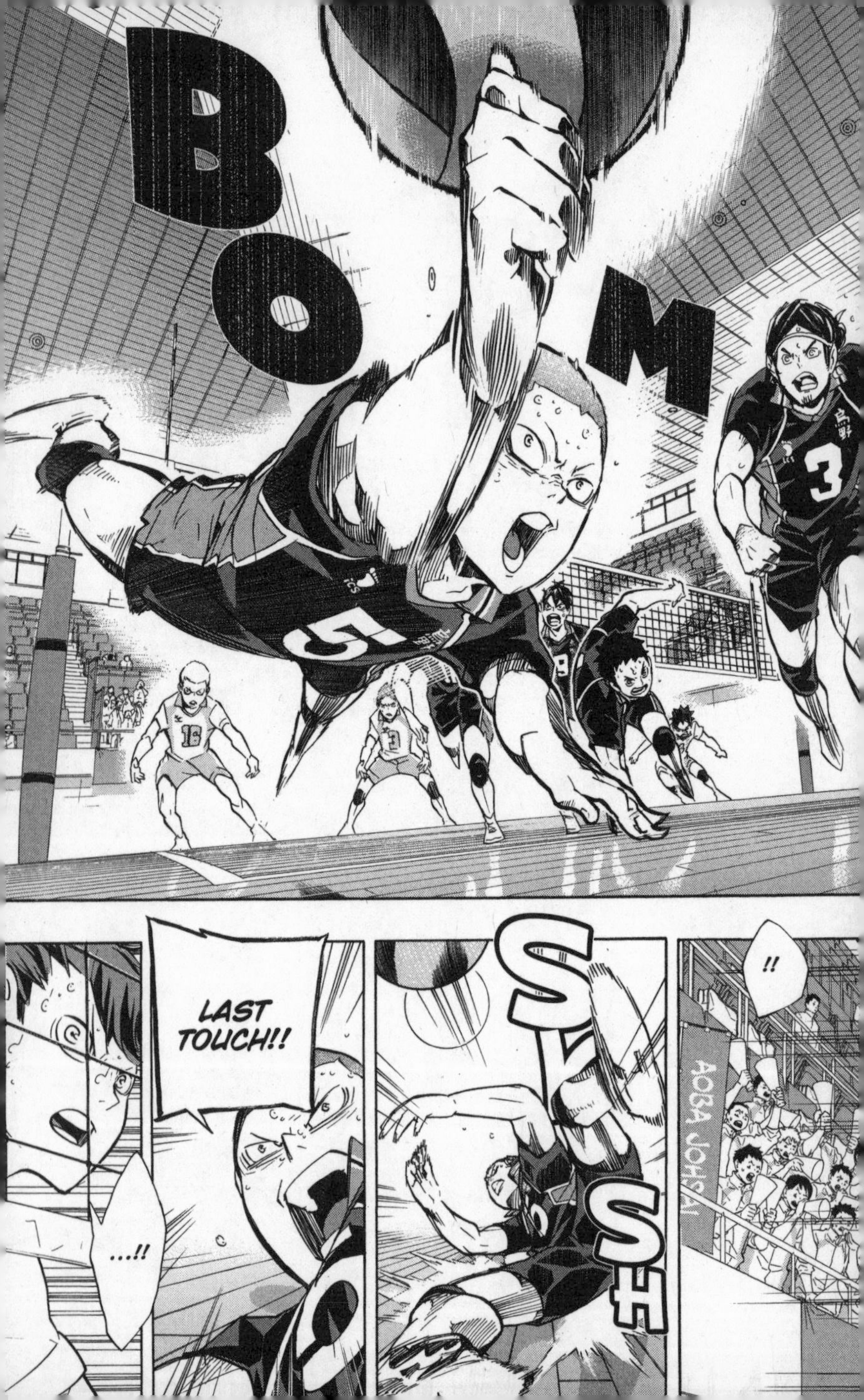
BOOM
!!
AOBA JOHSAI
SHSH
LAST TOUCH!!
...!!

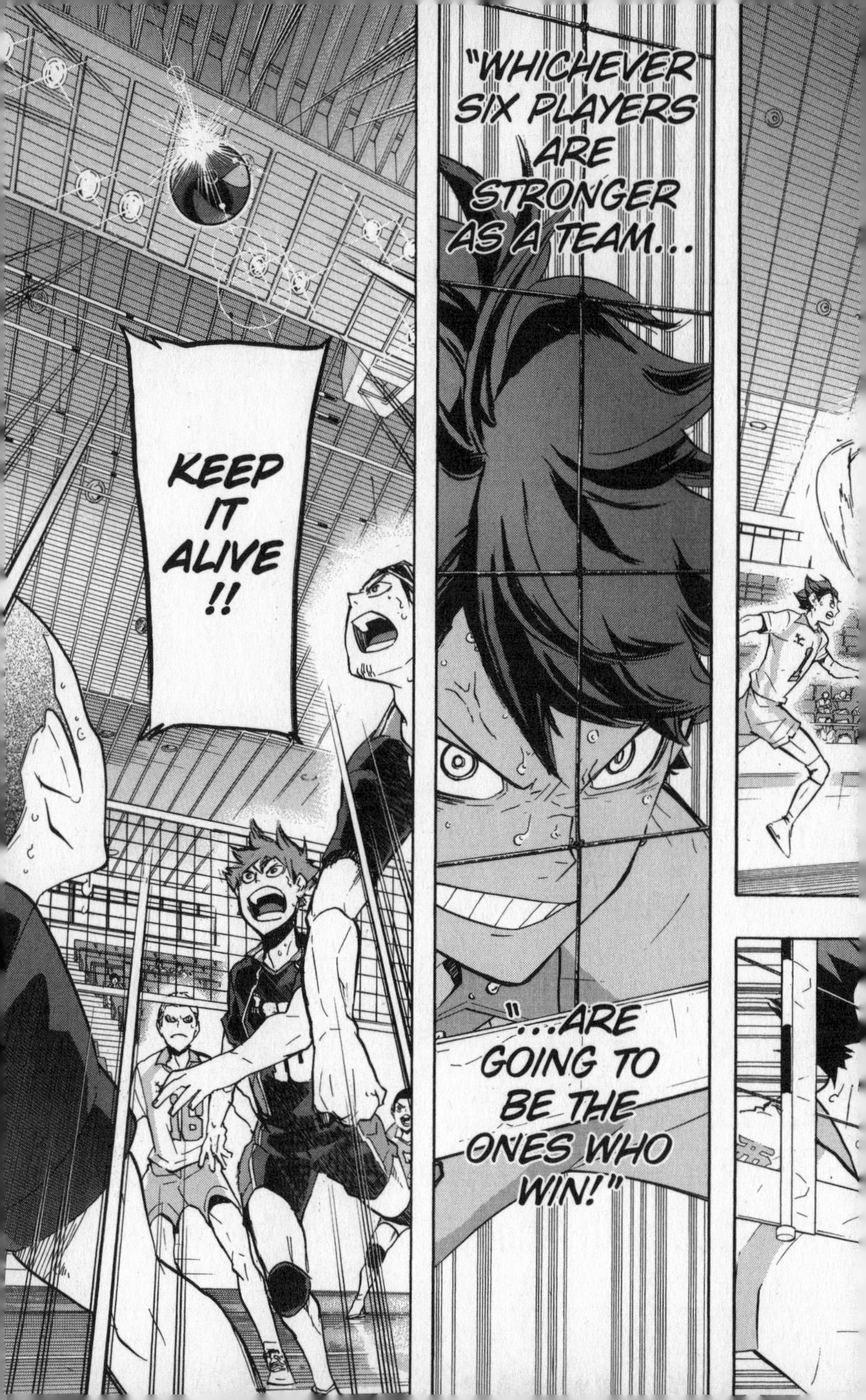
"WHICHEVER SIX PLAYERS ARE STRONGER AS A TEAM...
"...ARE GOING TO BE THE ONES WHO WIN!"
KEEP IT ALIVE!!

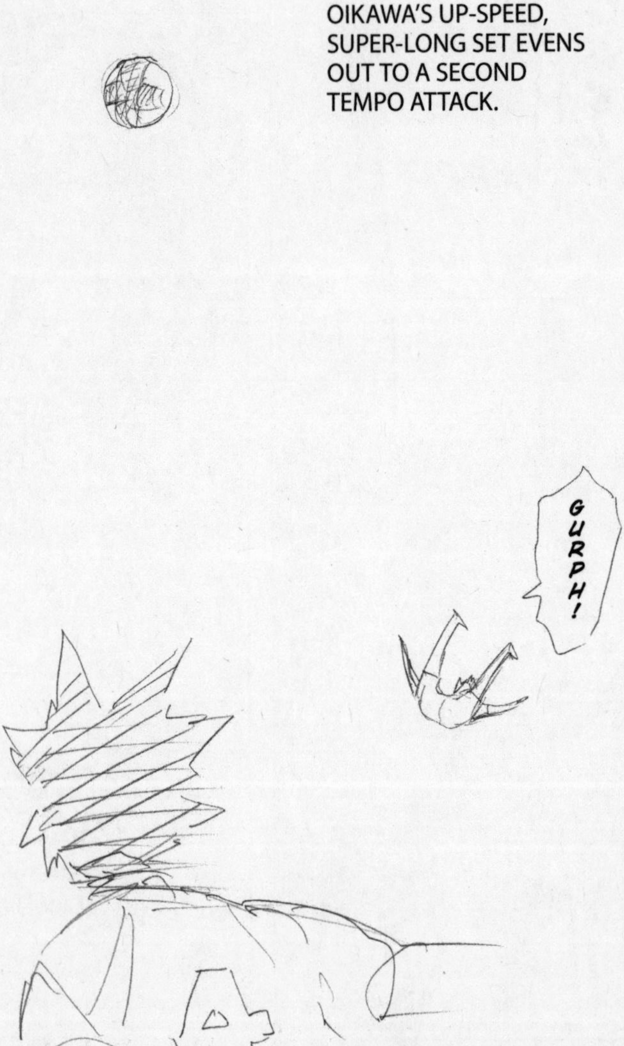
OIKAWA'S UP-SPEED, SUPER-LONG SET EVENS OUT TO A SECOND TEMPO ATTACK.
GURPH!

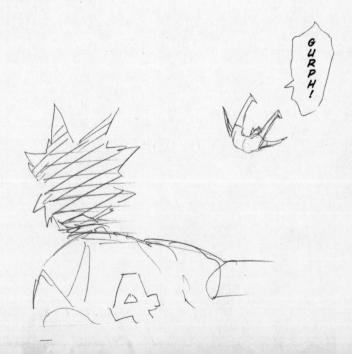

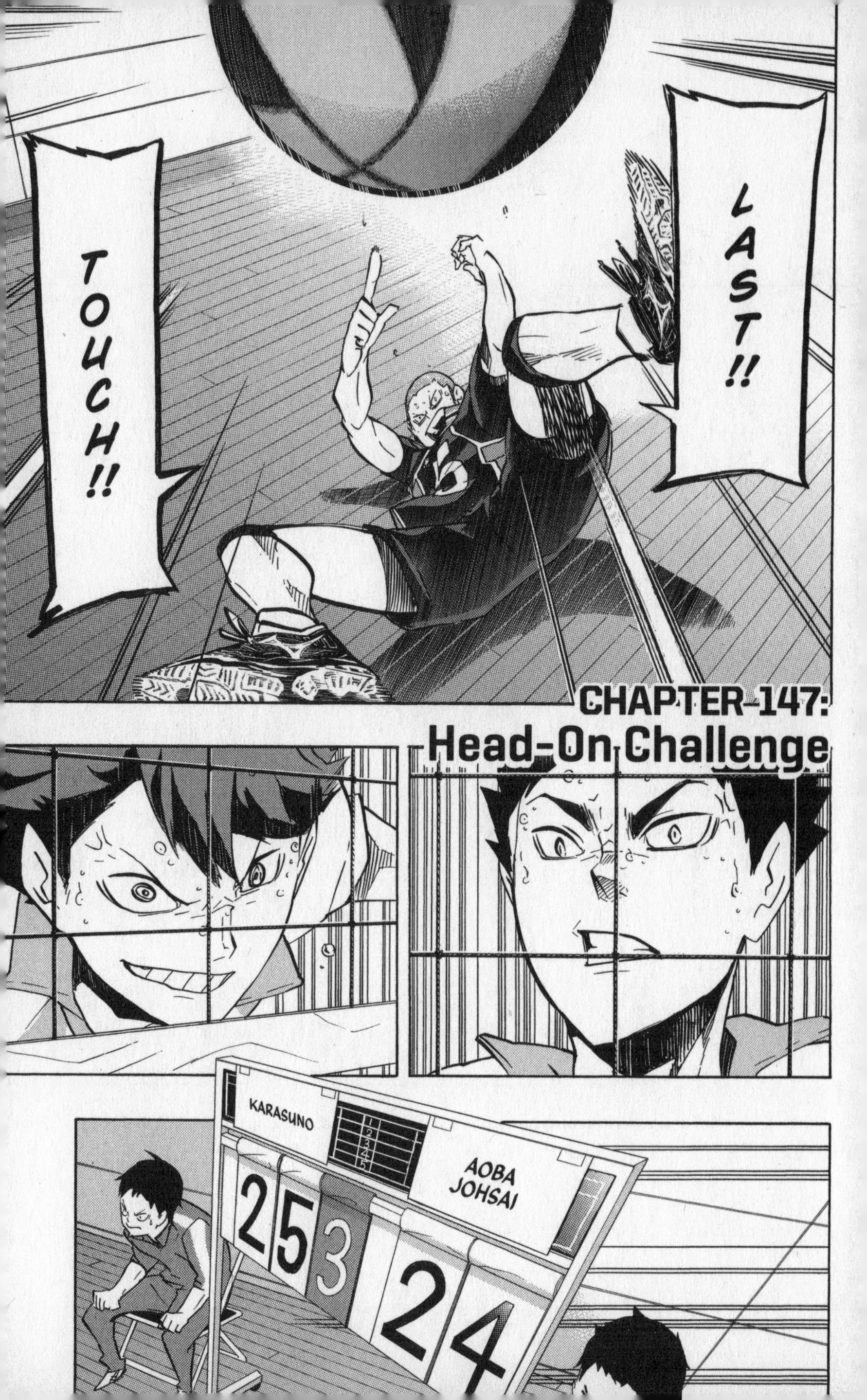
LAST!!
TOUCH!!
CHAPTER 147:
Head-On Challenge
KARASUNO
AOBA JOHSAI
25
3
24

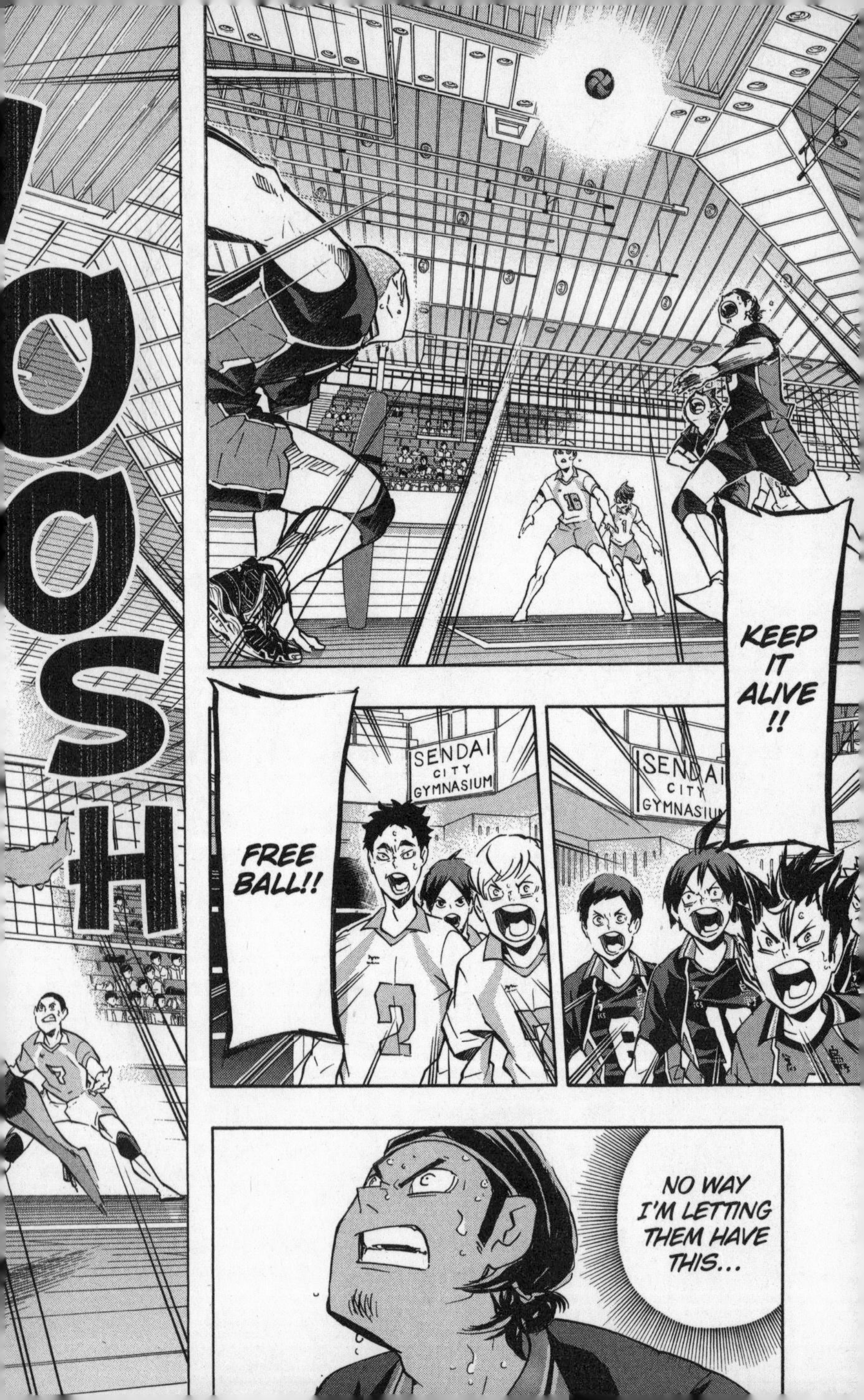
KEEP IT ALIVE!!
SENDAI CITY GYMNASIUM
SENDAI CITY GYMNASIUM
FREE BALL!!
NO WAY I'M LETTING THEM HAVE THIS...

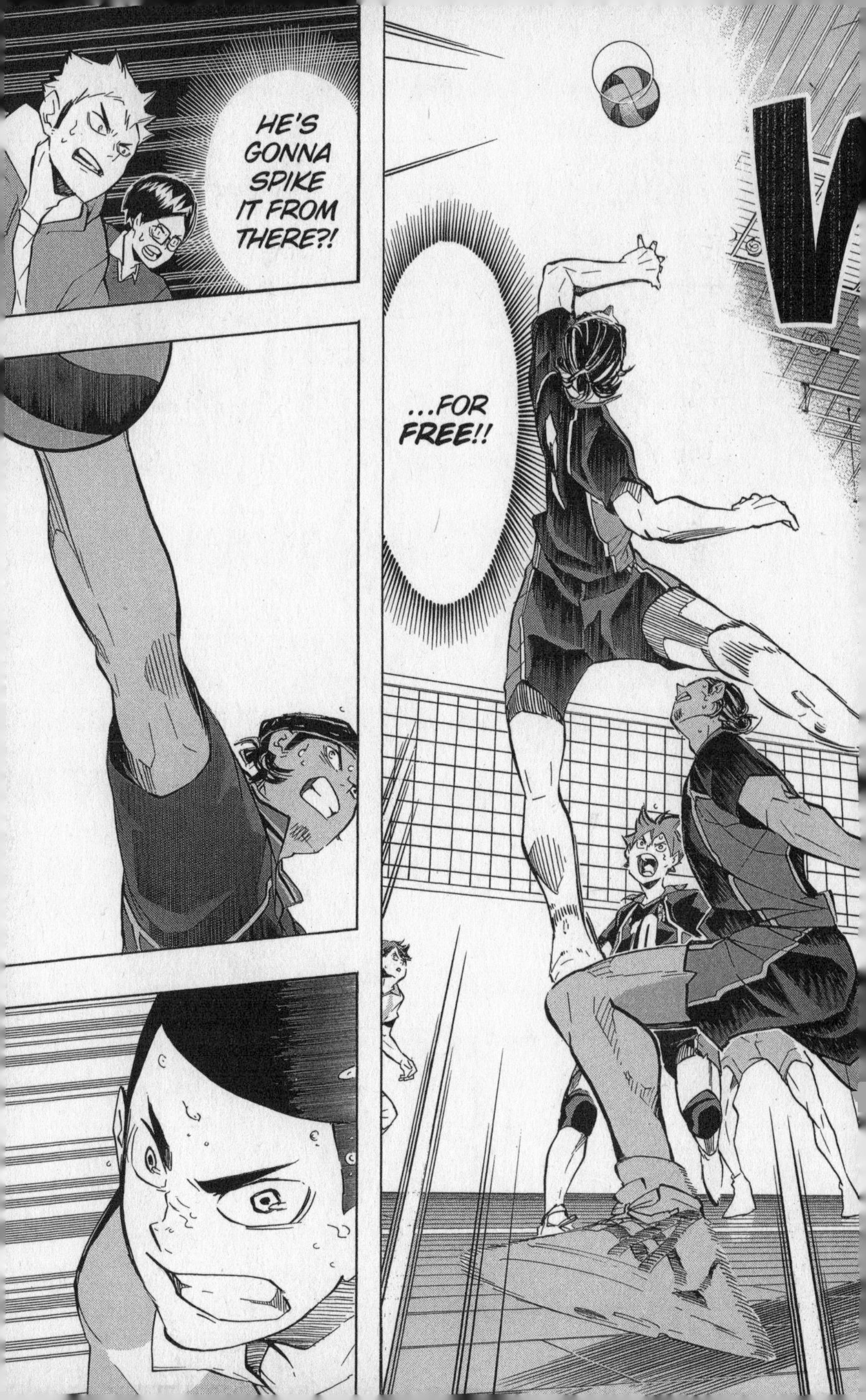
...FOR FREE!!
HE'S GONNA SPIKE IT FROM THERE?!

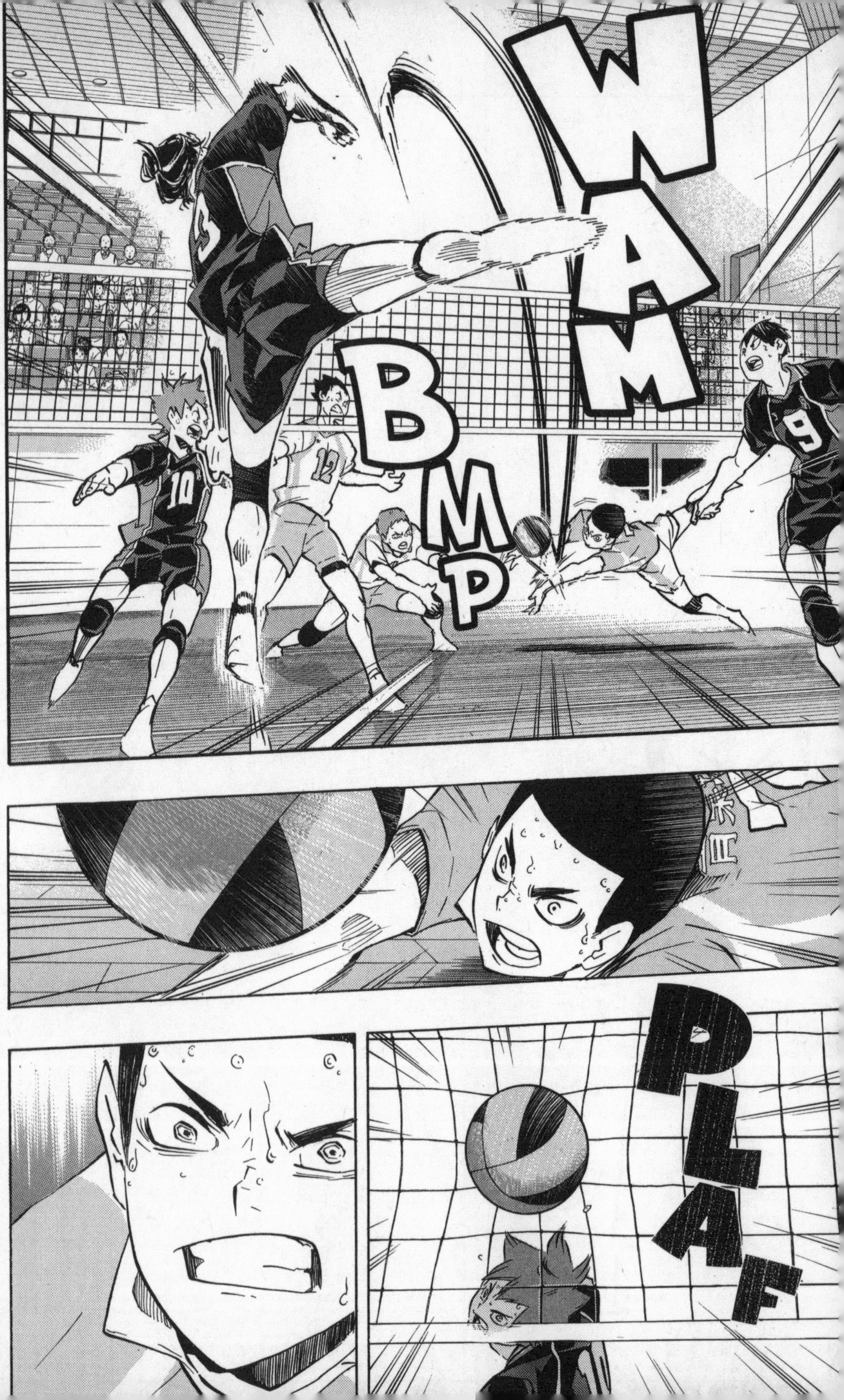
WAM
BMP
PLAF

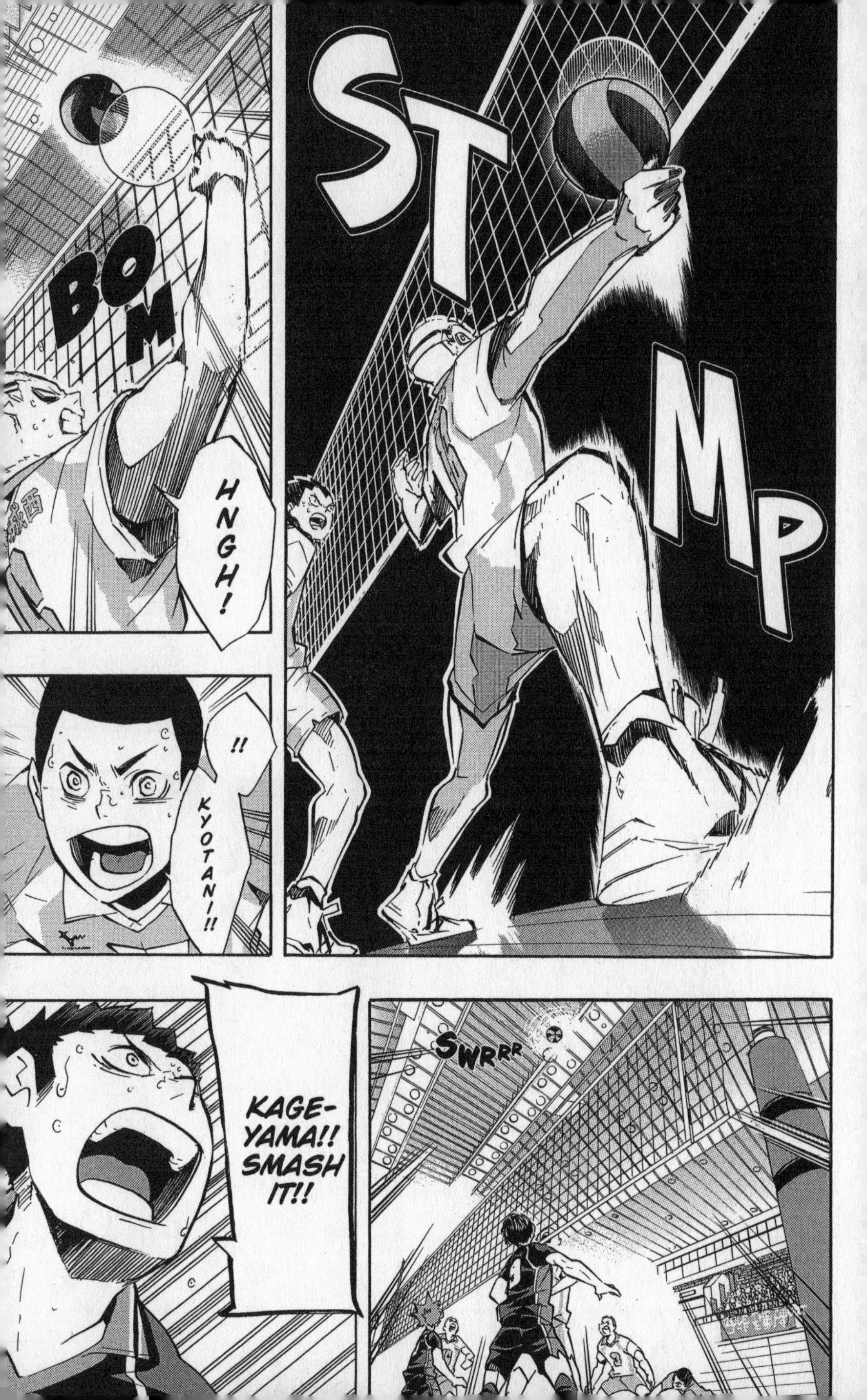
STOMP
BOOM
HNGH!
!!
KYOTANI!!
SWRRR
KAGE-YAMA!! SMASH IT!!

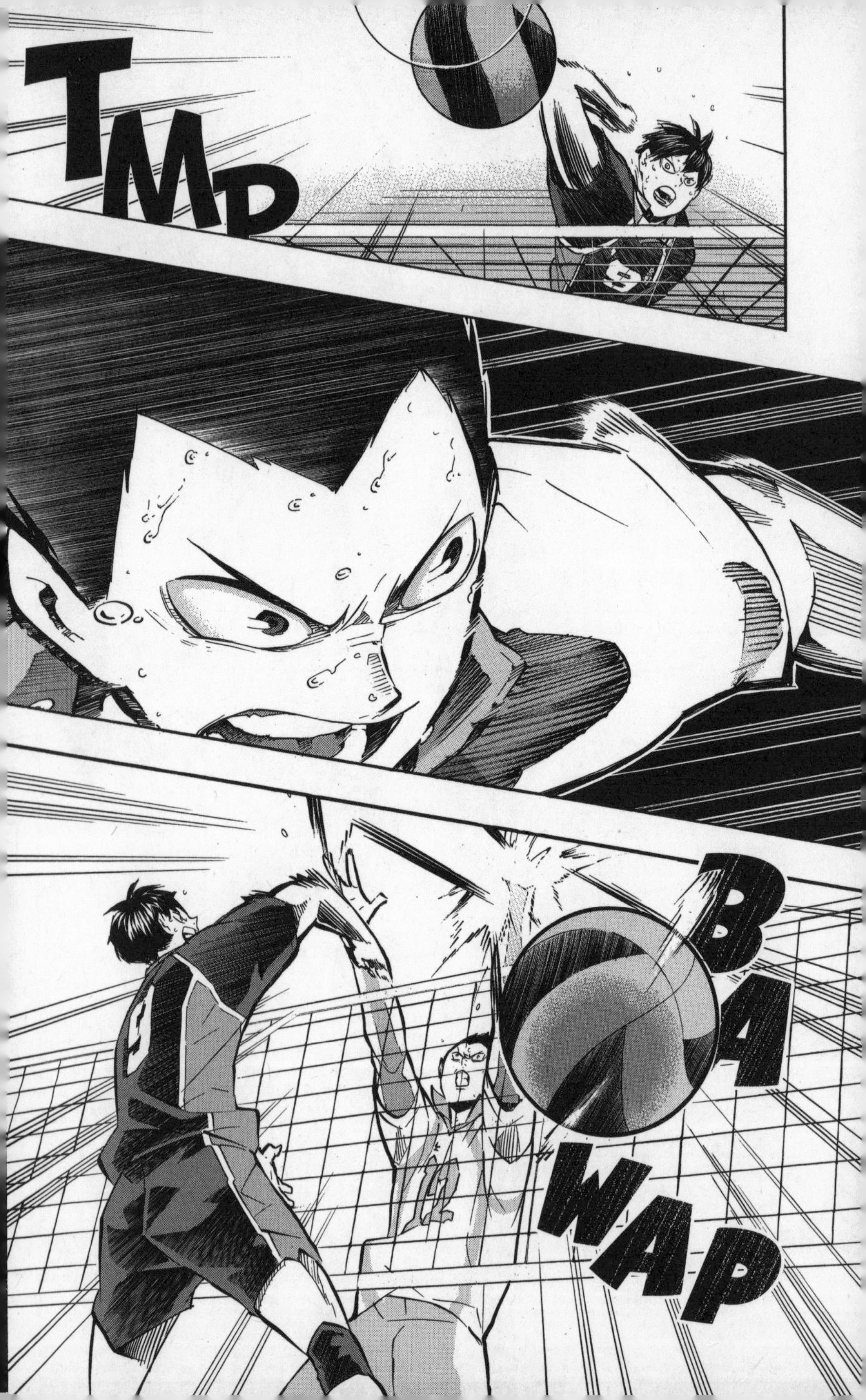
TMP
BA
WAP

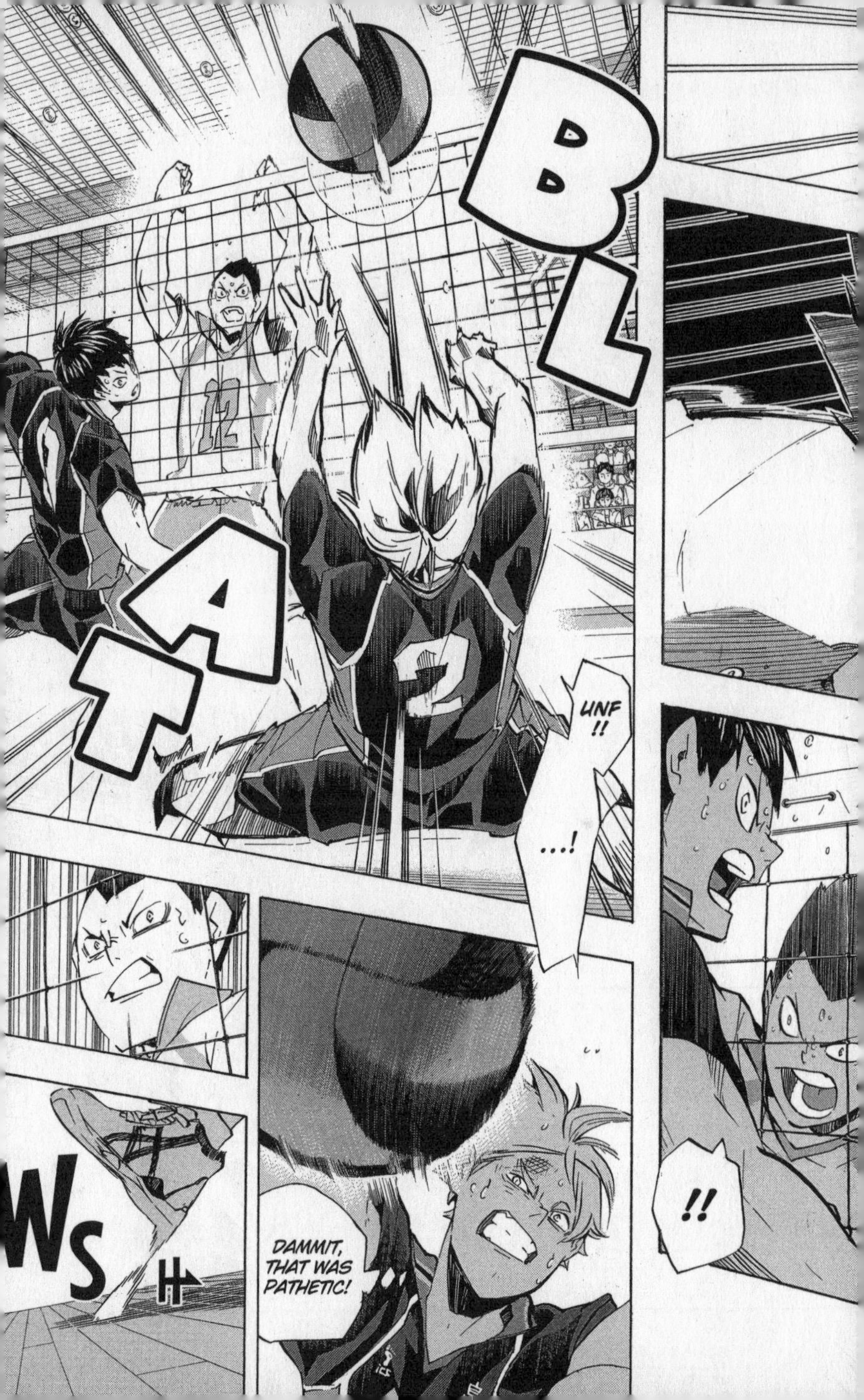
BLAT
UNF !!
...!
!!
DAMMIT, THAT WAS PATHETIC!
WSH

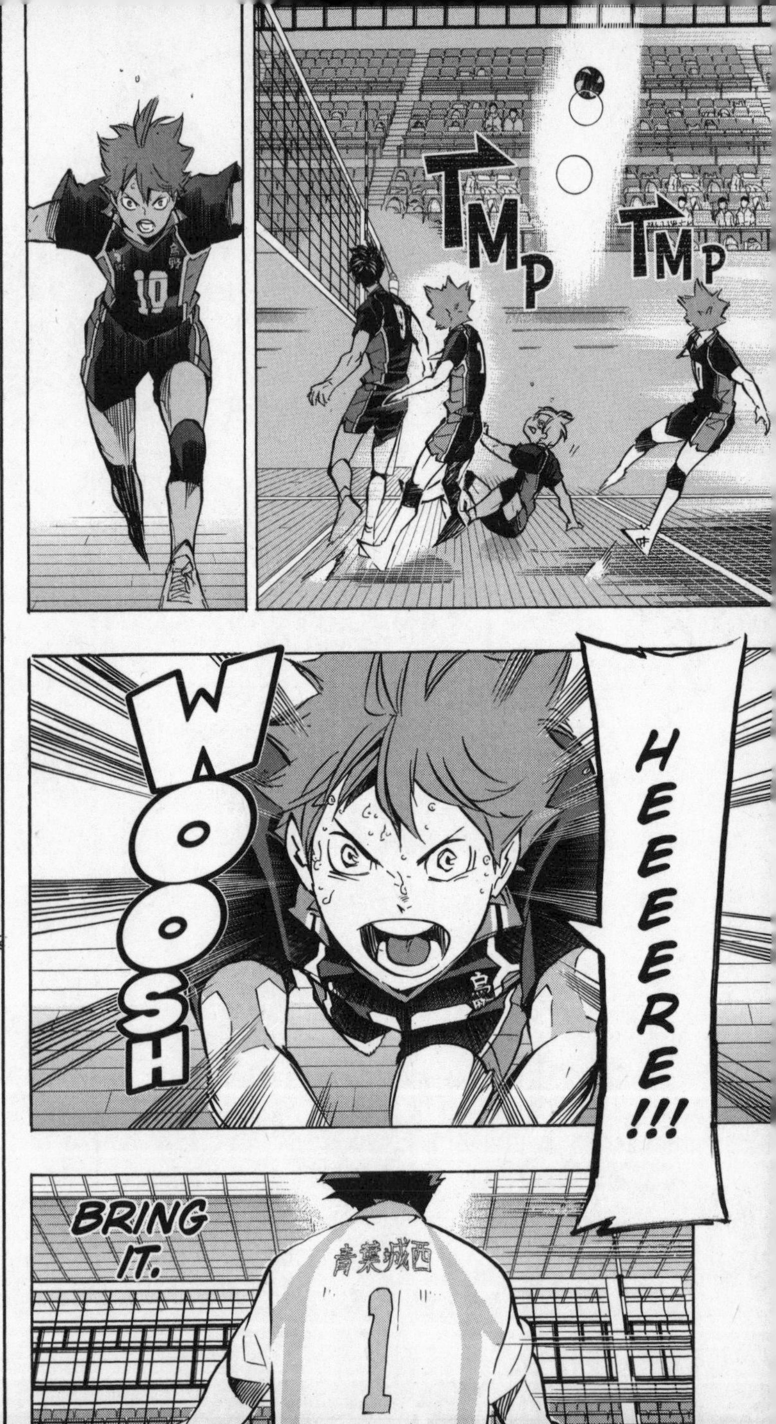
TMP
TMP
HEEEEERE!!!
WOOSH
BRING IT.
青葉城西

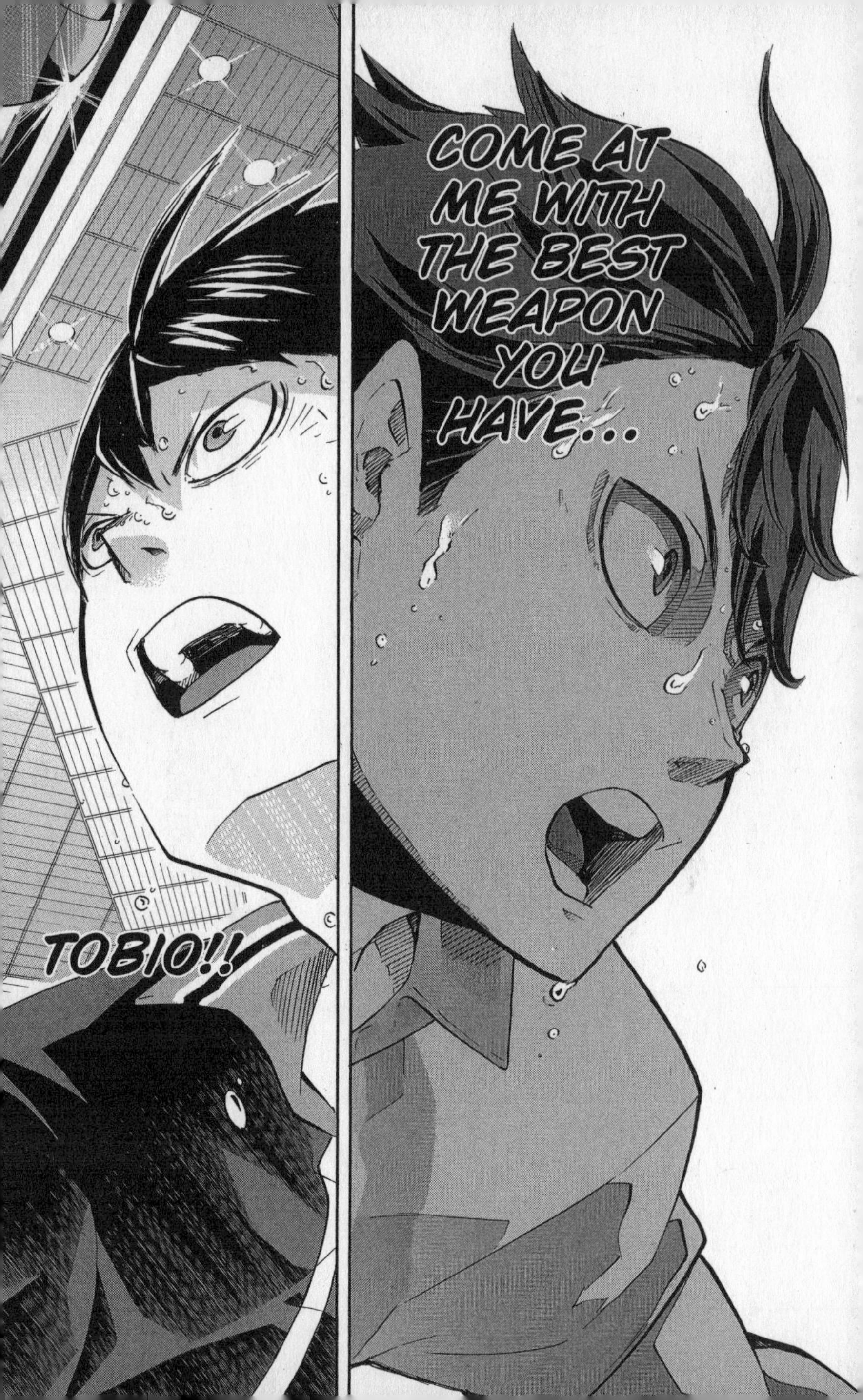
COME AT ME WITH THE BEST WEAPON YOU HAVE...
TOBIO!!

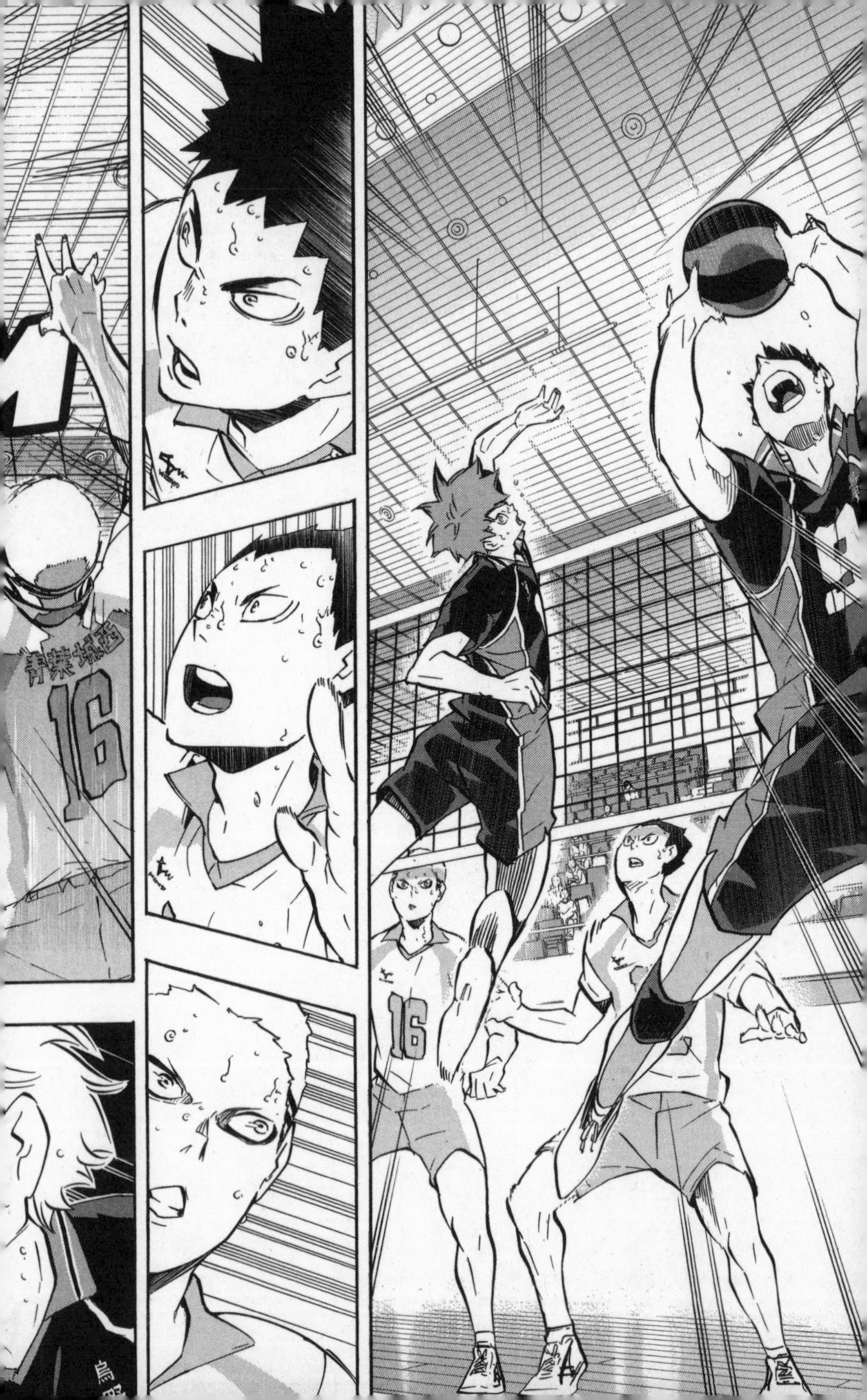
青葉城西
16
16

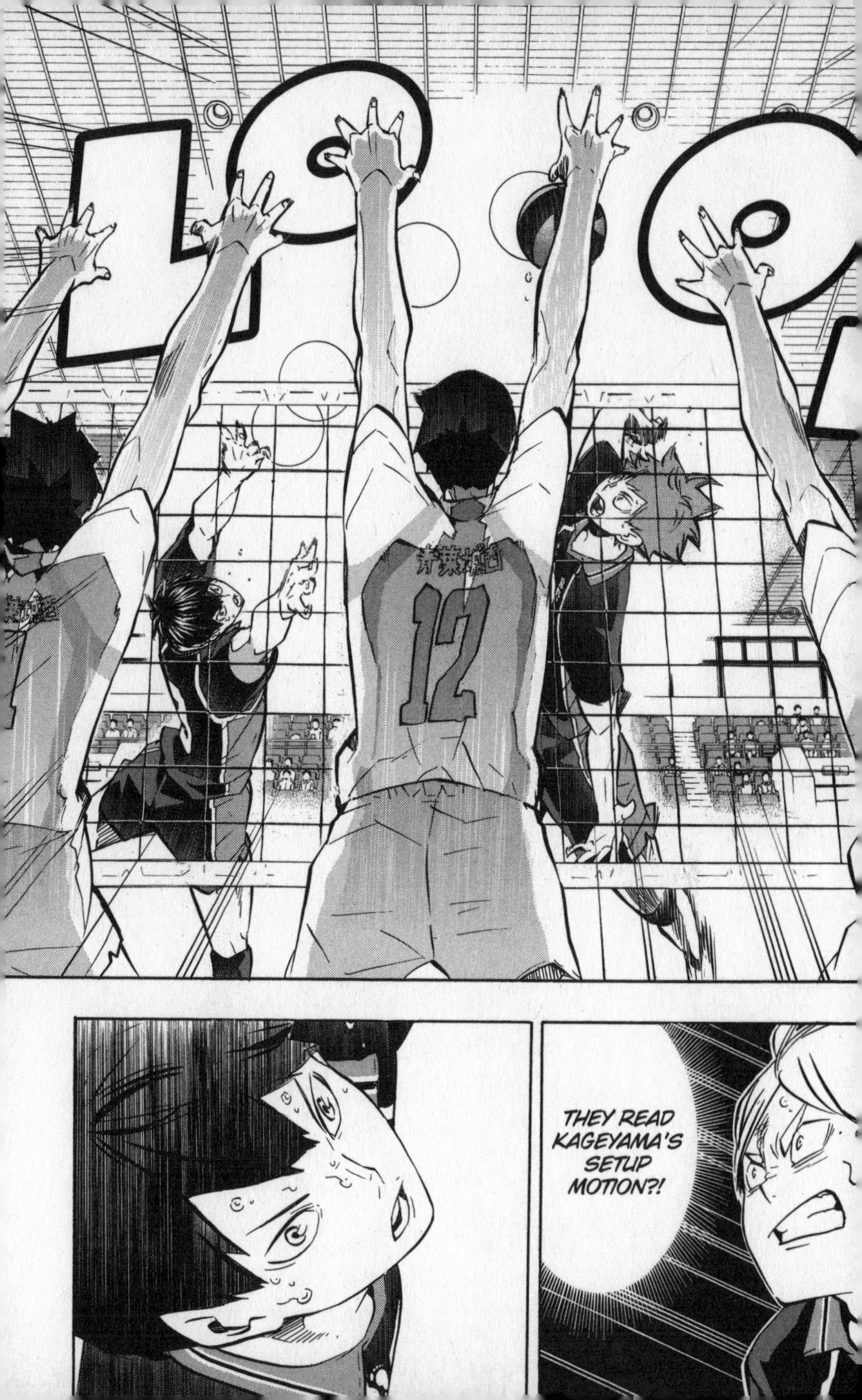
THEY READ KAGEYAMA'S SETUP MOTION?!

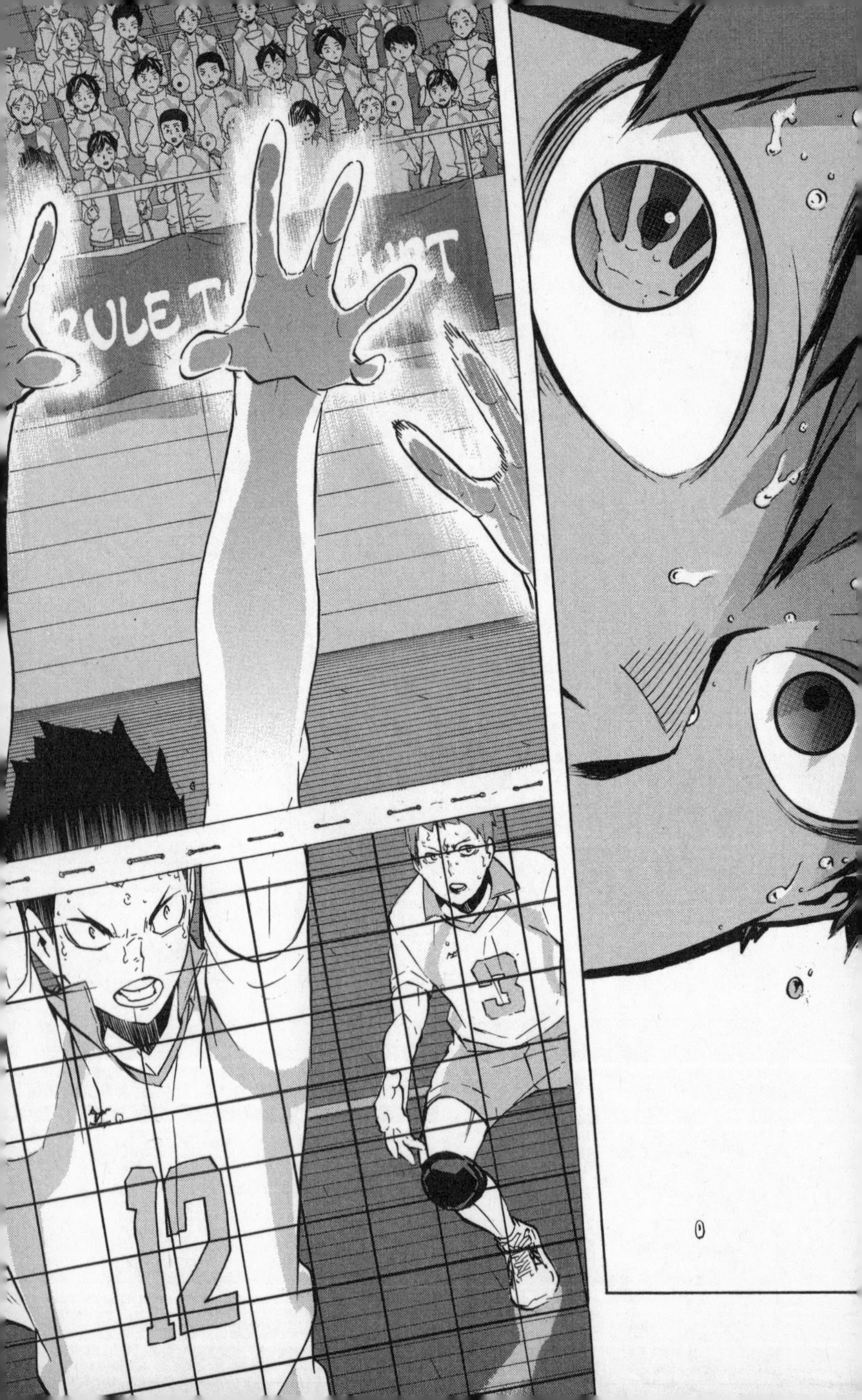

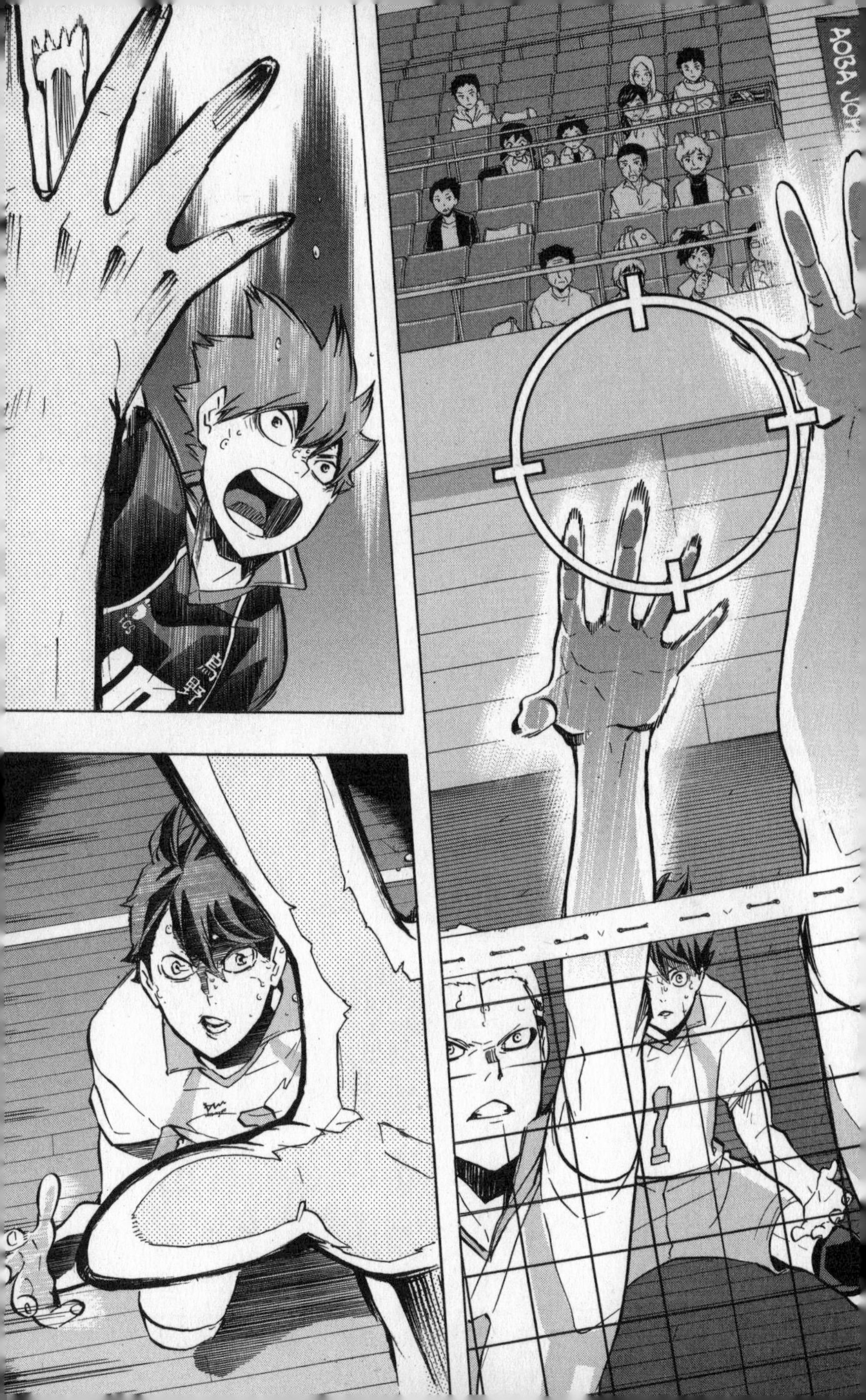
AOBA JOH

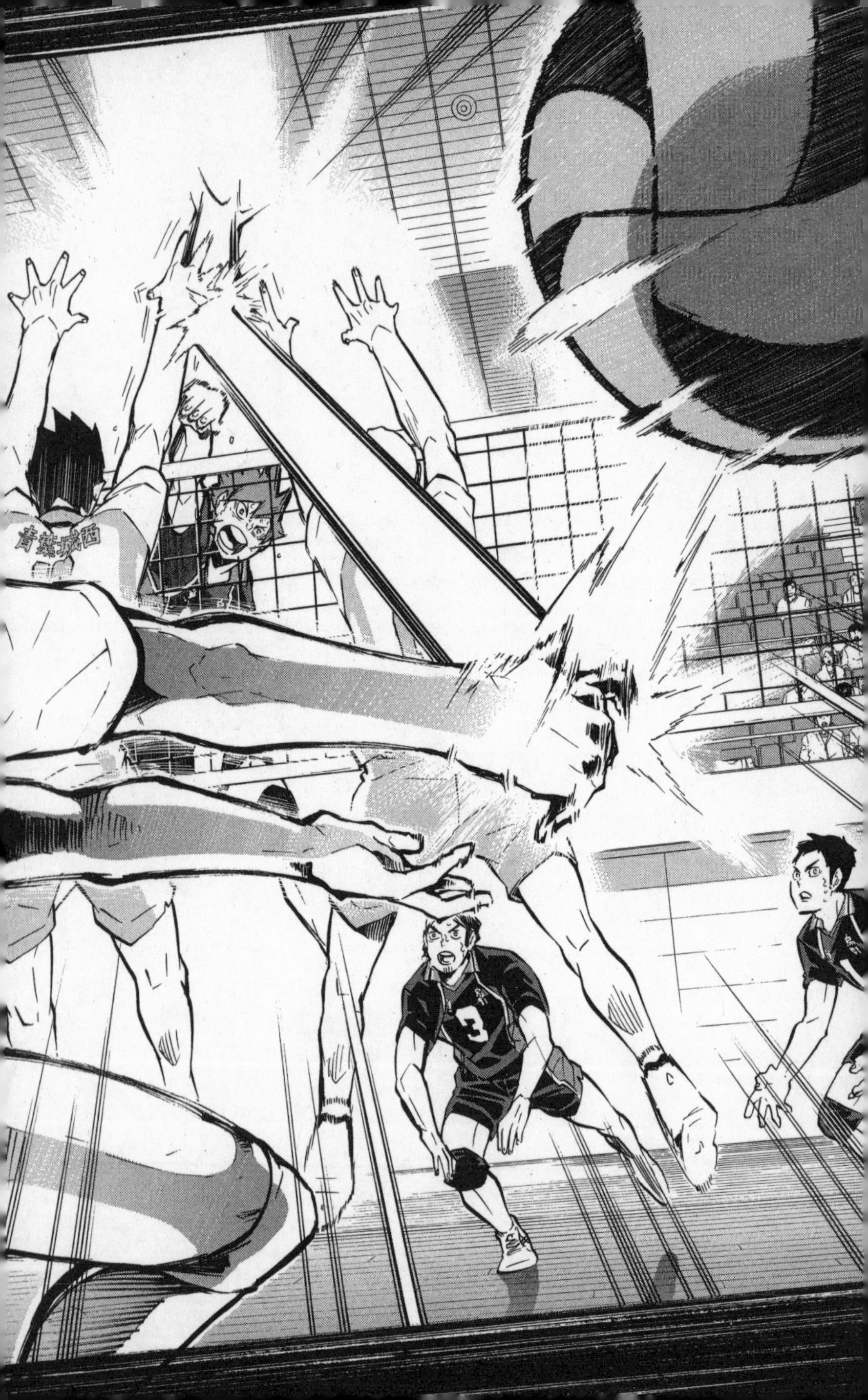
青葉城西

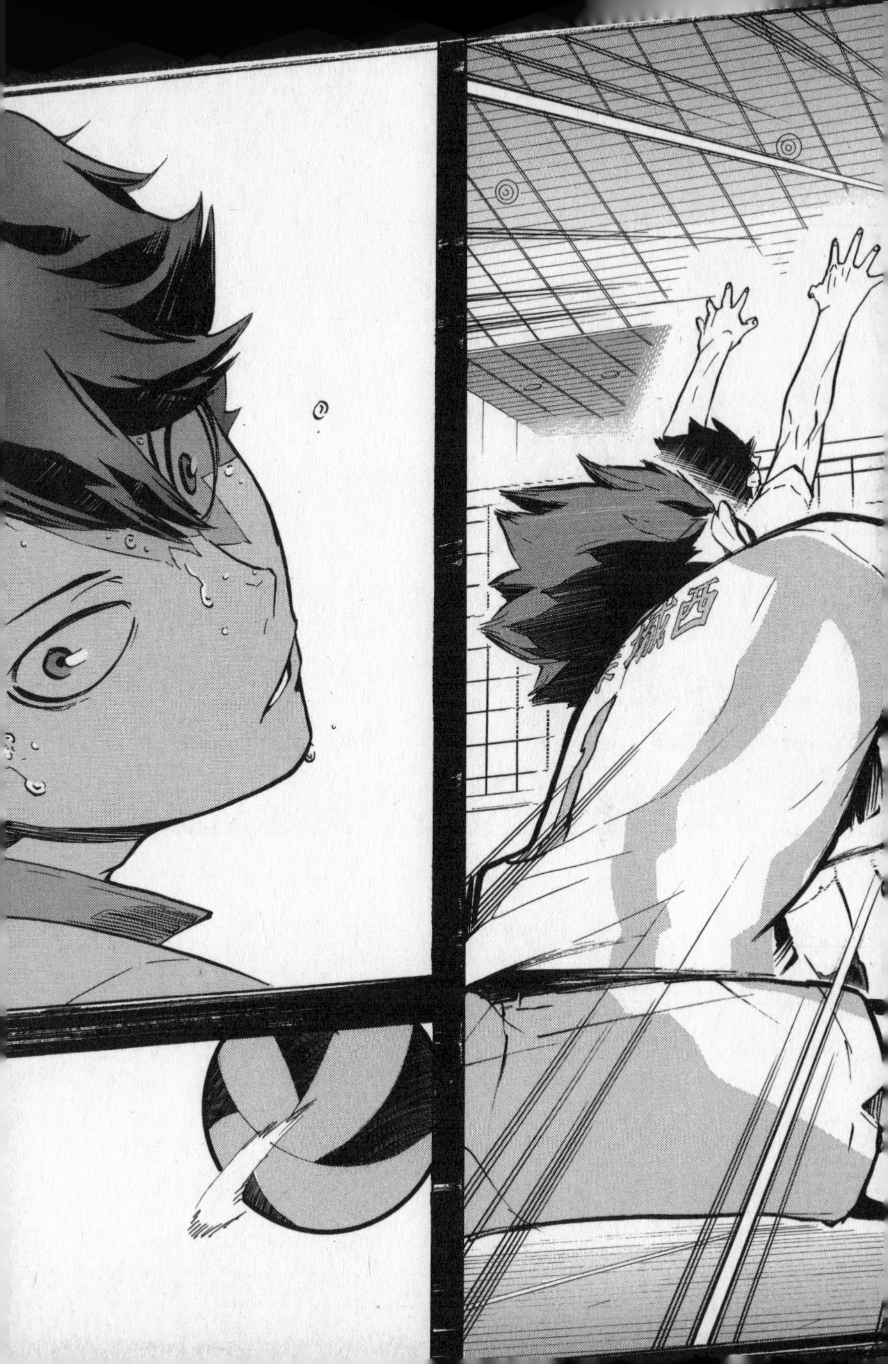
城西

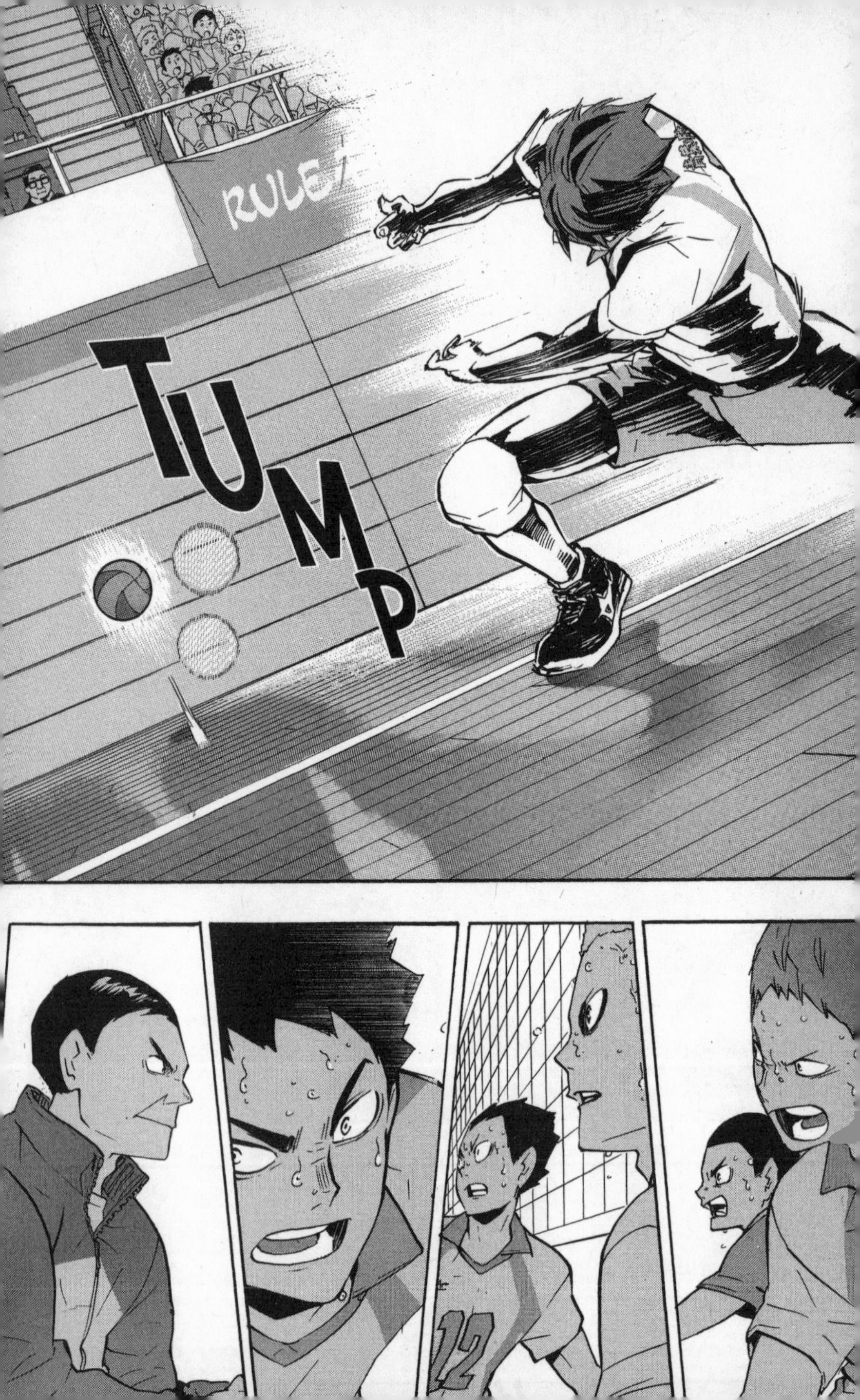
RULE
TUMP

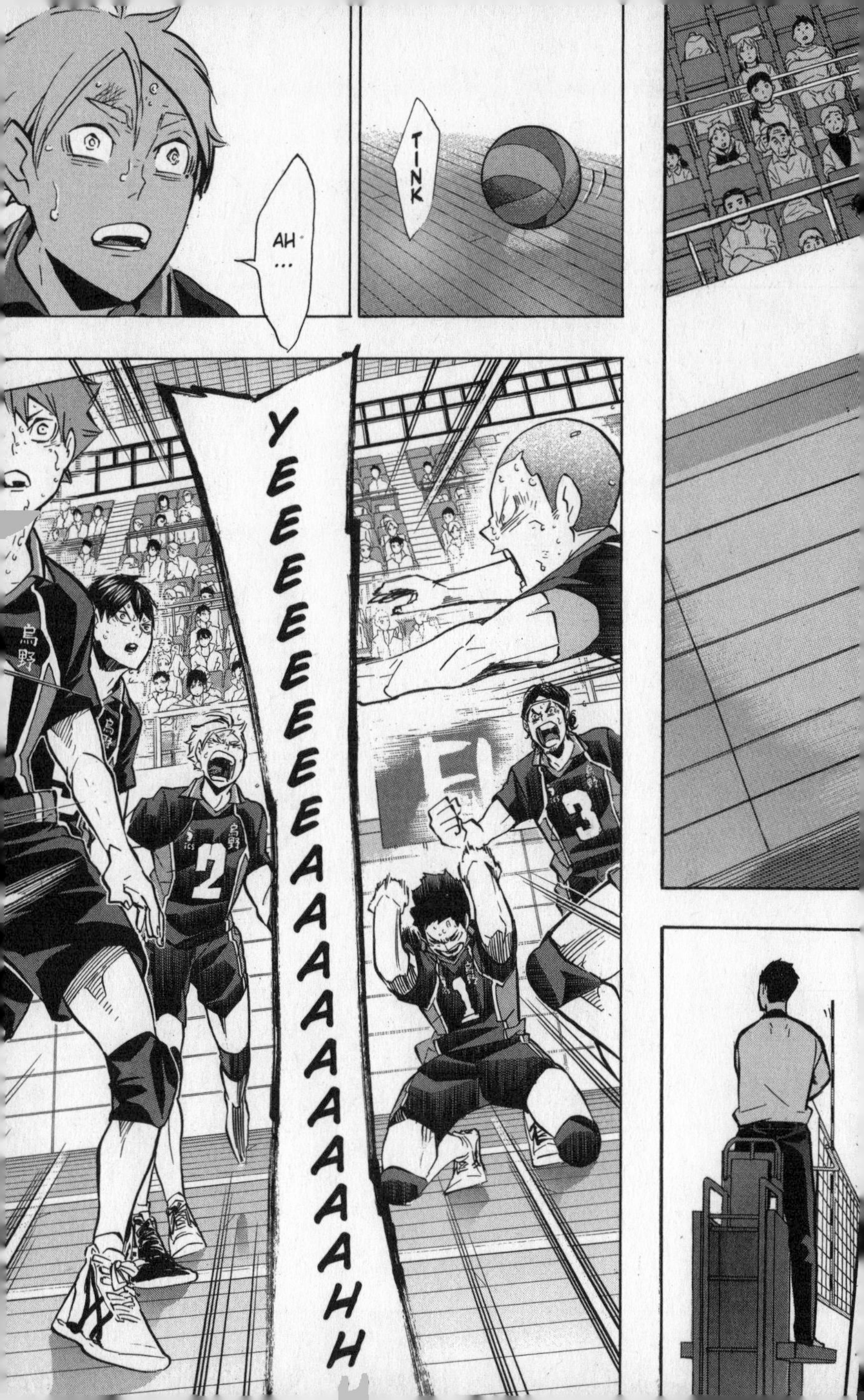
TINK
AH...
YEEEEEEEEEAAAAAAAAAAHH

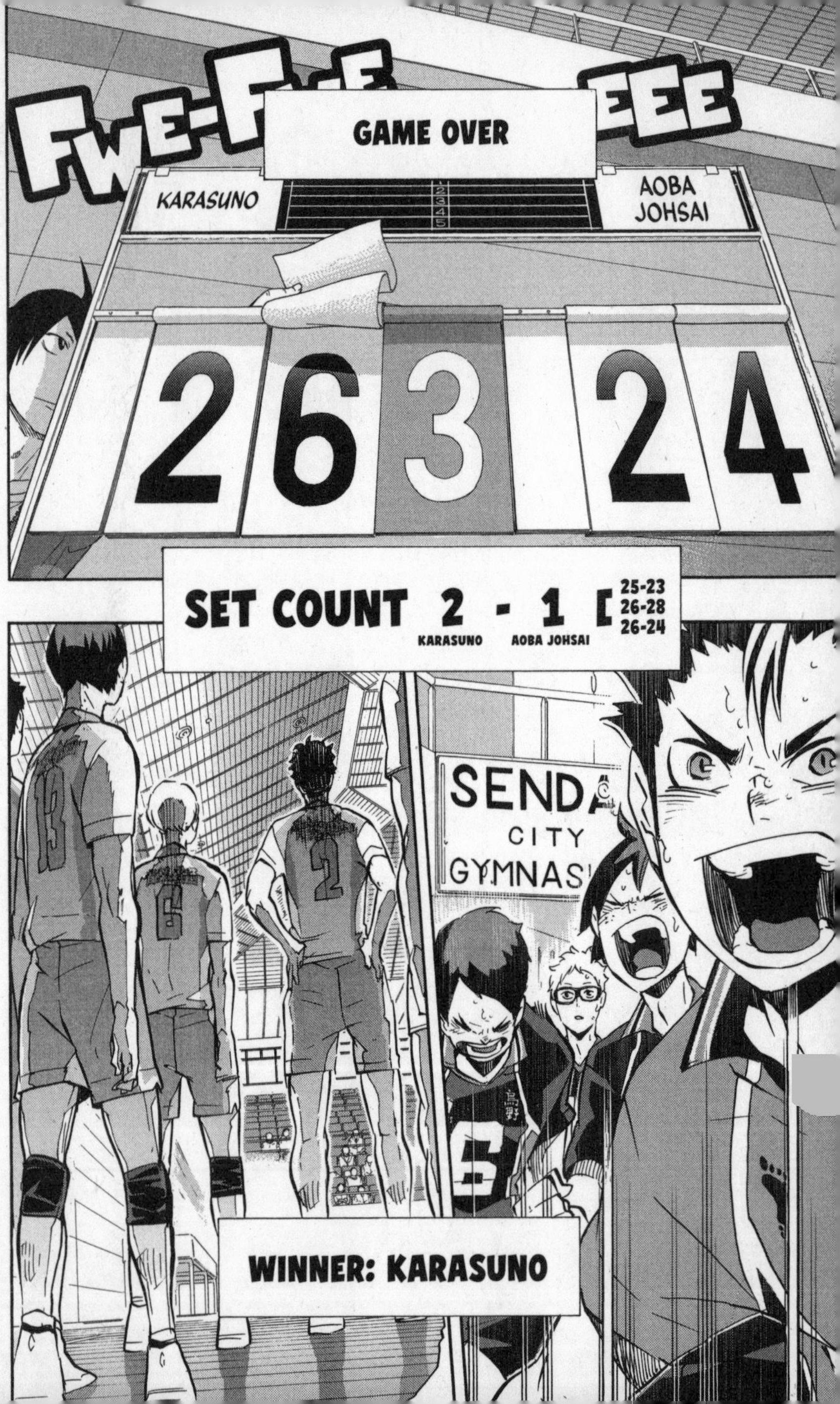
FWE-F-E EEE
GAME OVER
KARASUNO
AOBA JOHSAI
26 3 24
SET COUNT 2 - 1
KARASUNO
AOBA JOHSAI
25-23
26-28
26-24
SENDA
CITY
GYMNAS
WINNER: KARASUNO

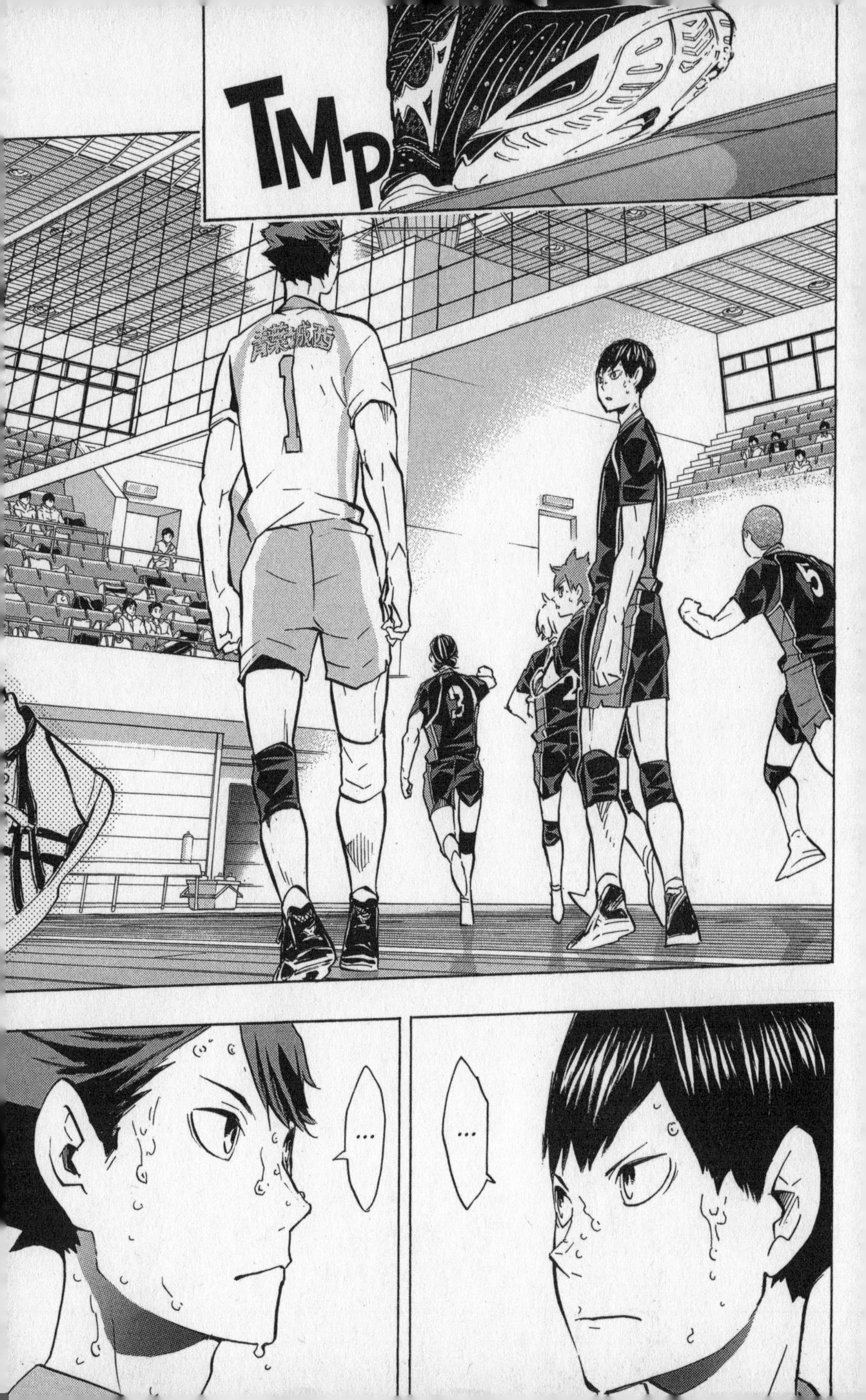
TMP
...
...

HAIKYU!!

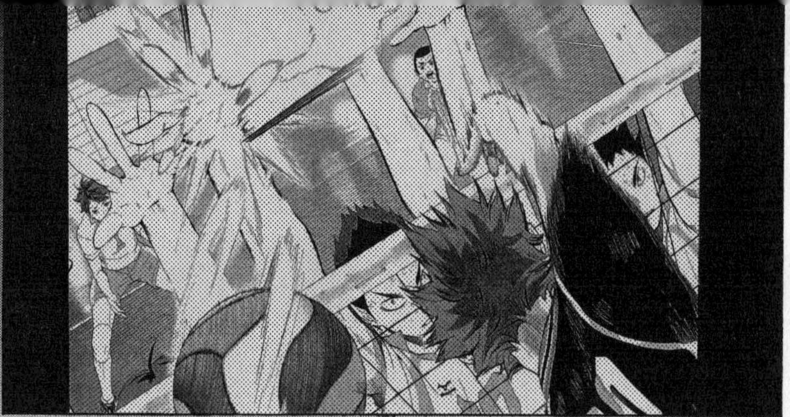

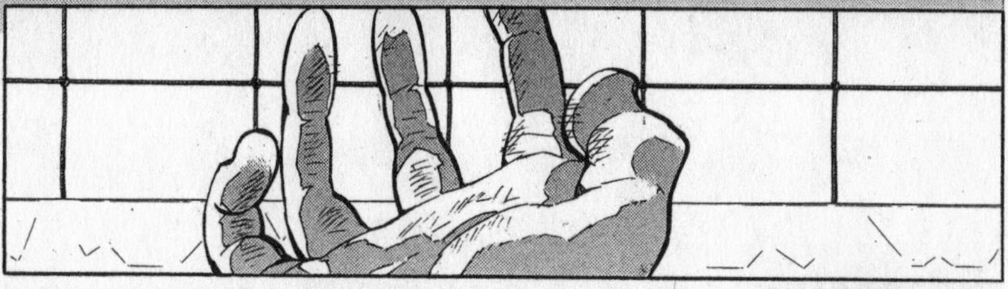

CHAPTER 148

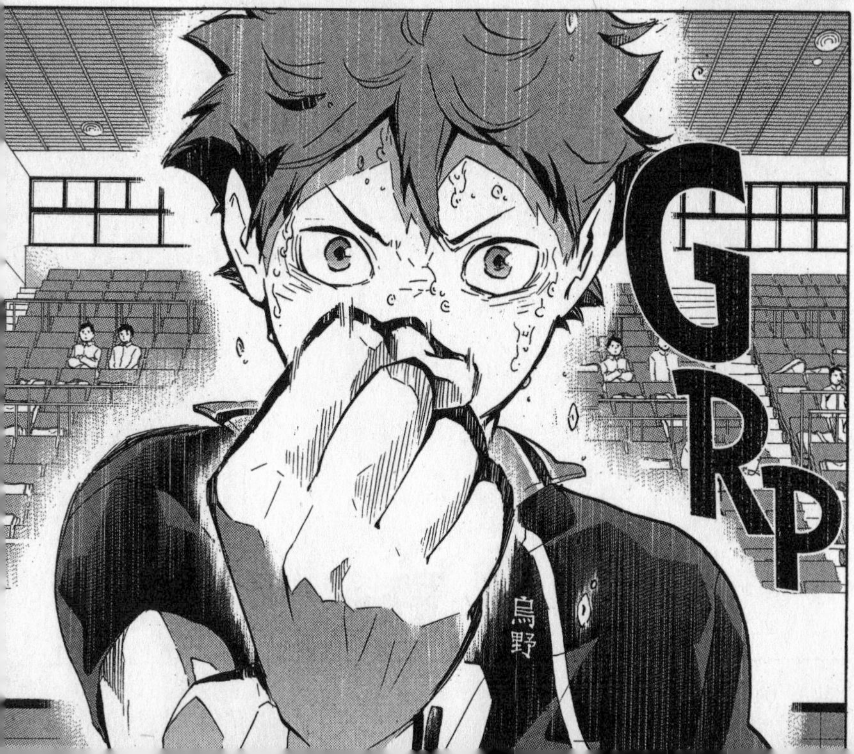
GRP
烏野

CHAPTER 148: Declaration of War

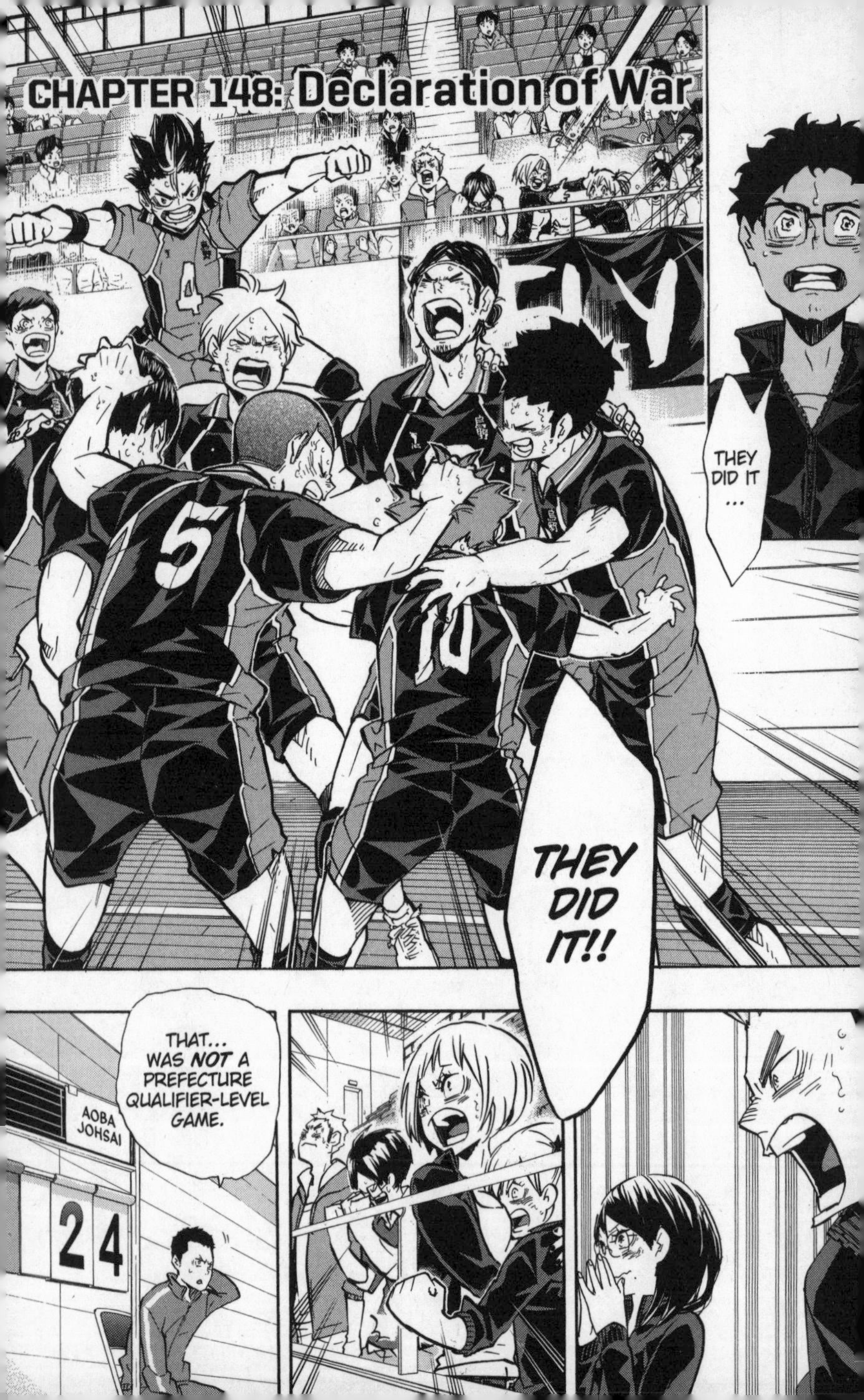

THEY DID IT ...
THEY DID IT!!
THAT... WAS *NOT* A PREFECTURE QUALIFIER-LEVEL GAME.
AOBA JOHSAI
24

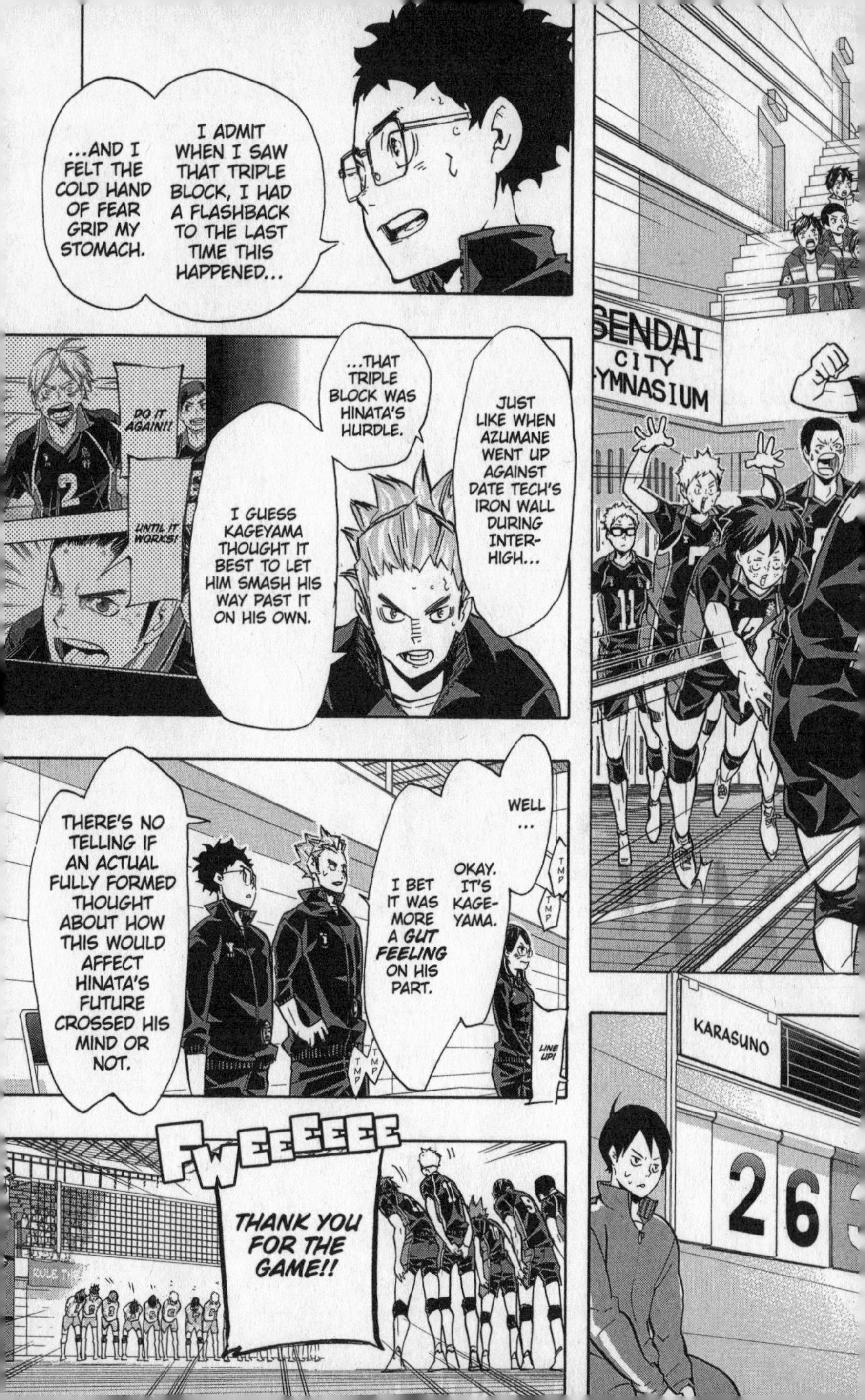
SENDAI CITY GYMNASIUM
I ADMIT WHEN I SAW THAT TRIPLE BLOCK, I HAD A FLASHBACK TO THE LAST TIME THIS HAPPENED...
...AND I FELT THE COLD HAND OF FEAR GRIP MY STOMACH.
JUST LIKE WHEN AZUMANE WENT UP AGAINST DATE TECH'S IRON WALL DURING INTER-HIGH...
...THAT TRIPLE BLOCK WAS HINATA'S HURDLE.
I GUESS KAGEYAMA THOUGHT IT BEST TO LET HIM SMASH HIS WAY PAST IT ON HIS OWN.
DO IT AGAIN!!
UNTIL IT WORKS!
WELL...
OKAY. IT'S KAGE-YAMA.
I BET IT WAS MORE A GUT FEELING ON HIS PART.
TMP TMP
LINE UP!
TMP TMP
THERE'S NO TELLING IF AN ACTUAL FULLY FORMED THOUGHT ABOUT HOW THIS WOULD AFFECT HINATA'S FUTURE CROSSED HIS MIND OR NOT.
KARASUNO
26
FWEEEEEE
THANK YOU FOR THE GAME!!

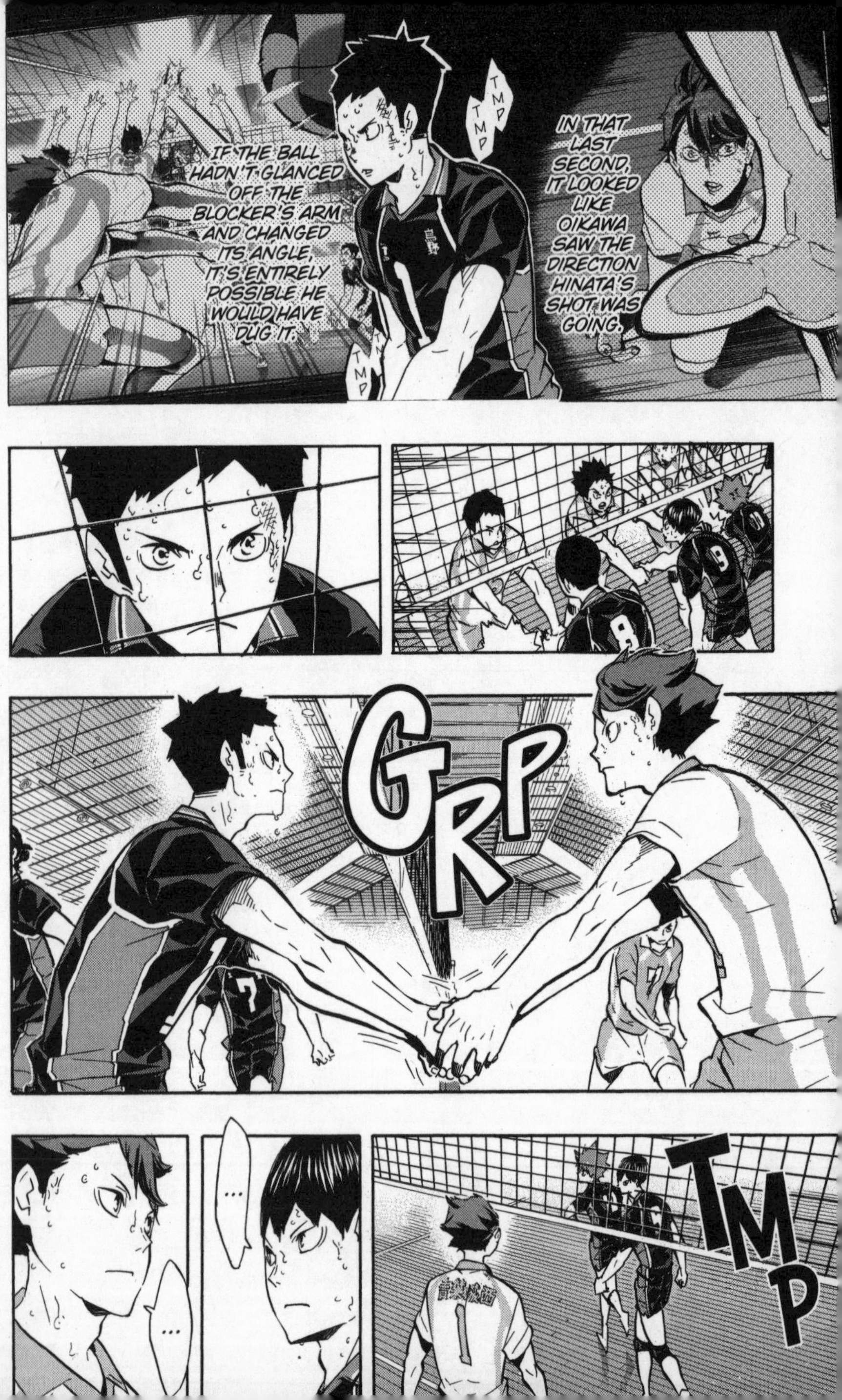
IN THAT LAST SECOND, IT LOOKED LIKE OIKAWA SAW THE DIRECTION HINATA'S SHOT WAS GOING.
TMP TMP
IF THE BALL HADN'T GLANCED OFF THE BLOCKER'S ARM AND CHANGED ITS ANGLE, IT'S ENTIRELY POSSIBLE HE WOULD HAVE DUG IT.
TMP
GRP
TMP
...
...

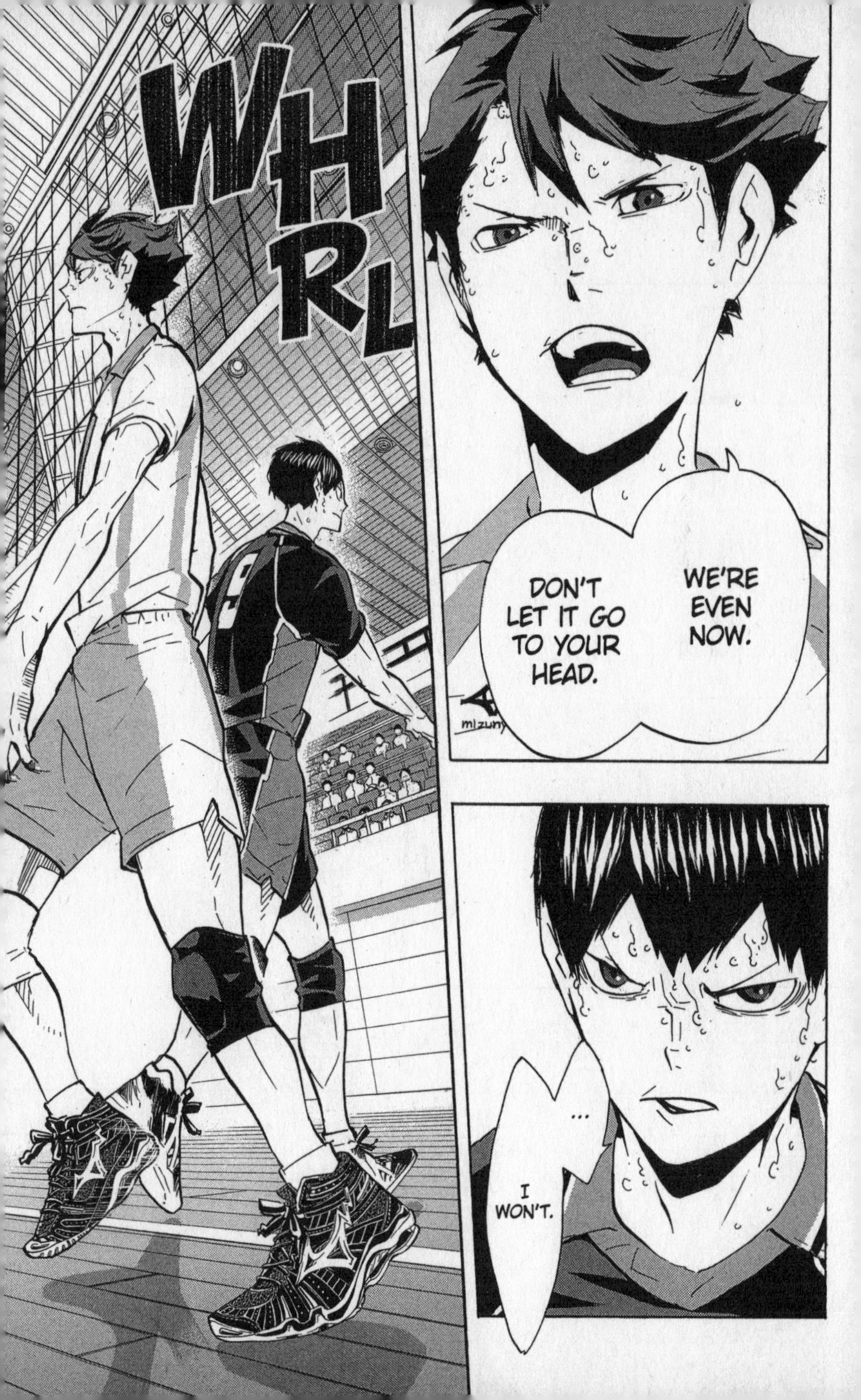
WE'RE EVEN NOW.
DON'T LET IT GO TO YOUR HEAD.
...
I WON'T.
WHRL

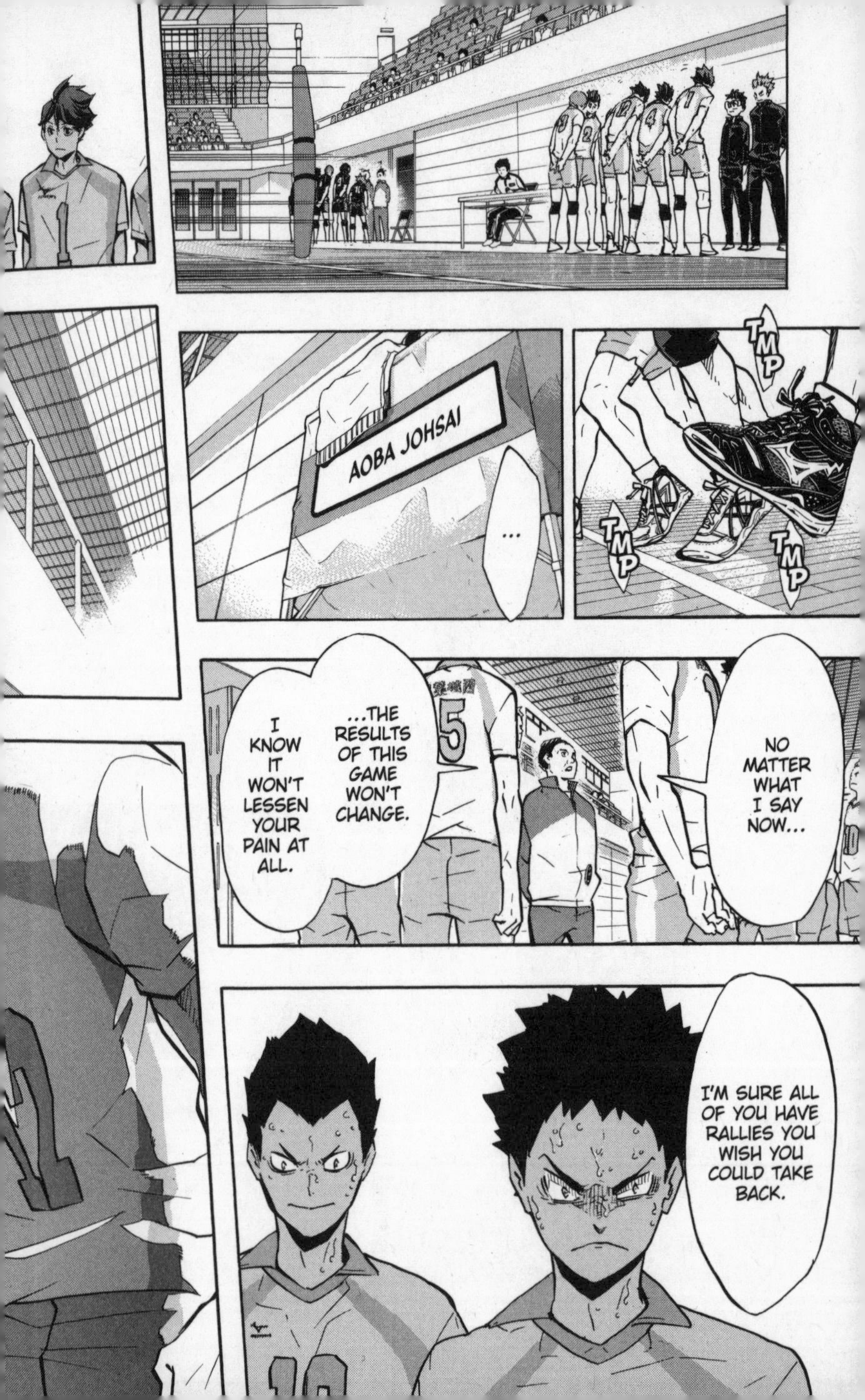
TMP
TMP
TMP
AOBA JOHSAI
...
NO MATTER WHAT I SAY NOW...
...THE RESULTS OF THIS GAME WON'T CHANGE.
I KNOW IT WON'T LESSEN YOUR PAIN AT ALL.
I'M SURE ALL OF YOU HAVE RALLIES YOU WISH YOU COULD TAKE BACK.

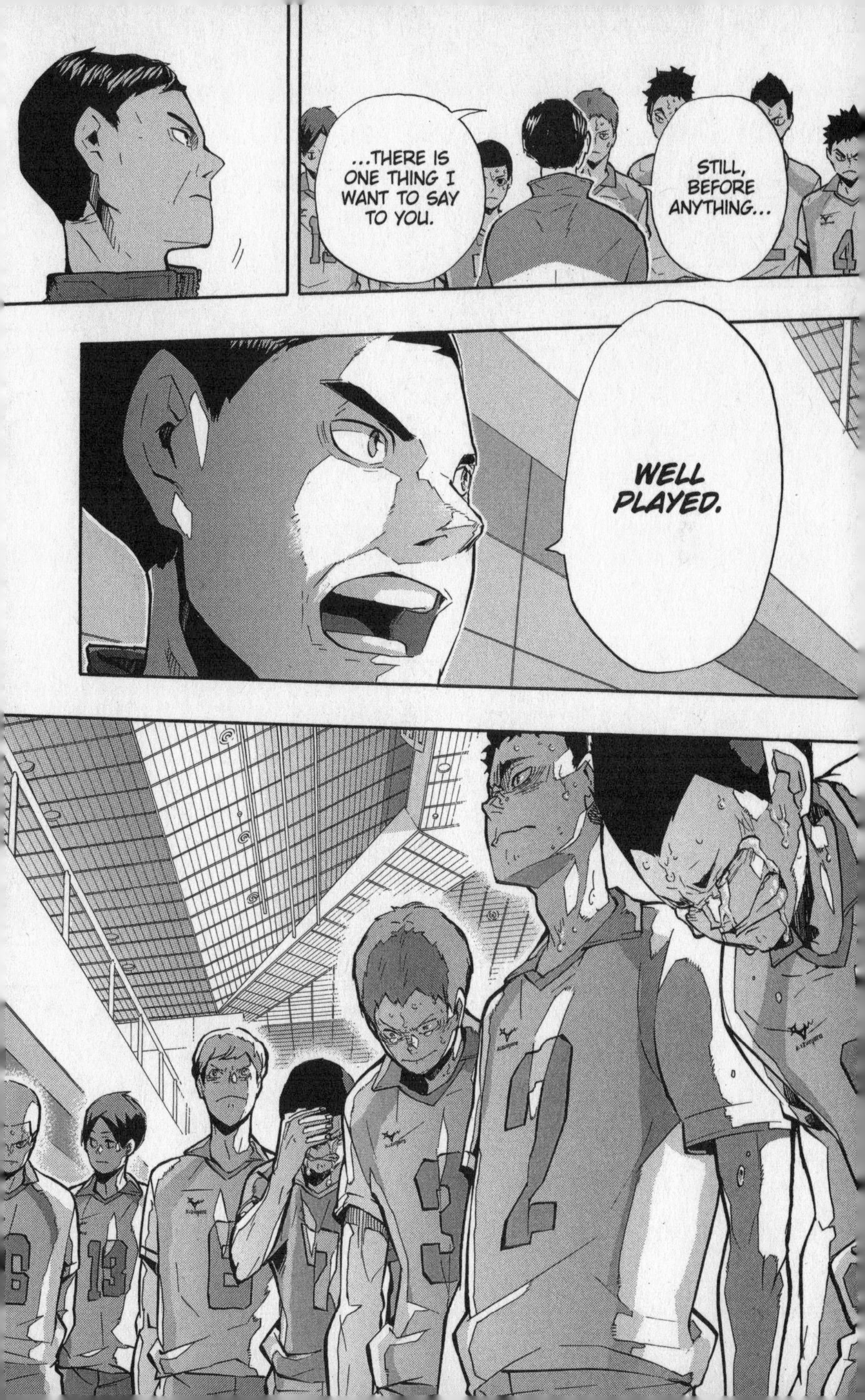
STILL, BEFORE ANYTHING...
...THERE IS ONE THING I WANT TO SAY TO YOU.
WELL PLAYED.

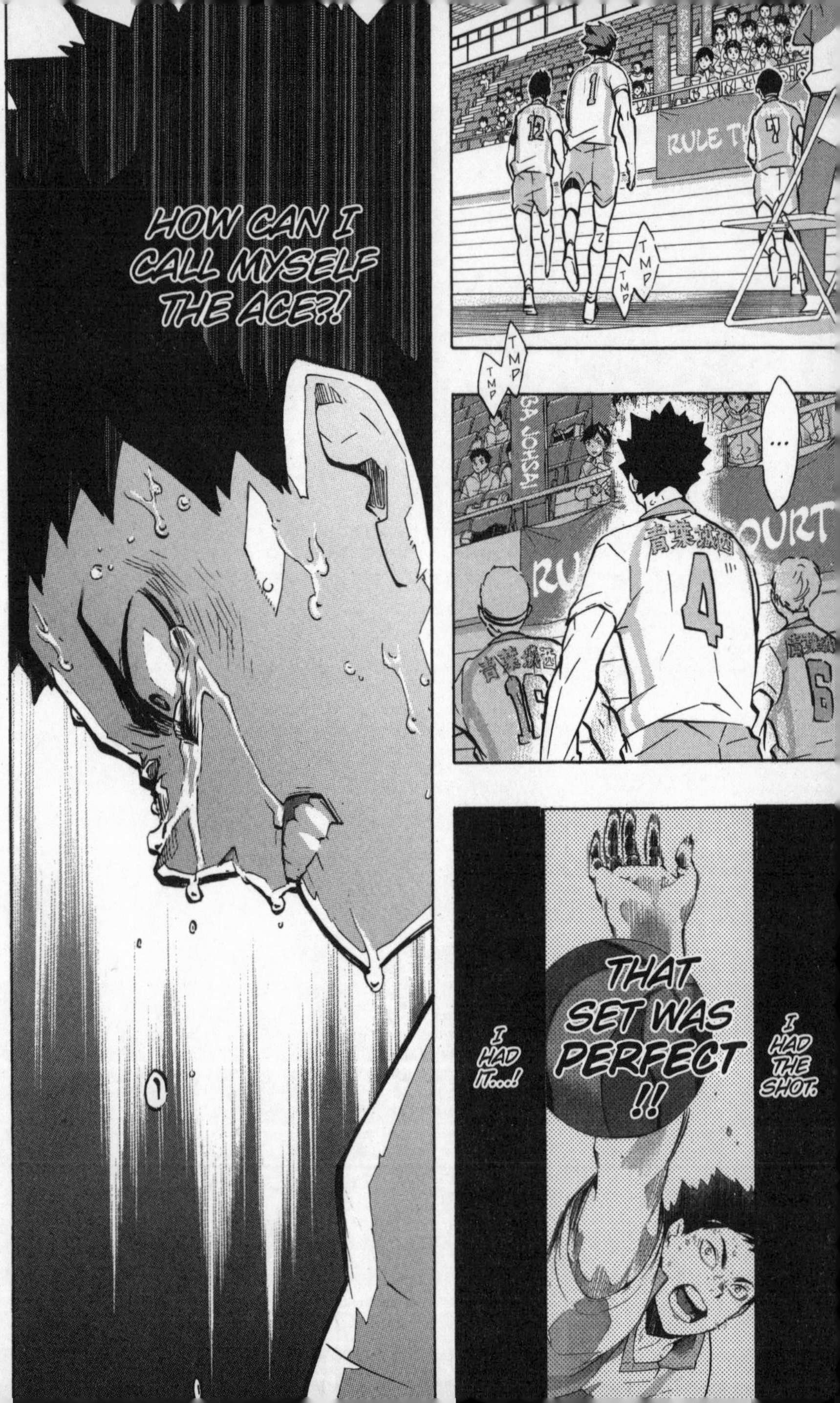
TMP TMP TMP
TMP TMP
...
I HAD THE SHOT.
THAT SET WAS PERFECT!!
I HAD IT...!
HOW CAN I CALL MYSELF THE ACE?!

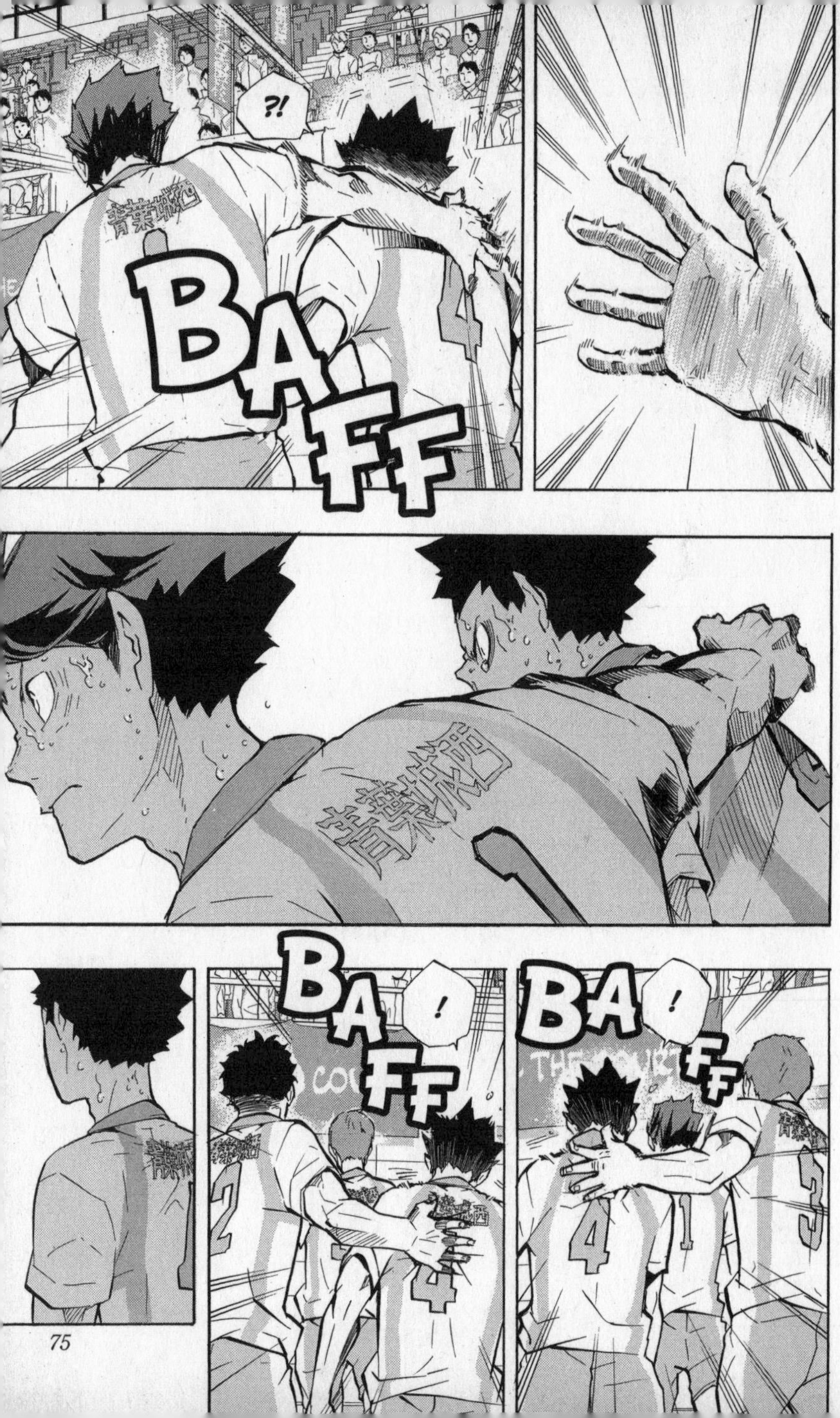
?!
BAFF
BAFF
!
BAFF
!

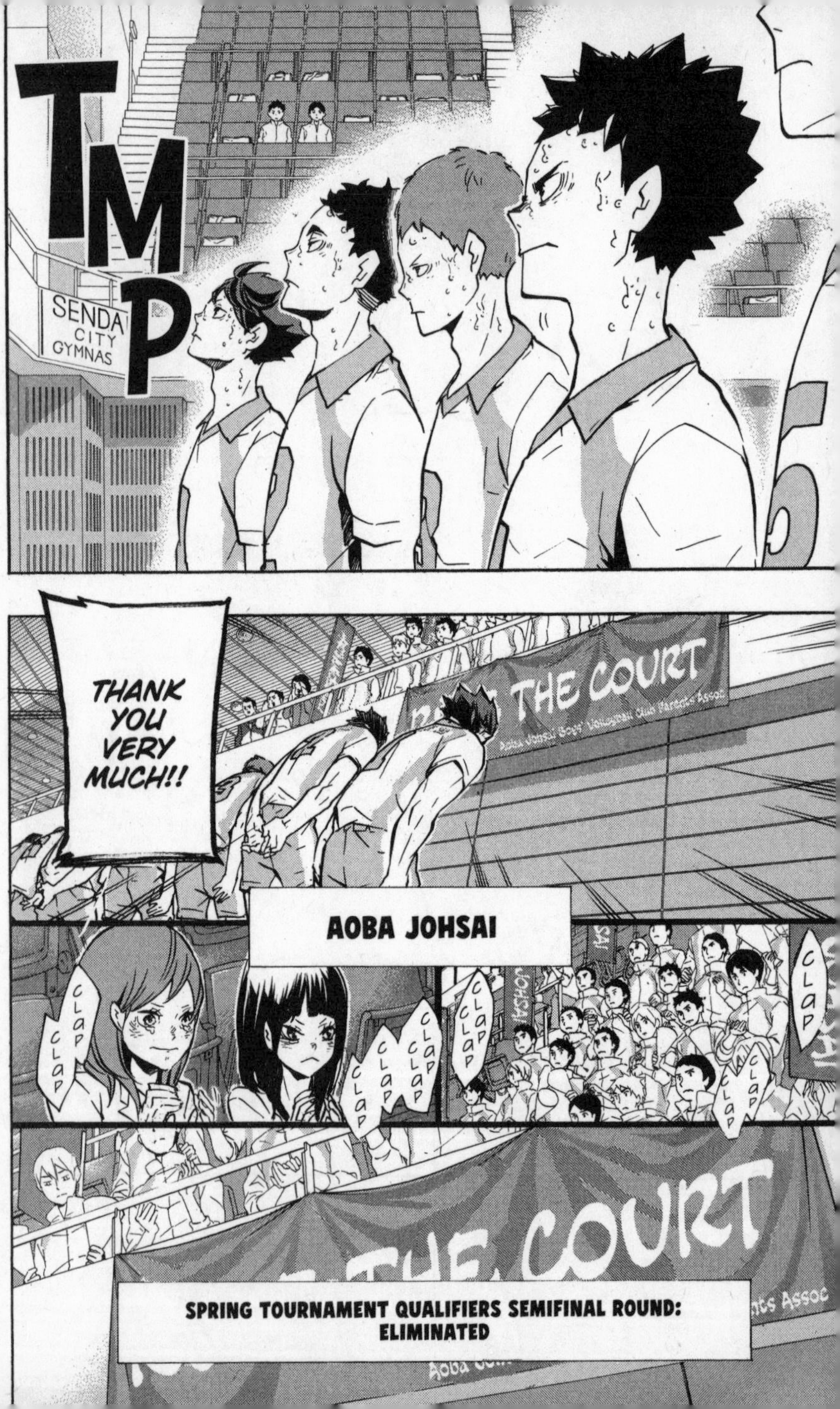

TMP
SENDA
CITY
GYMNAS
THANK YOU VERY MUCH!!
THE COURT
AOBA JOHSAI
CLAP CLAP
CLAP
CLAP
CLAP CLAP
CLAP CLAP
CLAP CLAP
CLAP CLAP
CLAP CLAP
COURT
SPRING TOURNAMENT QUALIFIERS SEMIFINAL ROUND: ELIMINATED

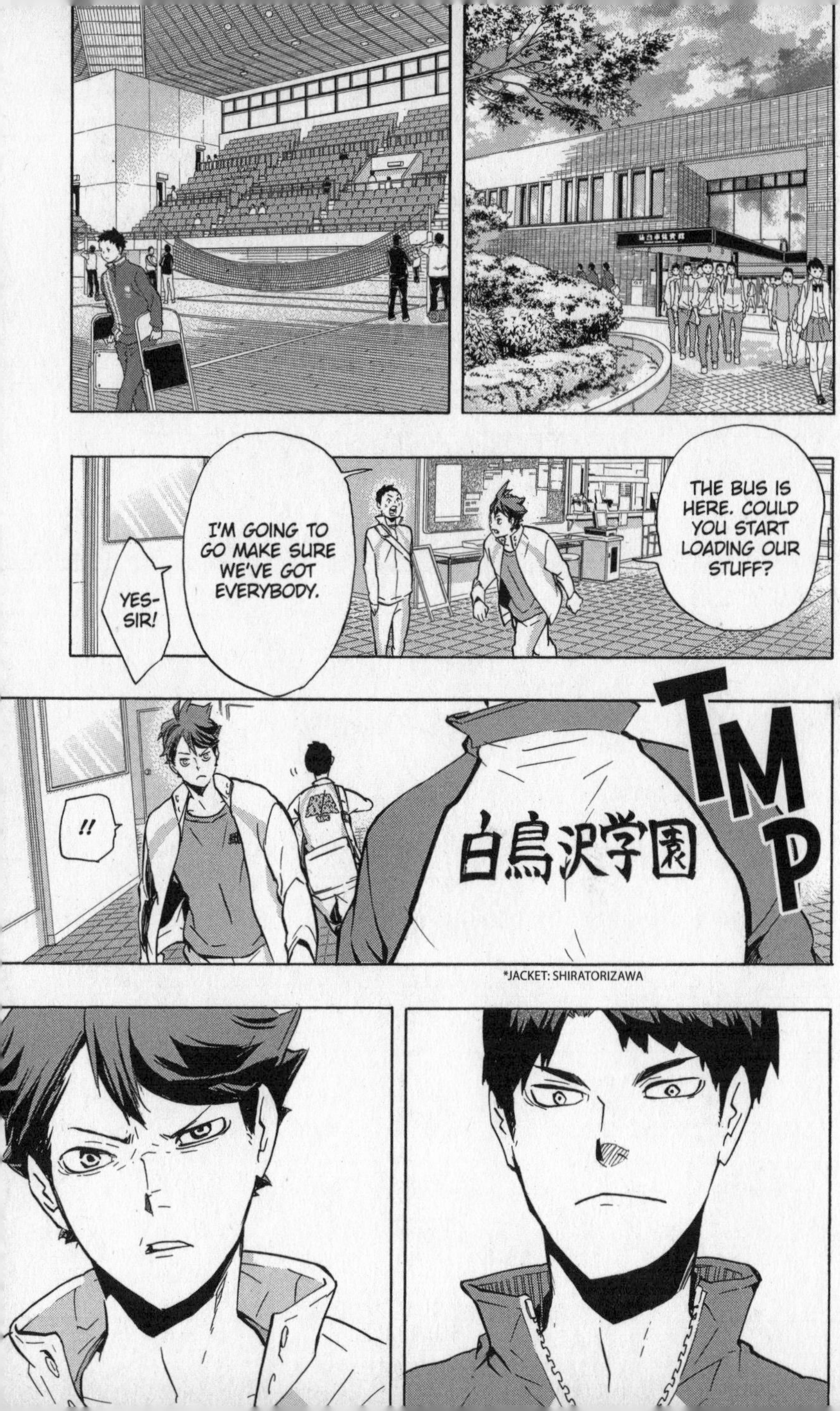
THE BUS IS HERE. COULD YOU START LOADING OUR STUFF?
I'M GOING TO GO MAKE SURE WE'VE GOT EVERYBODY.
YES-SIR!
TMP
白鳥沢学園
!!
*JACKET: SHIRATORIZAWA

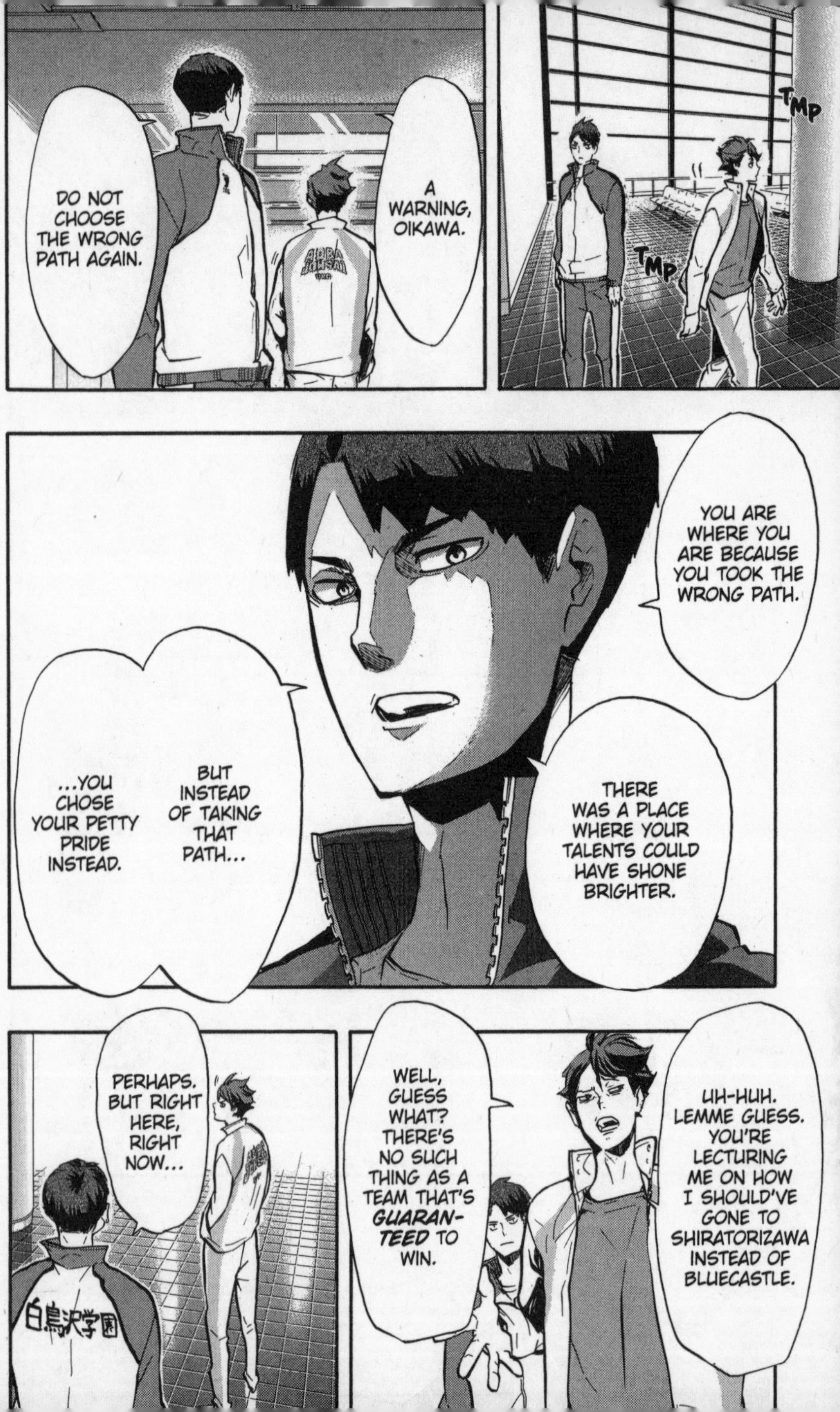
TMP
TMP
A WARNING, OIKAWA.
DO NOT CHOOSE THE WRONG PATH AGAIN.
YOU ARE WHERE YOU ARE BECAUSE YOU TOOK THE WRONG PATH.
THERE WAS A PLACE WHERE YOUR TALENTS COULD HAVE SHONE BRIGHTER.
BUT INSTEAD OF TAKING THAT PATH...
...YOU CHOSE YOUR PETTY PRIDE INSTEAD.
UH-HUH. LEMME GUESS. YOU'RE LECTURING ME ON HOW I SHOULD'VE GONE TO SHIRATORIZAWA INSTEAD OF BLUECASTLE.
WELL, GUESS WHAT? THERE'S NO SUCH THING AS A TEAM THAT'S ***GUARAN-TEED*** TO WIN.
PERHAPS. BUT RIGHT HERE, RIGHT NOW...
白鳥沢学園

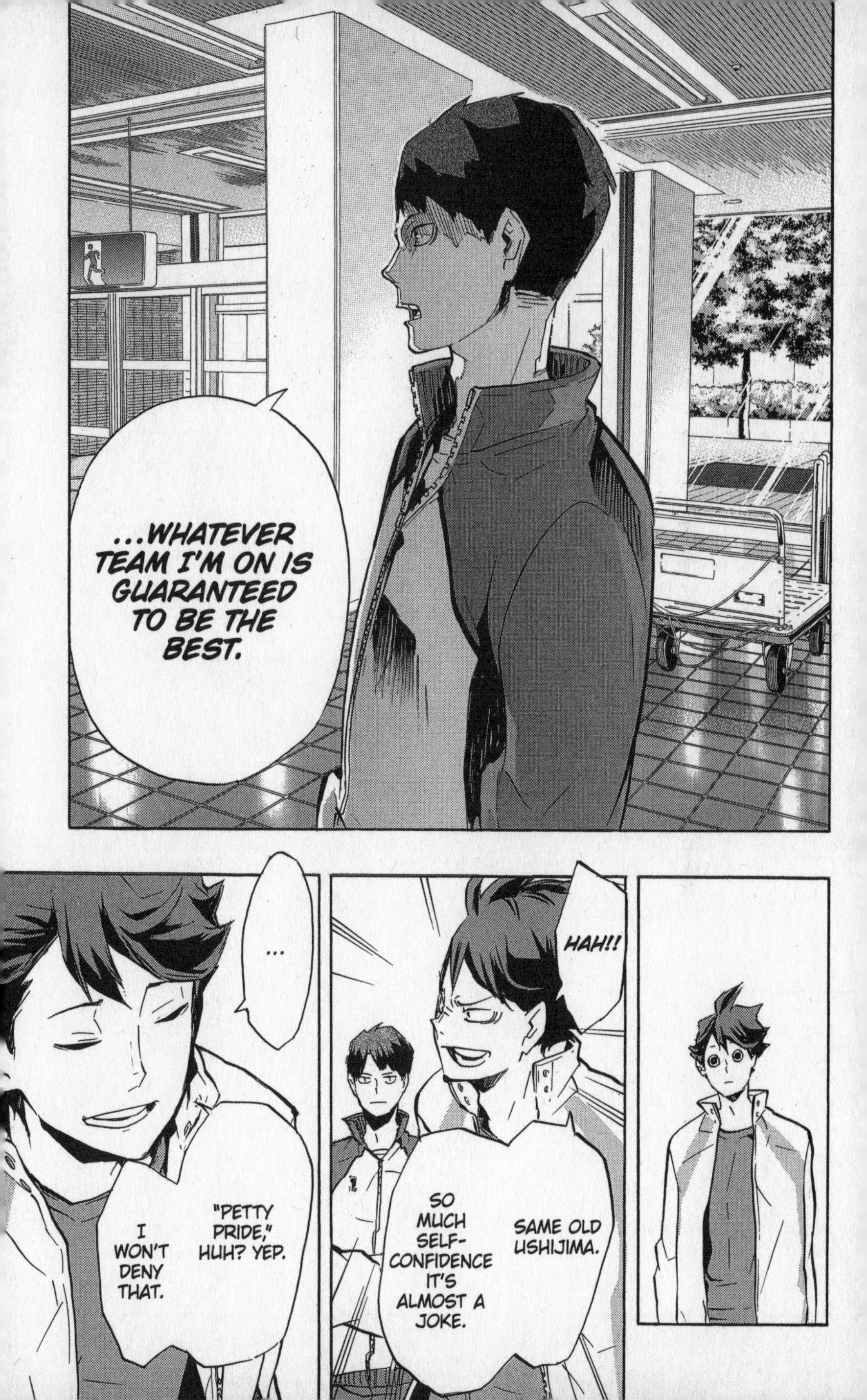
...WHATEVER TEAM I'M ON IS GUARANTEED TO BE THE BEST.
HAH!!
SAME OLD USHIJIMA.
SO MUCH SELF-CONFIDENCE IT'S ALMOST A JOKE.
...
"PETTY PRIDE," HUH? YEP.
I WON'T DENY THAT.

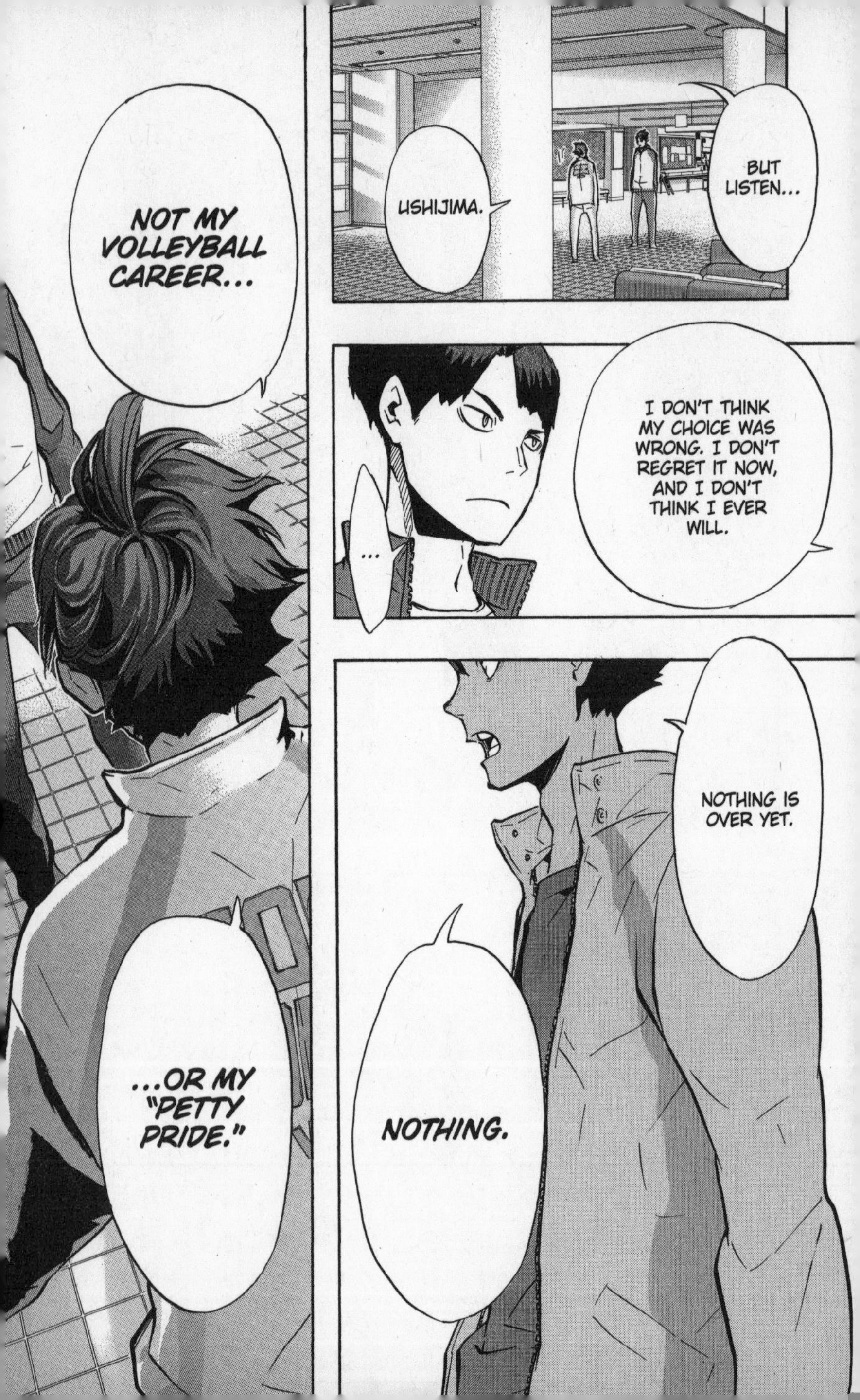
BUT LISTEN...
USHIJIMA.
I DON'T THINK MY CHOICE WAS WRONG. I DON'T REGRET IT NOW, AND I DON'T THINK I EVER WILL.
...
NOTHING IS OVER YET.
NOTHING.
NOT MY VOLLEYBALL CAREER...
...OR MY "PETTY PRIDE."

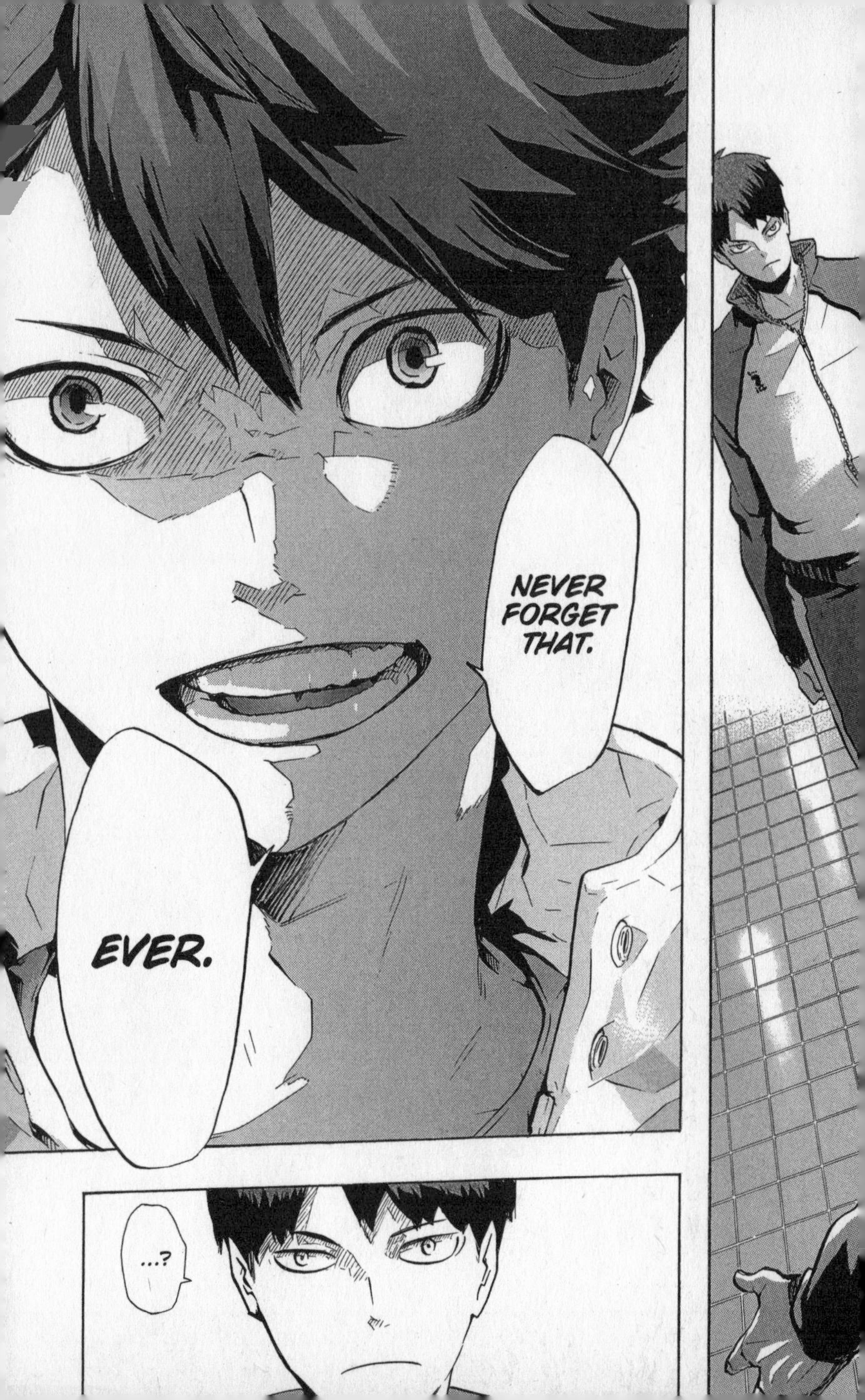
NEVER FORGET THAT.
EVER.
...?

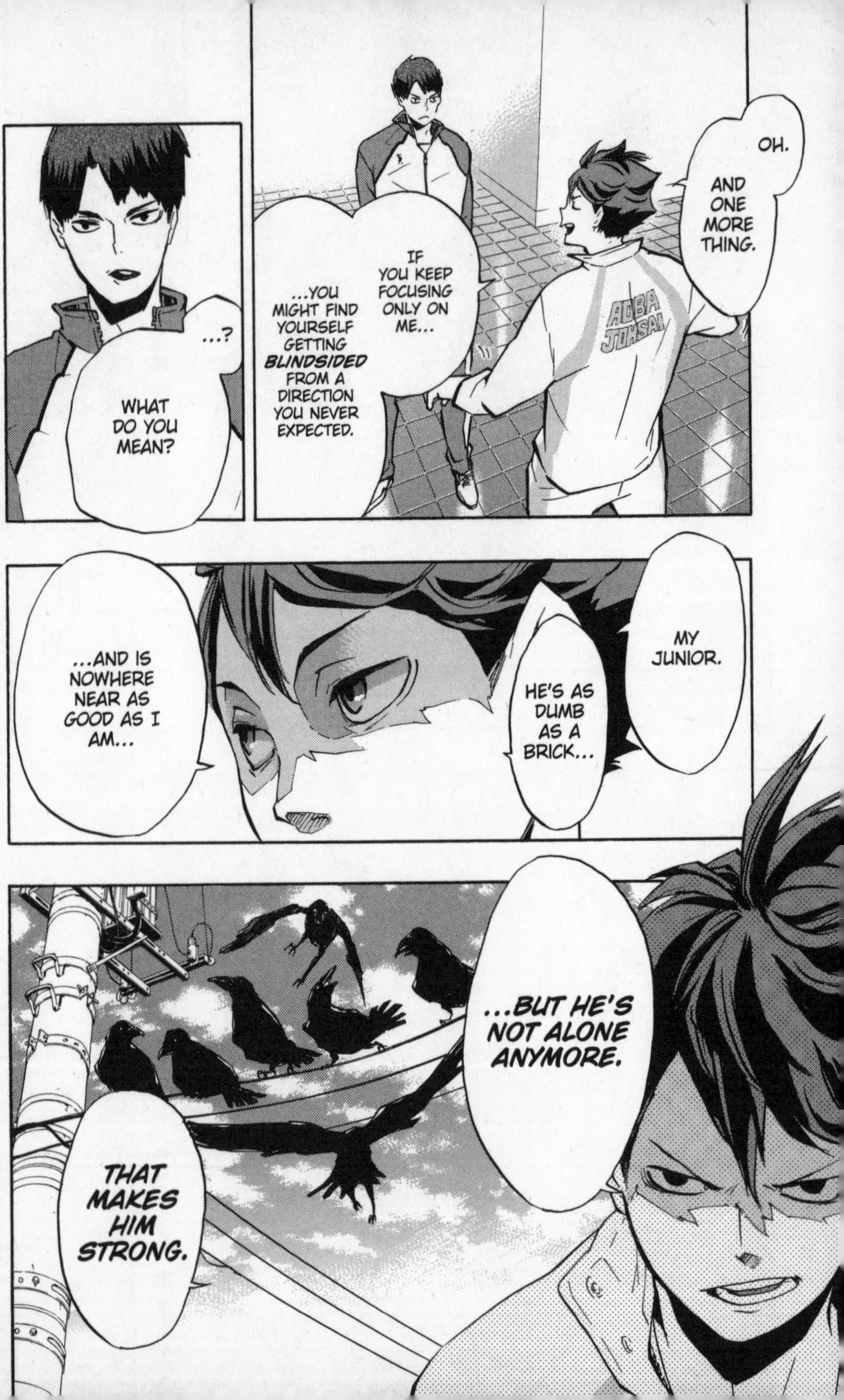
OH.
AND ONE MORE THING.
AOBA JOHSAI
IF YOU KEEP FOCUSING ONLY ON ME...
...YOU MIGHT FIND YOURSELF GETTING BLINDSIDED FROM A DIRECTION YOU NEVER EXPECTED.
...?
WHAT DO YOU MEAN?
MY JUNIOR.
HE'S AS DUMB AS A BRICK...
...AND IS NOWHERE NEAR AS GOOD AS I AM...
...BUT HE'S NOT ALONE ANYMORE.
THAT MAKES HIM STRONG.

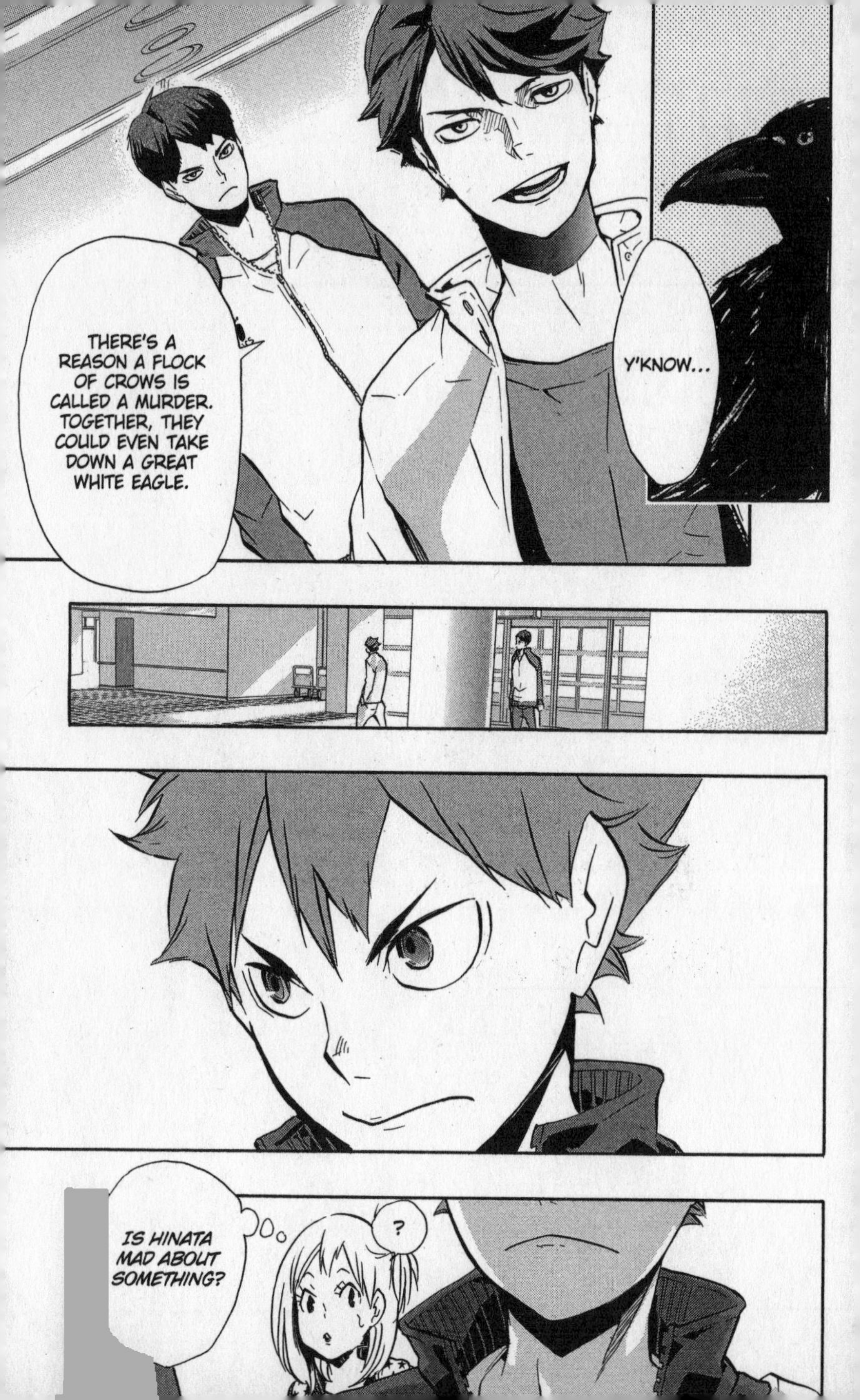
Y'KNOW...
THERE'S A REASON A FLOCK OF CROWS IS CALLED A MURDER. TOGETHER, THEY COULD EVEN TAKE DOWN A GREAT WHITE EAGLE.
?
IS HINATA MAD ABOUT SOMETHING?

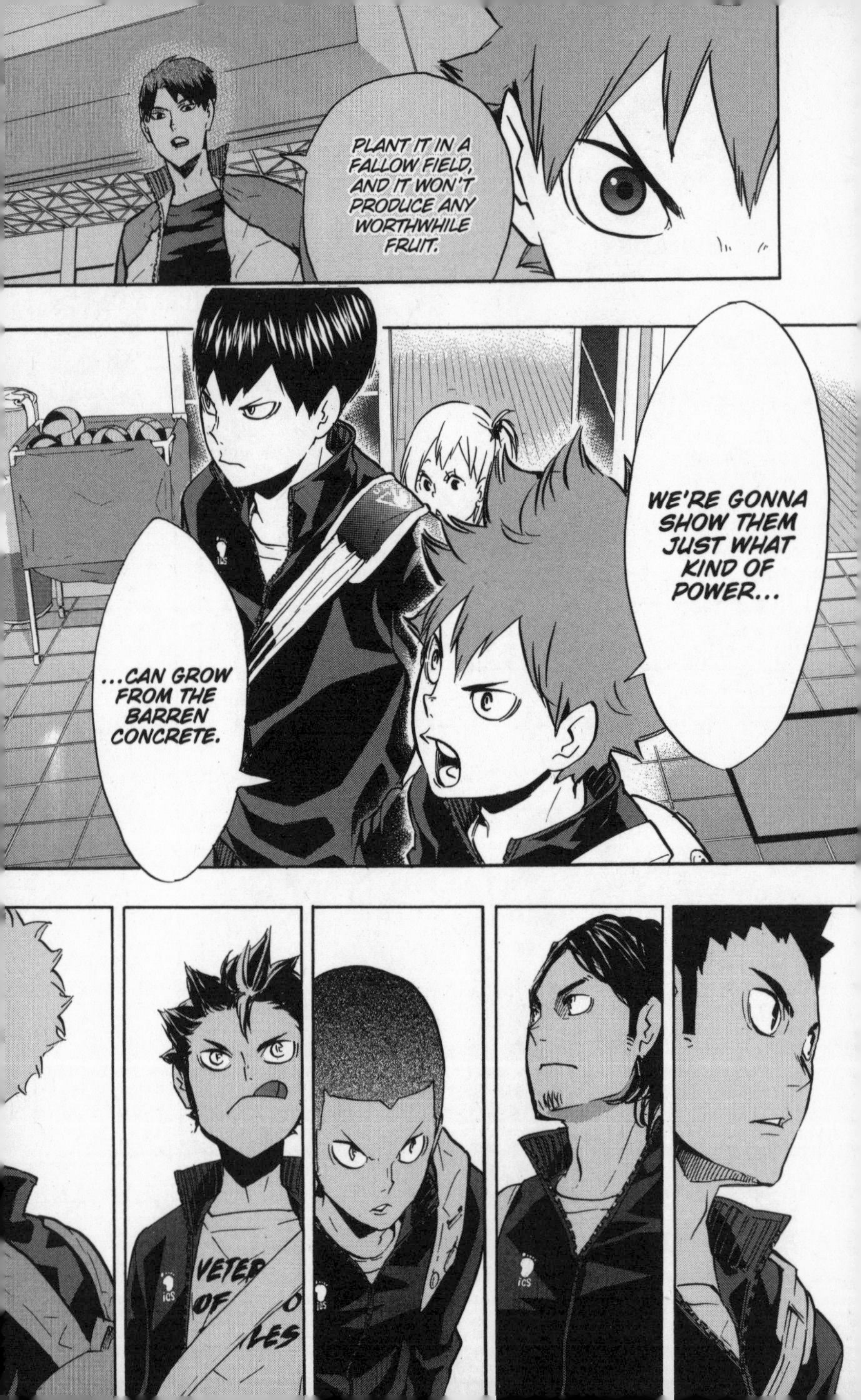
PLANT IT IN A FALLOW FIELD, AND IT WON'T PRODUCE ANY WORTHWHILE FRUIT.
WE'RE GONNA SHOW THEM JUST WHAT KIND OF POWER...
...CAN GROW FROM THE BARREN CONCRETE.

新井2
KAJI
加　持3
HAKUSUIKAN
白水館4
MIDORIKAWA
翠　川5
MINE NISHI
峰　西6
SAKUI
佐久井7

SPRING TOURNAMENT MIYAGI PREFECTURE QUALIFIERS...

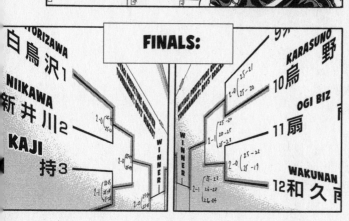

FINALS:

白鳥沢1

NIIKAWA
新井川2

KAJI
持3

KARASUNO
10 烏 野

OGI BIZ
11 扇

WAKUNAN
12 和久南

W I N N E R

W I N N E R

KARASUNO VS. SHIRATORIZAWA

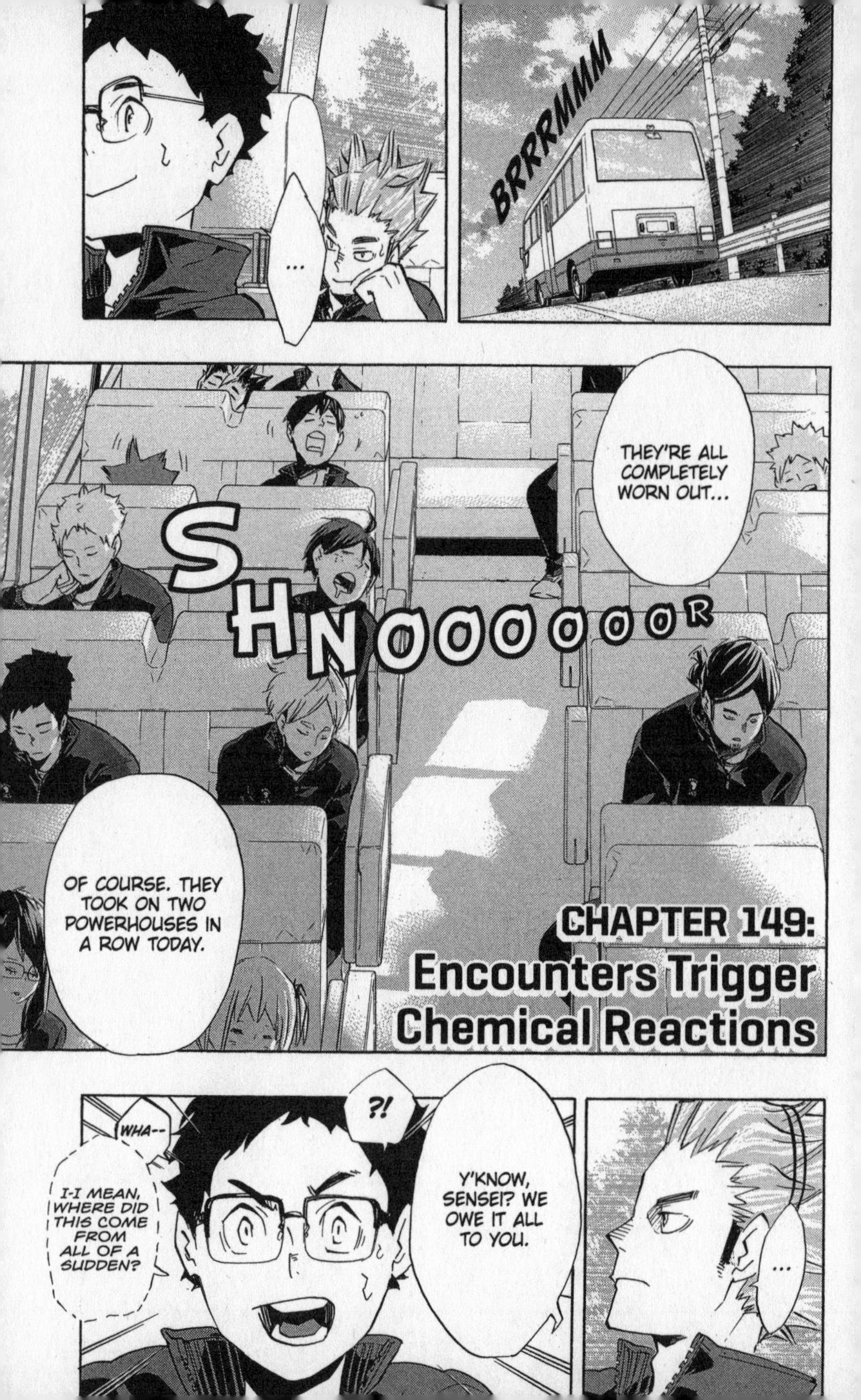
BRRRMMM
...
THEY'RE ALL COMPLETELY WORN OUT...
SHNOOOOOOOR
OF COURSE. THEY TOOK ON TWO POWERHOUSES IN A ROW TODAY.
CHAPTER 149: Encounters Trigger Chemical Reactions
...
Y'KNOW, SENSEI? WE OWE IT ALL TO YOU.
?!
WHA--
I-I MEAN, WHERE DID THIS COME FROM ALL OF A SUDDEN?

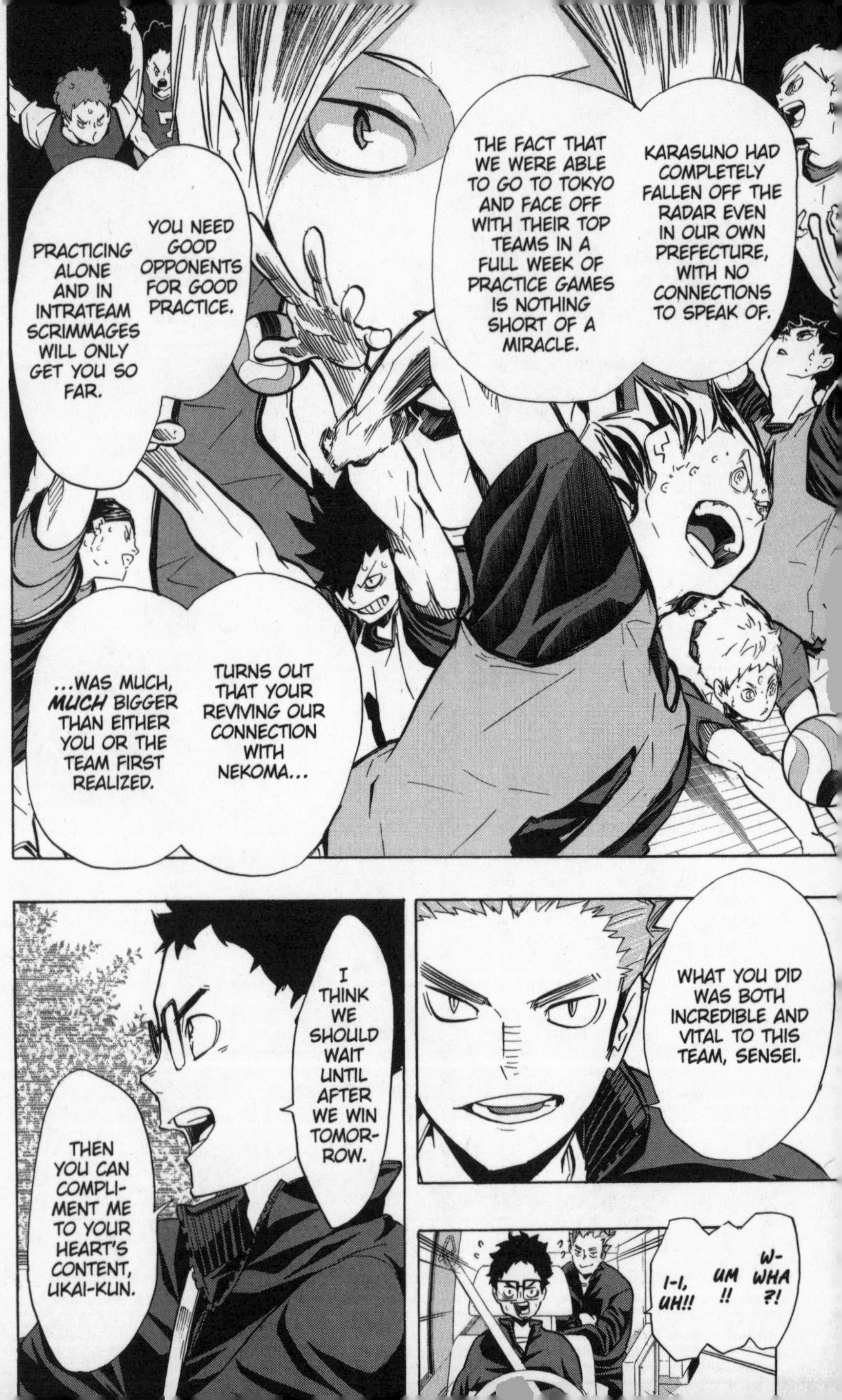
KARASUNO HAD COMPLETELY FALLEN OFF THE RADAR EVEN IN OUR OWN PREFECTURE, WITH NO CONNECTIONS TO SPEAK OF.
THE FACT THAT WE WERE ABLE TO GO TO TOKYO AND FACE OFF WITH THEIR TOP TEAMS IN A FULL WEEK OF PRACTICE GAMES IS NOTHING SHORT OF A MIRACLE.
YOU NEED GOOD OPPONENTS FOR GOOD PRACTICE.
PRACTICING ALONE AND IN INTRATEAM SCRIMMAGES WILL ONLY GET YOU SO FAR.
TURNS OUT THAT YOUR REVIVING OUR CONNECTION WITH NEKOMA...
...WAS MUCH, *MUCH* BIGGER THAN EITHER YOU OR THE TEAM FIRST REALIZED.
WHAT YOU DID WAS BOTH INCREDIBLE AND VITAL TO THIS TEAM, SENSEI.
W-WHA?!
UM!!
I-I, UH!!
I THINK WE SHOULD WAIT UNTIL AFTER WE WIN TOMOR-ROW.
THEN YOU CAN COMPLI-MENT ME TO YOUR HEART'S CONTENT, UKAI-KUN.

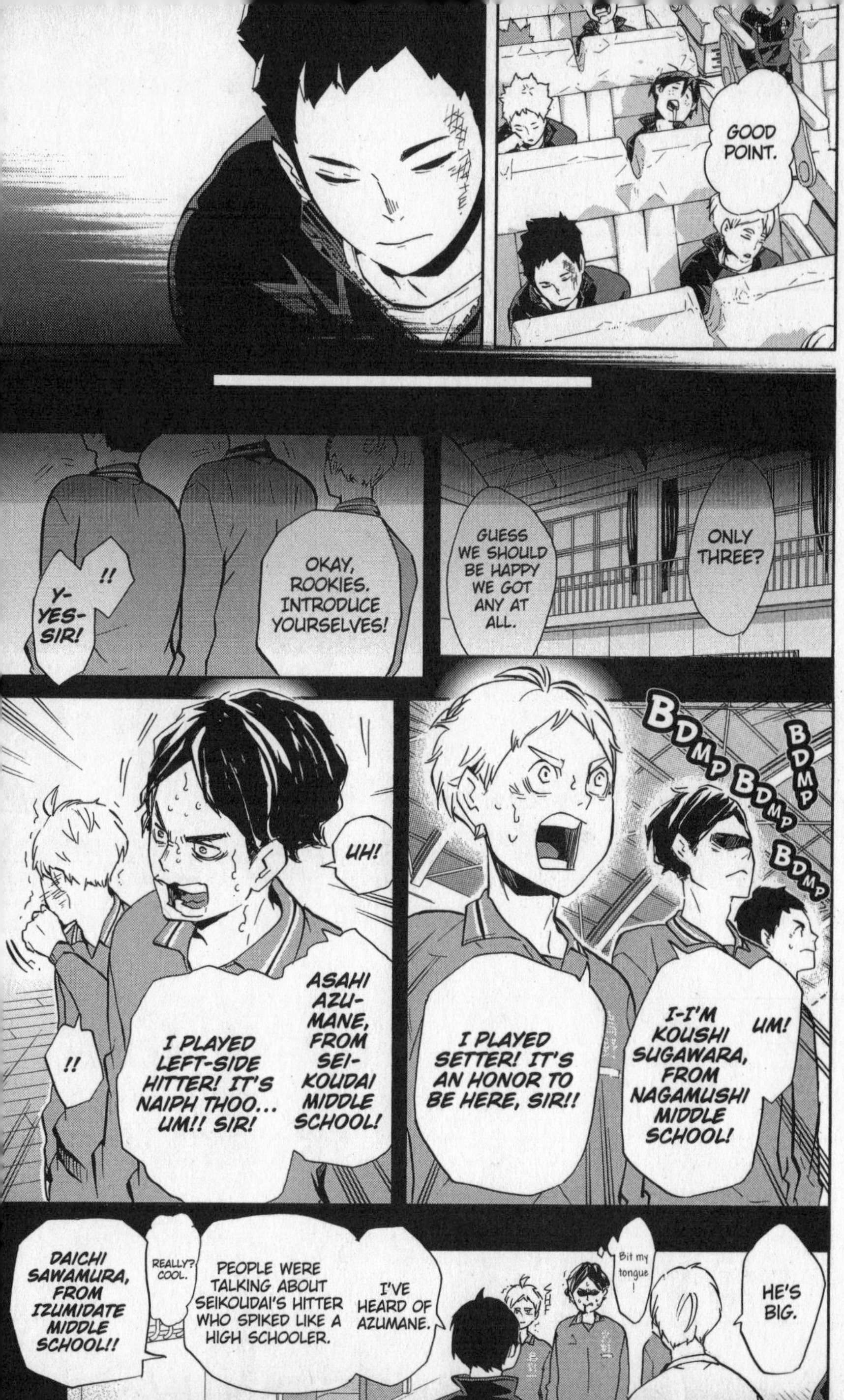
GOOD POINT.
ONLY THREE?
GUESS WE SHOULD BE HAPPY WE GOT ANY AT ALL.
OKAY, ROOKIES. INTRODUCE YOURSELVES!
!!
Y-YES-SIR!
BDMP BDMP BDMP BDMP
UM!
I-I'M KOUSHI SUGAWARA, FROM NAGAMUSHI MIDDLE SCHOOL!
I PLAYED SETTER! IT'S AN HONOR TO BE HERE, SIR!!
UH!
ASAHI AZUMANE, FROM SEIKOUDAI MIDDLE SCHOOL!
I PLAYED LEFT-SIDE HITTER! IT'S NAIPH THOO... UM!! SIR!
!!
HE'S BIG.
Bit my tongue!
SHF
I'VE HEARD OF AZUMANE.
PEOPLE WERE TALKING ABOUT SEIKOUDAI'S HITTER WHO SPIKED LIKE A HIGH SCHOOLER.
REALLY? COOL.
DAICHI SAWAMURA, FROM IZUMIDATE MIDDLE SCHOOL!!

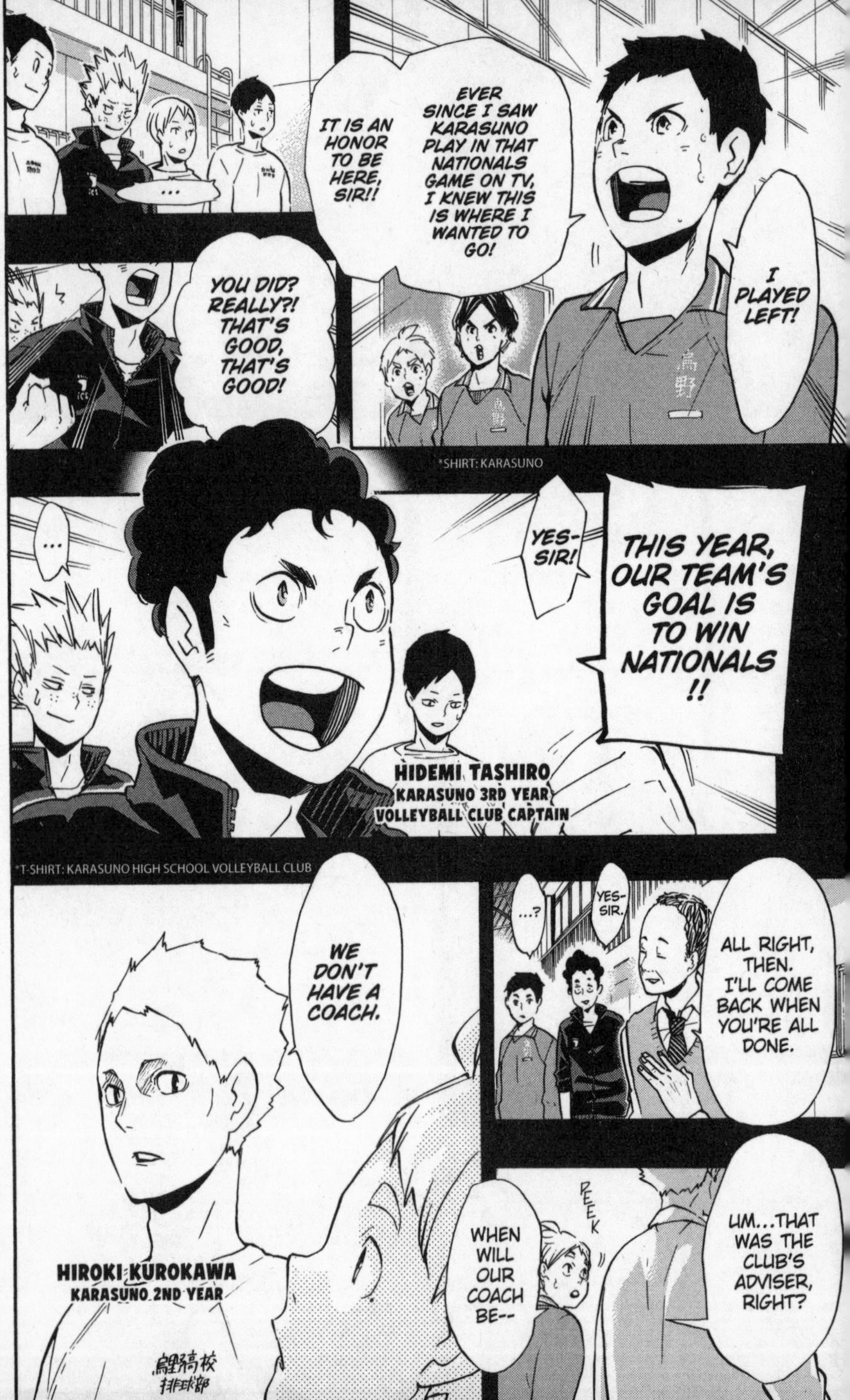
I PLAYED LEFT!
EVER SINCE I SAW KARASUNO PLAY IN THAT NATIONALS GAME ON TV, I KNEW THIS IS WHERE I WANTED TO GO!
IT IS AN HONOR TO BE HERE, SIR!!
...
YOU DID? REALLY?! THAT'S GOOD, THAT'S GOOD!
*SHIRT: KARASUNO
THIS YEAR, OUR TEAM'S GOAL IS TO WIN NATIONALS !!
YES-SIR!
...
HIDEMI TASHIRO
KARASUNO 3RD YEAR
VOLLEYBALL CLUB CAPTAIN
*T-SHIRT: KARASUNO HIGH SCHOOL VOLLEYBALL CLUB
ALL RIGHT, THEN. I'LL COME BACK WHEN YOU'RE ALL DONE.
YES-SIR.
...?
UM...THAT WAS THE CLUB'S ADVISER, RIGHT?
PEEK
WHEN WILL OUR COACH BE--
WE DON'T HAVE A COACH.
HIROKI KUROKAWA
KARASUNO 2ND YEAR
烏野高校
排球部

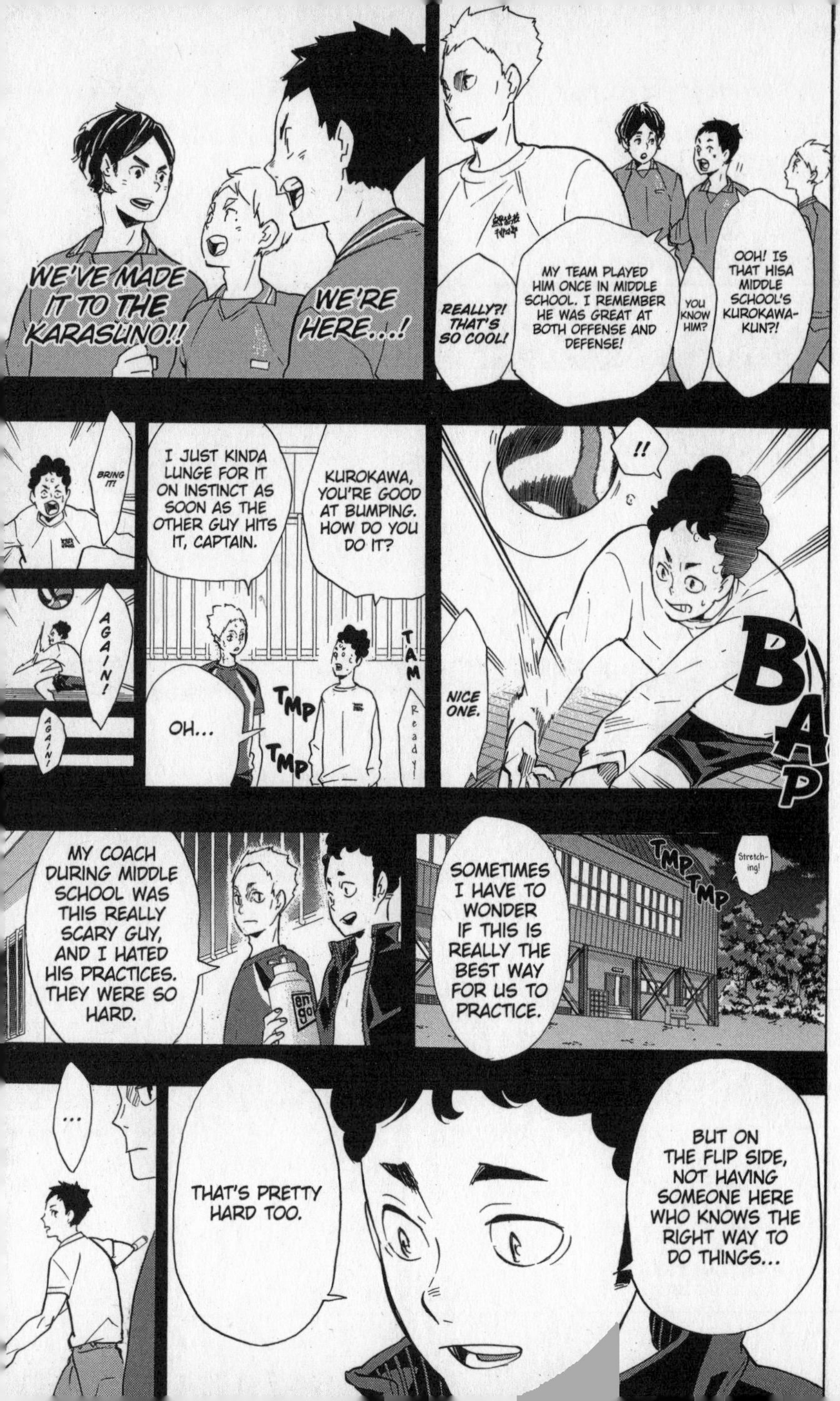
OOH! IS THAT HISA MIDDLE SCHOOL'S KUROKAWA-KUN?!
YOU KNOW HIM?
MY TEAM PLAYED HIM ONCE IN MIDDLE SCHOOL. I REMEMBER HE WAS GREAT AT BOTH OFFENSE AND DEFENSE!
REALLY?! THAT'S SO COOL!
WE'RE HERE...!
WE'VE MADE IT TO THE KARASUNO!!
!!
BAP
NICE ONE.
KUROKAWA, YOU'RE GOOD AT BUMPING. HOW DO YOU DO IT?
I JUST KINDA LUNGE FOR IT ON INSTINCT AS SOON AS THE OTHER GUY HITS IT, CAPTAIN.
TAM
Ready!
TMP
TMP
OH...
BRING IT!
AGAIN!
AGAIN!
Stretching!
TMP TMP TMP
SOMETIMES I HAVE TO WONDER IF THIS IS REALLY THE BEST WAY FOR US TO PRACTICE.
MY COACH DURING MIDDLE SCHOOL WAS THIS REALLY SCARY GUY, AND I HATED HIS PRACTICES. THEY WERE SO HARD.
BUT ON THE FLIP SIDE, NOT HAVING SOMEONE HERE WHO KNOWS THE RIGHT WAY TO DO THINGS...
THAT'S PRETTY HARD TOO.
...

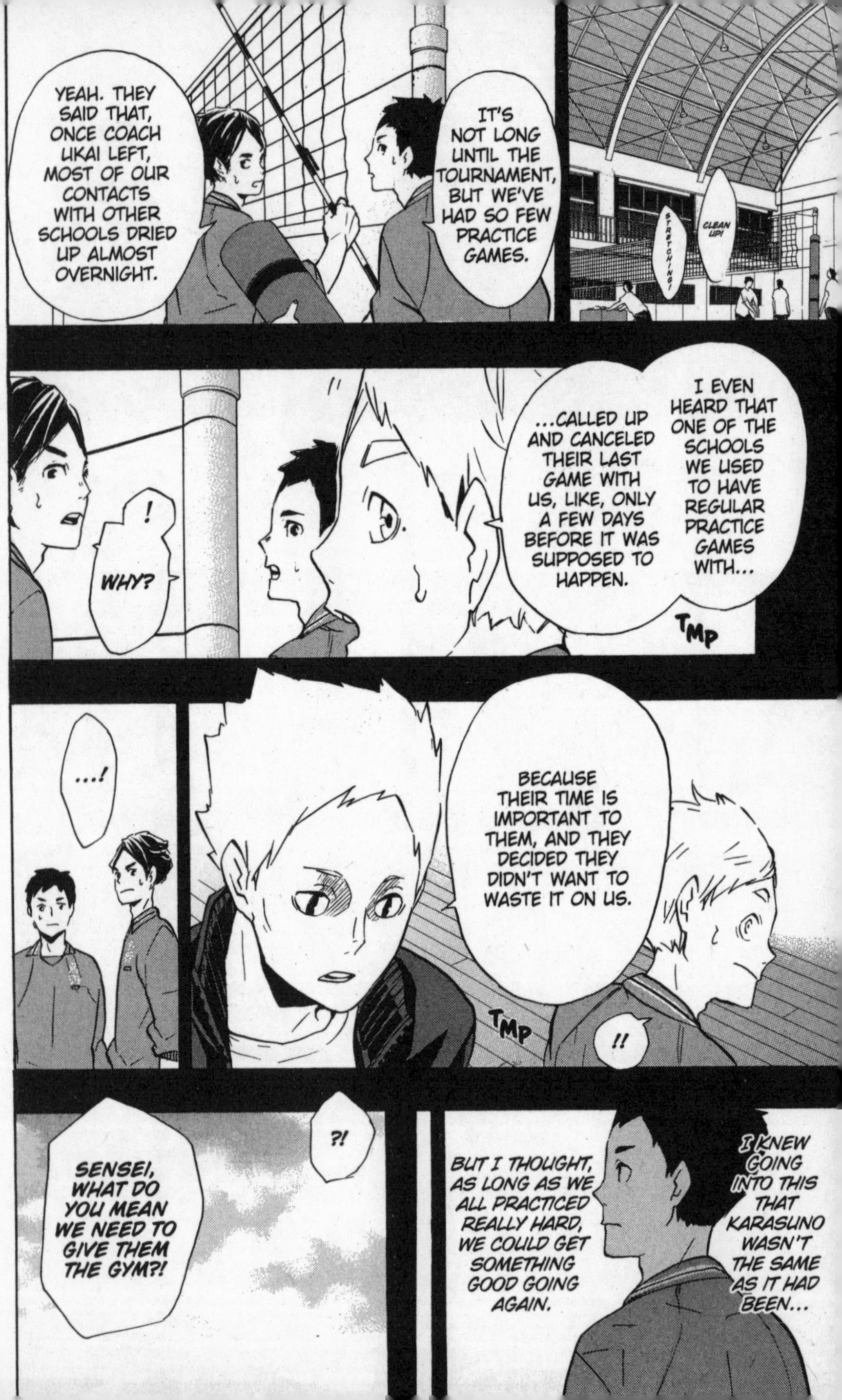
CLEAN UP!
STRETCHING!
IT'S NOT LONG UNTIL THE TOURNAMENT, BUT WE'VE HAD SO FEW PRACTICE GAMES.
YEAH. THEY SAID THAT, ONCE COACH UKAI LEFT, MOST OF OUR CONTACTS WITH OTHER SCHOOLS DRIED UP ALMOST OVERNIGHT.
I EVEN HEARD THAT ONE OF THE SCHOOLS WE USED TO HAVE REGULAR PRACTICE GAMES WITH...
...CALLED UP AND CANCELED THEIR LAST GAME WITH US, LIKE, ONLY A FEW DAYS BEFORE IT WAS SUPPOSED TO HAPPEN.
TMP
!
WHY?
BECAUSE THEIR TIME IS IMPORTANT TO THEM, AND THEY DECIDED THEY DIDN'T WANT TO WASTE IT ON US.
!!
TMP
...!
I KNEW GOING INTO THIS THAT KARASUNO WASN'T THE SAME AS IT HAD BEEN...
BUT I THOUGHT, AS LONG AS WE ALL PRACTICED REALLY HARD, WE COULD GET SOMETHING GOOD GOING AGAIN.
?!
SENSEI, WHAT DO YOU MEAN WE NEED TO GIVE THEM THE GYM?!

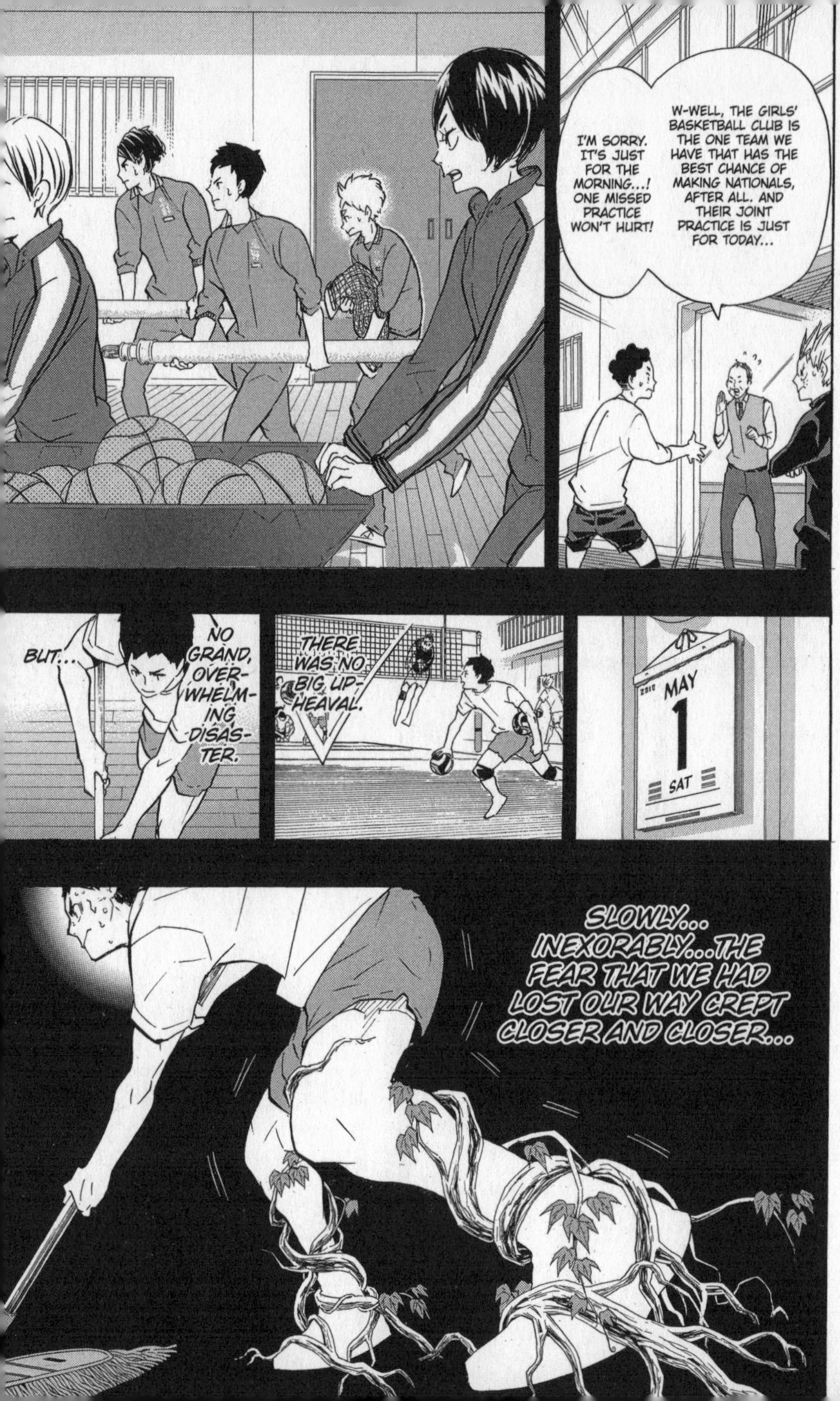
W-WELL, THE GIRLS' BASKETBALL CLUB IS THE ONE TEAM WE HAVE THAT HAS THE BEST CHANCE OF MAKING NATIONALS, AFTER ALL. AND THEIR JOINT PRACTICE IS JUST FOR TODAY...
I'M SORRY. IT'S JUST FOR THE MORNING...! ONE MISSED PRACTICE WON'T HURT!
2010 MAY 1 SAT
THERE WAS NO BIG UP-HEAVAL.
NO GRAND, OVER-WHELM-ING DISAS-TER.
BUT...
SLOWLY... INEXORABLY...THE FEAR THAT WE HAD LOST OUR WAY CREPT CLOSER AND CLOSER...

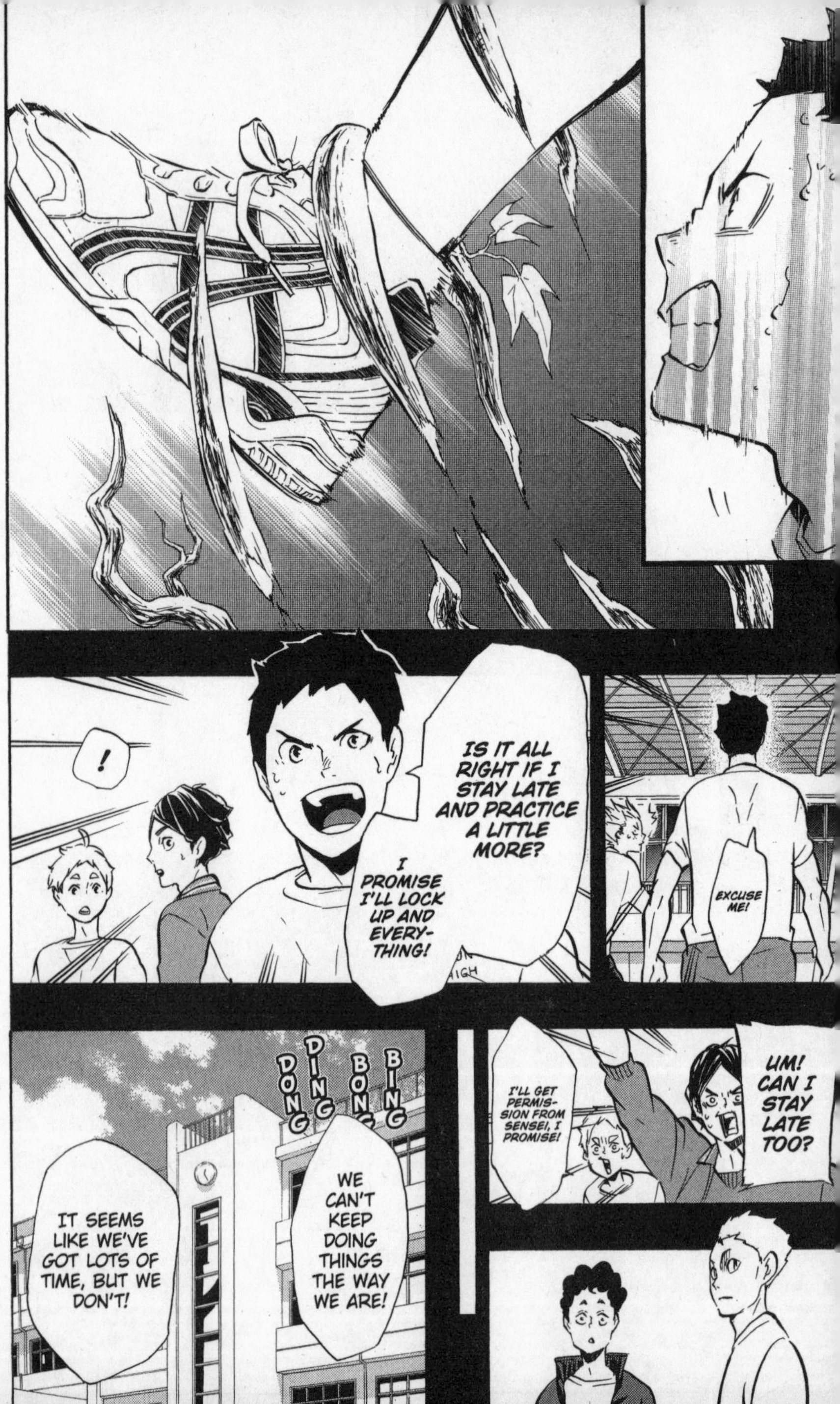
EXCUSE ME!
!
IS IT ALL RIGHT IF I STAY LATE AND PRACTICE A LITTLE MORE?
I PROMISE I'LL LOCK UP AND EVERYTHING!
UM! CAN I STAY LATE TOO?
I'LL GET PERMISSION FROM SENSEI, I PROMISE!
BING BONG DING DONG
WE CAN'T KEEP DOING THINGS THE WAY WE ARE!
IT SEEMS LIKE WE'VE GOT LOTS OF TIME, BUT WE DON'T!

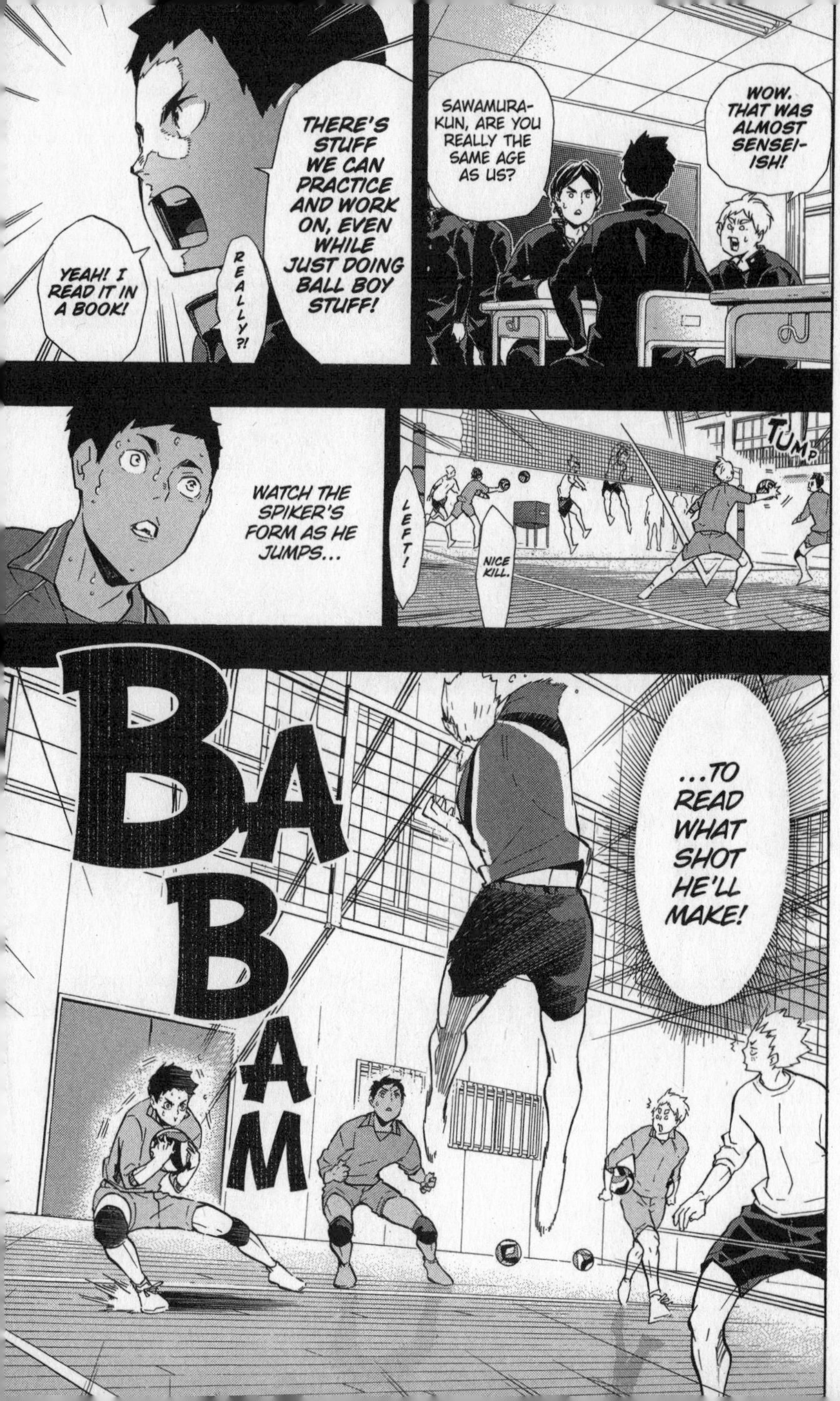
WOW. THAT WAS ALMOST SENSEI-ISH!
SAWAMURA-KUN, ARE YOU REALLY THE SAME AGE AS US?
THERE'S STUFF WE CAN PRACTICE AND WORK ON, EVEN WHILE JUST DOING BALL BOY STUFF!
REALLY?!
YEAH! I READ IT IN A BOOK!
TUMP
LEFT!
NICE KILL.
WATCH THE SPIKER'S FORM AS HE JUMPS...
...TO READ WHAT SHOT HE'LL MAKE!
BABAM

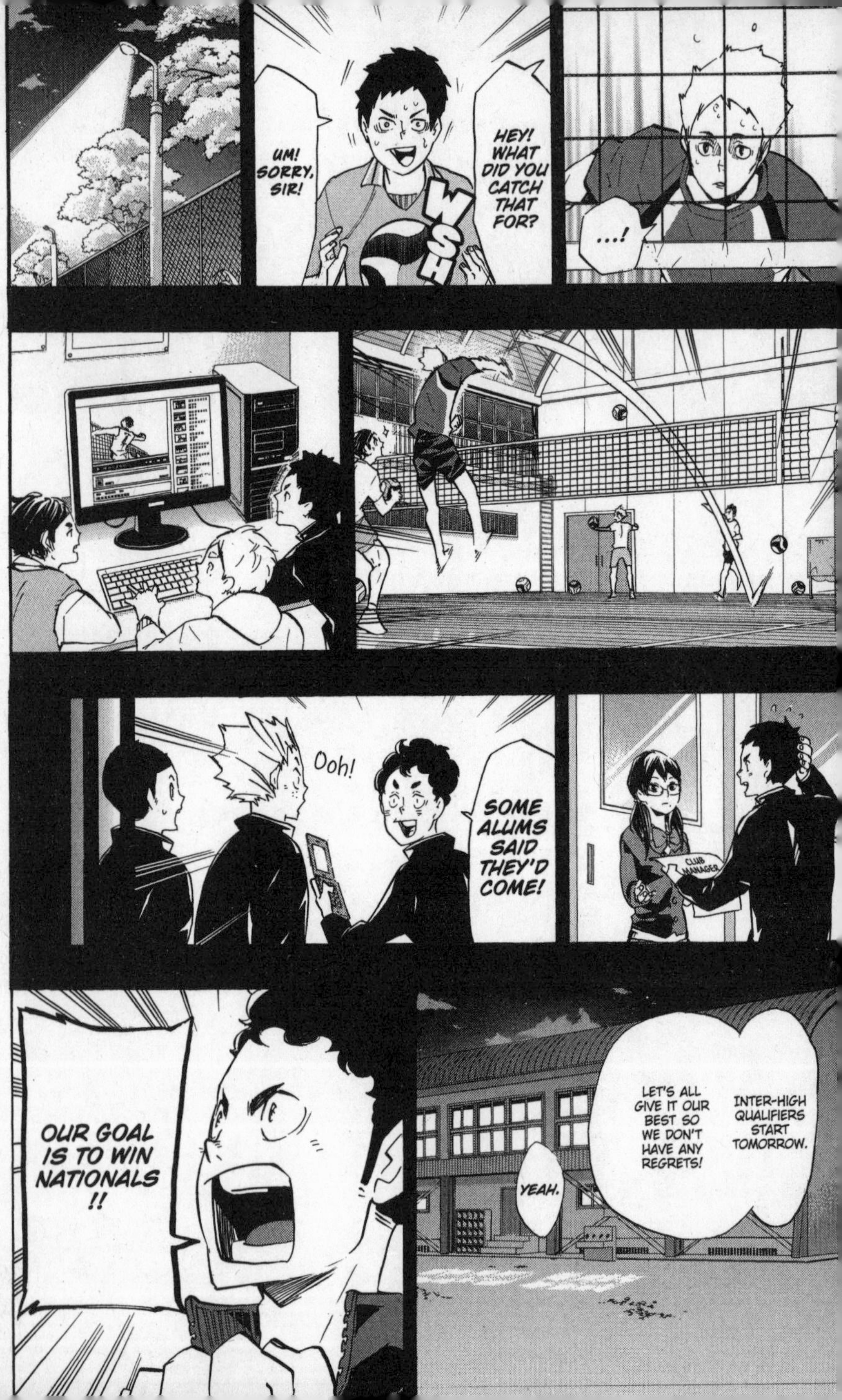
...!
HEY! WHAT DID YOU CATCH THAT FOR?
WSH
UM! SORRY, SIR!
CLUB MANAGER
SOME ALUMS SAID THEY'D COME!
Ooh!
INTER-HIGH QUALIFIERS START TOMORROW.
LET'S ALL GIVE IT OUR BEST SO WE DON'T HAVE ANY REGRETS!
YEAH.
OUR GOAL IS TO WIN NATIONALS !!

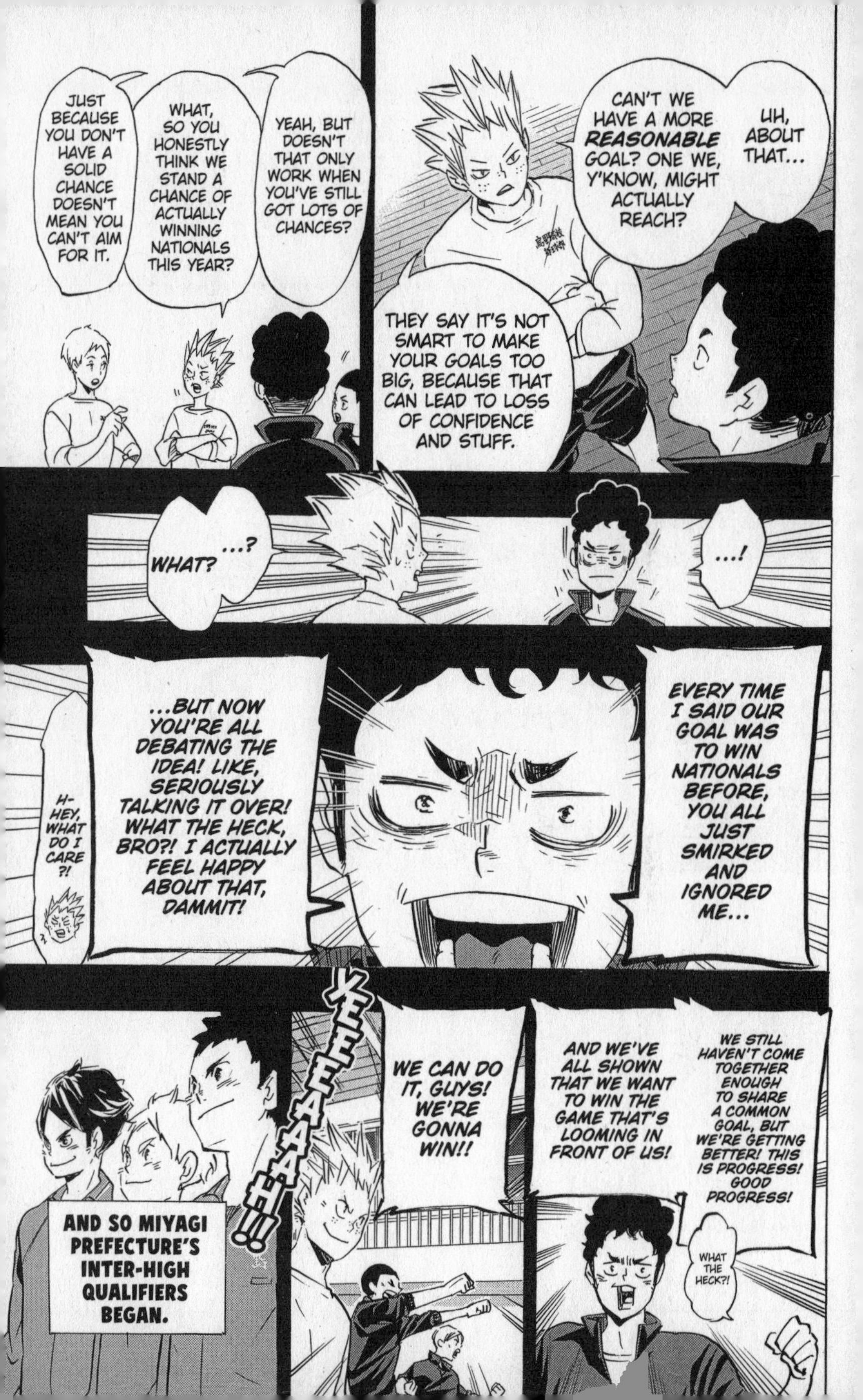
UH, ABOUT THAT...
CAN'T WE HAVE A MORE REASONABLE GOAL? ONE WE, Y'KNOW, MIGHT ACTUALLY REACH?
THEY SAY IT'S NOT SMART TO MAKE YOUR GOALS TOO BIG, BECAUSE THAT CAN LEAD TO LOSS OF CONFIDENCE AND STUFF.
YEAH, BUT DOESN'T THAT ONLY WORK WHEN YOU'VE STILL GOT LOTS OF CHANCES?
WHAT, SO YOU HONESTLY THINK WE STAND A CHANCE OF ACTUALLY WINNING NATIONALS THIS YEAR?
JUST BECAUSE YOU DON'T HAVE A SOLID CHANCE DOESN'T MEAN YOU CAN'T AIM FOR IT.
...!
...? WHAT?
EVERY TIME I SAID OUR GOAL WAS TO WIN NATIONALS BEFORE, YOU ALL JUST SMIRKED AND IGNORED ME...
...BUT NOW YOU'RE ALL DEBATING THE IDEA! LIKE, SERIOUSLY TALKING IT OVER! WHAT THE HECK, BRO?! I ACTUALLY FEEL HAPPY ABOUT THAT, DAMMIT!
H-HEY, WHAT DO I CARE ?!
WE STILL HAVEN'T COME TOGETHER ENOUGH TO SHARE A COMMON GOAL, BUT WE'RE GETTING BETTER! THIS IS PROGRESS! GOOD PROGRESS!
WHAT THE HECK?!
AND WE'VE ALL SHOWN THAT WE WANT TO WIN THE GAME THAT'S LOOMING IN FRONT OF US!
WE CAN DO IT, GUYS! WE'RE GONNA WIN!!
YEEEEAAAAH!!
AND SO MIYAGI PREFECTURE'S INTER-HIGH QUALIFIERS BEGAN.

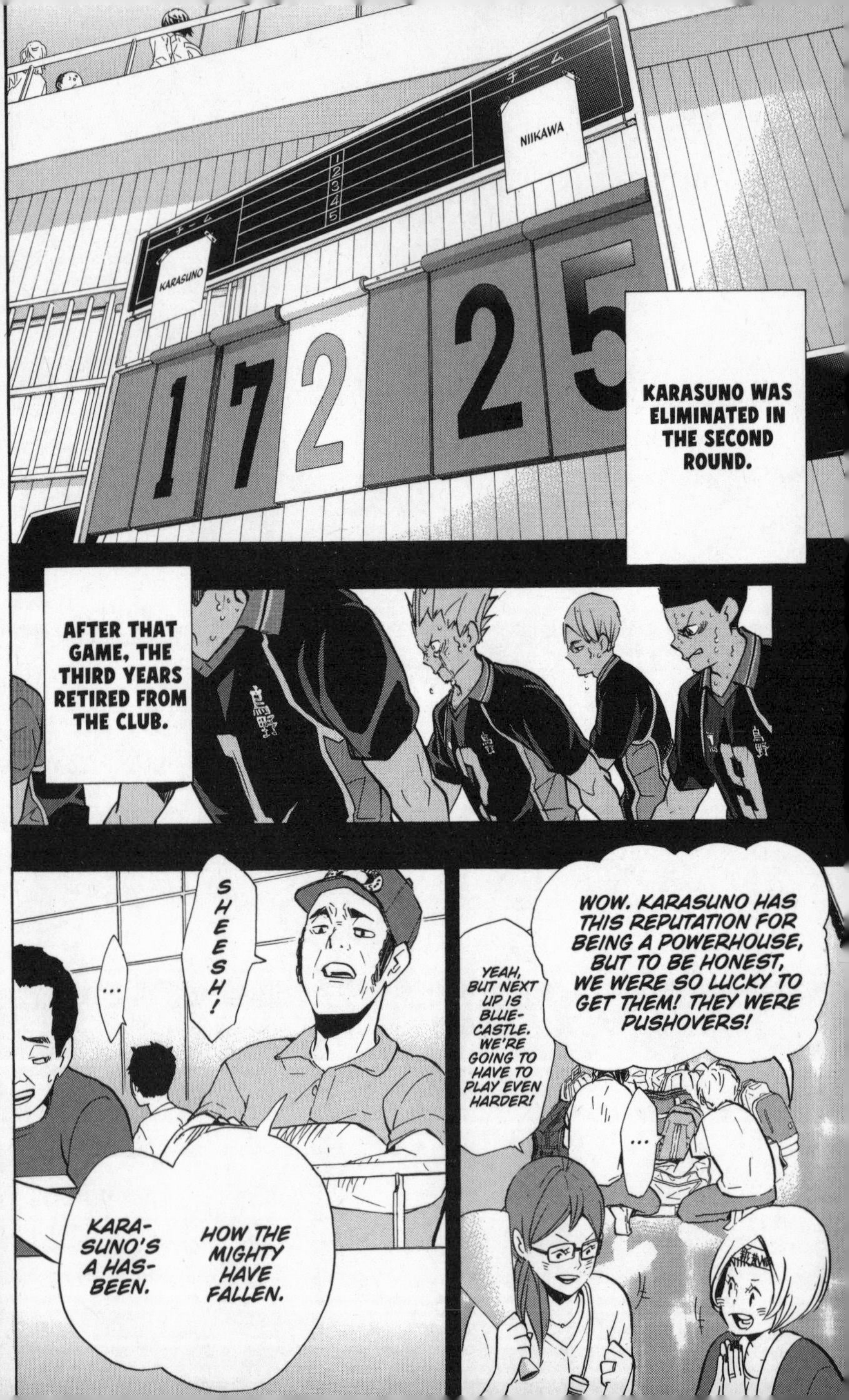
NIIKAWA
KARASUNO
17
25
KARASUNO WAS ELIMINATED IN THE SECOND ROUND.
AFTER THAT GAME, THE THIRD YEARS RETIRED FROM THE CLUB.
WOW. KARASUNO HAS THIS REPUTATION FOR BEING A POWERHOUSE, BUT TO BE HONEST, WE WERE SO LUCKY TO GET THEM! THEY WERE PUSHOVERS!
YEAH, BUT NEXT UP IS BLUE-CASTLE. WE'RE GOING TO HAVE TO PLAY EVEN HARDER!
...
SHEESH!
...
HOW THE MIGHTY HAVE FALLEN.
KARA-SUNO'S A HAS-BEEN.

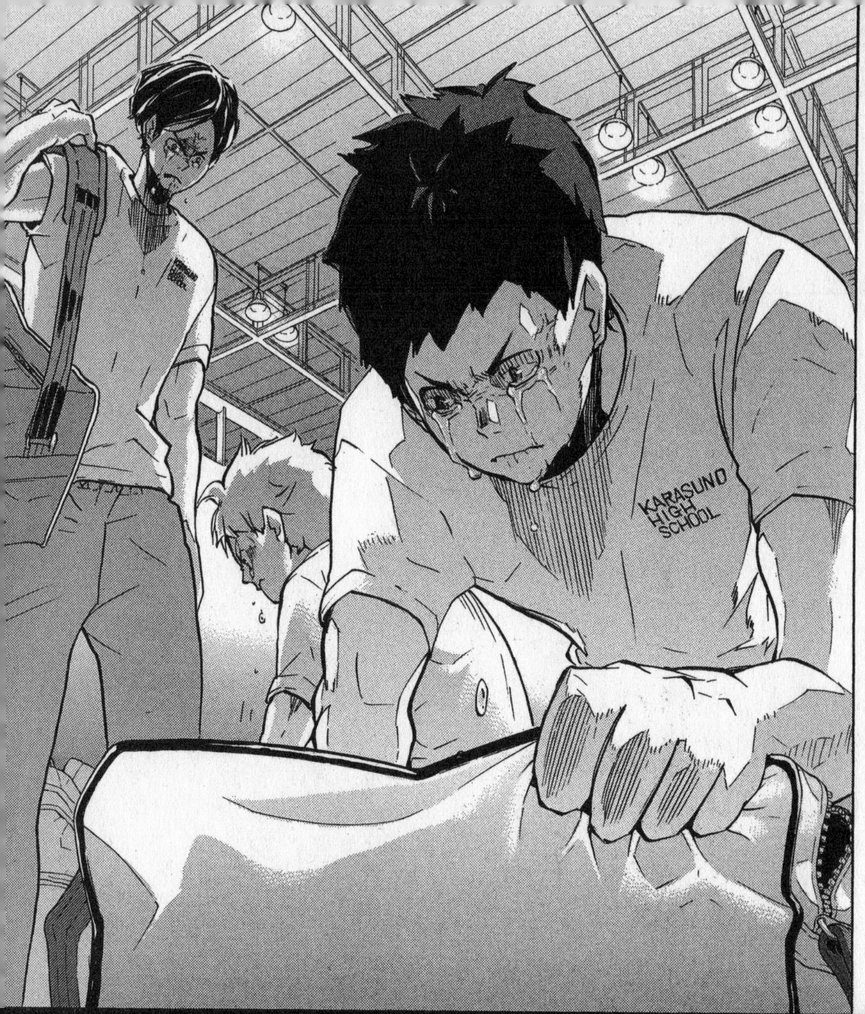
KARASUNO HIGH SCHOOL

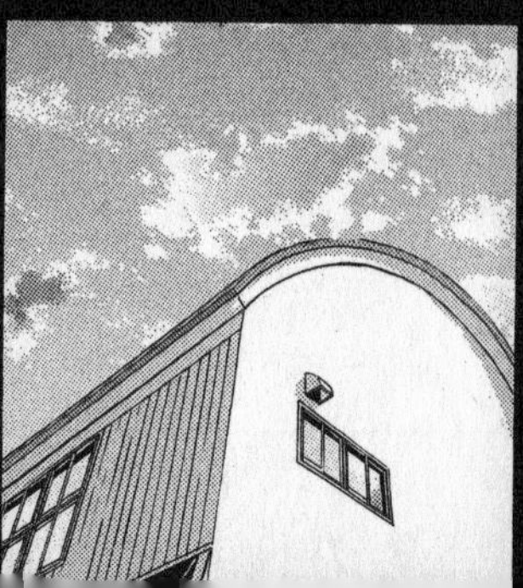

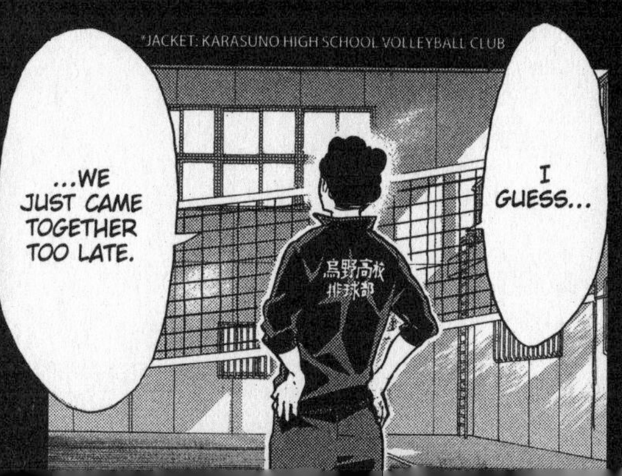
I GUESS...
...WE JUST CAME TOGETHER TOO LATE.
烏野高校 排球部

*JACKET: KARASUNO HIGH SCHOOL VOLLEYBALL CLUB

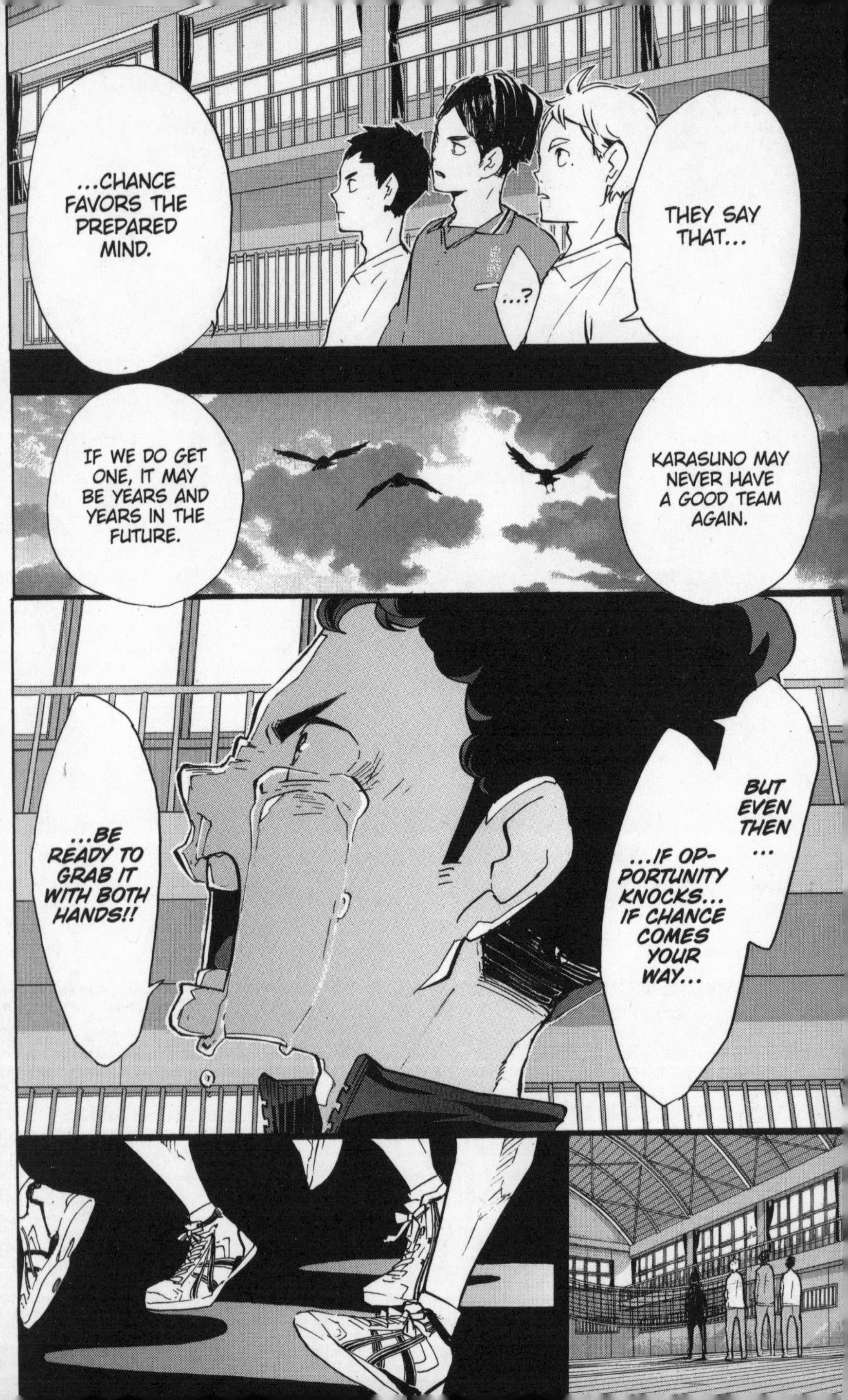
THEY SAY THAT...
...?
...CHANCE FAVORS THE PREPARED MIND.
KARASUNO MAY NEVER HAVE A GOOD TEAM AGAIN.
IF WE DO GET ONE, IT MAY BE YEARS AND YEARS IN THE FUTURE.
BUT EVEN THEN...
...IF OP-PORTUNITY KNOCKS... IF CHANCE COMES YOUR WAY...
...BE READY TO GRAB IT WITH BOTH HANDS!!

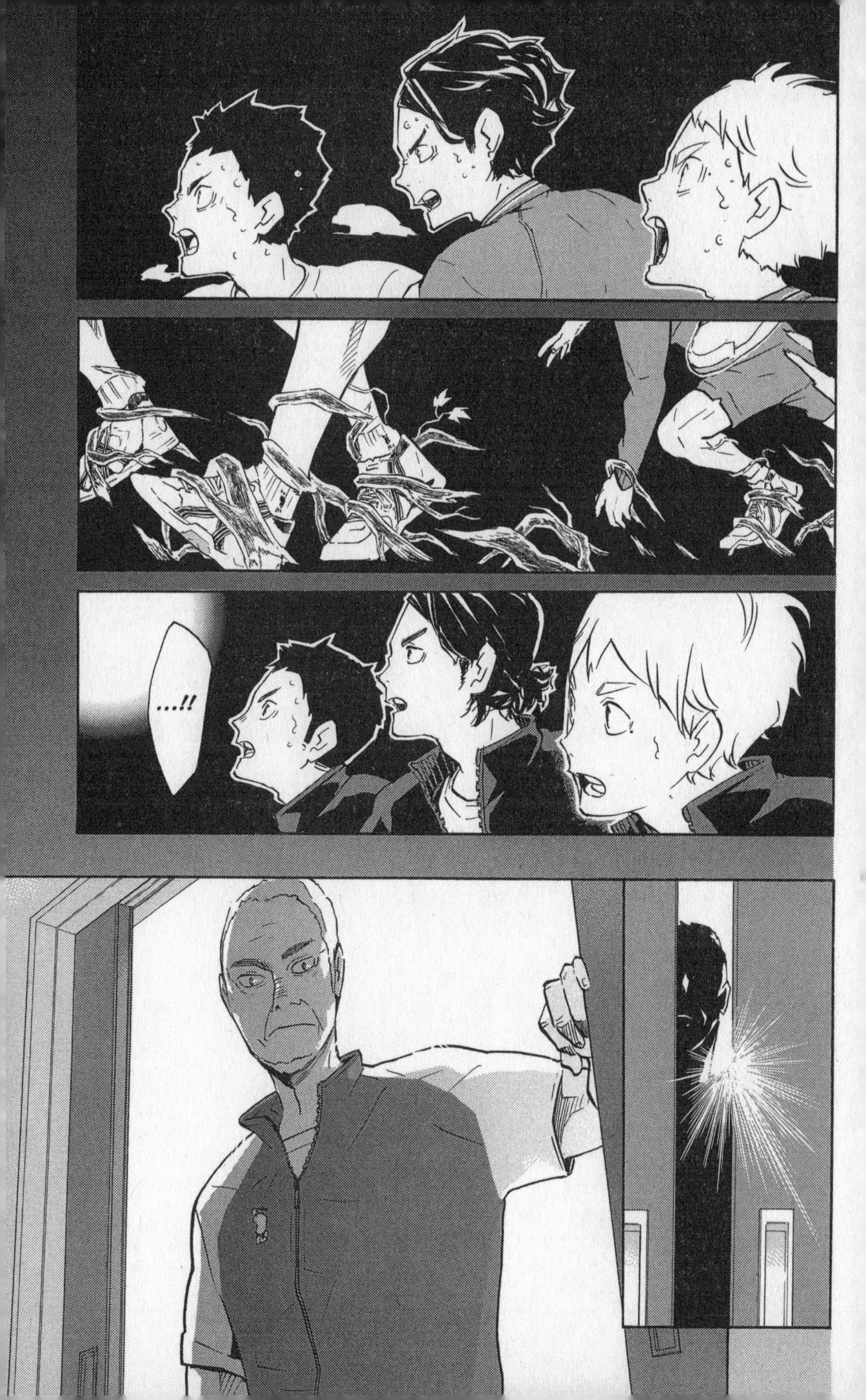
...!!

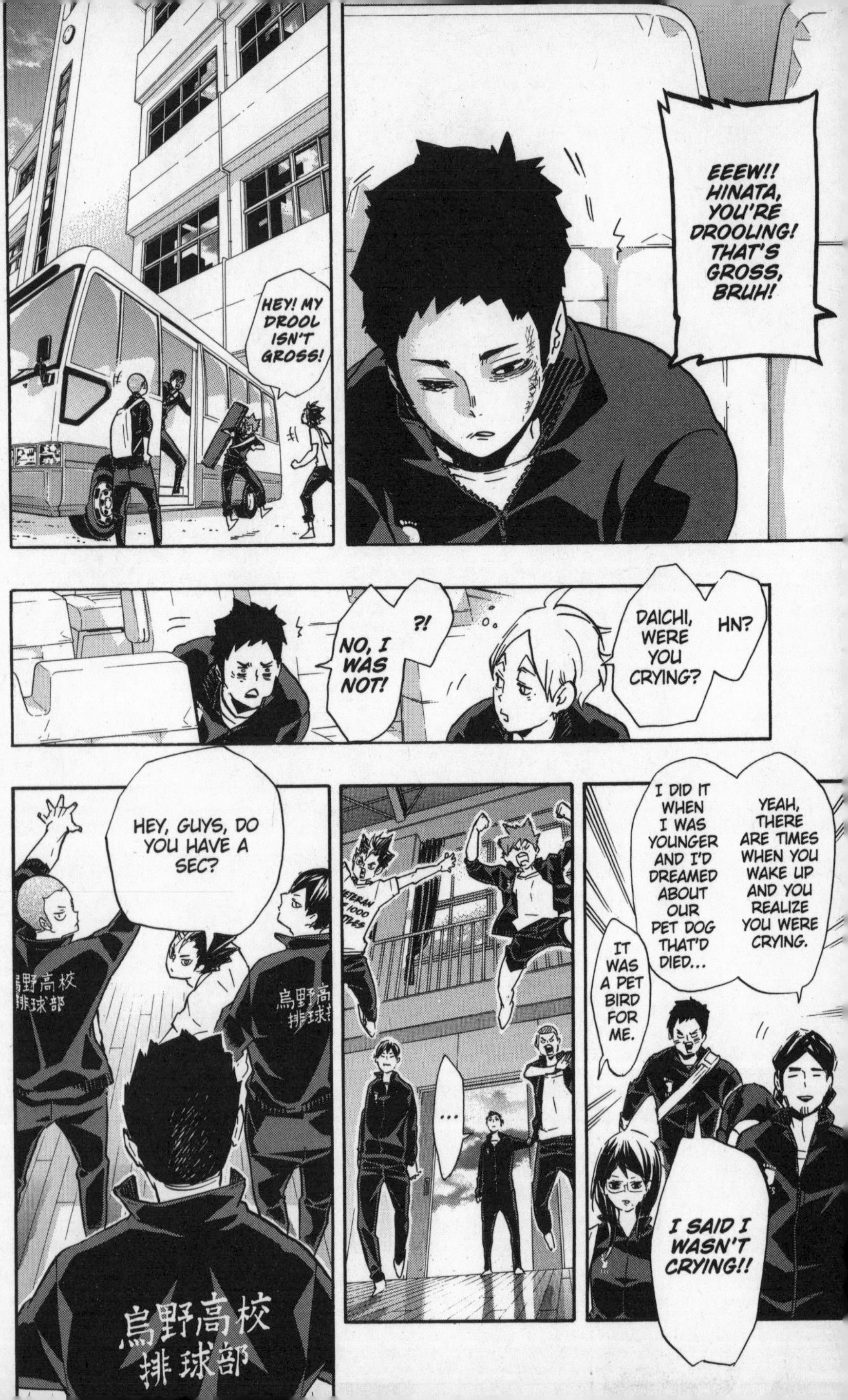
EEEW!! HINATA, YOU'RE DROOLING! THAT'S GROSS, BRUH!
HEY! MY DROOL ISN'T GROSS!
HN?
DAICHI, WERE YOU CRYING?
?!
NO, I WAS NOT!
YEAH, THERE ARE TIMES WHEN YOU WAKE UP AND YOU REALIZE YOU WERE CRYING.
I DID IT WHEN I WAS YOUNGER AND I'D DREAMED ABOUT OUR PET DOG THAT'D DIED...
IT WAS A PET BIRD FOR ME.
I SAID I WASN'T CRYING!!
...
HEY, GUYS, DO YOU HAVE A SEC?
烏野高校
排球部

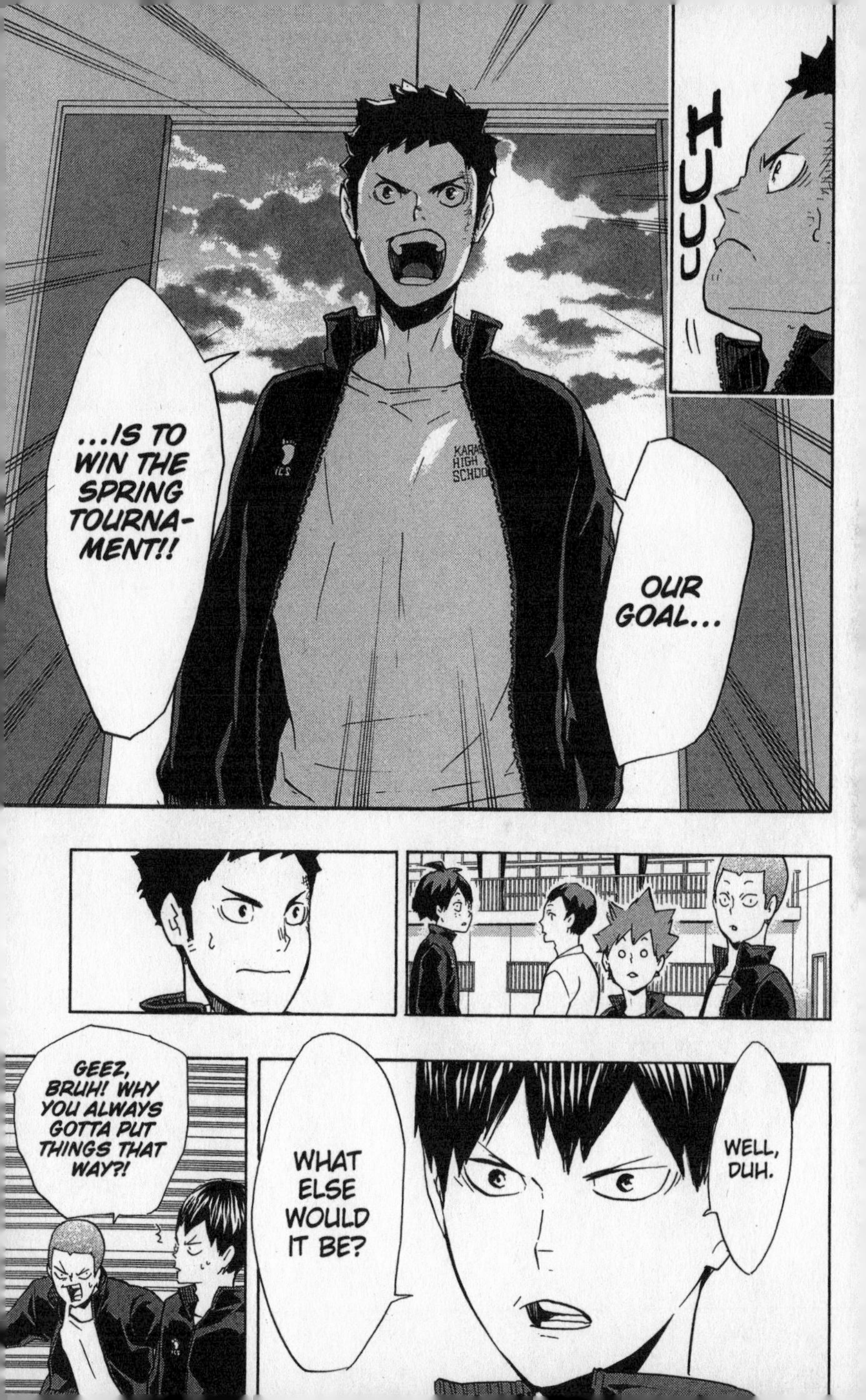
HUUUU
OUR GOAL...
...IS TO WIN THE SPRING TOURNAMENT!!
WELL, DUH.
WHAT ELSE WOULD IT BE?
GEEZ, BRUH! WHY YOU ALWAYS GOTTA PUT THINGS THAT WAY?!

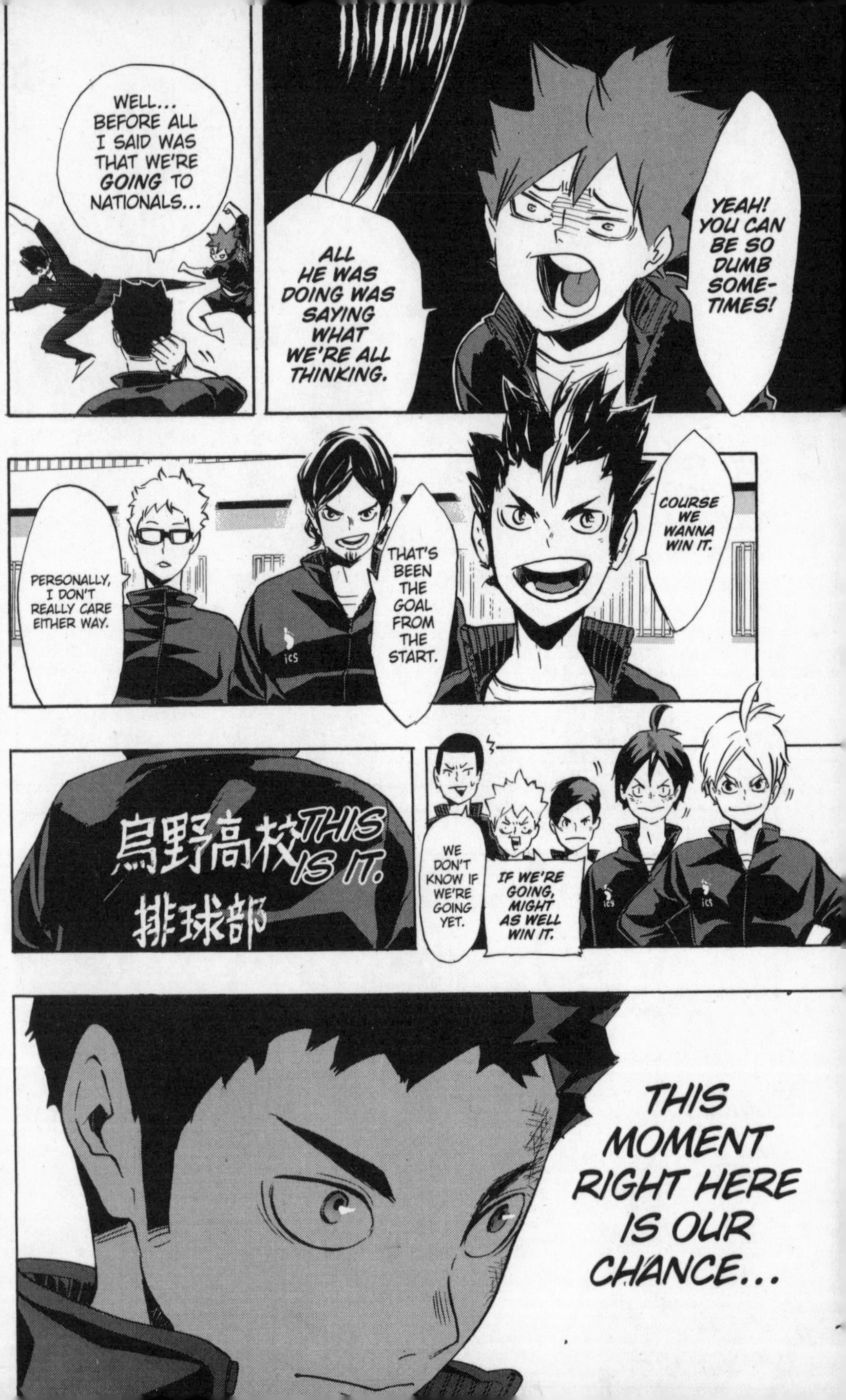
YEAH! YOU CAN BE SO DUMB SOME-TIMES!
ALL HE WAS DOING WAS SAYING WHAT WE'RE ALL THINKING.
WELL... BEFORE ALL I SAID WAS THAT WE'RE GOING TO NATIONALS...
COURSE WE WANNA WIN IT.
THAT'S BEEN THE GOAL FROM THE START.
PERSONALLY, I DON'T REALLY CARE EITHER WAY.
IF WE'RE GOING, MIGHT AS WELL WIN IT.
WE DON'T KNOW IF WE'RE GOING YET.
烏野高校
排球部
THIS IS IT.
THIS MOMENT RIGHT HERE IS OUR CHANCE...

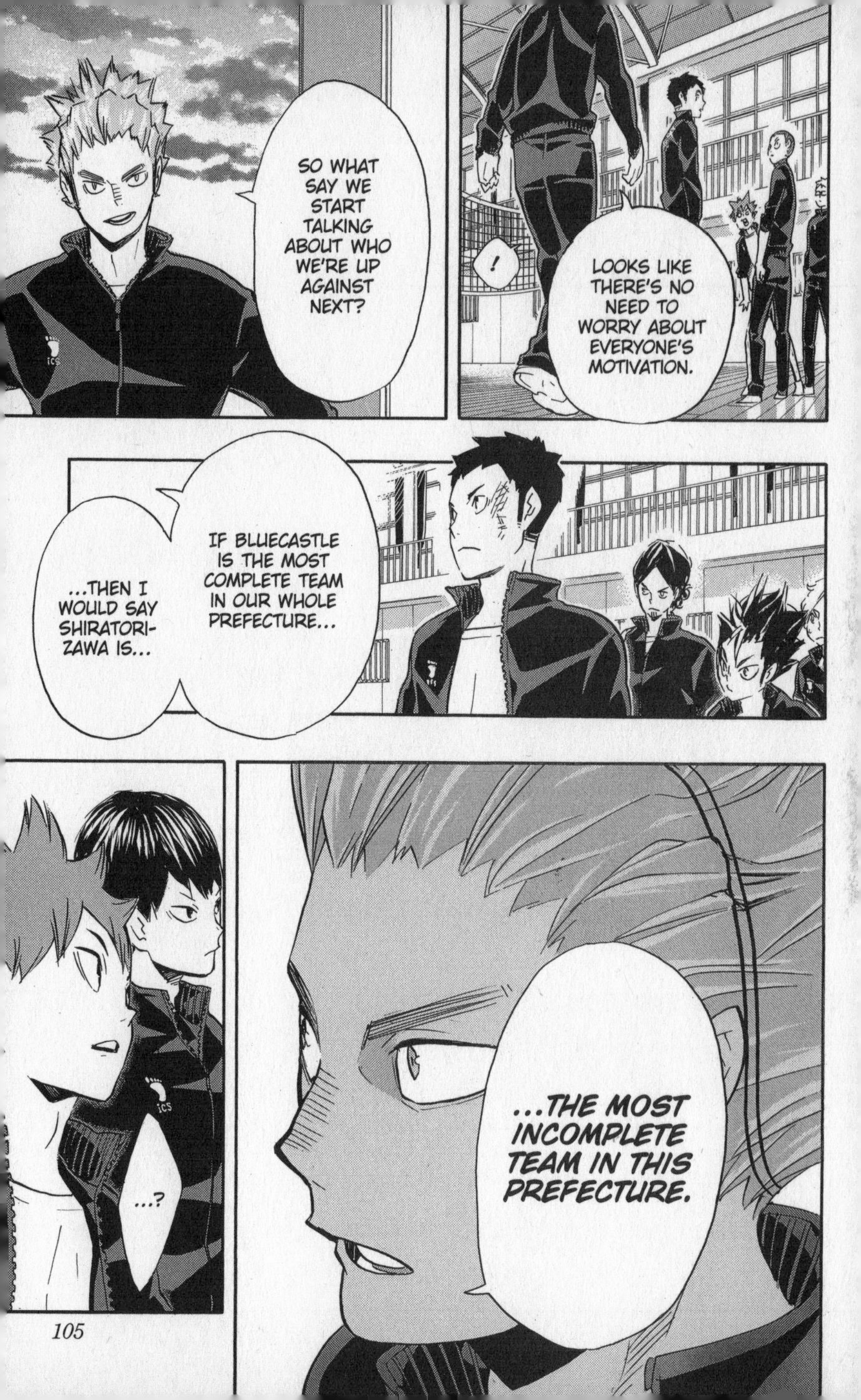
!
LOOKS LIKE THERE'S NO NEED TO WORRY ABOUT EVERYONE'S MOTIVATION.
SO WHAT SAY WE START TALKING ABOUT WHO WE'RE UP AGAINST NEXT?
IF BLUECASTLE IS THE MOST COMPLETE TEAM IN OUR WHOLE PREFECTURE...
...THEN I WOULD SAY SHIRATORI-ZAWA IS...
...THE MOST INCOMPLETE TEAM IN THIS PREFECTURE.
...?

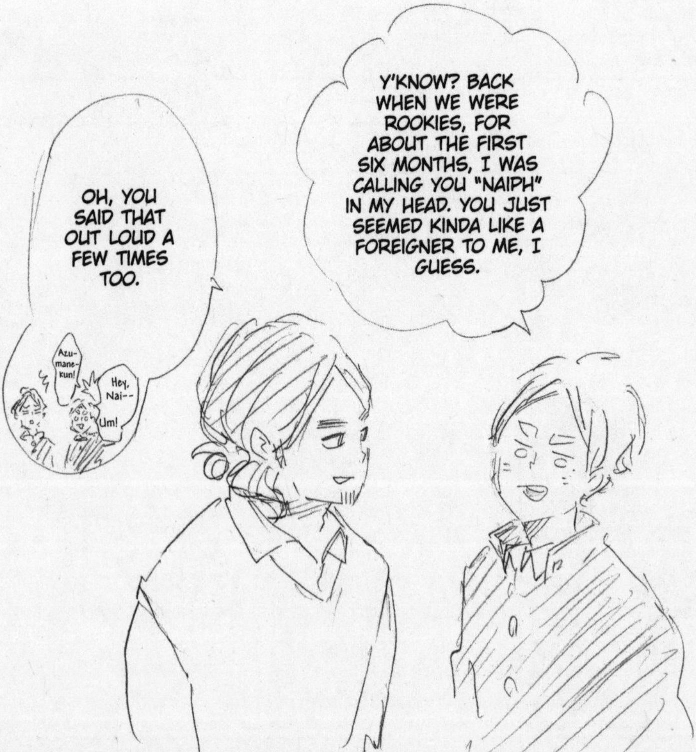
Y'KNOW? BACK WHEN WE WERE ROOKIES, FOR ABOUT THE FIRST SIX MONTHS, I WAS CALLING YOU "NAIPH" IN MY HEAD. YOU JUST SEEMED KINDA LIKE A FOREIGNER TO ME, I GUESS.
OH, YOU SAID THAT OUT LOUD A FEW TIMES TOO.
Hey, Nai--
Azu-mane-kun!
Um!

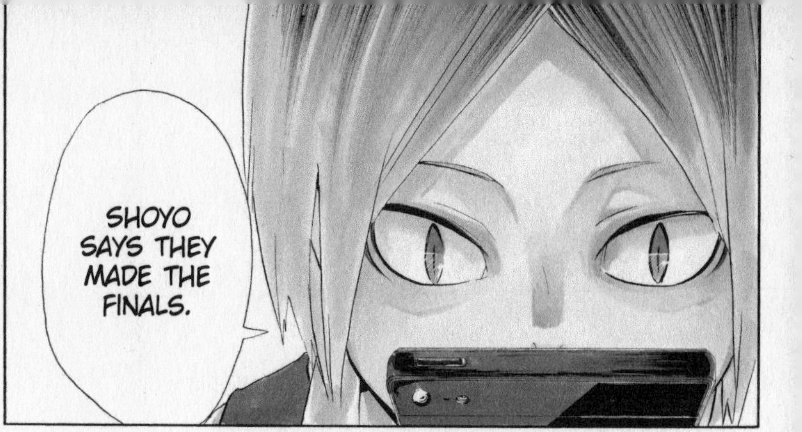
SHOYO SAYS THEY MADE THE FINALS.

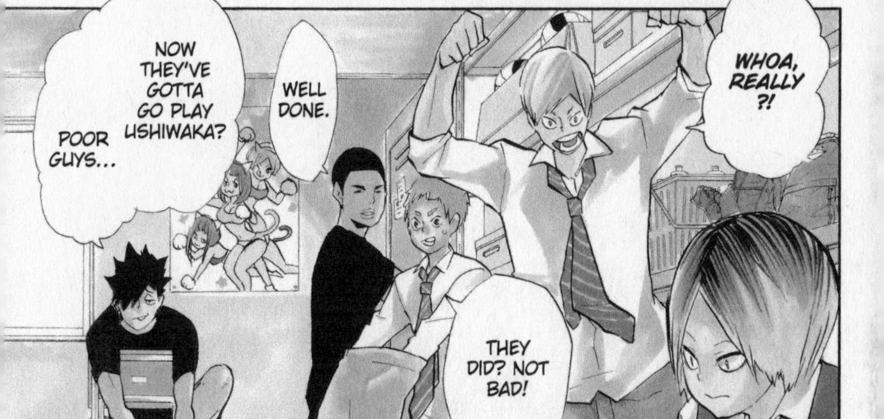
WHOA, REALLY ?!
THEY DID? NOT BAD!
WELL DONE.
NOW THEY'VE GOTTA GO PLAY USHIWAKA?
POOR GUYS...

CHAPTER 150

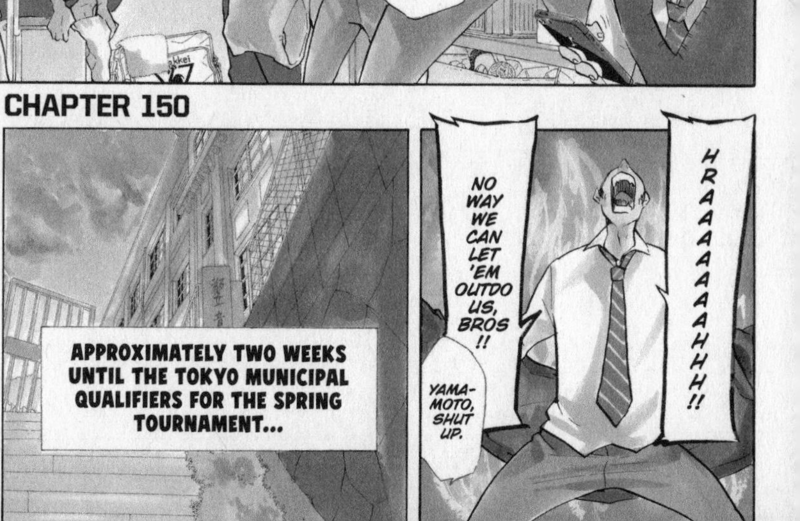
HRAAAAAAAAHHH!!
NO WAY WE CAN LET 'EM OUTDO US, BROS !!
YAMAMOTO, SHUT UP.
APPROXIMATELY TWO WEEKS UNTIL THE TOKYO MUNICIPAL QUALIFIERS FOR THE SPRING TOURNAMENT...

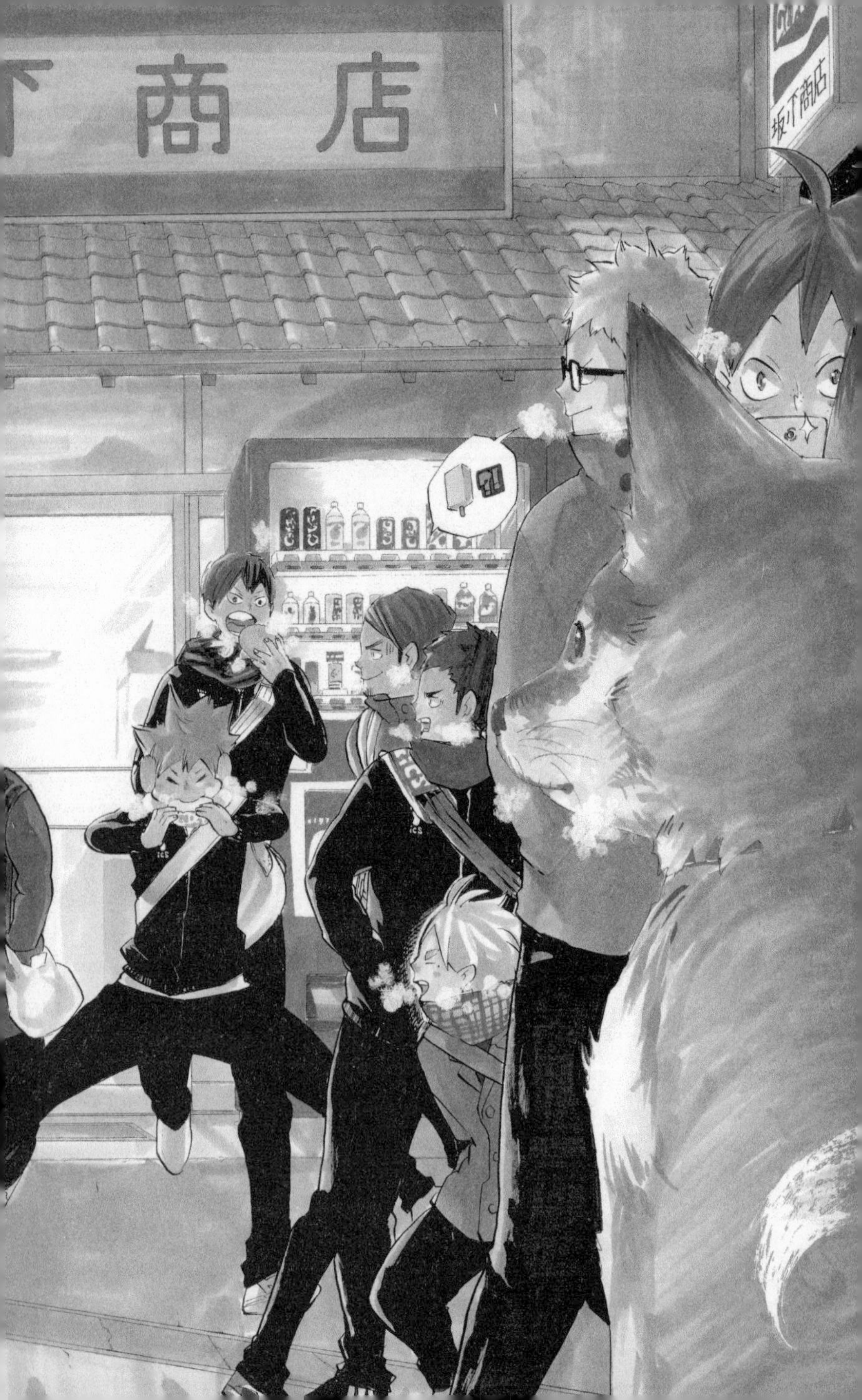

商店
坂ノ下商店
?!

CHAPTER 150: Greetings

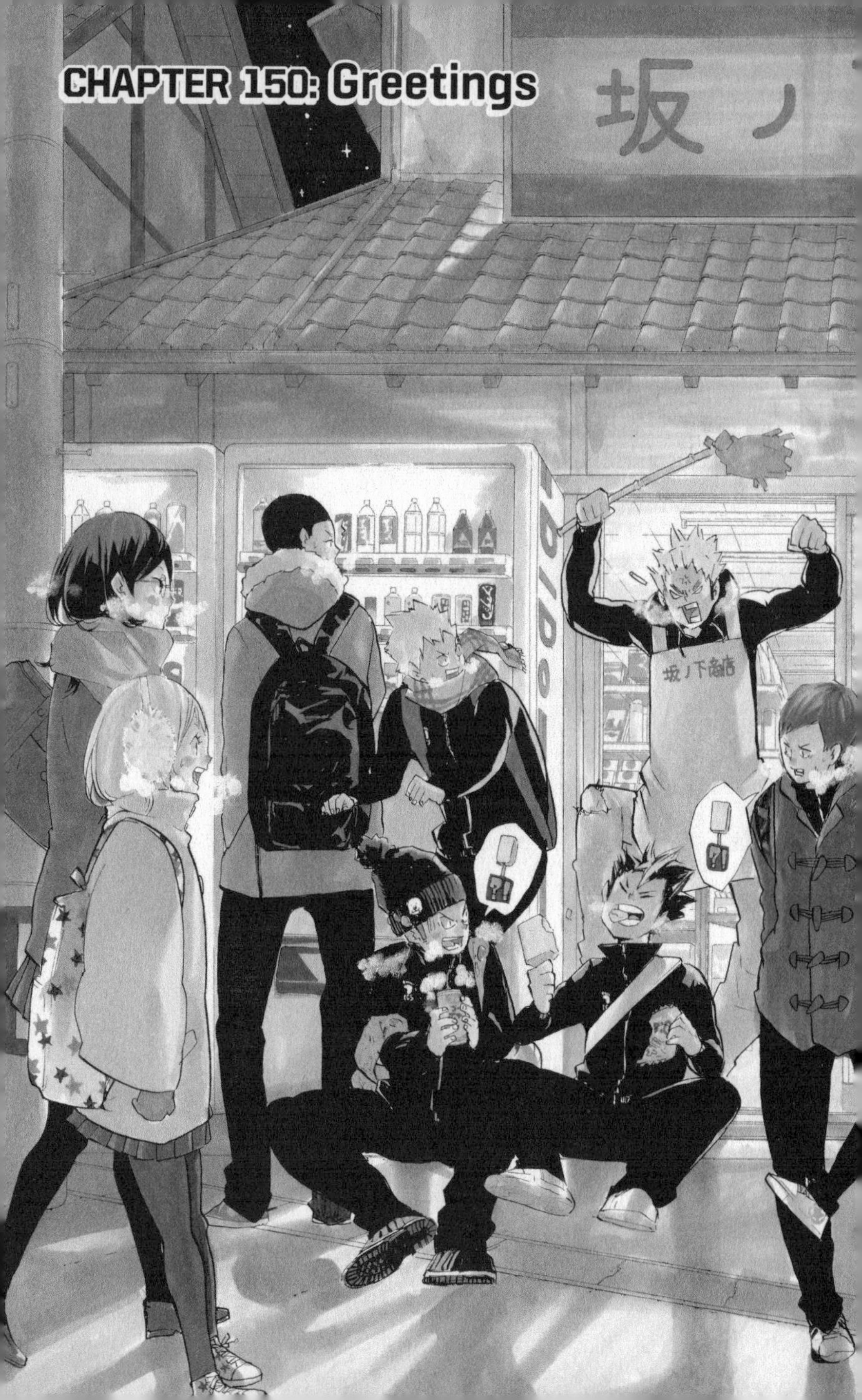
坂ノ
坂ノ下商店
?!
?!

HAIKYU!!

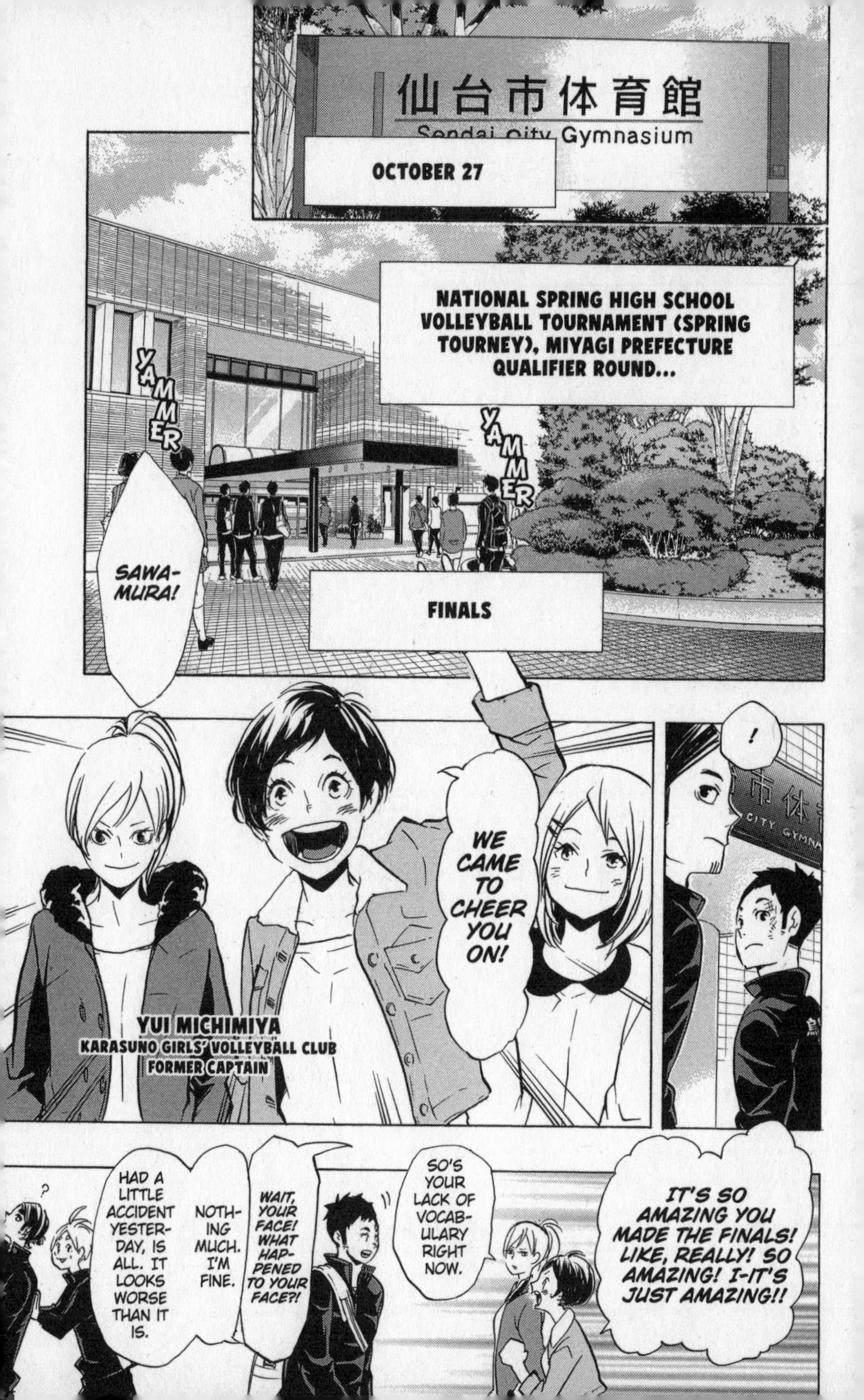

仙台市体育館
Sendai city Gymnasium
OCTOBER 27
NATIONAL SPRING HIGH SCHOOL VOLLEYBALL TOURNAMENT (SPRING TOURNEY), MIYAGI PREFECTURE QUALIFIER ROUND...
YAMMER
YAMMER
FINALS
SAWA-MURA!
!
WE CAME TO CHEER YOU ON!
YUI MICHIMIYA
KARASUNO GIRLS' VOLLEYBALL CLUB FORMER CAPTAIN
IT'S SO AMAZING YOU MADE THE FINALS! LIKE, REALLY! SO AMAZING! I-IT'S JUST AMAZING!!
SO'S YOUR LACK OF VOCAB-ULARY RIGHT NOW.
WAIT, YOUR FACE! WHAT HAP-PENED TO YOUR FACE?!
NOTH-ING MUCH. I'M FINE.
HAD A LITTLE ACCIDENT YESTER-DAY, IS ALL. IT LOOKS WORSE THAN IT IS.
?

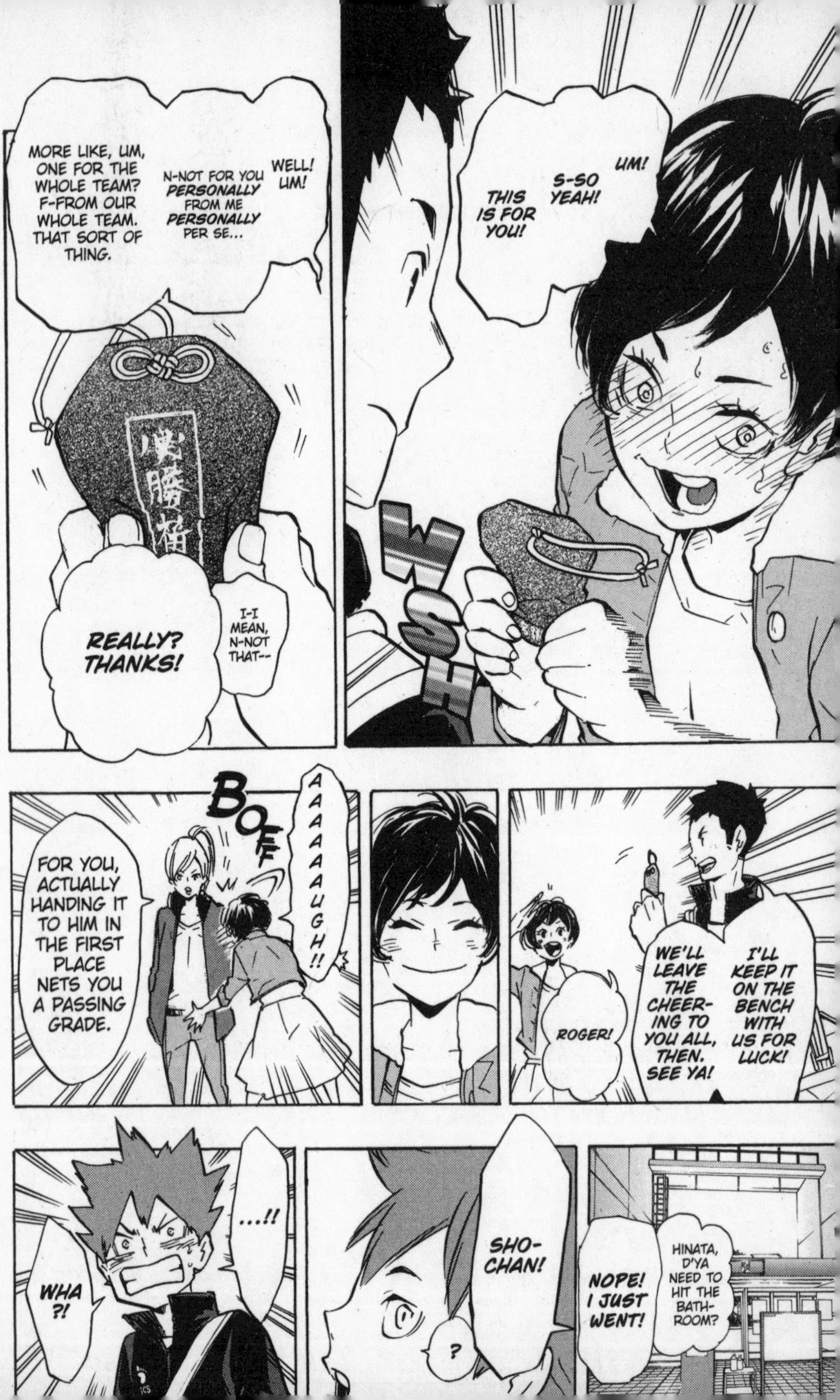
UM!
S-SO YEAH!
THIS IS FOR YOU!
WSH
WELL! UM!
N-NOT FOR YOU PERSONALLY FROM ME PERSONALLY PER SE...
MORE LIKE, UM, ONE FOR THE WHOLE TEAM? F-FROM OUR WHOLE TEAM. THAT SORT OF THING.
I-I MEAN, N-NOT THAT--
REALLY? THANKS!
I'LL KEEP IT ON THE BENCH WITH US FOR LUCK!
WE'LL LEAVE THE CHEERING TO YOU ALL, THEN. SEE YA!
ROGER!
AAAAAAAUGH!!
BOFF
FOR YOU, ACTUALLY HANDING IT TO HIM IN THE FIRST PLACE NETS YOU A PASSING GRADE.
HINATA, D'YA NEED TO HIT THE BATH-ROOM?
NOPE! I JUST WENT!
SHO-CHAN!
?
...!!
WHA?!

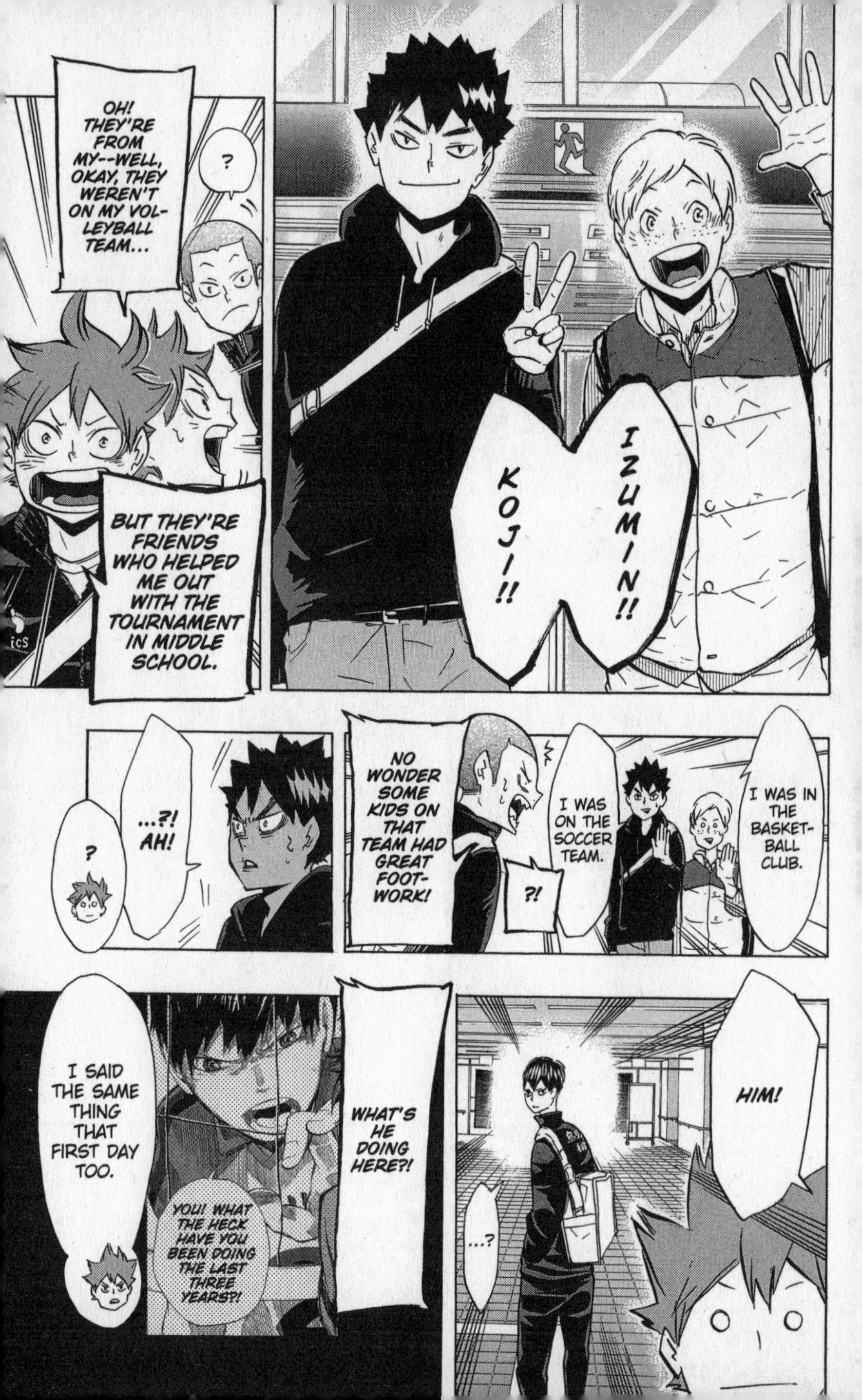
IZUMIN!!
KOJI!!
?
OH! THEY'RE FROM MY--WELL, OKAY, THEY WEREN'T ON MY VOLLEYBALL TEAM...
BUT THEY'RE FRIENDS WHO HELPED ME OUT WITH THE TOURNAMENT IN MIDDLE SCHOOL.
I WAS IN THE BASKETBALL CLUB.
I WAS ON THE SOCCER TEAM.
?!
NO WONDER SOME KIDS ON THAT TEAM HAD GREAT FOOTWORK!
...?! AH!
?
HIM!
...?
WHAT'S HE DOING HERE?!
I SAID THE SAME THING THAT FIRST DAY TOO.
YOU! WHAT THE HECK HAVE YOU BEEN DOING THE LAST THREE YEARS?!

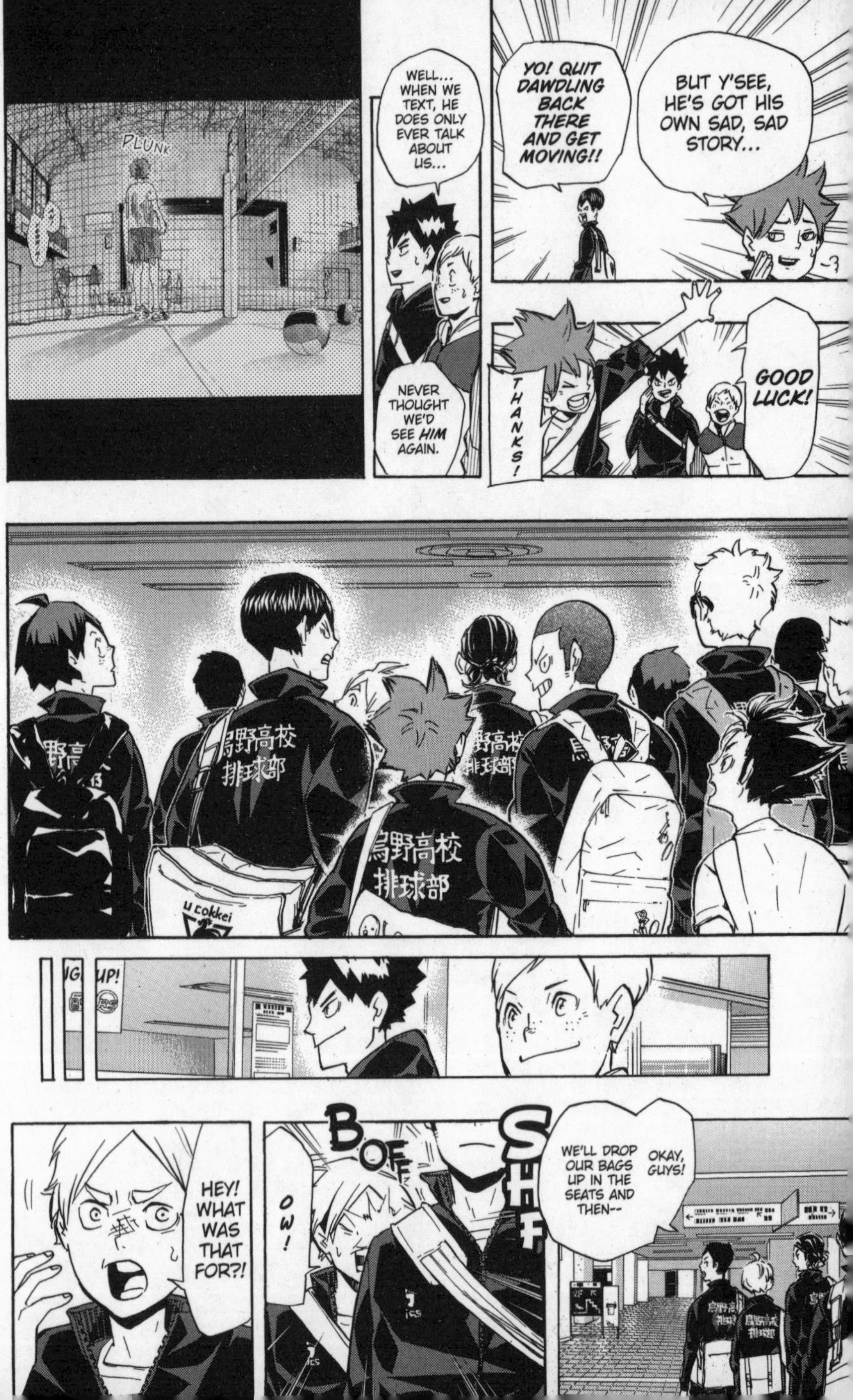
BUT Y'SEE, HE'S GOT HIS OWN SAD, SAD STORY...
YO! QUIT DAWDLING BACK THERE AND GET MOVING!!
GOOD LUCK!
THANKS!
WELL... WHEN WE TEXT, HE DOES ONLY EVER TALK ABOUT US...
NEVER THOUGHT WE'D SEE HIM AGAIN.
PLUNK
OKAY, GUYS!
WE'LL DROP OUR BAGS UP IN THE SEATS AND THEN--
SHF
BOFF
OW!
HEY! WHAT WAS THAT FOR?!

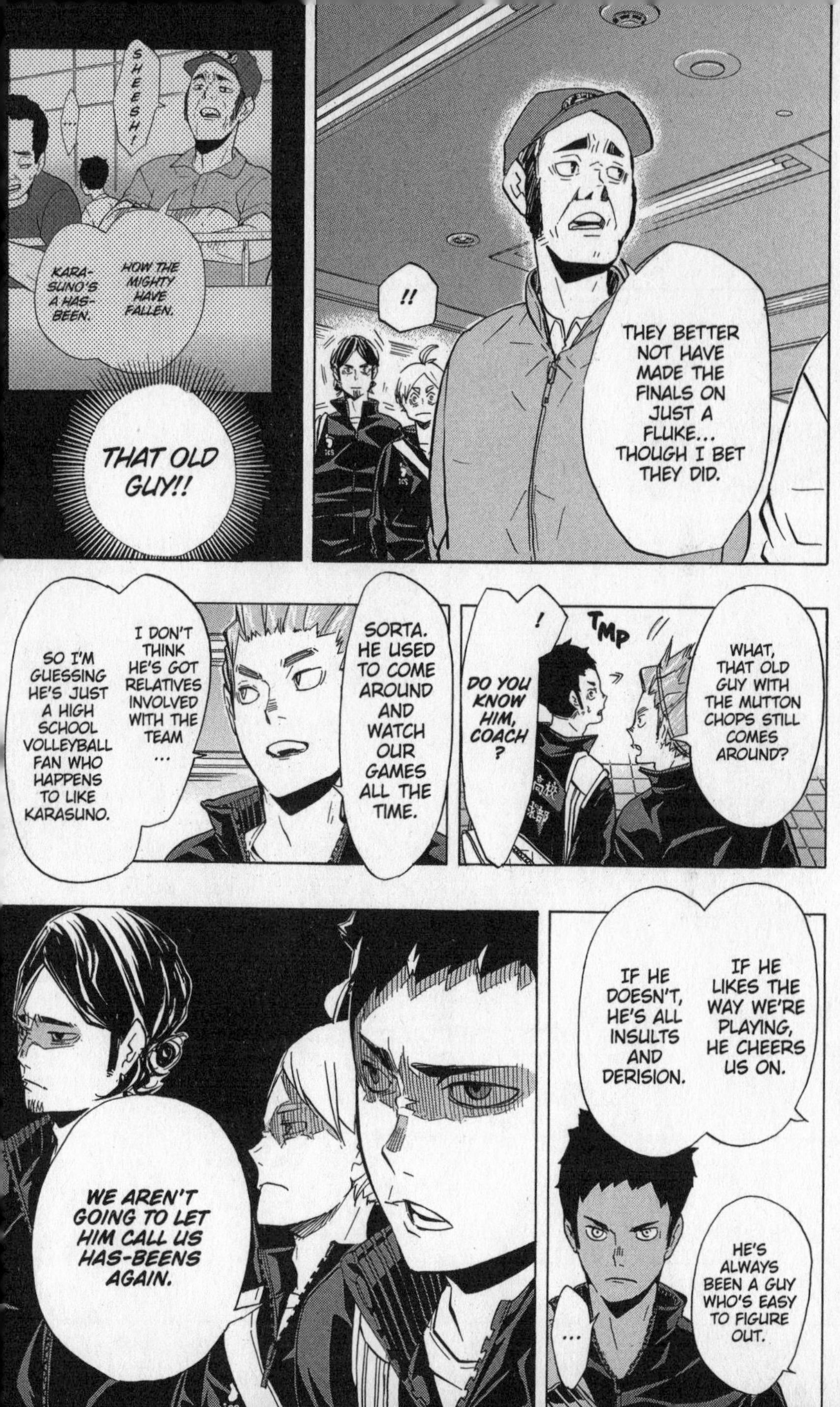
!!
THEY BETTER NOT HAVE MADE THE FINALS ON JUST A FLUKE... THOUGH I BET THEY DID.
SHEESH!
...
HOW THE MIGHTY HAVE FALLEN.
KARA-SUNO'S A HAS-BEEN.
THAT OLD GUY!!
WHAT, THAT OLD GUY WITH THE MUTTON CHOPS STILL COMES AROUND?
TMP
!
DO YOU KNOW HIM, COACH?
SORTA. HE USED TO COME AROUND AND WATCH OUR GAMES ALL THE TIME.
I DON'T THINK HE'S GOT RELATIVES INVOLVED WITH THE TEAM...
SO I'M GUESSING HE'S JUST A HIGH SCHOOL VOLLEYBALL FAN WHO HAPPENS TO LIKE KARASUNO.
IF HE LIKES THE WAY WE'RE PLAYING, HE CHEERS US ON.
IF HE DOESN'T, HE'S ALL INSULTS AND DERISION.
HE'S ALWAYS BEEN A GUY WHO'S EASY TO FIGURE OUT.
...
WE AREN'T GOING TO LET HIM CALL US HAS-BEENS AGAIN.

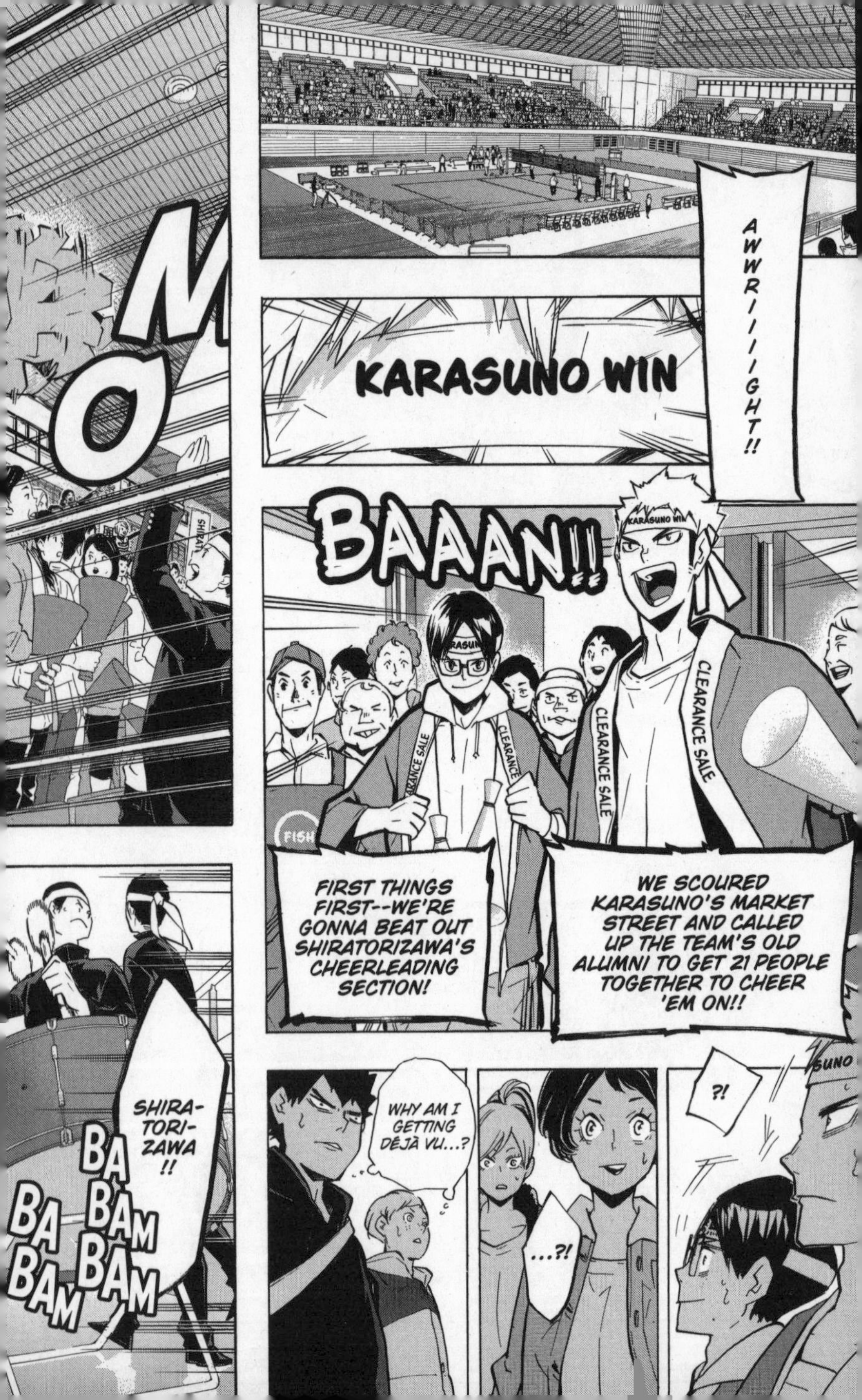
AWWRIIIIIGHT!!
KARASUNO WIN
BAAAN!!
KARASUNO WIN
CLEARANCE SALE
CLEARANCE SALE
CLEARANCE
CLEARANCE SALE
FISH
WE SCOURED KARASUNO'S MARKET STREET AND CALLED UP THE TEAM'S OLD ALUMNI TO GET 21 PEOPLE TOGETHER TO CHEER 'EM ON!!
FIRST THINGS FIRST--WE'RE GONNA BEAT OUT SHIRATORIZAWA'S CHEERLEADING SECTION!
MO
SHIRA
?!
...?!
WHY AM I GETTING DÉJÀ VU...?
SHIRATORIZAWA!!
BA BAM BAM
BA BAM BAM

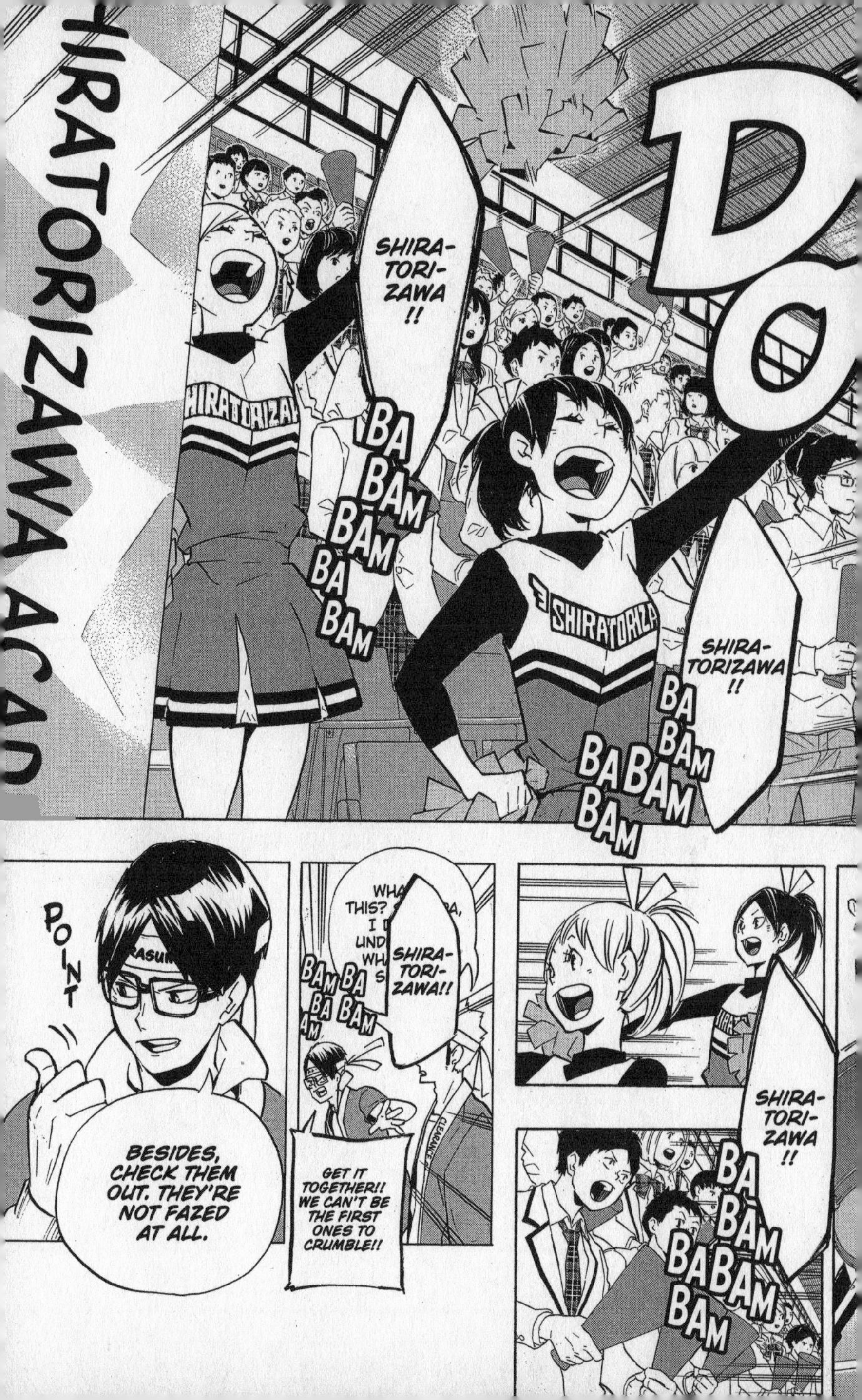
DO
SHIRA-TORIZAWA!!
BA BAM BABAM BAM
SHIRA-TORI-ZAWA!!
BA BAM BAM BA BAM
SHIRATORIZAWA ACAD
SHIRA-TORI-ZAWA!!
BA BAM BABAM BAM
SHIRA-TORI-ZAWA!!
BAM BA BA BAM
GET IT TOGETHER!! WE CAN'T BE THE FIRST ONES TO CRUMBLE!!
POINT
BESIDES, CHECK THEM OUT. THEY'RE NOT FAZED AT ALL.

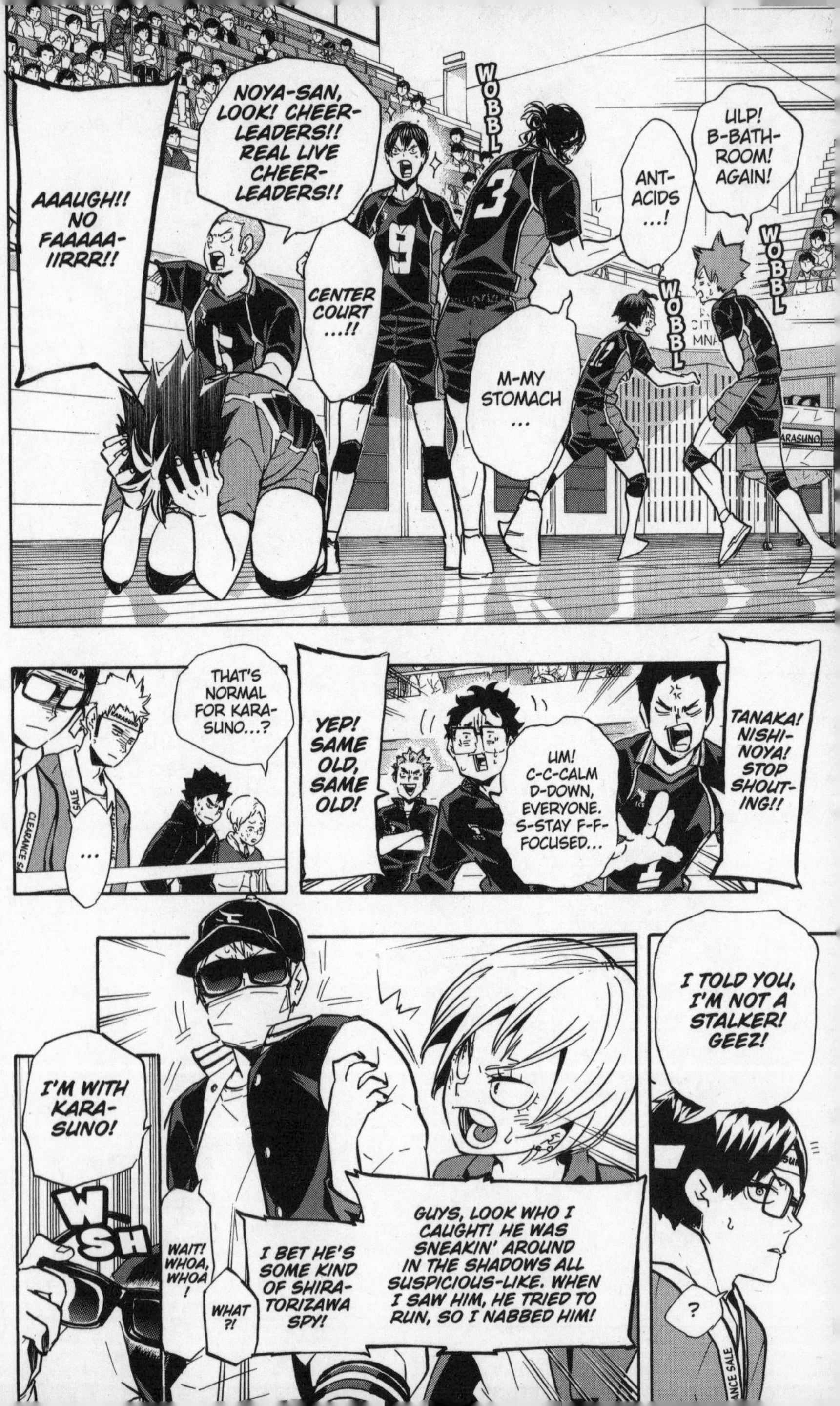
ULP! B-BATH-ROOM! AGAIN!
WOBBL
ANT-ACIDS ...!
WOBBL
M-MY STOMACH ...
WOBBL
NOYA-SAN, LOOK! CHEER-LEADERS!! REAL LIVE CHEER-LEADERS!!
CENTER COURT ...!!
AAAUGH!! NO FAAAAA-IIRRR!!
KARASUNO
TANAKA! NISHI-NOYA! STOP SHOUT-ING!!
UM! C-C-CALM D-DOWN, EVERYONE. S-STAY F-F-FOCUSED...
YEP! SAME OLD, SAME OLD!
THAT'S NORMAL FOR KARA-SUNO...?
...
I TOLD YOU, I'M NOT A STALKER! GEEZ!
?
GUYS, LOOK WHO I CAUGHT! HE WAS SNEAKIN' AROUND IN THE SHADOWS ALL SUSPICIOUS-LIKE. WHEN I SAW HIM, HE TRIED TO RUN, SO I NABBED HIM!
I BET HE'S SOME KIND OF SHIRA-TORIZAWA SPY!
WAIT! WHOA, WHOA!
WHAT ?!
I'M WITH KARA-SUNO!
WSH

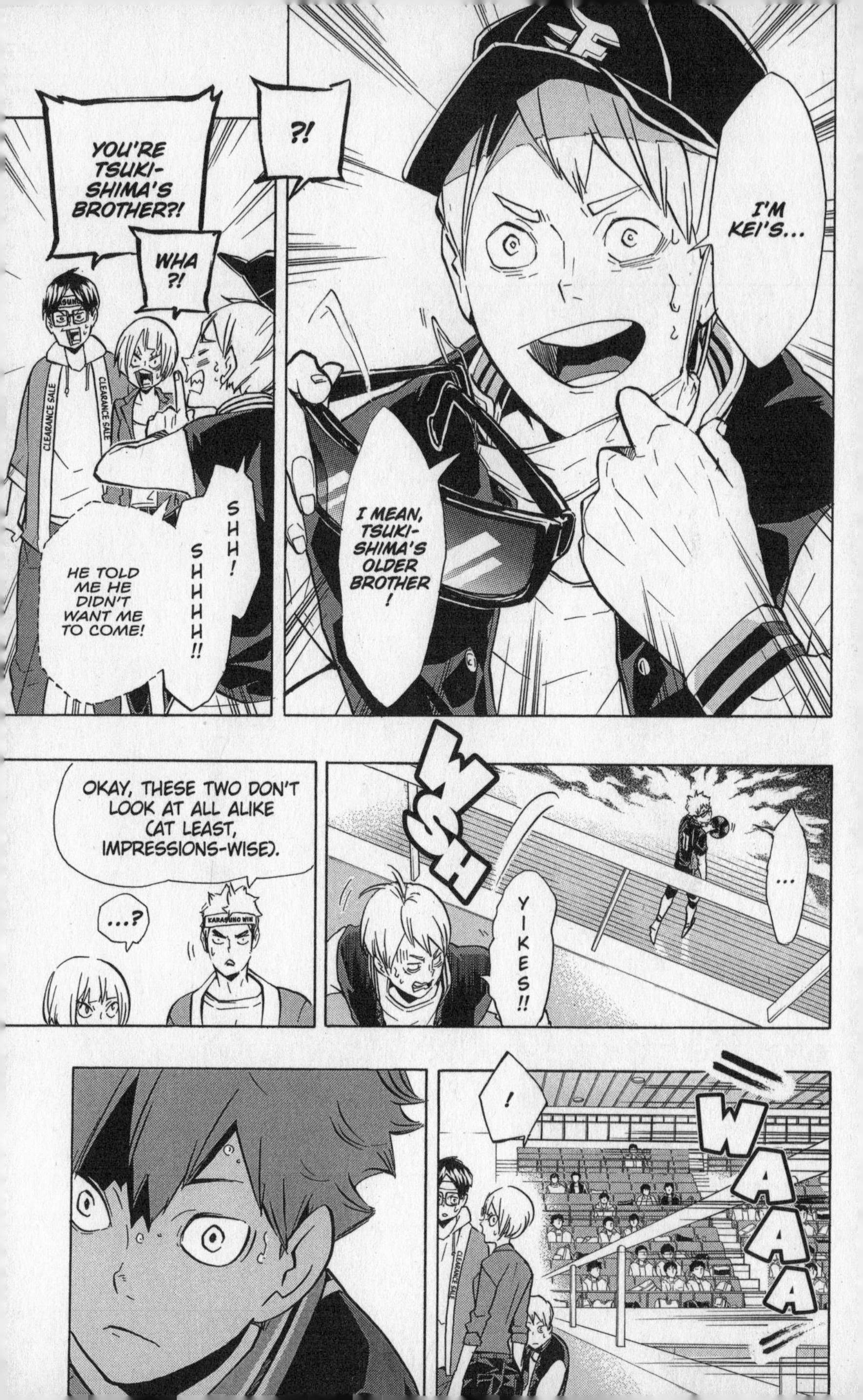
I'M KEI'S...
I MEAN, TSUKISHIMA'S OLDER BROTHER!
?!
YOU'RE TSUKISHIMA'S BROTHER?!
WHA?!
SHH! SHHHHH!!
HE TOLD ME HE DIDN'T WANT ME TO COME!
CLEARANCE SALE
WSH
...
YIKES!!
OKAY, THESE TWO DON'T LOOK AT ALL ALIKE (AT LEAST, IMPRESSIONS-WISE).
...?
KARASUNO WIN
!
WAAA

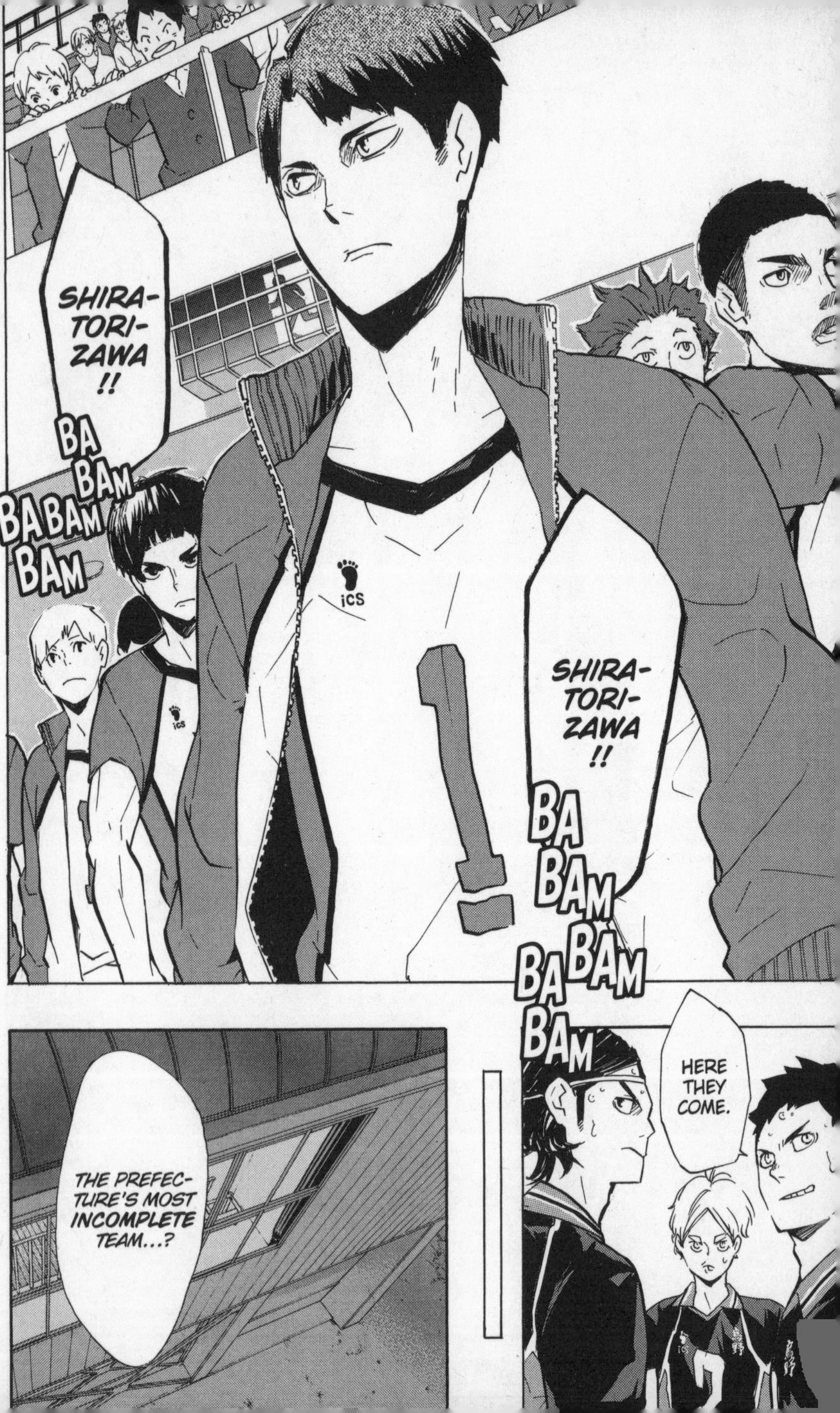
SHIRA-TORI-ZAWA !!
BA BAM BAM BA BAM BAM
SHIRA-TORI-ZAWA !!
BA BAM BABAM BAM
HERE THEY COME.
THE PREFECTURE'S MOST INCOMPLETE TEAM...?

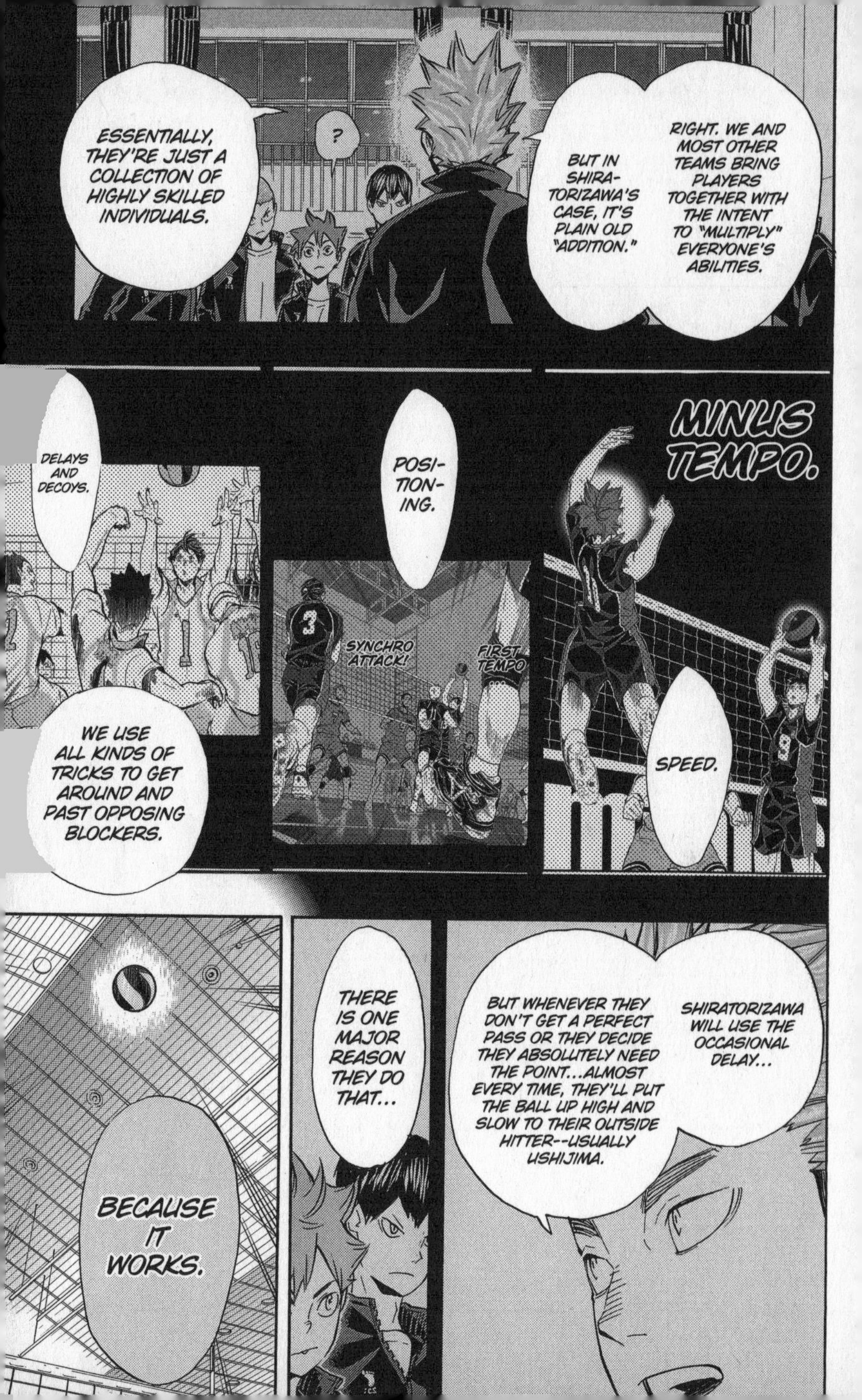
RIGHT. WE AND MOST OTHER TEAMS BRING PLAYERS TOGETHER WITH THE INTENT TO "MULTIPLY" EVERYONE'S ABILITIES.
BUT IN SHIRATORIZAWA'S CASE, IT'S PLAIN OLD "ADDITION."
?
ESSENTIALLY, THEY'RE JUST A COLLECTION OF HIGHLY SKILLED INDIVIDUALS.
MINUS TEMPO.
SPEED.
POSITIONING.
FIRST TEMPO...
SYNCHRO ATTACK!
DELAYS AND DECOYS.
WE USE ALL KINDS OF TRICKS TO GET AROUND AND PAST OPPOSING BLOCKERS.
SHIRATORIZAWA WILL USE THE OCCASIONAL DELAY...
BUT WHENEVER THEY DON'T GET A PERFECT PASS OR THEY DECIDE THEY ABSOLUTELY NEED THE POINT...ALMOST EVERY TIME, THEY'LL PUT THE BALL UP HIGH AND SLOW TO THEIR OUTSIDE HITTER--USUALLY USHIJIMA.
THERE IS ONE MAJOR REASON THEY DO THAT...
BECAUSE IT WORKS.

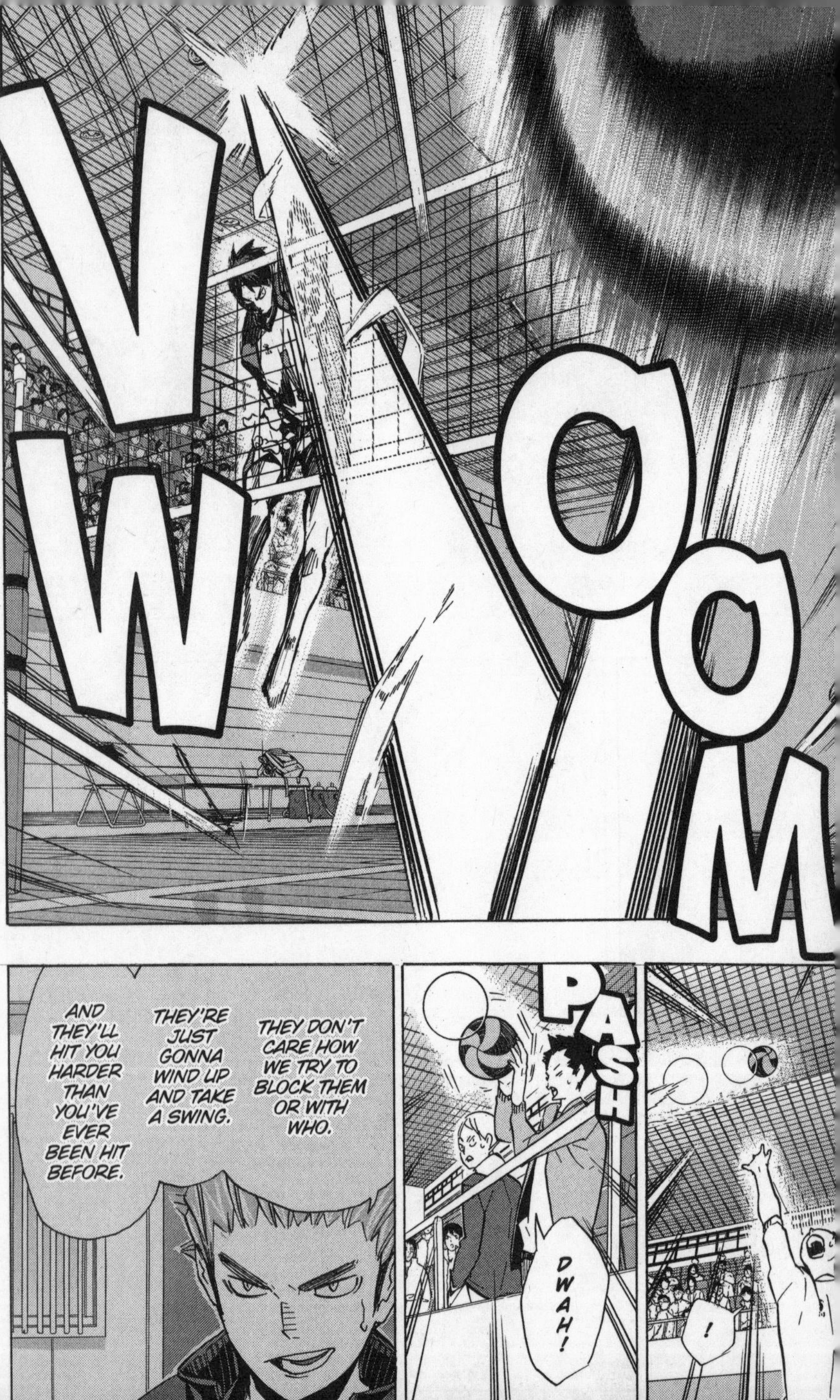
VWOOM
!
PASH
DWAH!
THEY DON'T CARE HOW WE TRY TO BLOCK THEM OR WITH WHO.
THEY'RE JUST GONNA WIND UP AND TAKE A SWING.
AND THEY'LL HIT YOU HARDER THAN YOU'VE EVER BEEN HIT BEFORE.

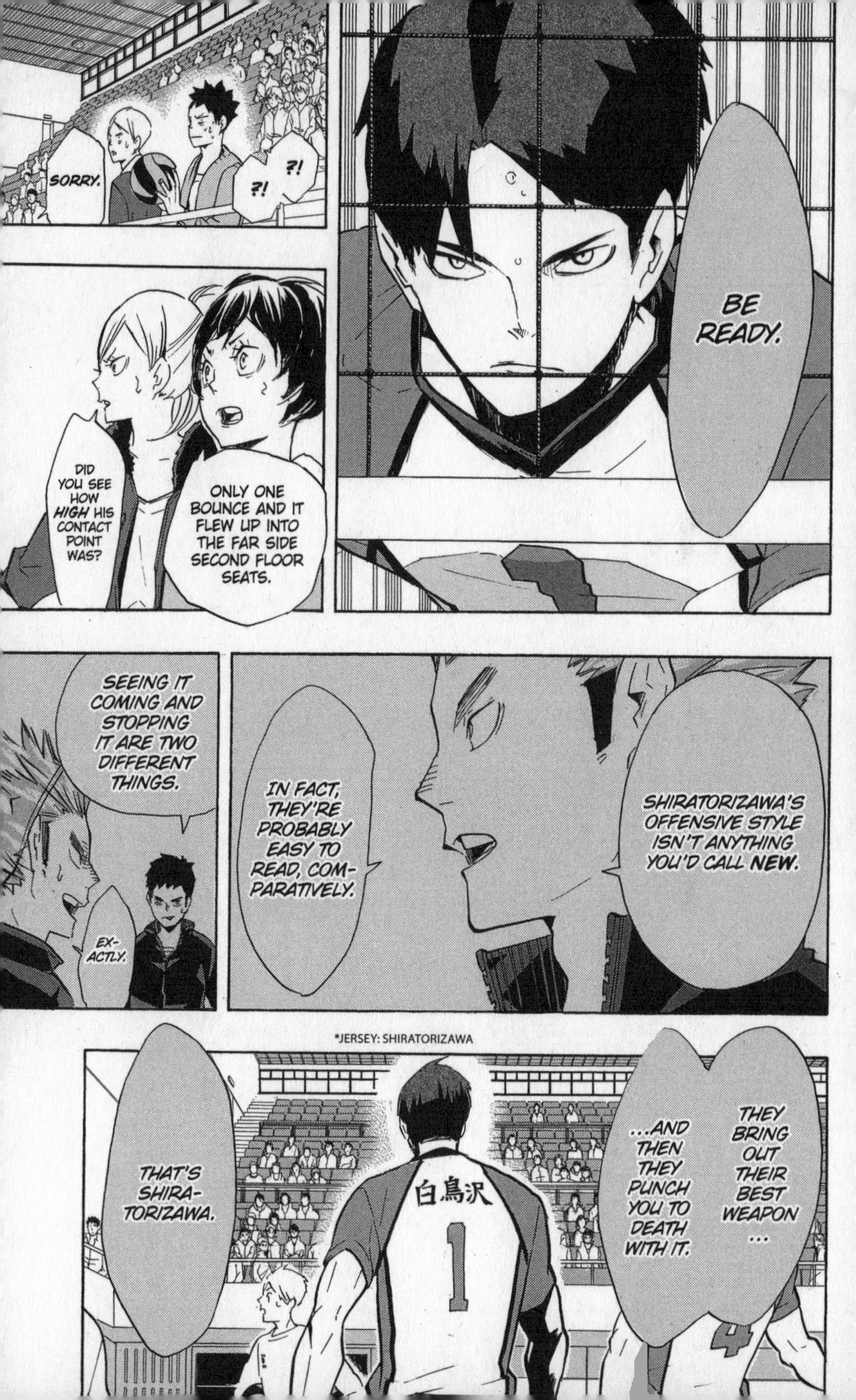
BE READY.
?!
?!
SORRY.
ONLY ONE BOUNCE AND IT FLEW UP INTO THE FAR SIDE SECOND FLOOR SEATS.
DID YOU SEE HOW *HIGH* HIS CONTACT POINT WAS?
SHIRATORIZAWA'S OFFENSIVE STYLE ISN'T ANYTHING YOU'D CALL **NEW**.
IN FACT, THEY'RE PROBABLY EASY TO READ, COMPARATIVELY.
SEEING IT COMING AND STOPPING IT ARE TWO DIFFERENT THINGS.
EXACTLY.
*JERSEY: SHIRATORIZAWA
THEY BRING OUT THEIR BEST WEAPON...
...AND THEN THEY PUNCH YOU TO DEATH WITH IT.
白鳥沢
1
THAT'S SHIRATORIZAWA.

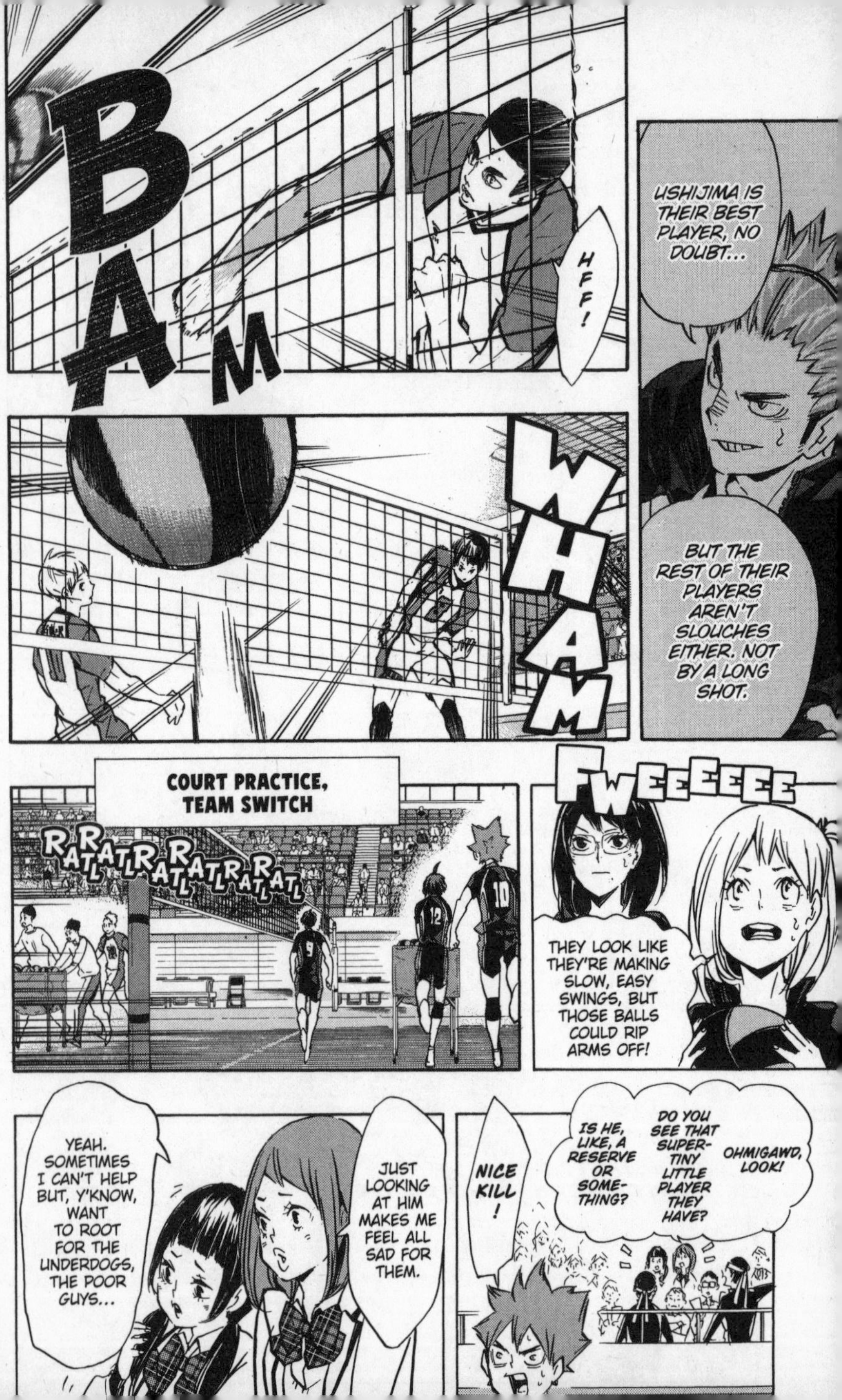
USHIJIMA IS THEIR BEST PLAYER, NO DOUBT...
BUT THE REST OF THEIR PLAYERS AREN'T SLOUCHES EITHER. NOT BY A LONG SHOT.
BAM
HFF!
WHAM
FWEEEEEE
THEY LOOK LIKE THEY'RE MAKING SLOW, EASY SWINGS, BUT THOSE BALLS COULD RIP ARMS OFF!
COURT PRACTICE, TEAM SWITCH
RATLRATLRATLRATLRATLRATL
OHMIGAWD, LOOK!
DO YOU SEE THAT SUPER-TINY LITTLE PLAYER THEY HAVE?
IS HE, LIKE, A RESERVE OR SOME-THING?
NICE KILL!
JUST LOOKING AT HIM MAKES ME FEEL ALL SAD FOR THEM.
YEAH. SOMETIMES I CAN'T HELP BUT, Y'KNOW, WANT TO ROOT FOR THE UNDERDOGS, THE POOR GUYS...

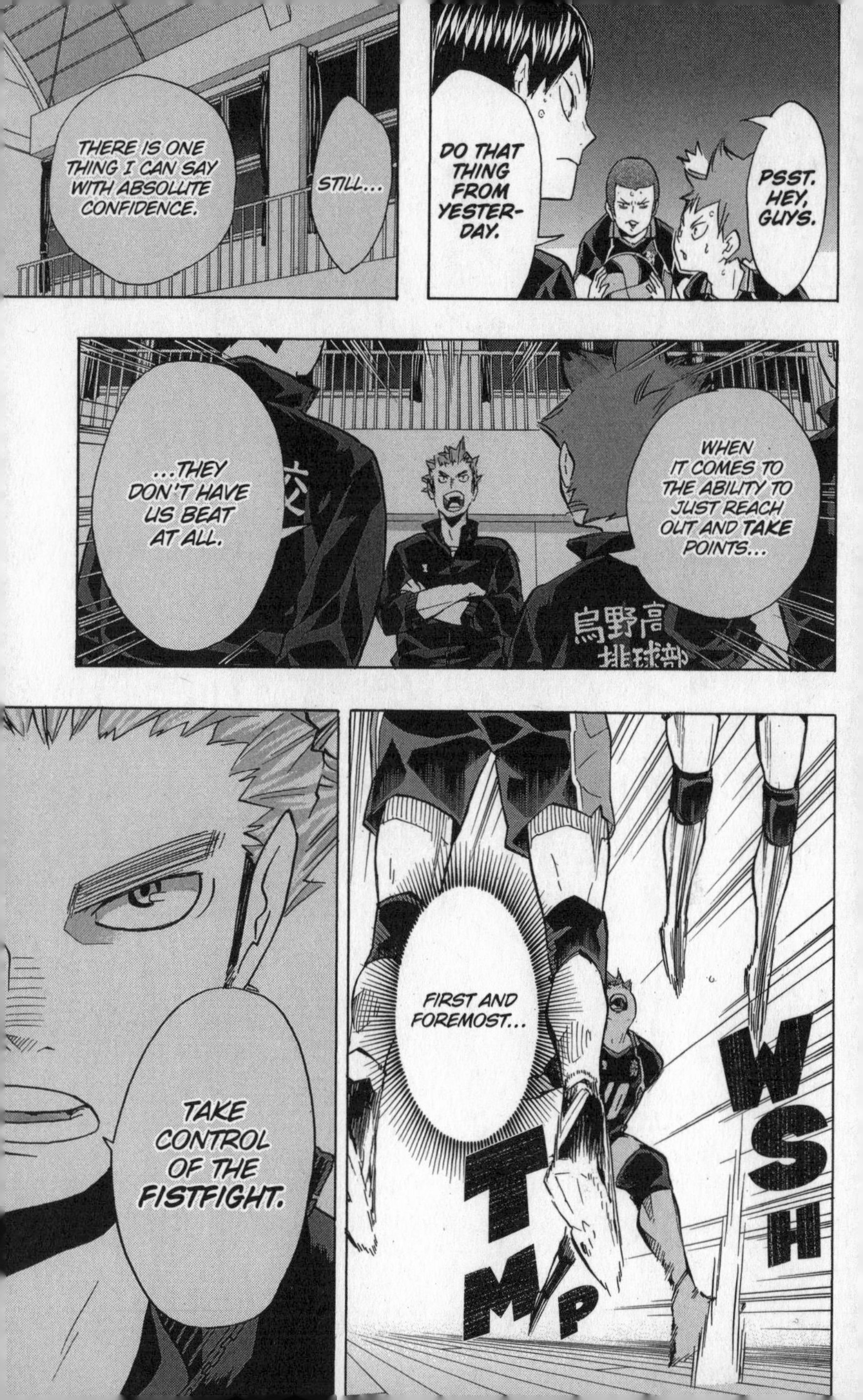
PSST. HEY, GUYS.
DO THAT THING FROM YESTER-DAY.
STILL...
THERE IS ONE THING I CAN SAY WITH ABSOLUTE CONFIDENCE.
WHEN IT COMES TO THE ABILITY TO JUST REACH OUT AND TAKE POINTS...
...THEY DON'T HAVE US BEAT AT ALL.
烏野高
排球部
FIRST AND FOREMOST...
WSH
TMP
TAKE CONTROL OF THE FISTFIGHT.

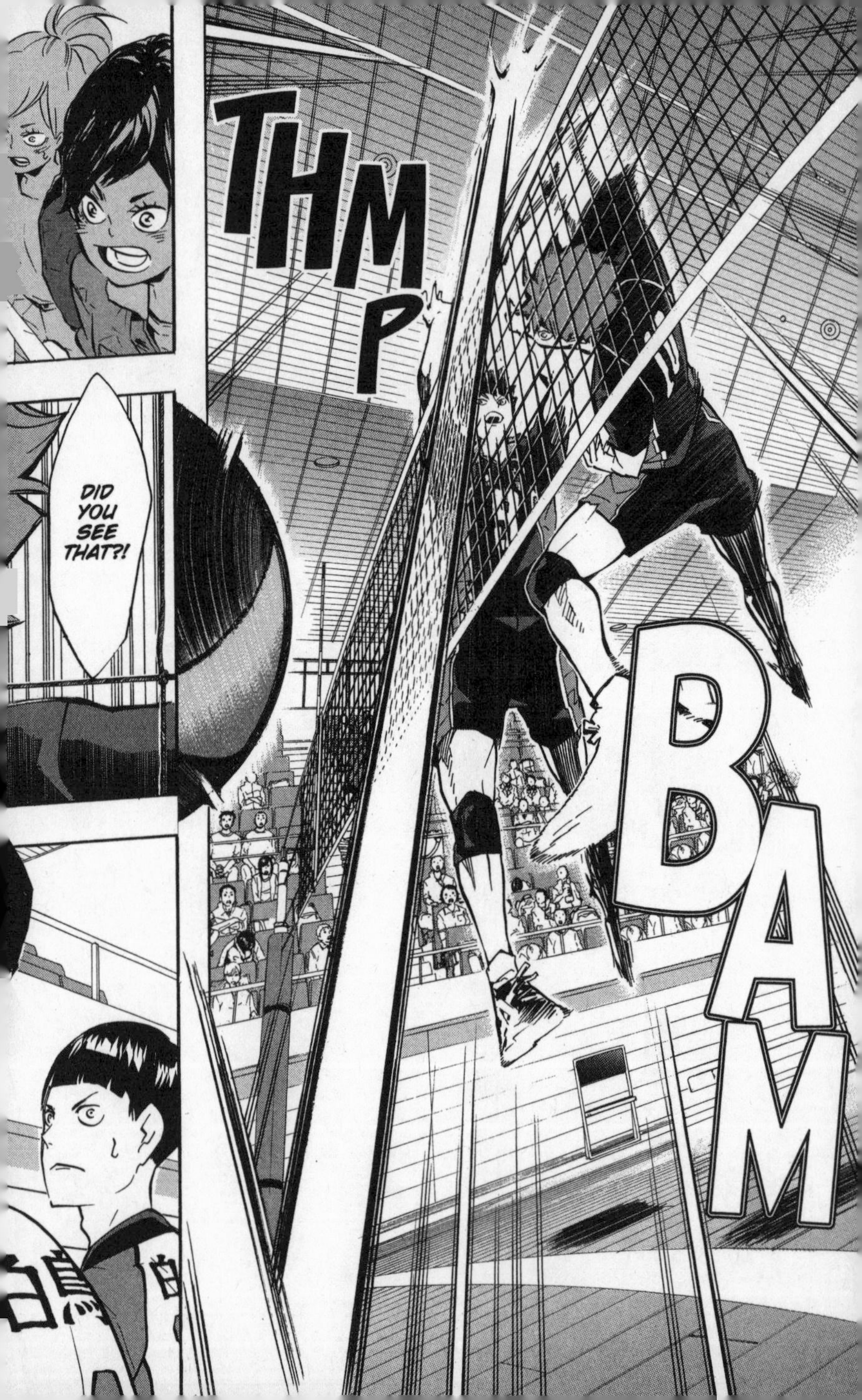
THMP
BAM
DID YOU SEE THAT?!

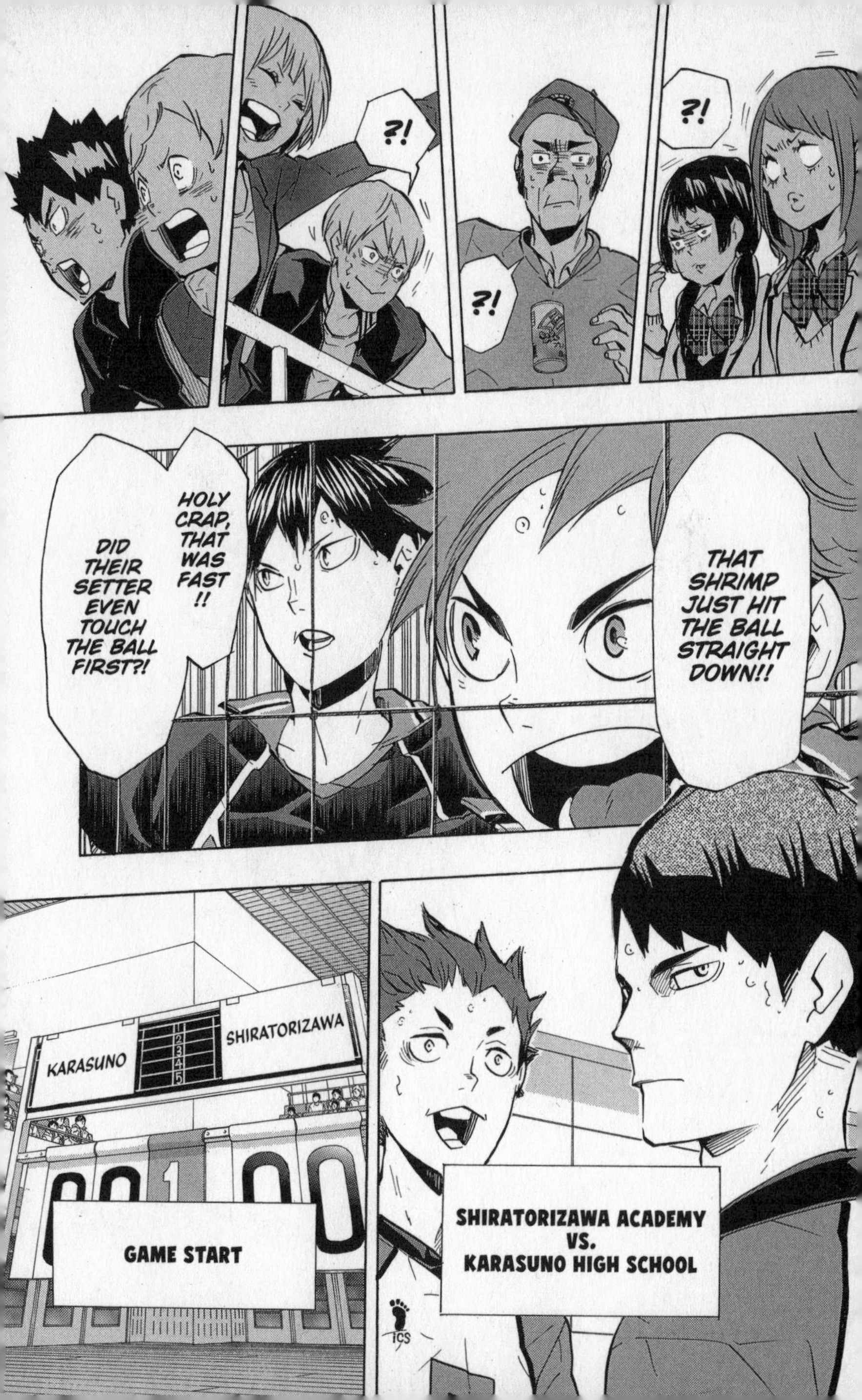
?!
?!
?!
THAT SHRIMP JUST HIT THE BALL STRAIGHT DOWN!!
HOLY CRAP, THAT WAS FAST!!
DID THEIR SETTER EVEN TOUCH THE BALL FIRST?!
SHIRATORIZAWA ACADEMY VS. KARASUNO HIGH SCHOOL
SHIRATORIZAWA
KARASUNO
GAME START

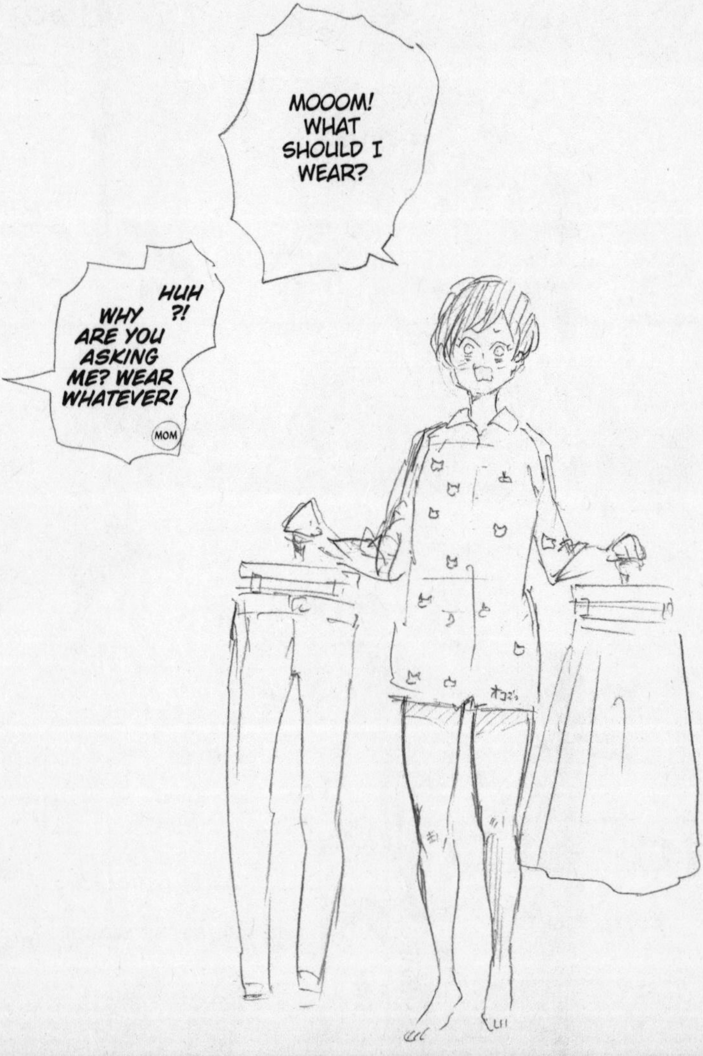
MOOOM! WHAT SHOULD I WEAR?
HUH ?! WHY ARE YOU ASKING ME? WEAR WHATEVER!
MOM

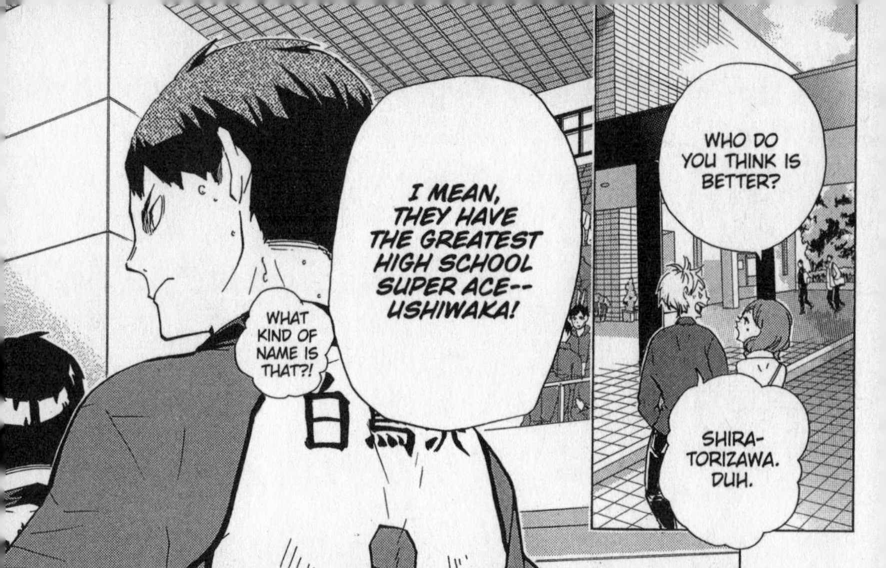
WHO DO YOU THINK IS BETTER?
SHIRA-TORIZAWA. DUH.
I MEAN, THEY HAVE THE GREATEST HIGH SCHOOL SUPER ACE-- USHIWAKA!
WHAT KIND OF NAME IS THAT?!

CHAPTER 151: First-Time Finalists

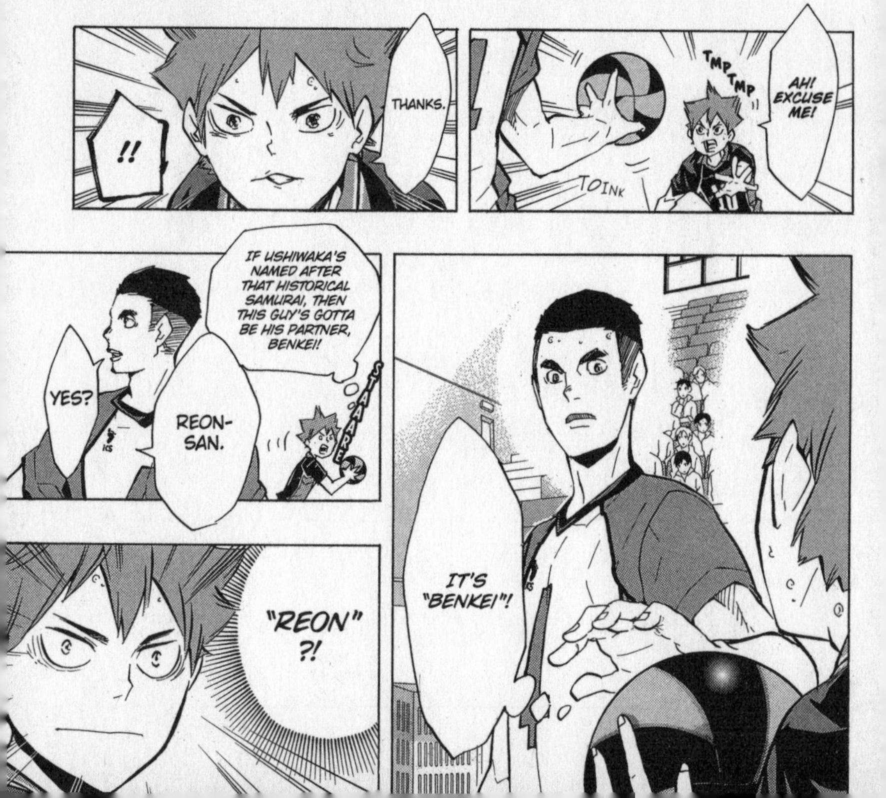
AH! EXCUSE ME!
TMP TMP
TOINK
THANKS.
!!
IT'S "BENKEI"!
IF USHIWAKA'S NAMED AFTER THAT HISTORICAL SAMURAI, THEN THIS GUY'S GOTTA BE HIS PARTNER, BENKEI!
STAAARE
REON-SAN.
YES?
"REON" ?!

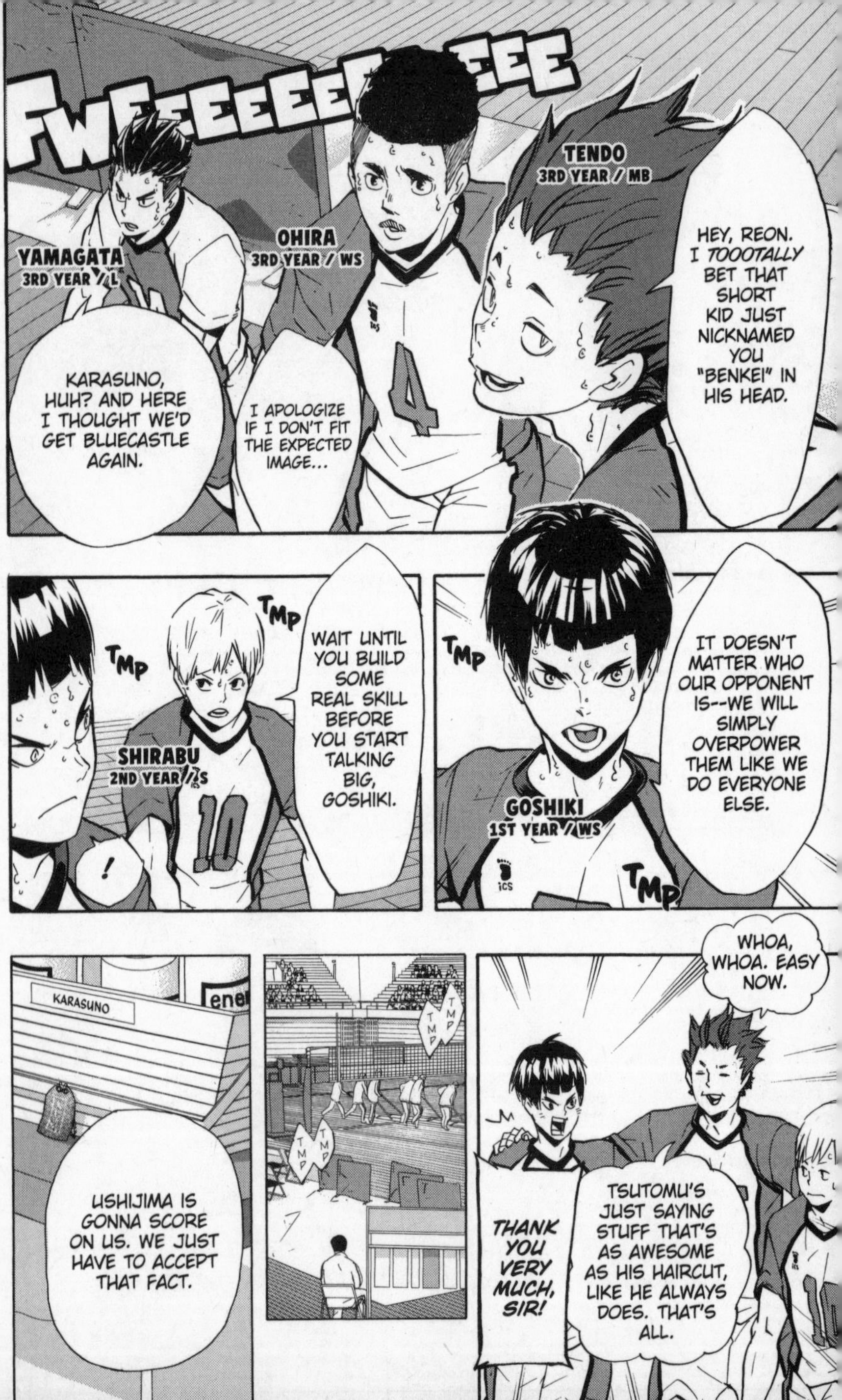
FWEEEEEEEEEEE
TENDO
3RD YEAR / MB
HEY, REON. I *TOOOTALLY* BET THAT SHORT KID JUST NICKNAMED YOU "BENKEI" IN HIS HEAD.
OHIRA
3RD YEAR / WS
I APOLOGIZE IF I DON'T FIT THE EXPECTED IMAGE...
YAMAGATA
3RD YEAR / L
KARASUNO, HUH? AND HERE I THOUGHT WE'D GET BLUECASTLE AGAIN.
TMP
IT DOESN'T MATTER WHO OUR OPPONENT IS--WE WILL SIMPLY OVERPOWER THEM LIKE WE DO EVERYONE ELSE.
GOSHIKI
1ST YEAR / WS
TMP
TMP
WAIT UNTIL YOU BUILD SOME REAL SKILL BEFORE YOU START TALKING BIG, GOSHIKI.
TMP
SHIRABU
2ND YEAR / S
!
WHOA, WHOA. EASY NOW.
TSUTOMU'S JUST SAYING STUFF THAT'S AS AWESOME AS HIS HAIRCUT, LIKE HE ALWAYS DOES. THAT'S ALL.
THANK YOU VERY MUCH, SIR!
TMP
TMP
TMP
TMP
KARASUNO
USHIJIMA IS GONNA SCORE ON US. WE JUST HAVE TO ACCEPT THAT FACT.

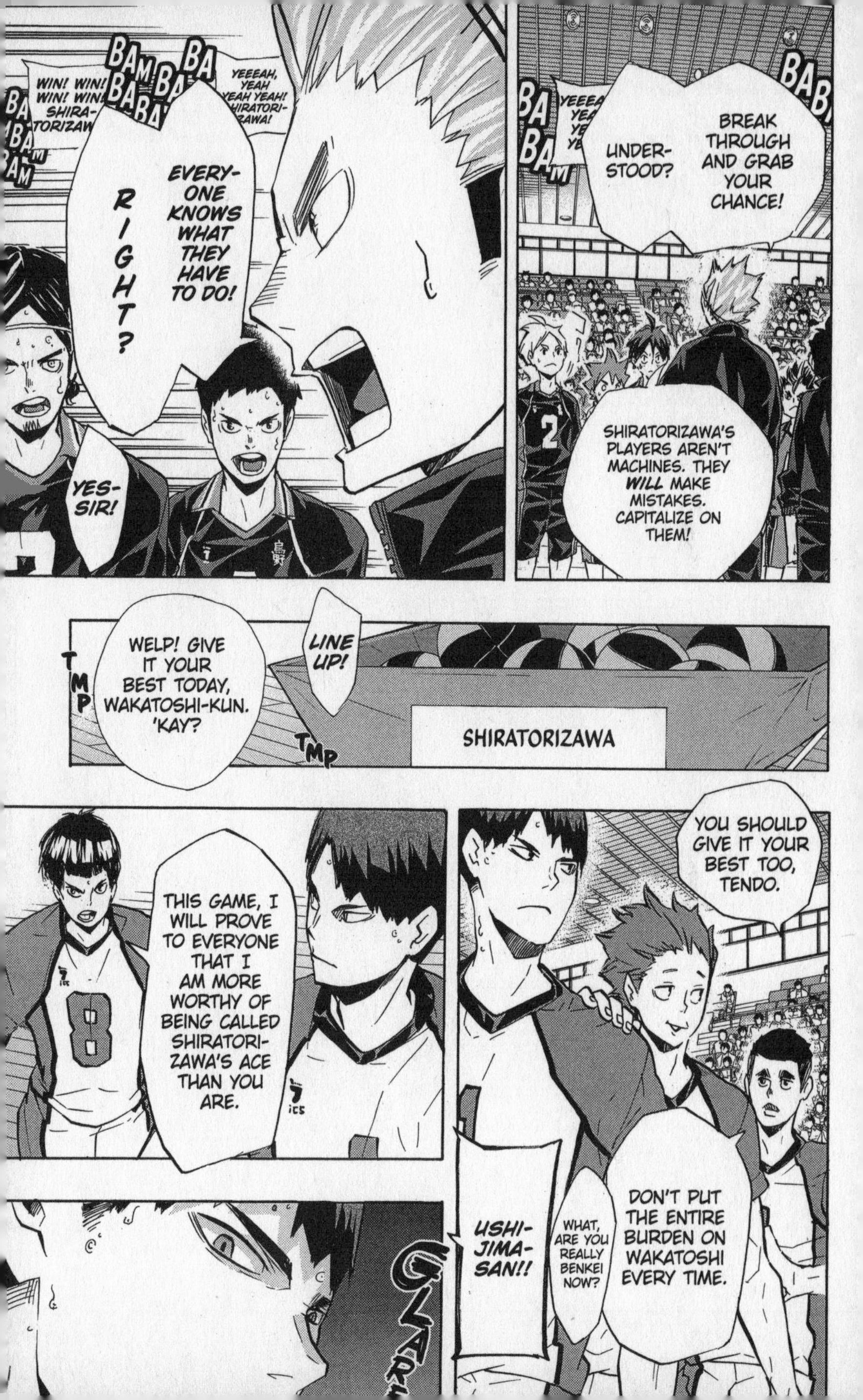BA
BA
BAM
YEEEA YEA YE YE
BREAK THROUGH AND GRAB YOUR CHANCE!
UNDER-STOOD?
BAB
SHIRATORIZAWA'S PLAYERS AREN'T MACHINES. THEY WILL MAKE MISTAKES. CAPITALIZE ON THEM!
YEEEAH, YEAH YEAH YEAH! HIRATORI-ZAWA!
BA BA BAM BA BA BA
EVERY-ONE KNOWS WHAT THEY HAVE TO DO!
RIGHT?
WIN! WIN! WIN! WIN! SHIRA-TORIZAW
BA BA BAM BAM
YES-SIR!
LINE UP!
TMP
SHIRATORIZAWA
WELP! GIVE IT YOUR BEST TODAY, WAKATOSHI-KUN. 'KAY?
TMP
YOU SHOULD GIVE IT YOUR BEST TOO, TENDO.
DON'T PUT THE ENTIRE BURDEN ON WAKATOSHI EVERY TIME.
WHAT, ARE YOU REALLY BENKEI NOW?
USHI-JIMA-SAN!!
THIS GAME, I WILL PROVE TO EVERYONE THAT I AM MORE WORTHY OF BEING CALLED SHIRATORI-ZAWA'S ACE THAN YOU ARE.
GLAR

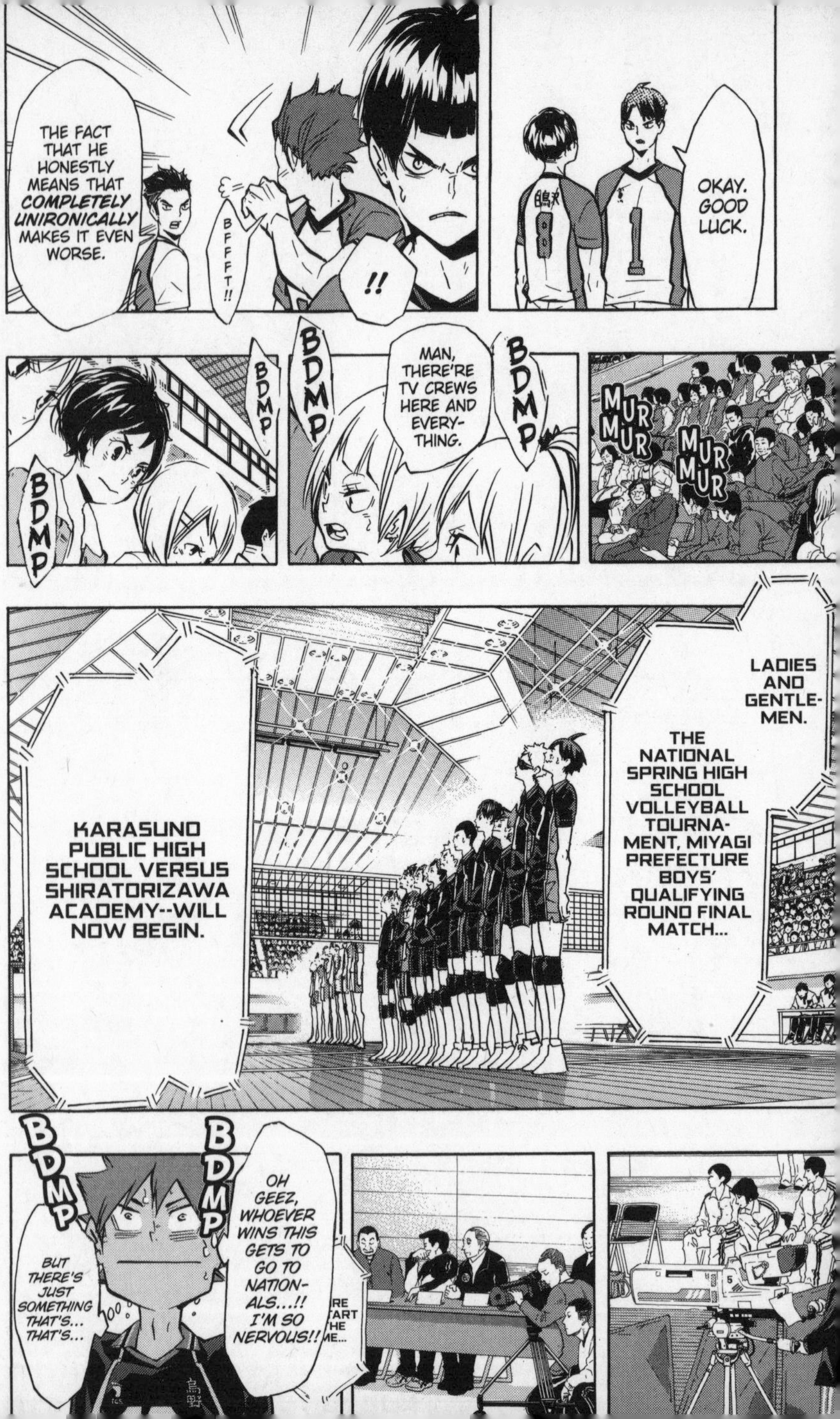
OKAY. GOOD LUCK.
!!
BFFFT!!
THE FACT THAT HE HONESTLY MEANS THAT COMPLETELY UNIRONICALLY MAKES IT EVEN WORSE.
MUR MUR
MUR MUR
BDMP
MAN, THERE'RE TV CREWS HERE AND EVERYTHING.
BDMP
BDMP
BDMP
LADIES AND GENTLEMEN.
THE NATIONAL SPRING HIGH SCHOOL VOLLEYBALL TOURNAMENT, MIYAGI PREFECTURE BOYS' QUALIFYING ROUND FINAL MATCH...
KARASUNO PUBLIC HIGH SCHOOL VERSUS SHIRATORIZAWA ACADEMY--WILL NOW BEGIN.
BDMP
OH GEEZ, WHOEVER WINS THIS GETS TO GO TO NATION-ALS...!! I'M SO NERVOUS!!
BDMP
BUT THERE'S JUST SOMETHING THAT'S... THAT'S...

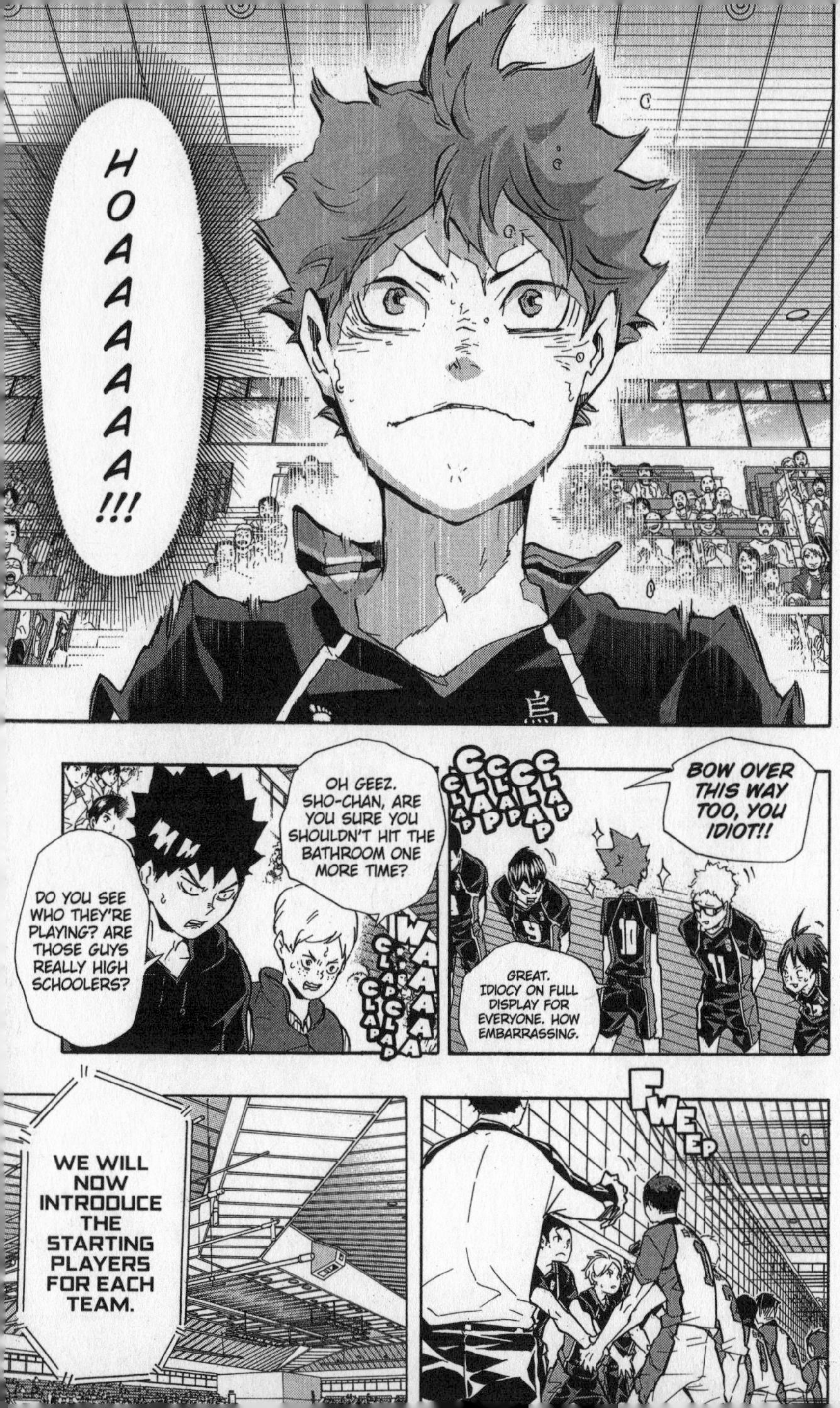
HOAAAAAA!!!
BOW OVER THIS WAY TOO, YOU IDIOT!!
CCCCC CLLLLL AAAAA PPPPP
GREAT. IDIOCY ON FULL DISPLAY FOR EVERYONE. HOW EMBARRASSING.
OH GEEZ. SHO-CHAN, ARE YOU SURE YOU SHOULDN'T HIT THE BATHROOM ONE MORE TIME?
DO YOU SEE WHO THEY'RE PLAYING? ARE THOSE GUYS REALLY HIGH SCHOOLERS?
WAAAAAA
CLAP CLAP CLAP CLAP
FWEEP
WE WILL NOW INTRODUCE THE STARTING PLAYERS FOR EACH TEAM.

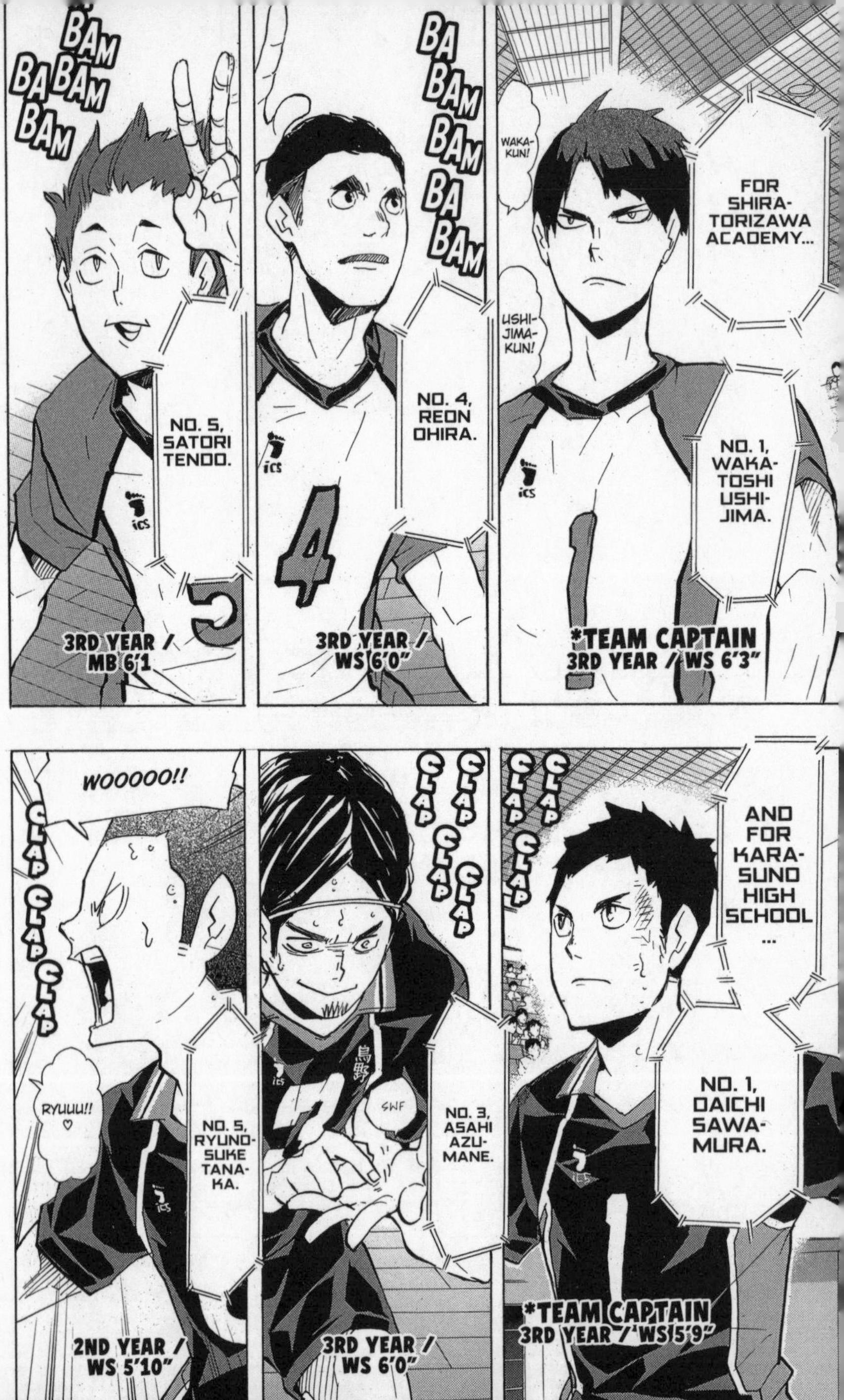
FOR SHIRA-TORIZAWA ACADEMY...
WAKA-KUN!
USHI-JIMA-KUN!
NO. 1, WAKA-TOSHI USHI-JIMA.
*TEAM CAPTAIN
3RD YEAR / WS 6'3"
BA BAM BAM BA BAM
NO. 4, REON OHIRA.
3RD YEAR / WS 6'0"
BAM BA BAM BAM
NO. 5, SATORI TENDO.
3RD YEAR / MB 6'1
AND FOR KARA-SUNO HIGH SCHOOL ...
CLAP CLAP CLAP CLAP
NO. 1, DAICHI SAWA-MURA.
*TEAM CAPTAIN
3RD YEAR / WS 5'9"
CLAP CLAP CLAP CLAP CLAP
SWF
NO. 3, ASAHI AZU-MANE.
3RD YEAR / WS 6'0"
WOOOOO!!
CLAP CLAP CLAP
RYUUU!! ♡
NO. 5, RYUNO-SUKE TANA-KA.
2ND YEAR / WS 5'10"

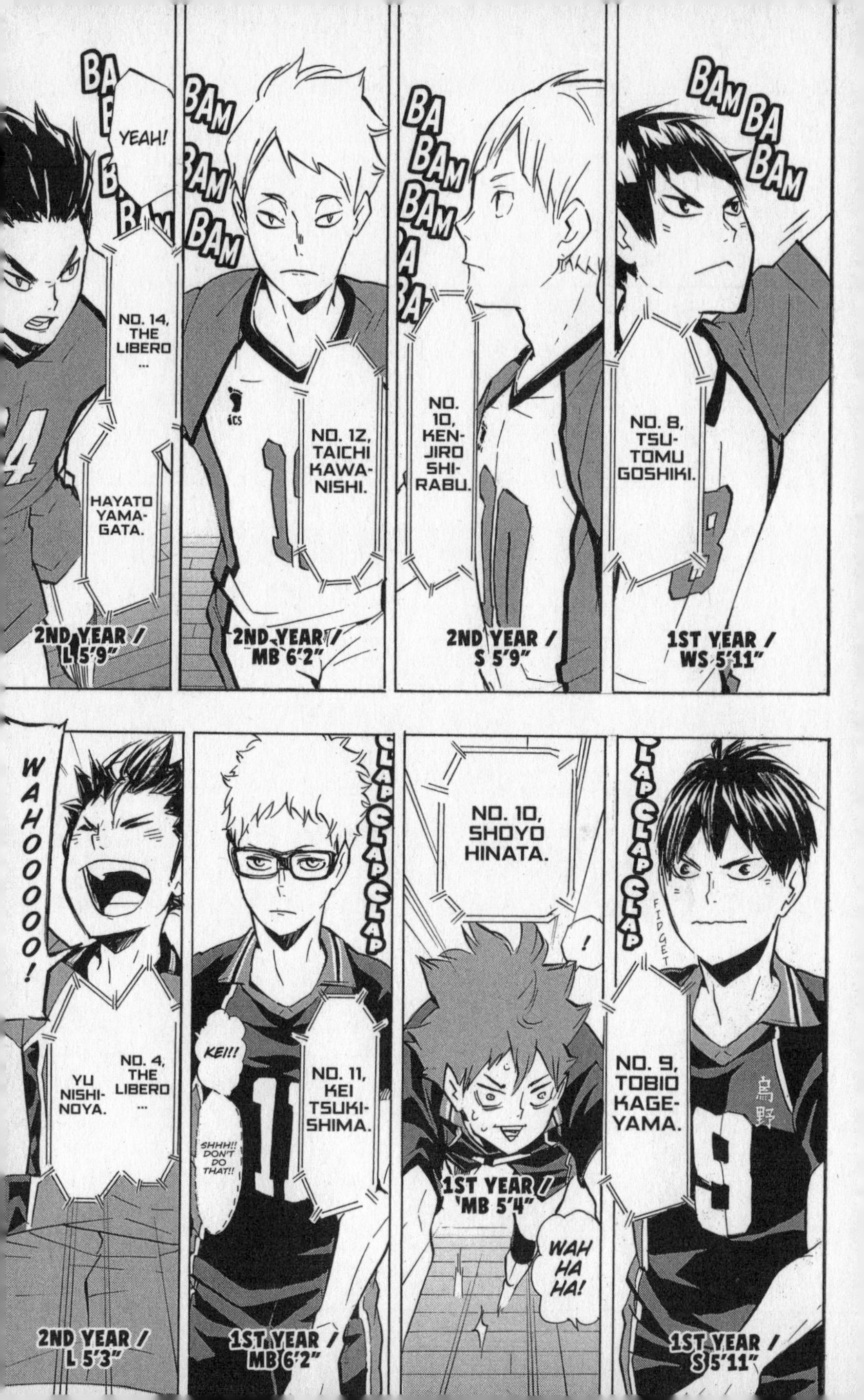
BAM BA BA BAM
NO. 8, TSUTOMU GOSHIKI.
1ST YEAR / WS 5'11"
BA BAM BAM BA BA BA
NO. 10, KENJIRO SHIRABU.
2ND YEAR / S 5'9"
BAM BAM BAM
NO. 12, TAICHI KAWANISHI.
2ND YEAR / MB 6'2"
YEAH!
NO. 14, THE LIBERO ...
HAYATO YAMAGATA.
2ND YEAR / L 5'9"
CLAP CLAP CLAP
FIDGET
NO. 9, TOBIO KAGEYAMA.
1ST YEAR / S 5'11"
NO. 10, SHOYO HINATA.
!
WAH HA HA!
1ST YEAR / MB 5'4"
CLAP CLAP CLAP CLAP
KEI!!
SHHH!! DON'T DO THAT!!
NO. 11, KEI TSUKISHIMA.
1ST YEAR / MB 6'2"
WAHOOOOOOO!
NO. 4, THE LIBERO ...
YU NISHINOYA.
2ND YEAR / L 5'3"

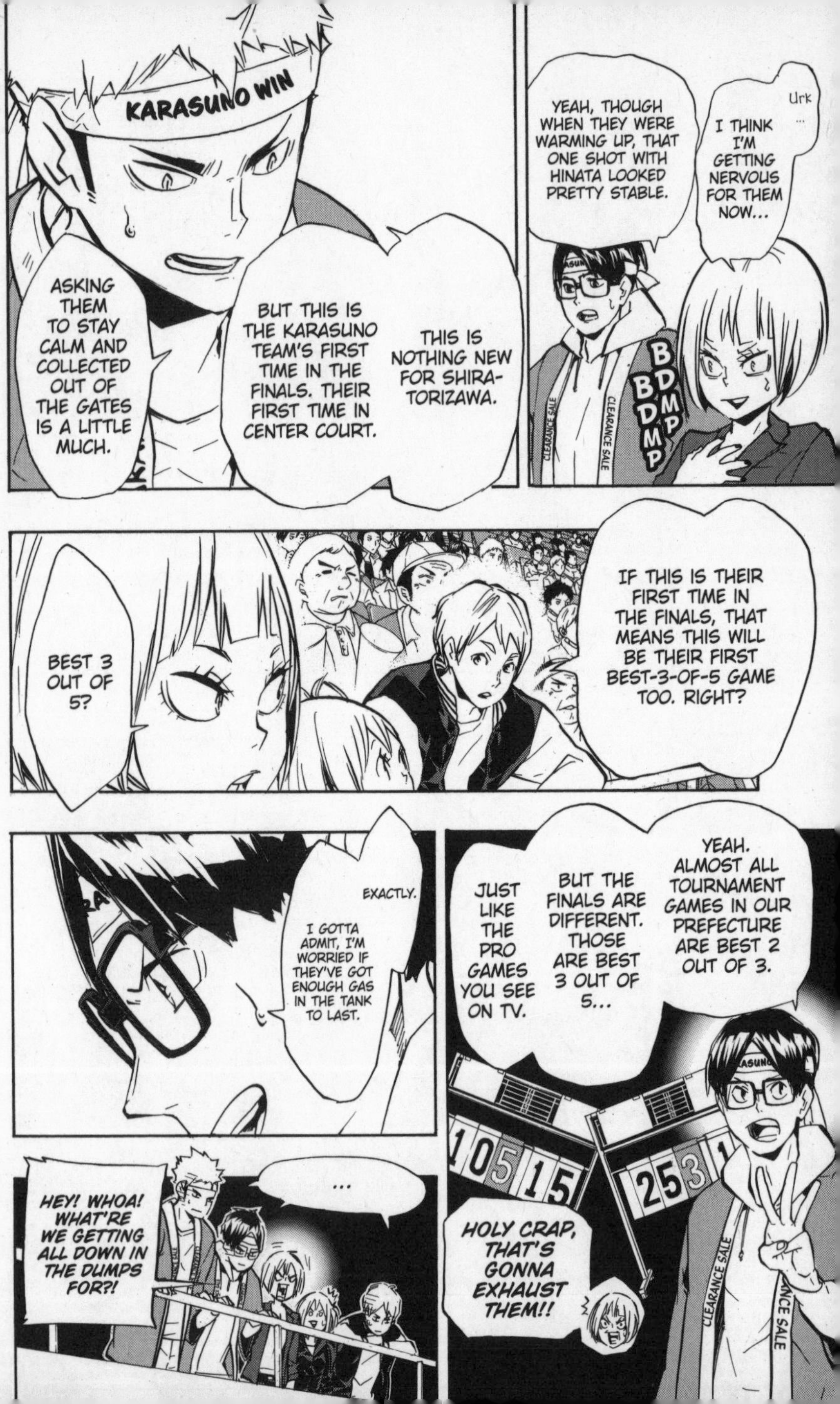
Urk ...
I THINK I'M GETTING NERVOUS FOR THEM NOW...
YEAH, THOUGH WHEN THEY WERE WARMING UP, THAT ONE SHOT WITH HINATA LOOKED PRETTY STABLE.
BDMP BDMP BDMP
KARASUNO WIN
THIS IS NOTHING NEW FOR SHIRATORIZAWA.
BUT THIS IS THE KARASUNO TEAM'S FIRST TIME IN THE FINALS. THEIR FIRST TIME IN CENTER COURT.
ASKING THEM TO STAY CALM AND COLLECTED OUT OF THE GATES IS A LITTLE MUCH.
IF THIS IS THEIR FIRST TIME IN THE FINALS, THAT MEANS THIS WILL BE THEIR FIRST BEST-3-OF-5 GAME TOO. RIGHT?
BEST 3 OUT OF 5?
YEAH. ALMOST ALL TOURNAMENT GAMES IN OUR PREFECTURE ARE BEST 2 OUT OF 3.
BUT THE FINALS ARE DIFFERENT. THOSE ARE BEST 3 OUT OF 5...
JUST LIKE THE PRO GAMES YOU SEE ON TV.
HOLY CRAP, THAT'S GONNA EXHAUST THEM!!
EXACTLY.
I GOTTA ADMIT, I'M WORRIED IF THEY'VE GOT ENOUGH GAS IN THE TANK TO LAST.
...
HEY! WHOA! WHAT'RE WE GETTING ALL DOWN IN THE DUMPS FOR?!

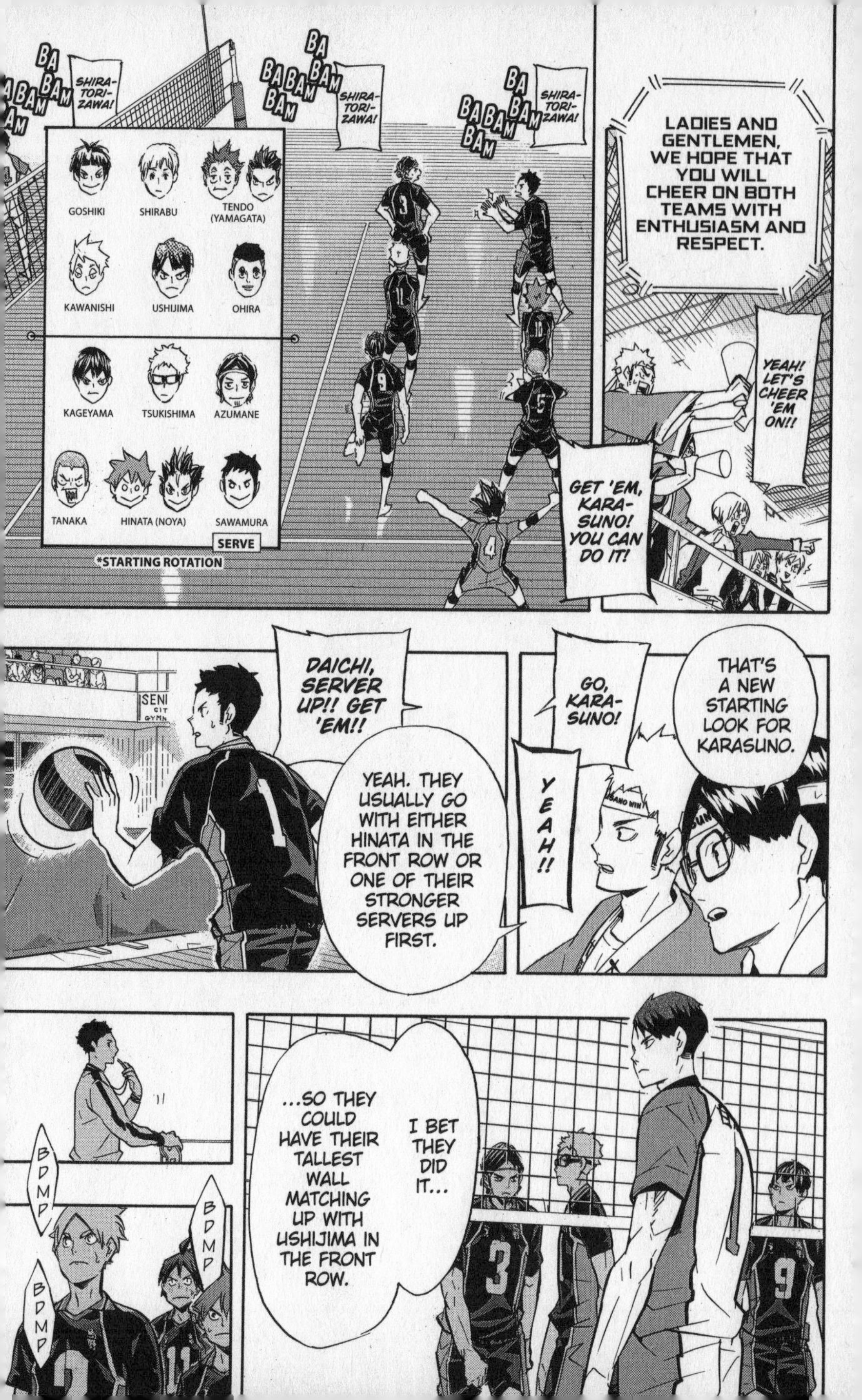
LADIES AND GENTLEMEN, WE HOPE THAT YOU WILL CHEER ON BOTH TEAMS WITH ENTHUSIASM AND RESPECT.
YEAH! LET'S CHEER 'EM ON!!
GET 'EM, KARA-SUNO! YOU CAN DO IT!
BA BA BAM BA BAM BAM
SHIRA-TORI-ZAWA!
BA BA BAM BA BAM BAM
SHIRA-TORI-ZAWA!
BA BA BAM BA BAM BAM
SHIRA-TORI-ZAWA!
GOSHIKI
SHIRABU
TENDO (YAMAGATA)
KAWANISHI
USHIJIMA
OHIRA
KAGEYAMA
TSUKISHIMA
AZUMANE
TANAKA
HINATA (NOYA)
SAWAMURA
SERVE
*STARTING ROTATION
THAT'S A NEW STARTING LOOK FOR KARASUNO.
GO, KARA-SUNO!
YEAH!!
YEAH. THEY USUALLY GO WITH EITHER HINATA IN THE FRONT ROW OR ONE OF THEIR STRONGER SERVERS UP FIRST.
DAICHI, SERVER UP!! GET 'EM!!
I BET THEY DID IT...
...SO THEY COULD HAVE THEIR TALLEST WALL MATCHING UP WITH USHIJIMA IN THE FRONT ROW.
BDMP
BDMP
BDMP

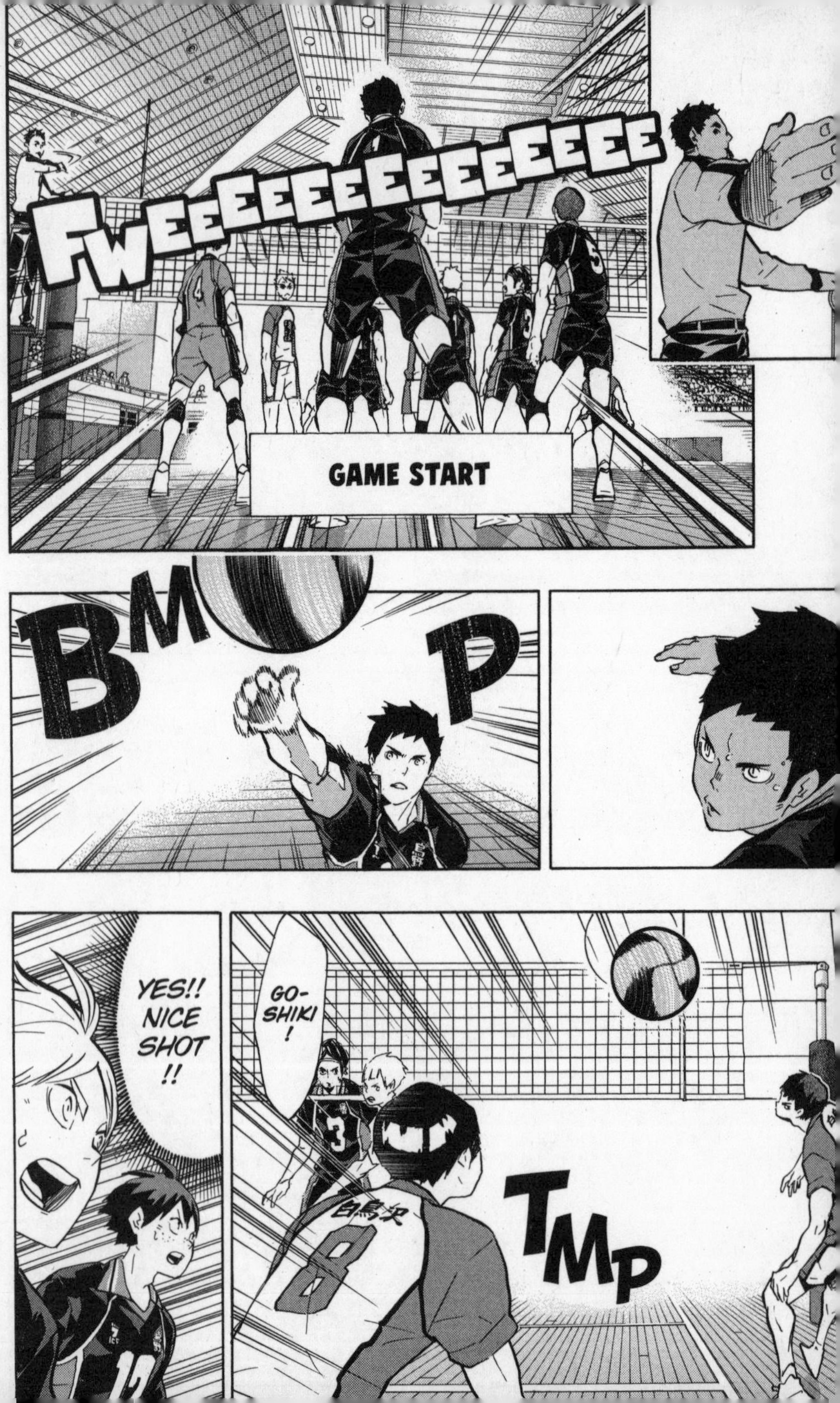
FWEEEEEEEEEEEEE
GAME START
BMP
GO-SHIKI!
TMP
YES!! NICE SHOT!!

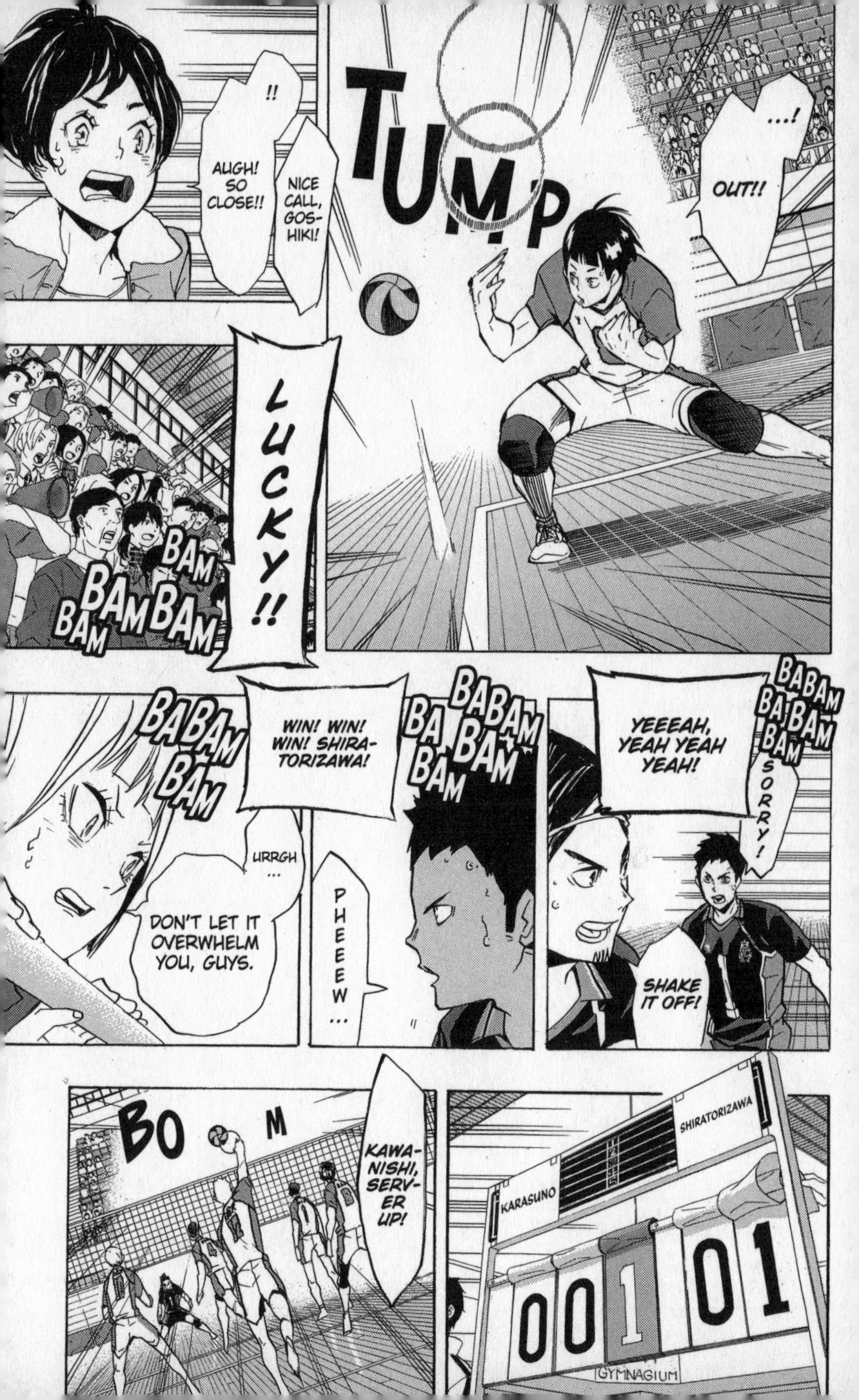

...!
OUT!!
TUMP
!!
NICE CALL, GOSHIKI!
AUGH! SO CLOSE!!
LUCKY!!
BAM BAM BAM BAM BAM
BABAM BABAM BAM
YEEEAH, YEAH YEAH YEAH!
SORRY!
SHAKE IT OFF!
BABAM BA BAM BAM
PHEEEW...
WIN! WIN! WIN! SHIRATORIZAWA!
BABAM BAM
URRGH...
DON'T LET IT OVERWHELM YOU, GUYS.
SHIRATORIZAWA
KARASUNO
00 1 01
GYMNAGIUM
KAWANISHI, SERVER UP!
BOM

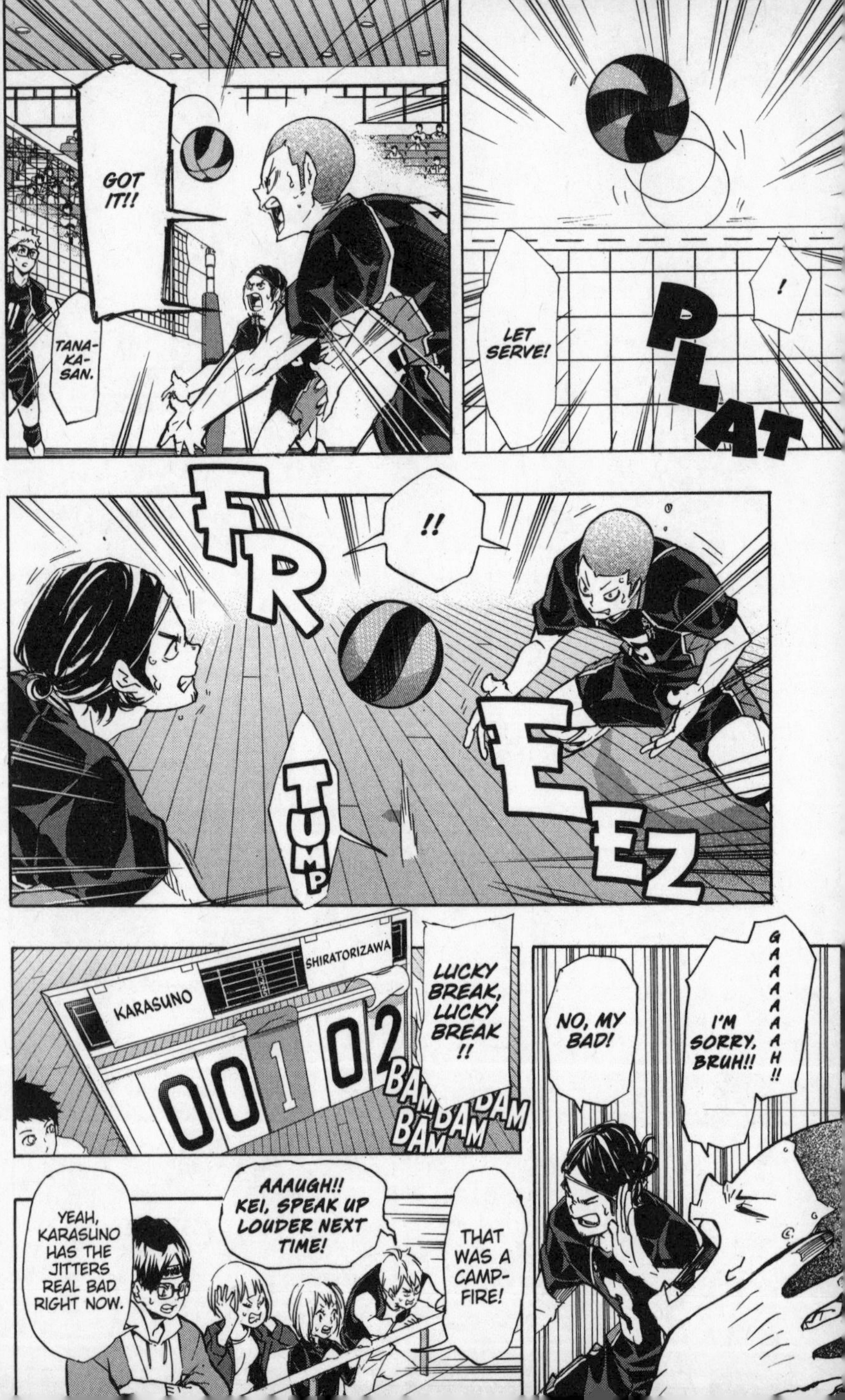
LET SERVE!
!
PLAT
GOT IT!!
TANAKA-SAN.
!!
FREEZ
TUMP
GAAAAAAAAH!!
I'M SORRY, BRUH!!
NO, MY BAD!
SHIRATORIZAWA
KARASUNO
00 1 02
LUCKY BREAK, LUCKY BREAK!!
BAM BAM BAM BAM
THAT WAS A CAMP-FIRE!
AAAUGH!! KEI, SPEAK UP LOUDER NEXT TIME!
YEAH, KARASUNO HAS THE JITTERS REAL BAD RIGHT NOW.

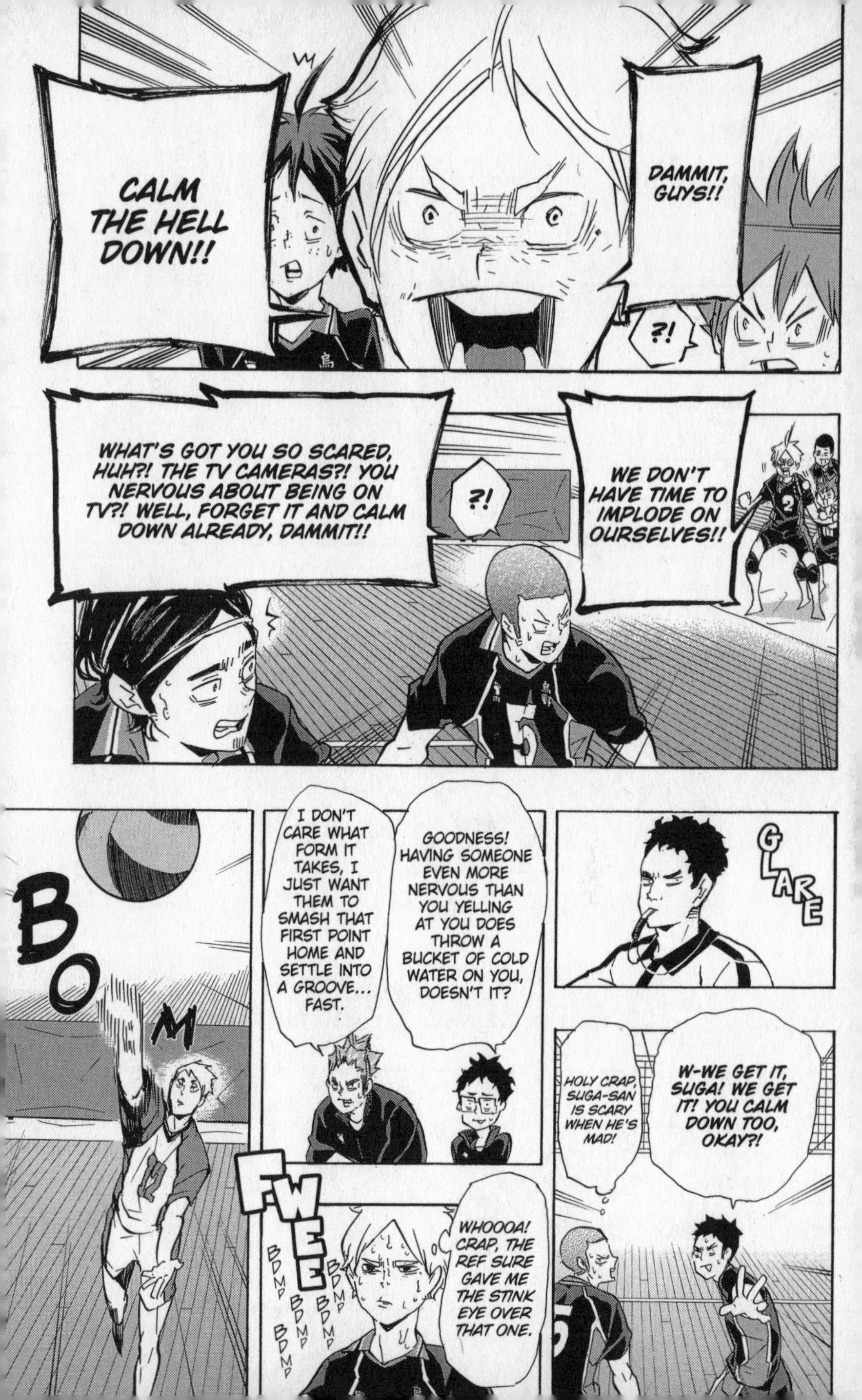
DAMMIT, GUYS!!
CALM THE HELL DOWN!!
?!
WE DON'T HAVE TIME TO IMPLODE ON OURSELVES!!
WHAT'S GOT YOU SO SCARED, HUH?! THE TV CAMERAS?! YOU NERVOUS ABOUT BEING ON TV?! WELL, FORGET IT AND CALM DOWN ALREADY, DAMMIT!!
?!
GLARE
W-WE GET IT, SUGA! WE GET IT! YOU CALM DOWN TOO, OKAY?!
HOLY CRAP, SUGA-SAN IS SCARY WHEN HE'S MAD!
GOODNESS! HAVING SOMEONE EVEN MORE NERVOUS THAN YOU YELLING AT YOU DOES THROW A BUCKET OF COLD WATER ON YOU, DOESN'T IT?
I DON'T CARE WHAT FORM IT TAKES, I JUST WANT THEM TO SMASH THAT FIRST POINT HOME AND SETTLE INTO A GROOVE... FAST.
WHOOOA! CRAP, THE REF SURE GAVE ME THE STINK EYE OVER THAT ONE.
FWEE
BDMP BDMP BDMP BDMP BDMP BDMP
BOOM

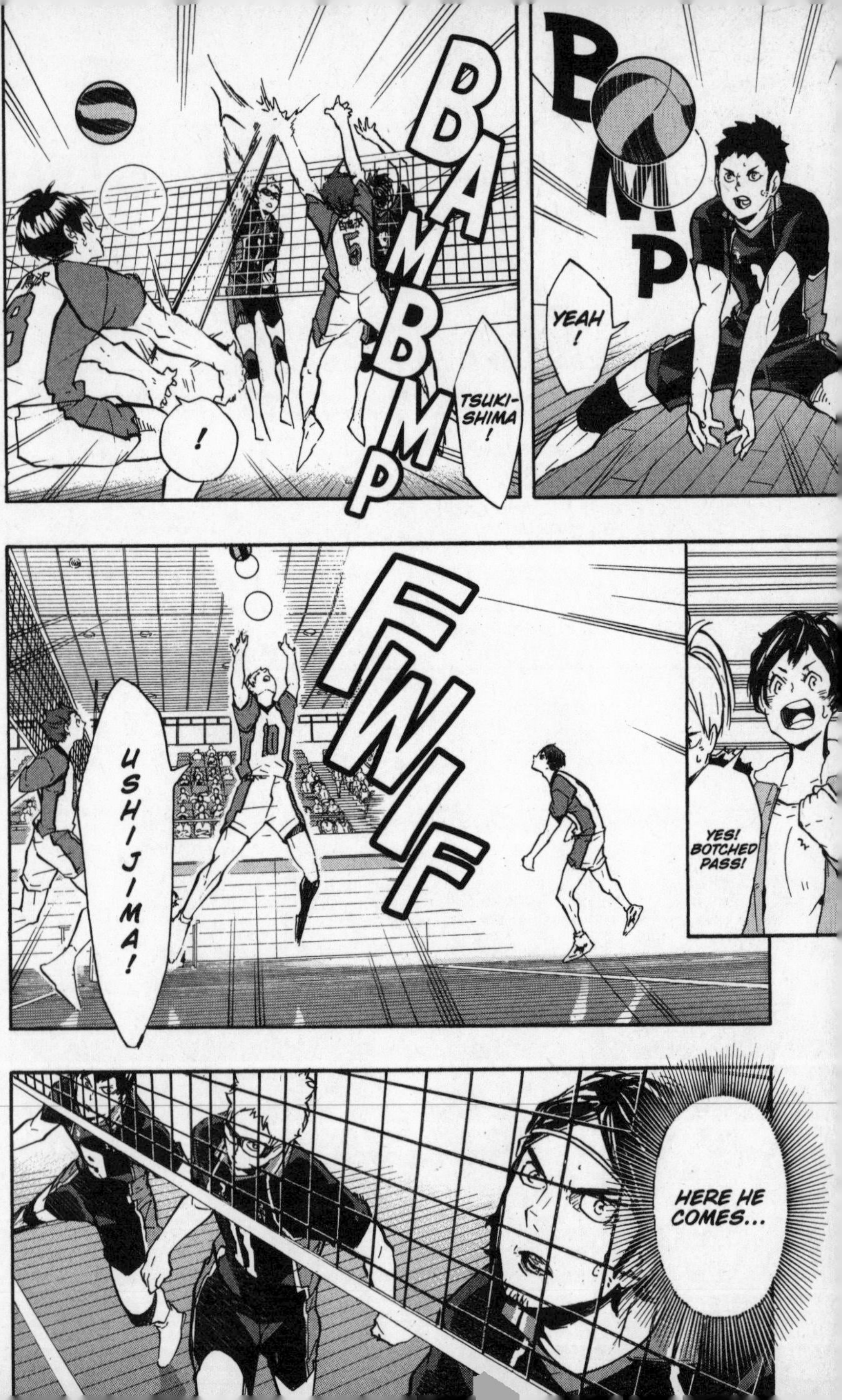
BUMP
YEAH!
BAMBIMP
TSUKI-SHIMA!
!
YES! BOTCHED PASS!
FWIF
USHIJIMA!
HERE HE COMES...

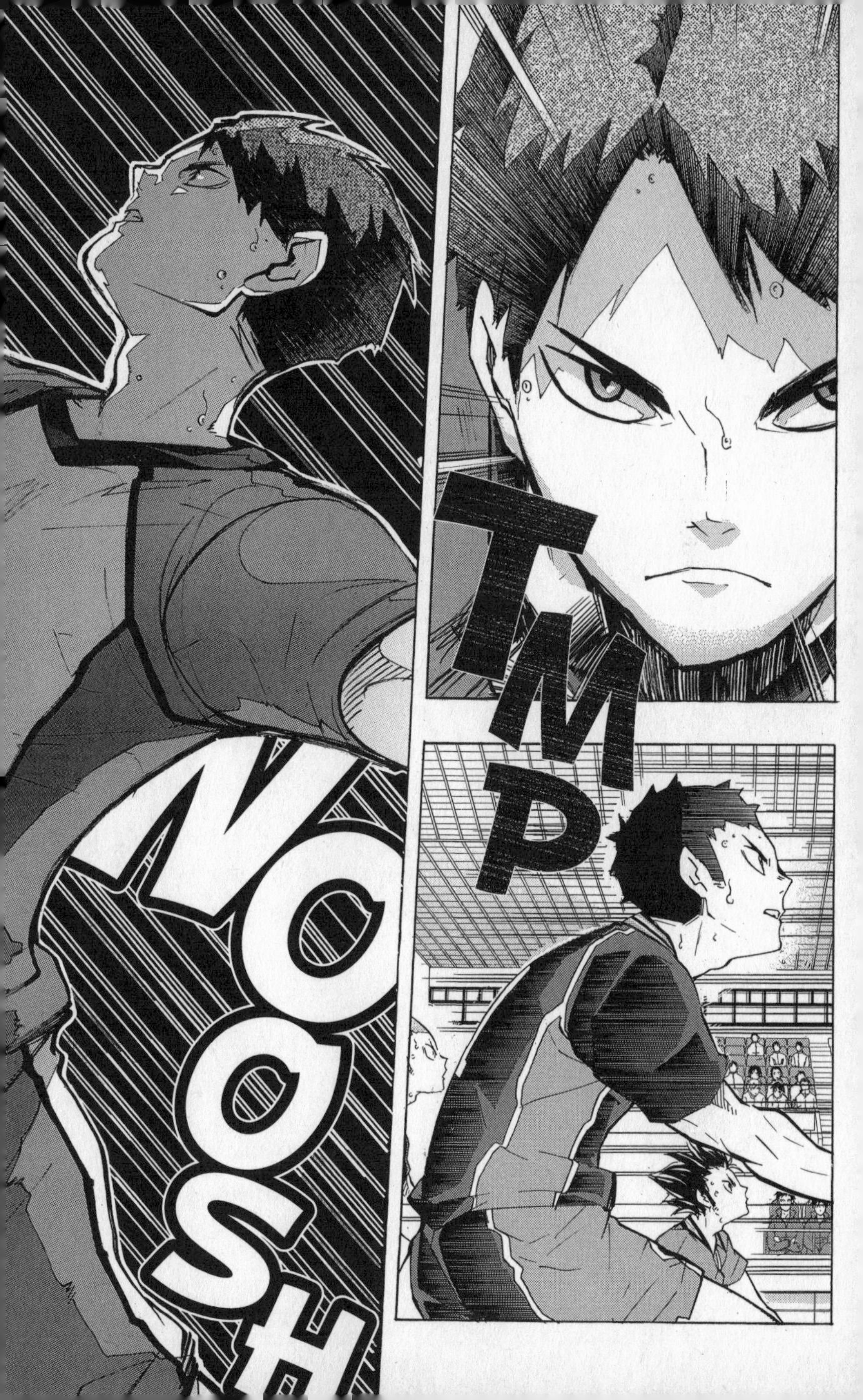
TMP
WOOSH

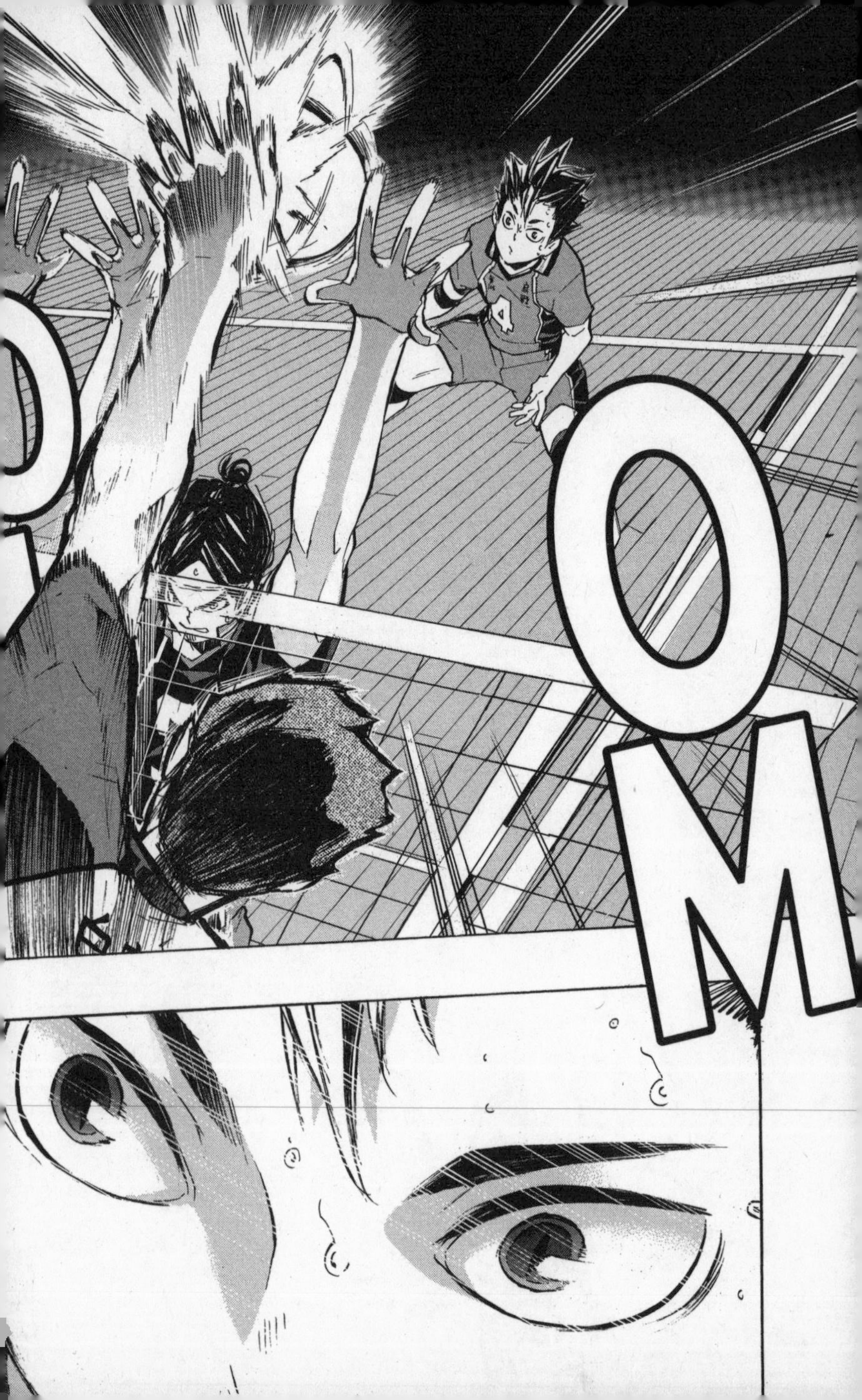
OOM

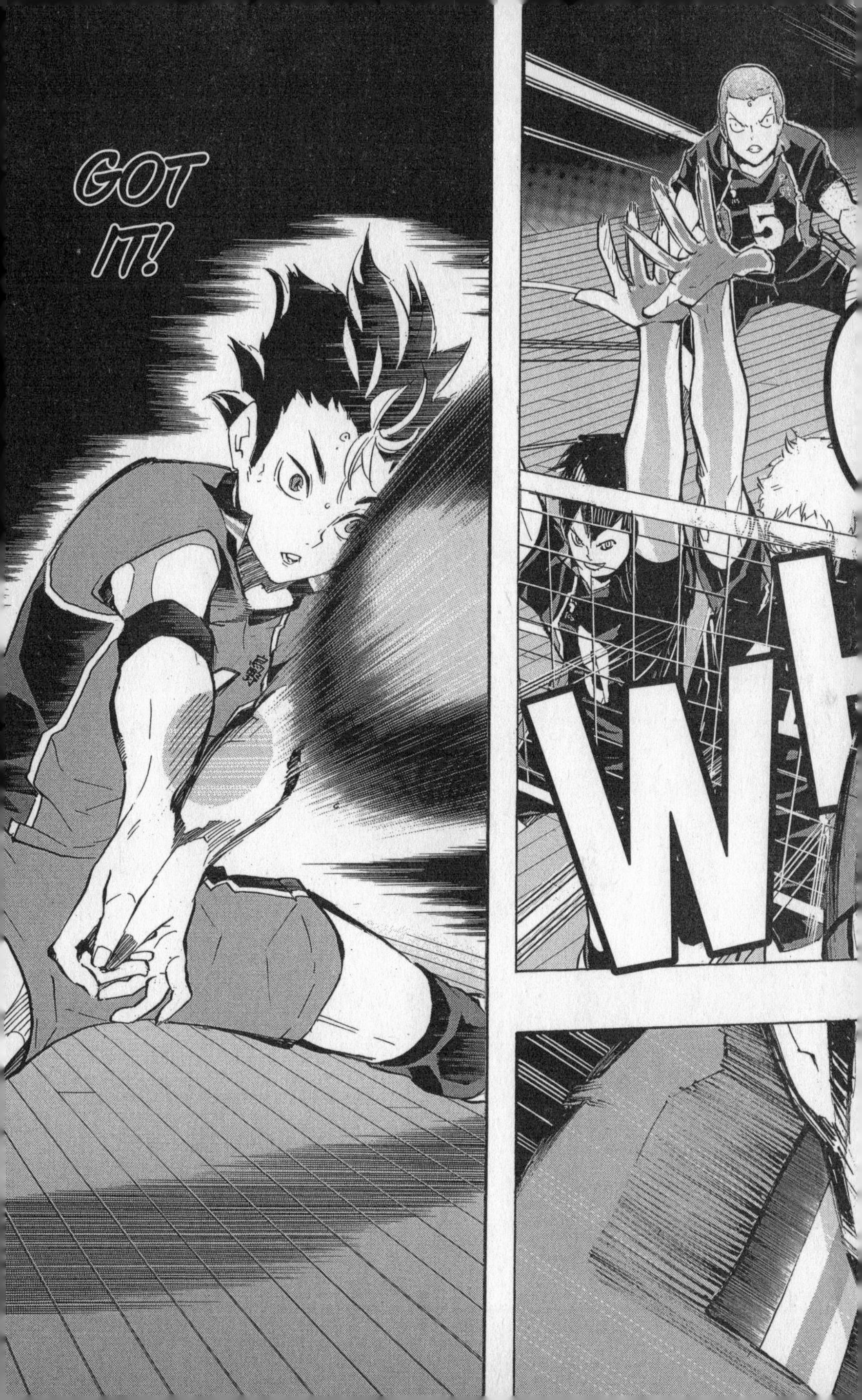
GOT IT!

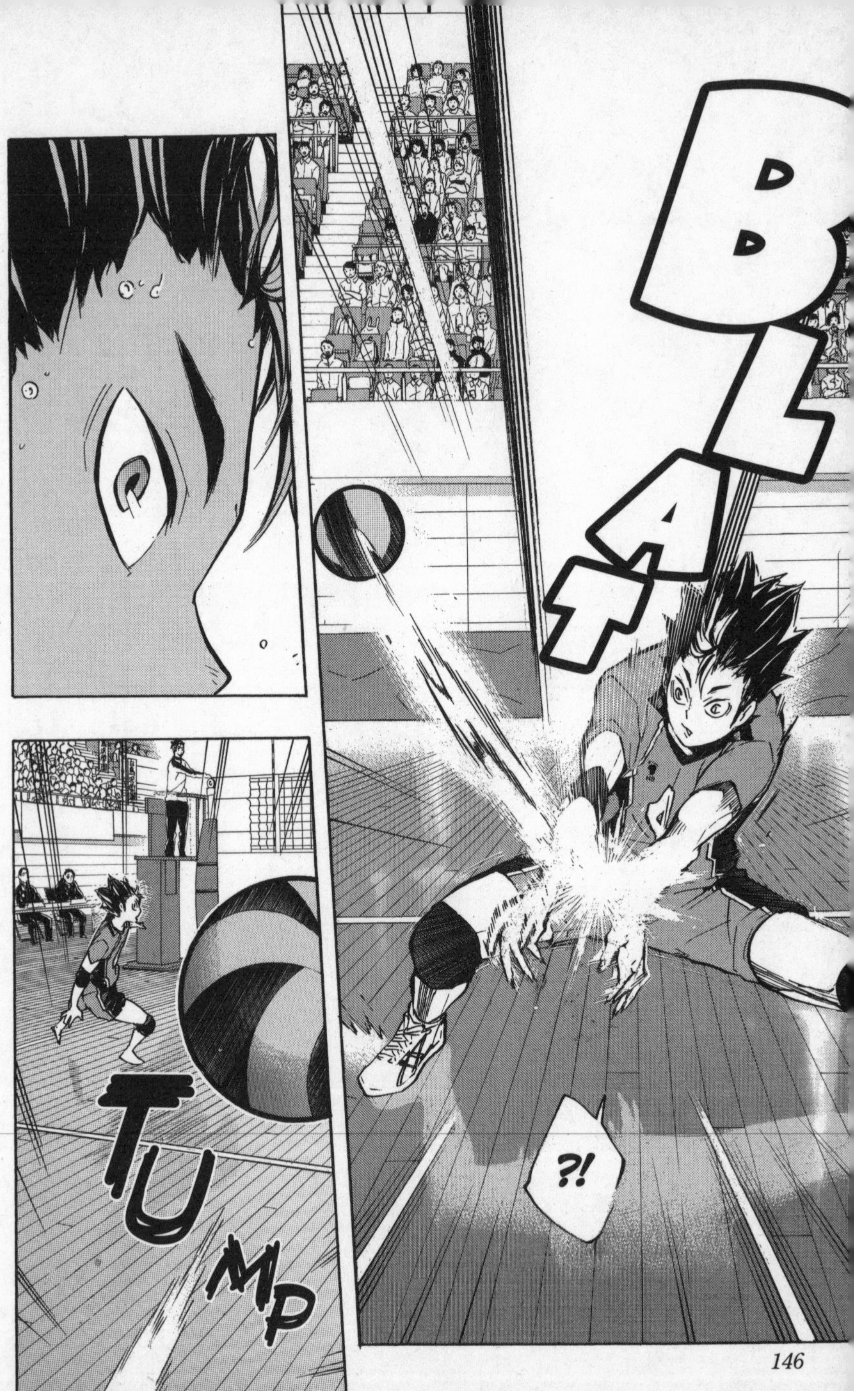
BLAT
?!
TUMP

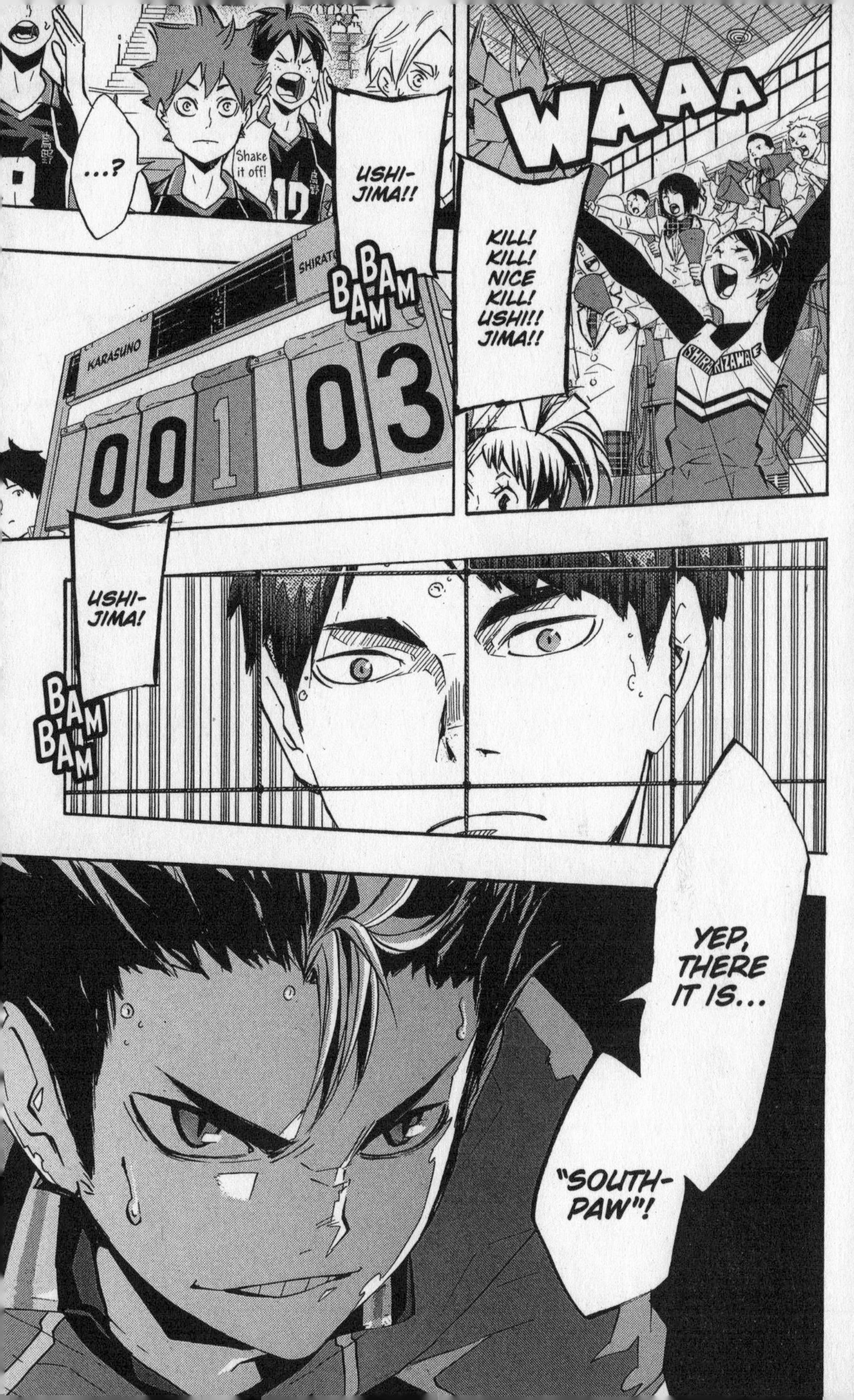
WAAAA
USHI-JIMA!!
KILL! KILL! NICE KILL! USHI!! JIMA!!
Shake it off!
...?
BAM BAM
SHIRATO
KARASUNO
00 1 03
USHI-JIMA!
BAM BAM
YEP, THERE IT IS...
"SOUTH-PAW"!

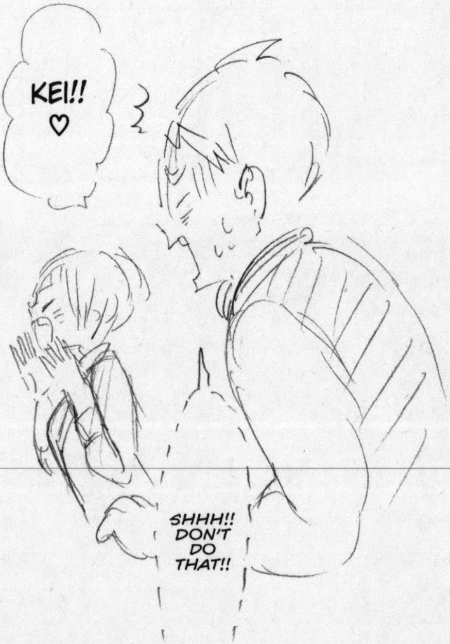
KEI!! ♡
SHHH!! DON'T DO THAT!!

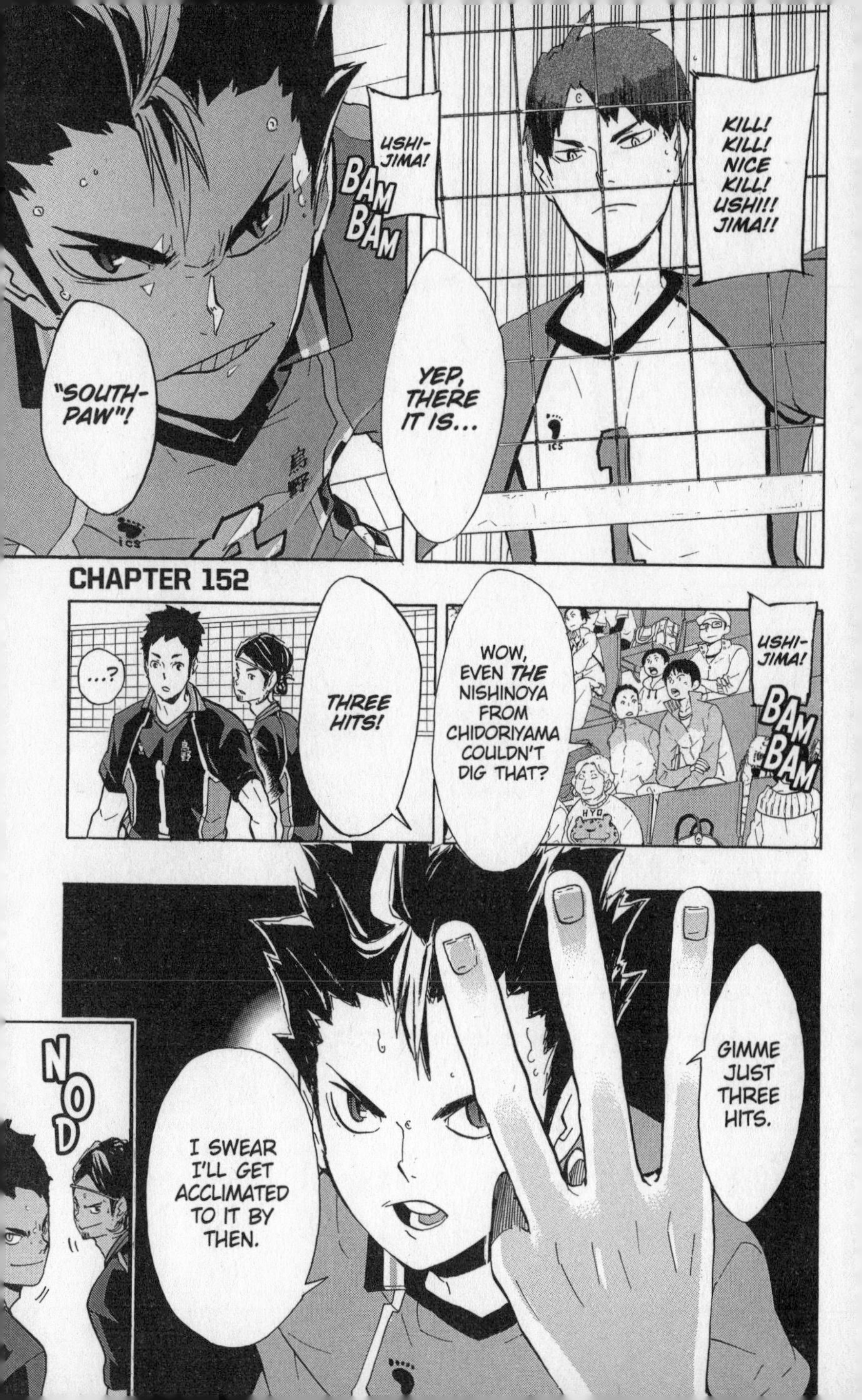
KILL! KILL! NICE KILL! USHI!! JIMA!!
USHI-JIMA!
BAM BAM
YEP, THERE IT IS...
"SOUTH-PAW"!
CHAPTER 152
USHI-JIMA!
BAM BAM
WOW, EVEN THE NISHINOYA FROM CHIDORIYAMA COULDN'T DIG THAT?
THREE HITS!
...?
GIMME JUST THREE HITS.
I SWEAR I'LL GET ACCLIMATED TO IT BY THEN.
NOD

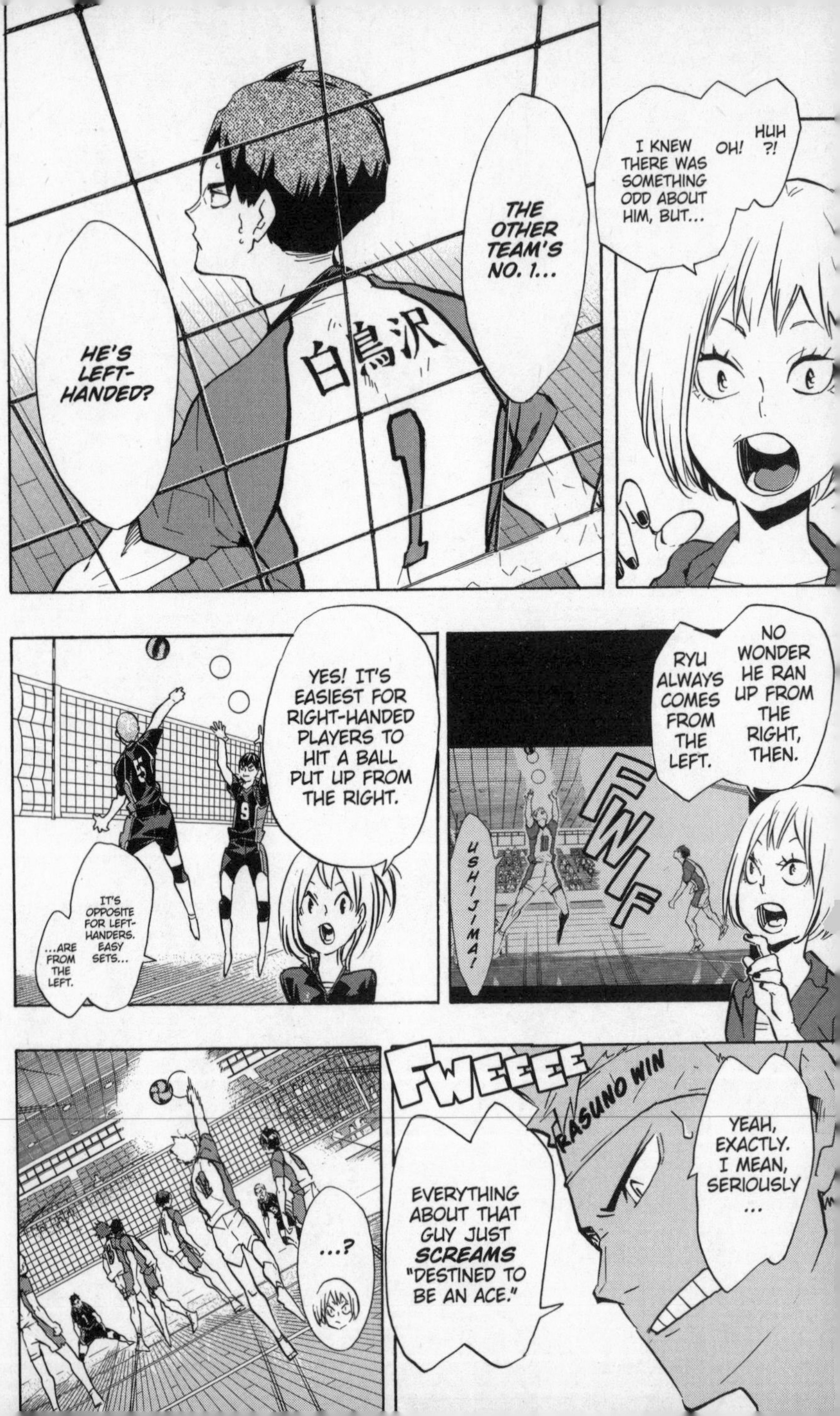
HUH ?!
OH!
I KNEW THERE WAS SOMETHING ODD ABOUT HIM, BUT...
THE OTHER TEAM'S NO. 1...
白鳥沢
HE'S LEFT-HANDED?
NO WONDER HE RAN UP FROM THE RIGHT, THEN.
RYU ALWAYS COMES FROM THE LEFT.
FWIF
USHIJIMA!
YES! IT'S EASIEST FOR RIGHT-HANDED PLAYERS TO HIT A BALL PUT UP FROM THE RIGHT.
IT'S OPPOSITE FOR LEFT-HANDERS. EASY SETS...
...ARE FROM THE LEFT.
FWEEEE
RASUNO WIN
YEAH, EXACTLY. I MEAN, SERIOUSLY...
EVERYTHING ABOUT THAT GUY JUST SCREAMS "DESTINED TO BE AN ACE."
...?

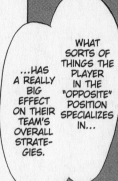

SEE, USHIWAKA'S POSITION IN HIS TEAM'S ROTATION IS CALLED *THE OPPOSITE.* BASICALLY, HE'S DIRECTLY OPPOSITE THE SETTER.
OPPOSITE
DIAGONALS
SETTER
ON KARASUNO'S SIDE, SAWAMURA IS IN THAT SPOT.
WHAT SORTS OF THINGS THE PLAYER IN THE "OPPOSITE" POSITION SPECIALIZES IN...
...HAS A REALLY BIG EFFECT ON THEIR TEAM'S OVERALL STRATE-GIES.
ONE BASIC PATTERN IS TO PUT A BALANCED PLAYER IN THAT SPOT--SOMEONE WHO'S NIMBLE, INTELLIGENT AND GOOD AT DEFENSE. KARASUNO DID THAT WITH SAWAMURA.
BMP
DAICHI!
MOST HIGH SCHOOLS TEND TO DO THAT.
ANOTHER STRATEGY IS TO PUT A *CANNON* LIKE USHIWAKA IN THAT SPOT.
THESE PLAYERS DON'T RECEIVE ANY SERVES. INSTEAD THEY STAY READY TO ATTACK AT ALL TIMES, FRONT OR BACK ROW.
IN THE OLD DAYS...
...THEY USED TO CALL THOSE PLAYERS "SUPER ACES."

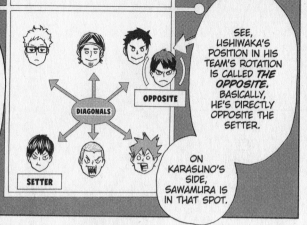

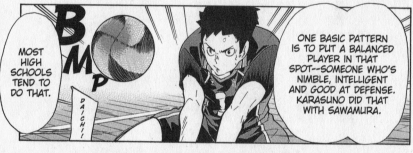

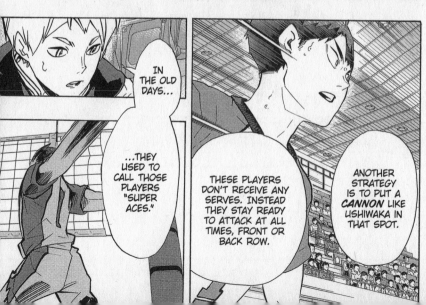

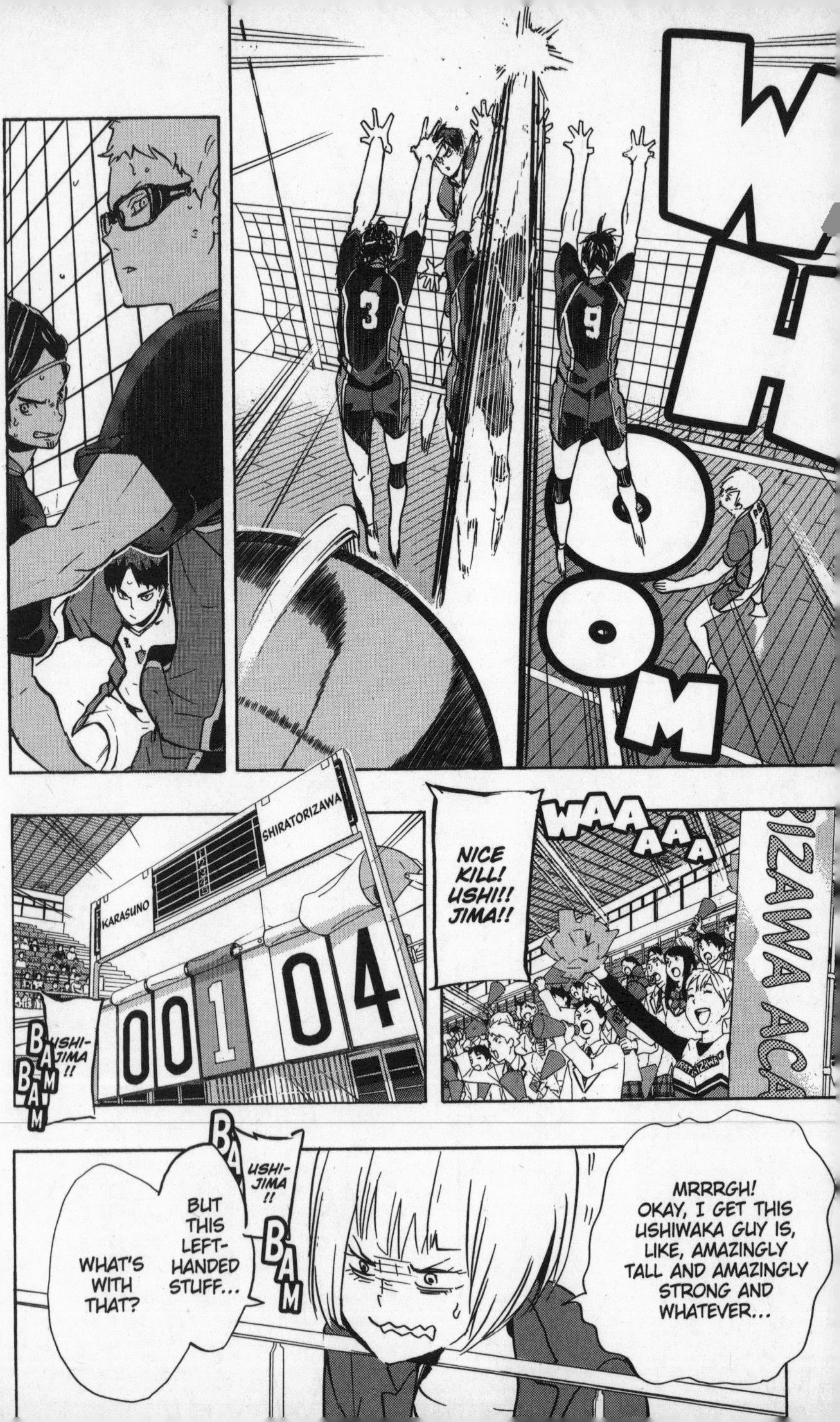
WHOOM
NICE KILL! USHI!! JIMA!!
WAAAAAA
SHIRATORIZAWA
KARASUNO
00 1 04
USHI-JIMA!!
BAM
BAM
MRRRGH! OKAY, I GET THIS USHIWAKA GUY IS, LIKE, AMAZINGLY TALL AND AMAZINGLY STRONG AND WHATEVER...
USHI-JIMA!!
BAM
BAM
BUT THIS LEFT-HANDED STUFF...
WHAT'S WITH THAT?

CHAPTER 152: Fear the Southpaw

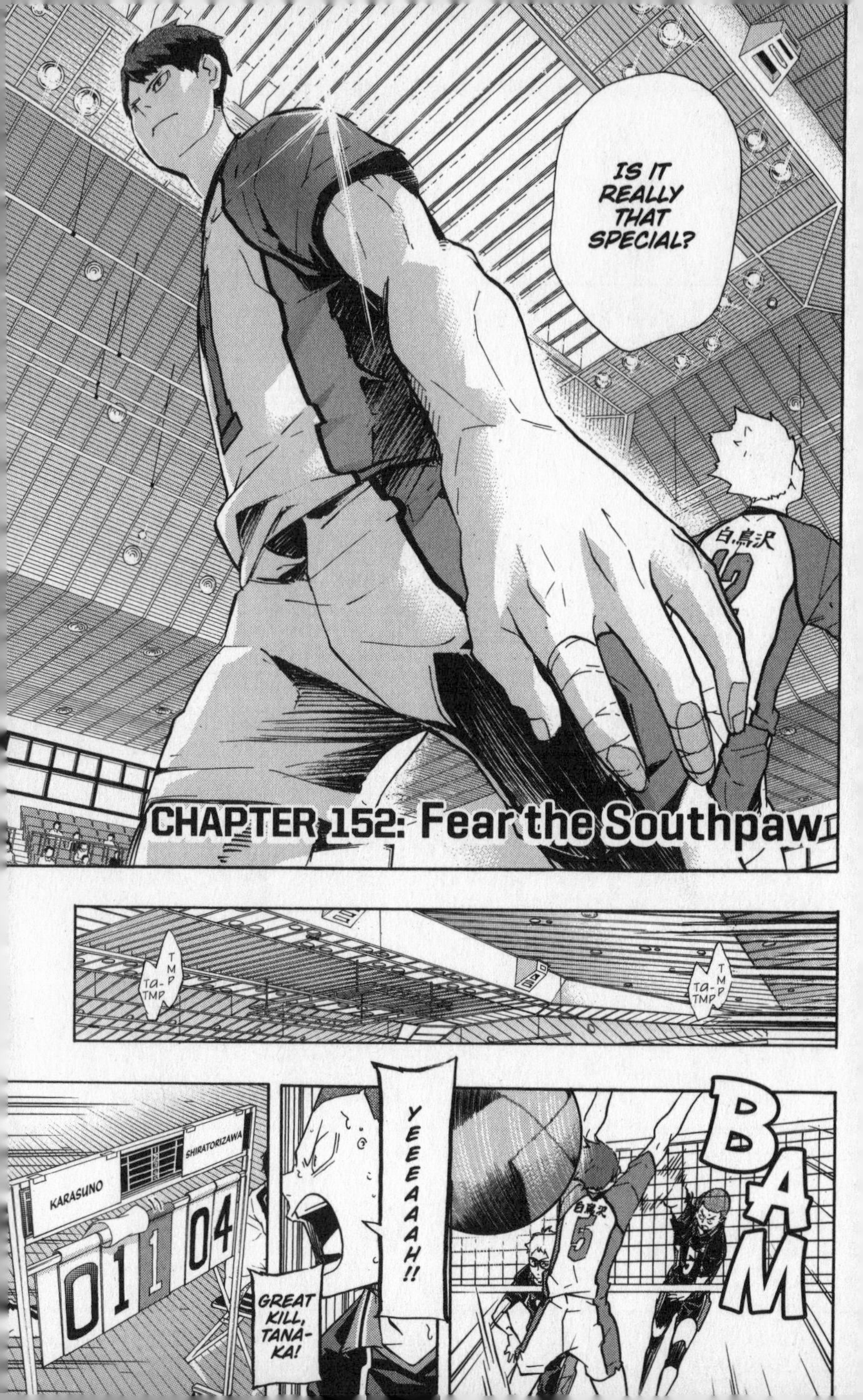
IS IT REALLY THAT SPECIAL?
白鳥沢
Ta-TMP TMP
Ta-TMP TMP
BAM
白鳥沢
YEEEAAAAH!!
GREAT KILL, TANAKA!
KARASUNO
SHIRATORIZAWA
01 1 04

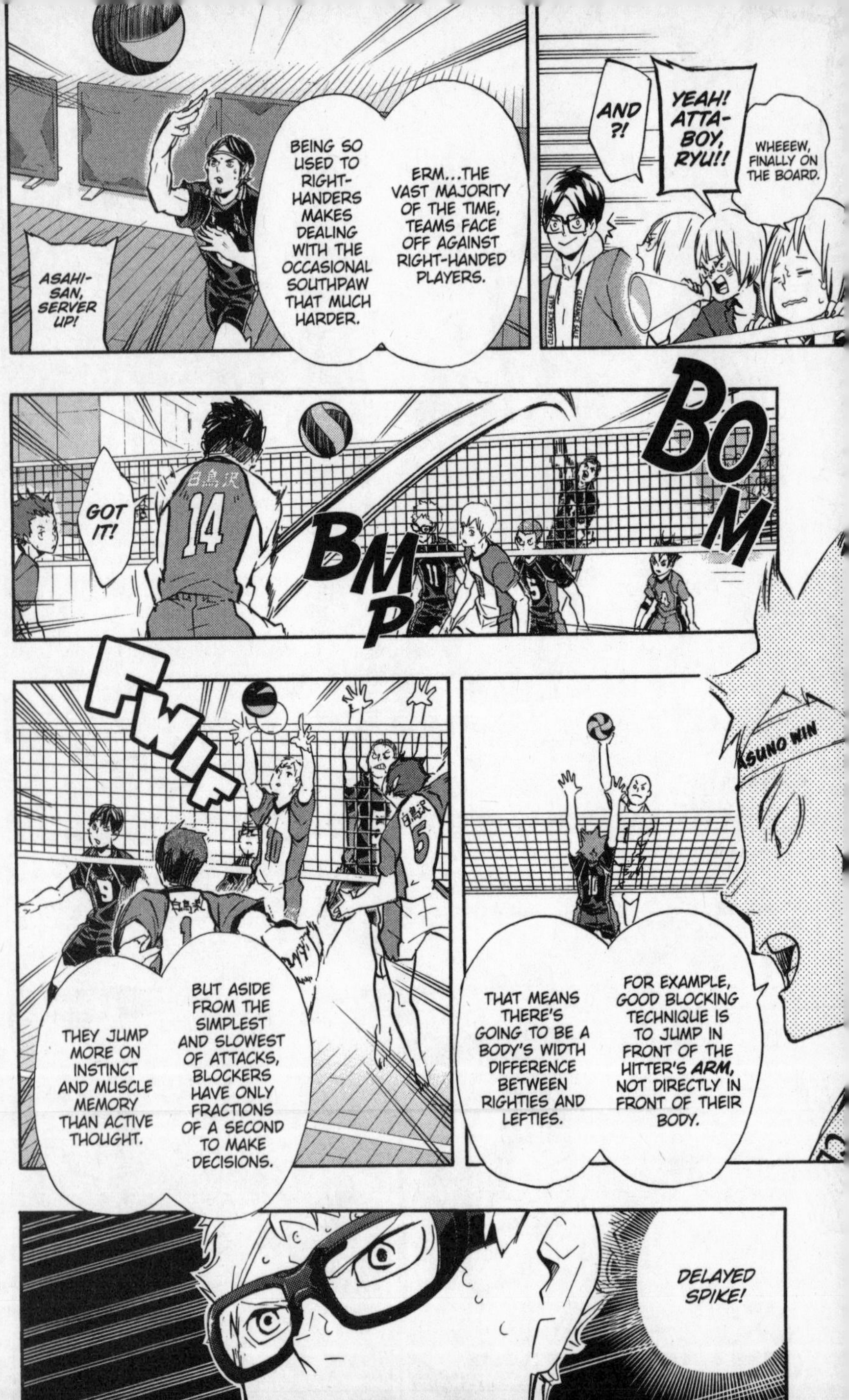
WHEEEW, FINALLY ON THE BOARD.
YEAH! ATTA-BOY, RYU!!
AND ?!
ERM...THE VAST MAJORITY OF THE TIME, TEAMS FACE OFF AGAINST RIGHT-HANDED PLAYERS.
BEING SO USED TO RIGHT-HANDERS MAKES DEALING WITH THE OCCASIONAL SOUTHPAW THAT MUCH HARDER.
ASAHI-SAN, SERVER UP!
BOM
GOT IT!
BMP
FOR EXAMPLE, GOOD BLOCKING TECHNIQUE IS TO JUMP IN FRONT OF THE HITTER'S ARM, NOT DIRECTLY IN FRONT OF THEIR BODY.
THAT MEANS THERE'S GOING TO BE A BODY'S WIDTH DIFFERENCE BETWEEN RIGHTIES AND LEFTIES.
FWIF
BUT ASIDE FROM THE SIMPLEST AND SLOWEST OF ATTACKS, BLOCKERS HAVE ONLY FRACTIONS OF A SECOND TO MAKE DECISIONS.
THEY JUMP MORE ON INSTINCT AND MUSCLE MEMORY THAN ACTIVE THOUGHT.
DELAYED SPIKE!

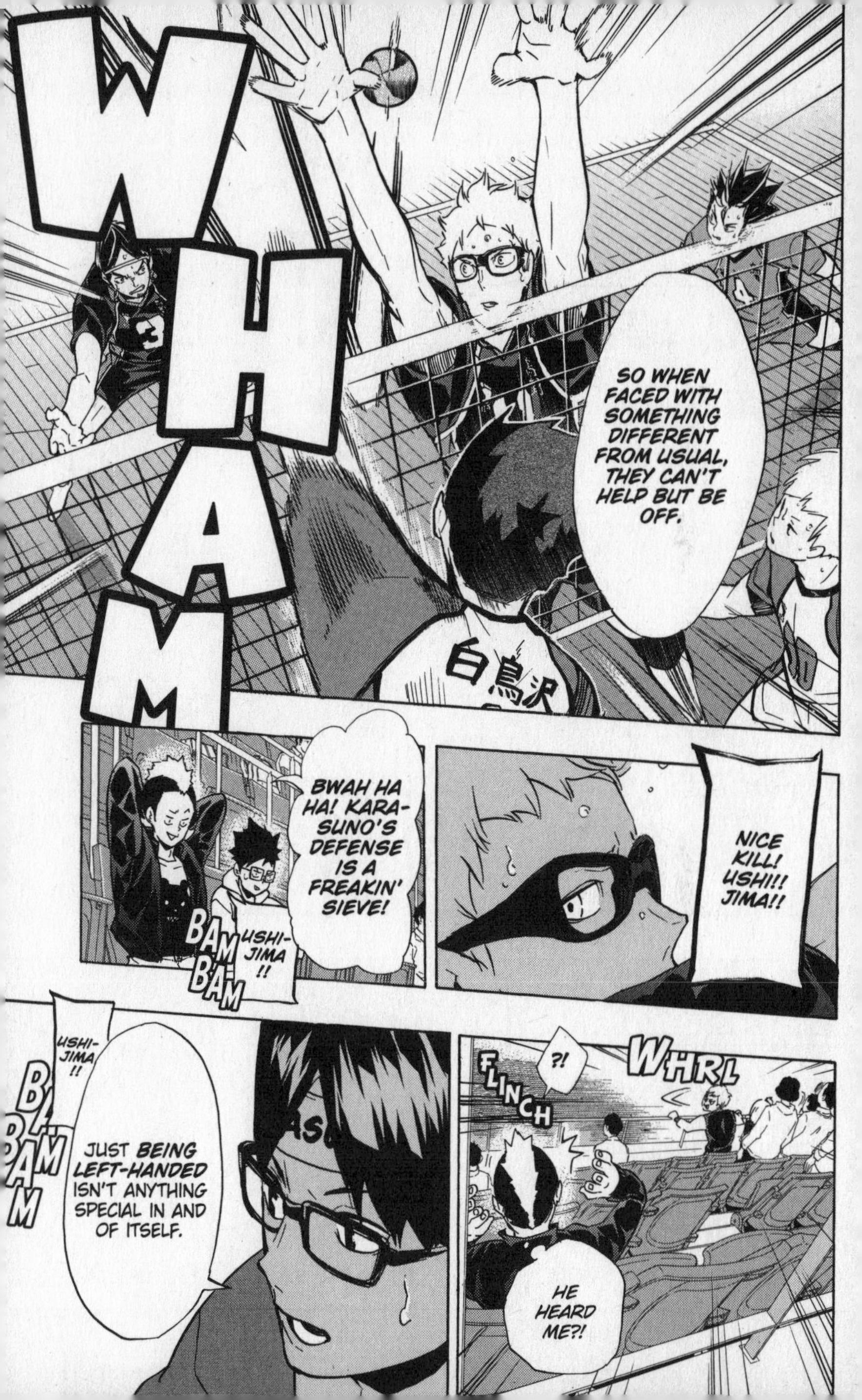
SO WHEN FACED WITH SOMETHING DIFFERENT FROM USUAL, THEY CAN'T HELP BUT BE OFF.
WHAM
NICE KILL! USHI!! JIMA!!
BWAH HA HA! KARA-SUNO'S DEFENSE IS A FREAKIN' SIEVE!
USHI-JIMA !!
BAM BAM
WHRL
?!
FLINCH
HE HEARD ME?!
USHI-JIMA !!
JUST BEING LEFT-HANDED ISN'T ANYTHING SPECIAL IN AND OF ITSELF.
BAM BAM

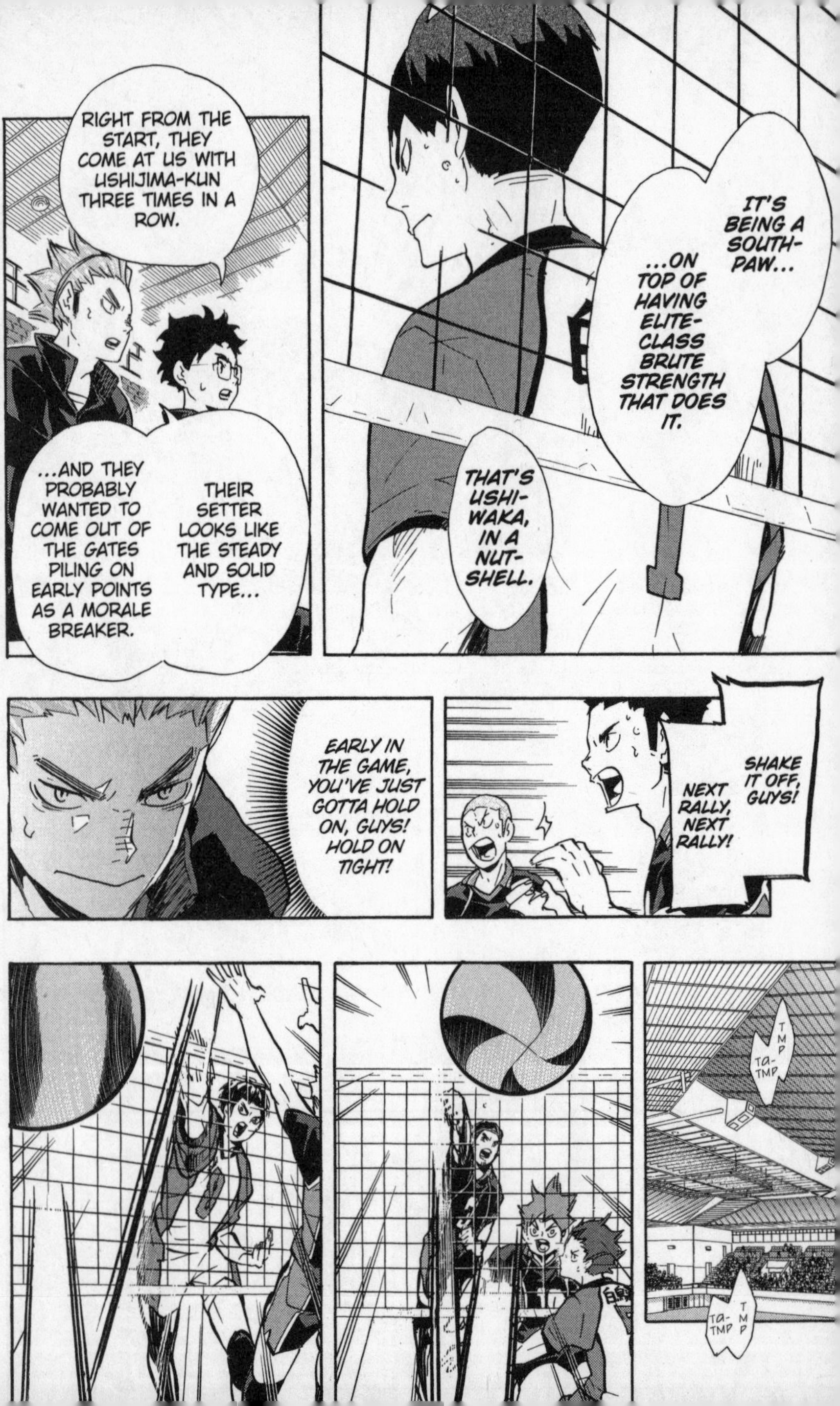
IT'S BEING A SOUTHPAW...
...ON TOP OF HAVING ELITE-CLASS BRUTE STRENGTH THAT DOES IT.
THAT'S USHIWAKA, IN A NUTSHELL.
RIGHT FROM THE START, THEY COME AT US WITH USHIJIMA-KUN THREE TIMES IN A ROW.
THEIR SETTER LOOKS LIKE THE STEADY AND SOLID TYPE...
...AND THEY PROBABLY WANTED TO COME OUT OF THE GATES PILING ON EARLY POINTS AS A MORALE BREAKER.
SHAKE IT OFF, GUYS!
NEXT RALLY, NEXT RALLY!
EARLY IN THE GAME, YOU'VE JUST GOTTA HOLD ON, GUYS! HOLD ON TIGHT!
TMP TA-TMP
TMP TA-TMP

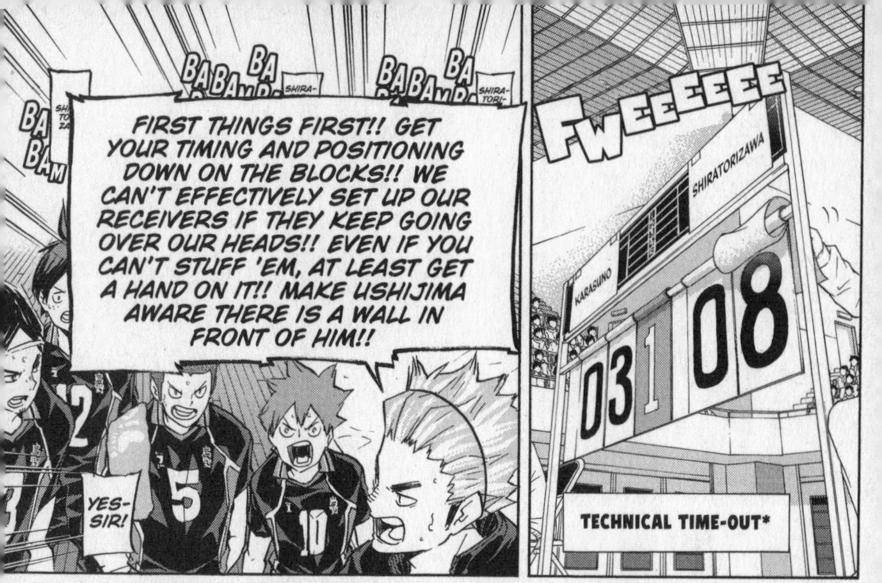
FWEEEEEEE
KARASUNO
SHIRATORIZAWA
03 1 08
TECHNICAL TIME-OUT*
BA BA BAM
BA BA BAM
BA BA BAM
FIRST THINGS FIRST!! GET YOUR TIMING AND POSITIONING DOWN ON THE BLOCKS!! WE CAN'T EFFECTIVELY SET UP OUR RECEIVERS IF THEY KEEP GOING OVER OUR HEADS!! EVEN IF YOU CAN'T STUFF 'EM, AT LEAST GET A HAND ON IT!! MAKE USHIJIMA AWARE THERE IS A WALL IN FRONT OF HIM!!
YES-SIR!

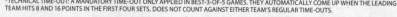

*TECHNICAL TIME-OUT: A MANDATORY TIME-OUT ONLY APPLIED IN BEST-3-OF-5 GAMES. THEY AUTOMATICALLY COME UP WHEN THE LEADING TEAM HITS 8 AND 16 POINTS IN THE FIRST FOUR SETS. DOES NOT COUNT AGAINST EITHER TEAM'S REGULAR TIME-OUTS.

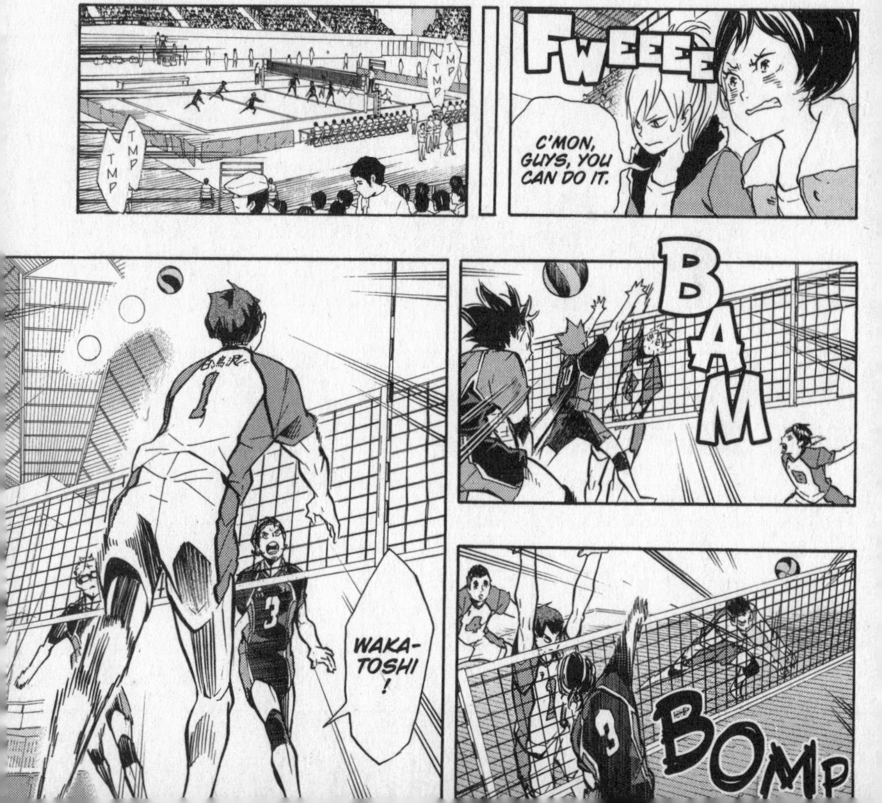
FWEEEE
C'MON, GUYS, YOU CAN DO IT.
TMP TMP
TMP TMP
BAM
BOMP
WAKA-TOSHI!

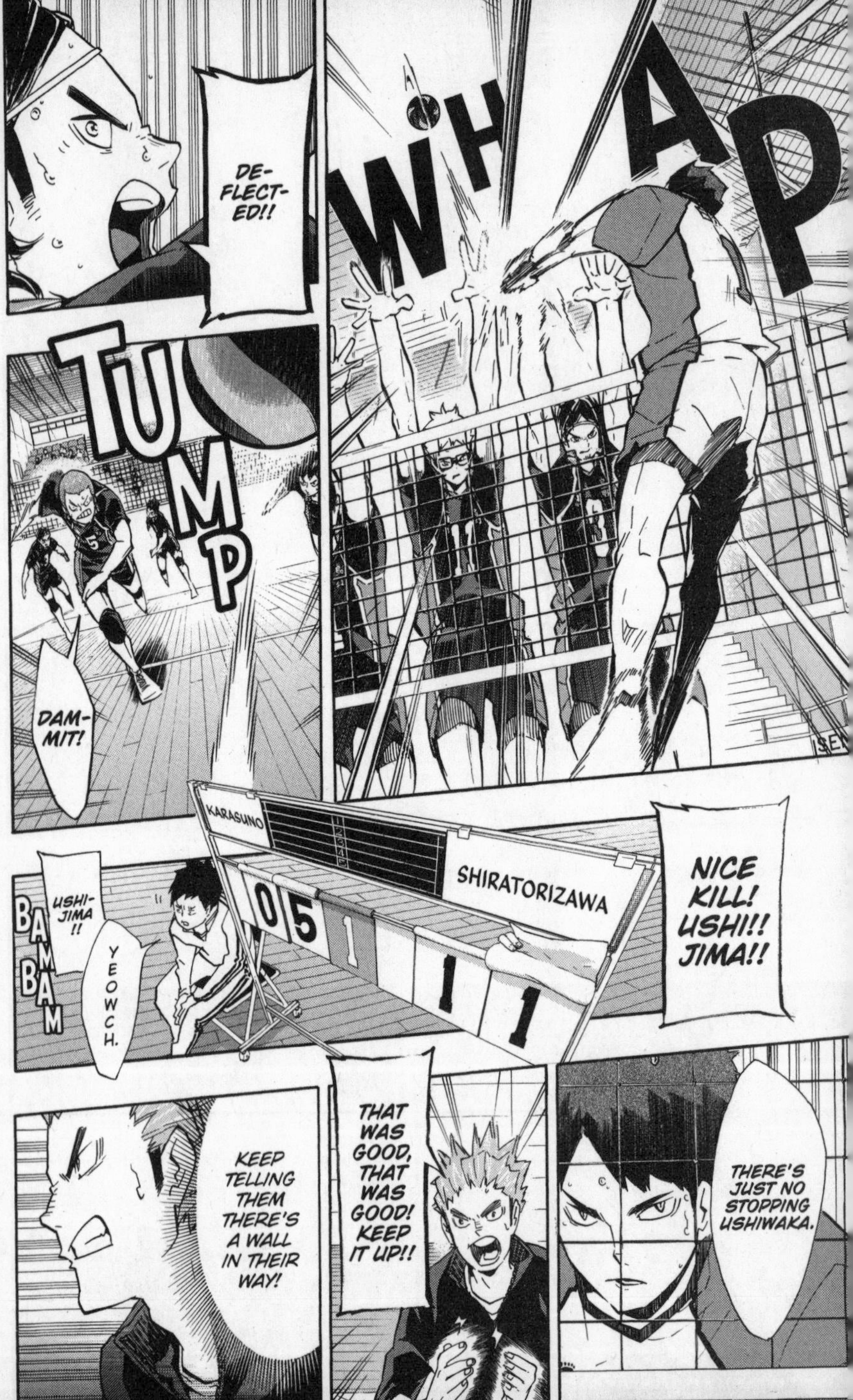
WHAP
DE-FLECT-ED!!
TUMP
DAM-MIT!
NICE KILL! USHI!! JIMA!!
KARASUNO
SHIRATORIZAWA
USHI-JIMA!!
YEOWCH.
BAMBAM
THERE'S JUST NO STOPPING USHIWAKA.
THAT WAS GOOD, THAT WAS GOOD! KEEP IT UP!!
KEEP TELLING THEM THERE'S A WALL IN THEIR WAY!

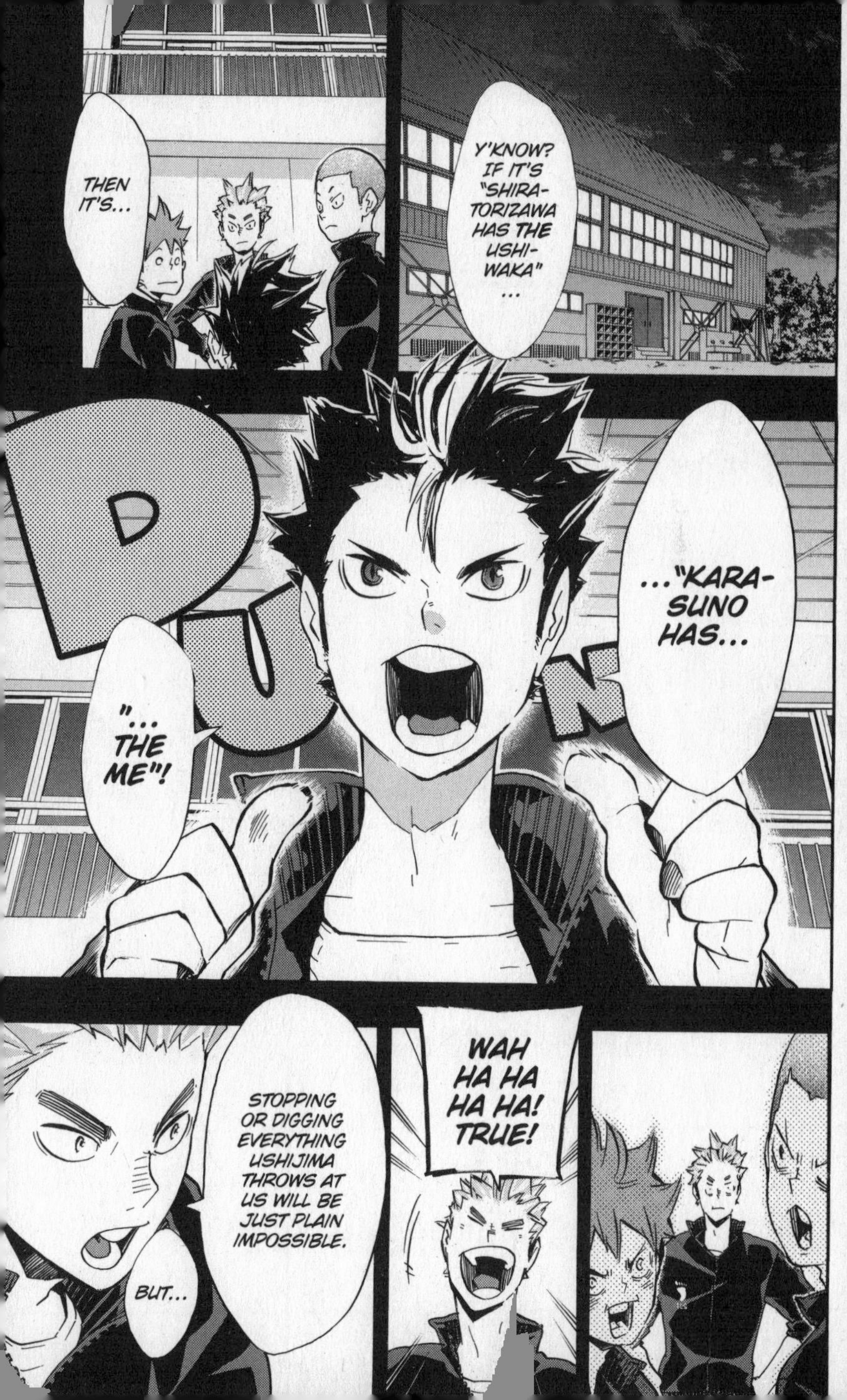
Y'KNOW? IF IT'S "SHIRATORIZAWA HAS THE USHIWAKA"...
THEN IT'S...
..."KARASUNO HAS...
D U N
"...THE ME"!
WAH HA HA HA HA! TRUE!
STOPPING OR DIGGING EVERYTHING USHIJIMA THROWS AT US WILL BE JUST PLAIN IMPOSSIBLE.
BUT...

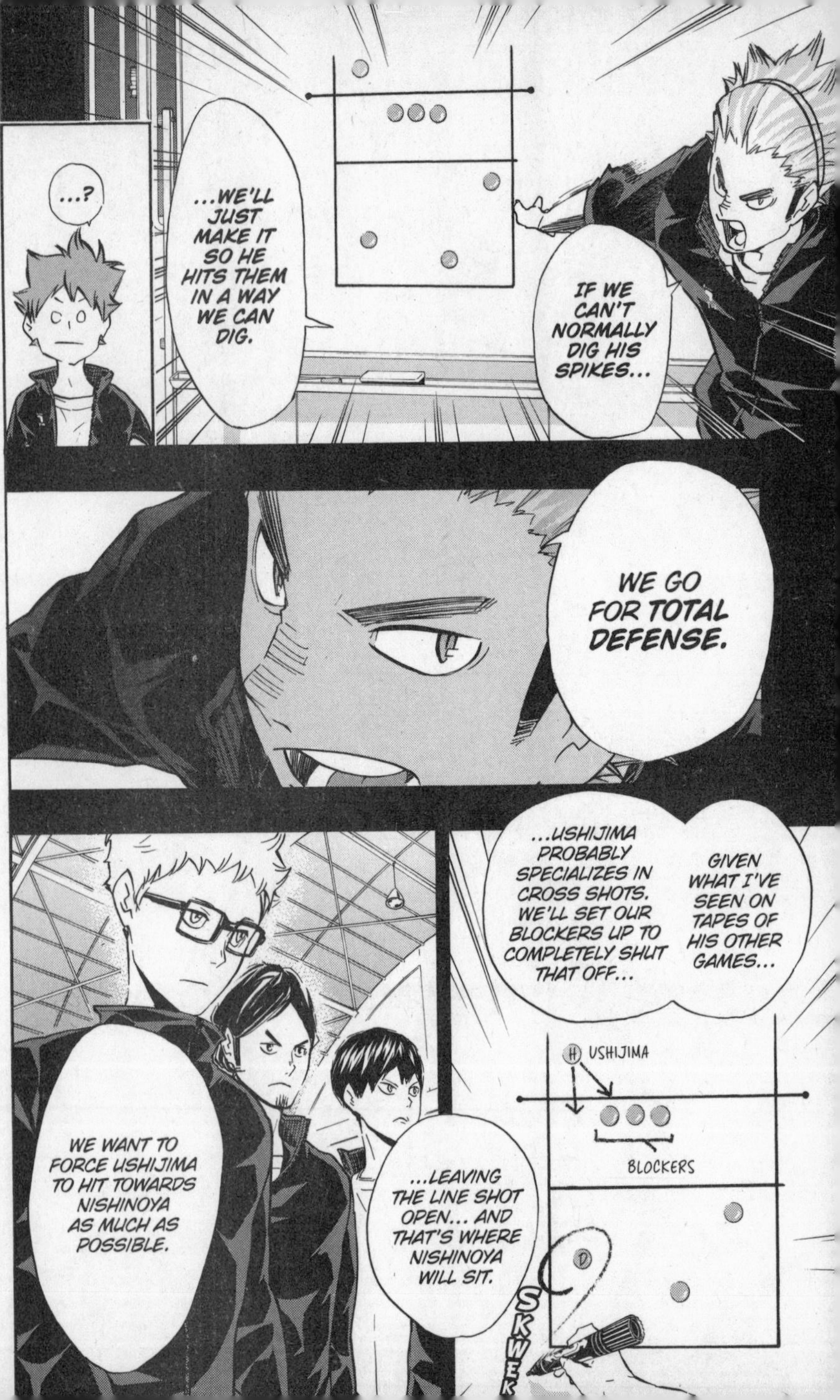
IF WE CAN'T NORMALLY DIG HIS SPIKES...
...WE'LL JUST MAKE IT SO HE HITS THEM IN A WAY WE CAN DIG.
...?
WE GO FOR TOTAL DEFENSE.
GIVEN WHAT I'VE SEEN ON TAPES OF HIS OTHER GAMES...
...USHIJIMA PROBABLY SPECIALIZES IN CROSS SHOTS. WE'LL SET OUR BLOCKERS UP TO COMPLETELY SHUT THAT OFF...
USHIJIMA
BLOCKERS
...LEAVING THE LINE SHOT OPEN... AND THAT'S WHERE NISHINOYA WILL SIT.
SKWEEK
WE WANT TO FORCE USHIJIMA TO HIT TOWARDS NISHINOYA AS MUCH AS POSSIBLE.

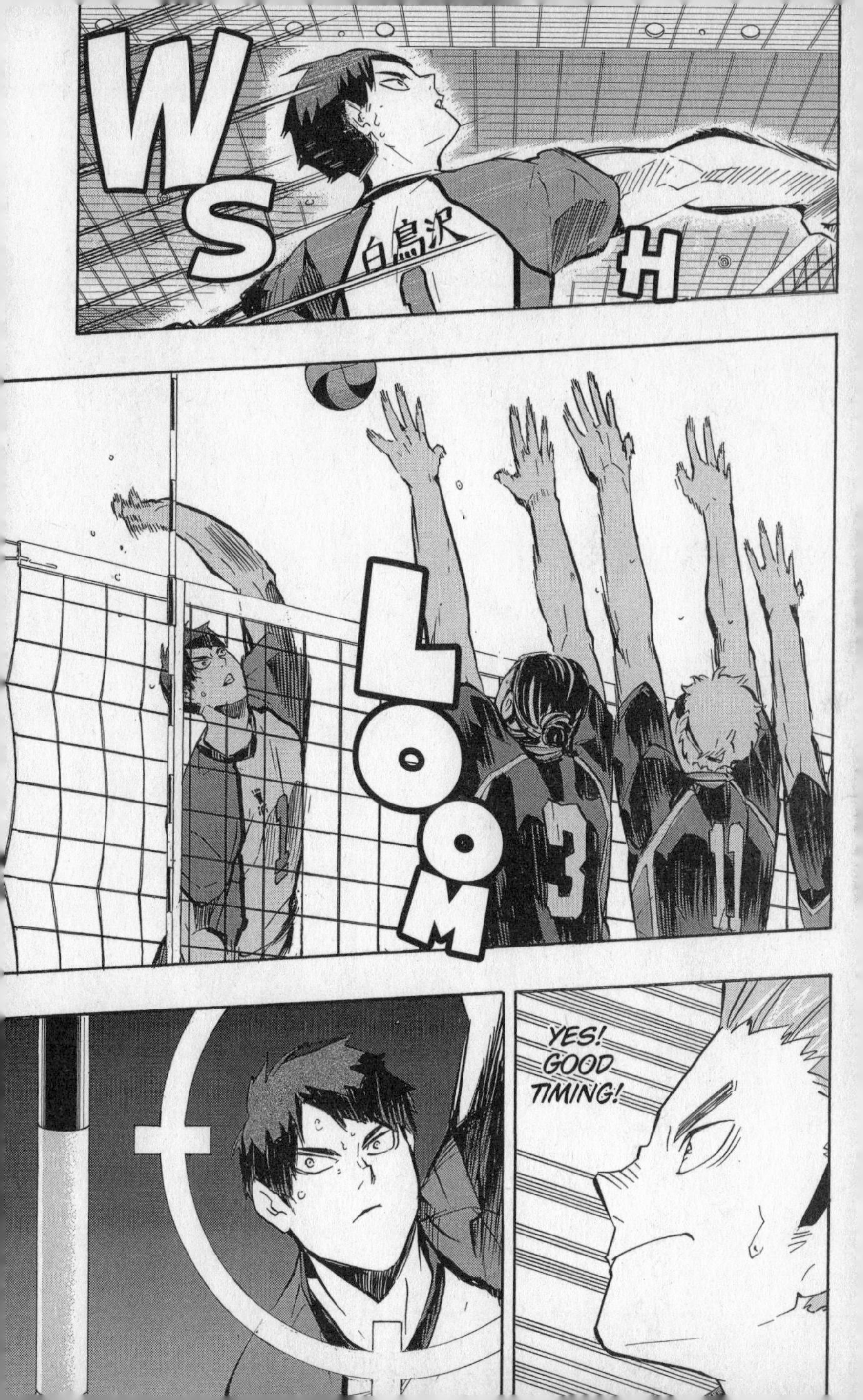
WSH
白鳥沢
LOOM
YES! GOOD TIMING!

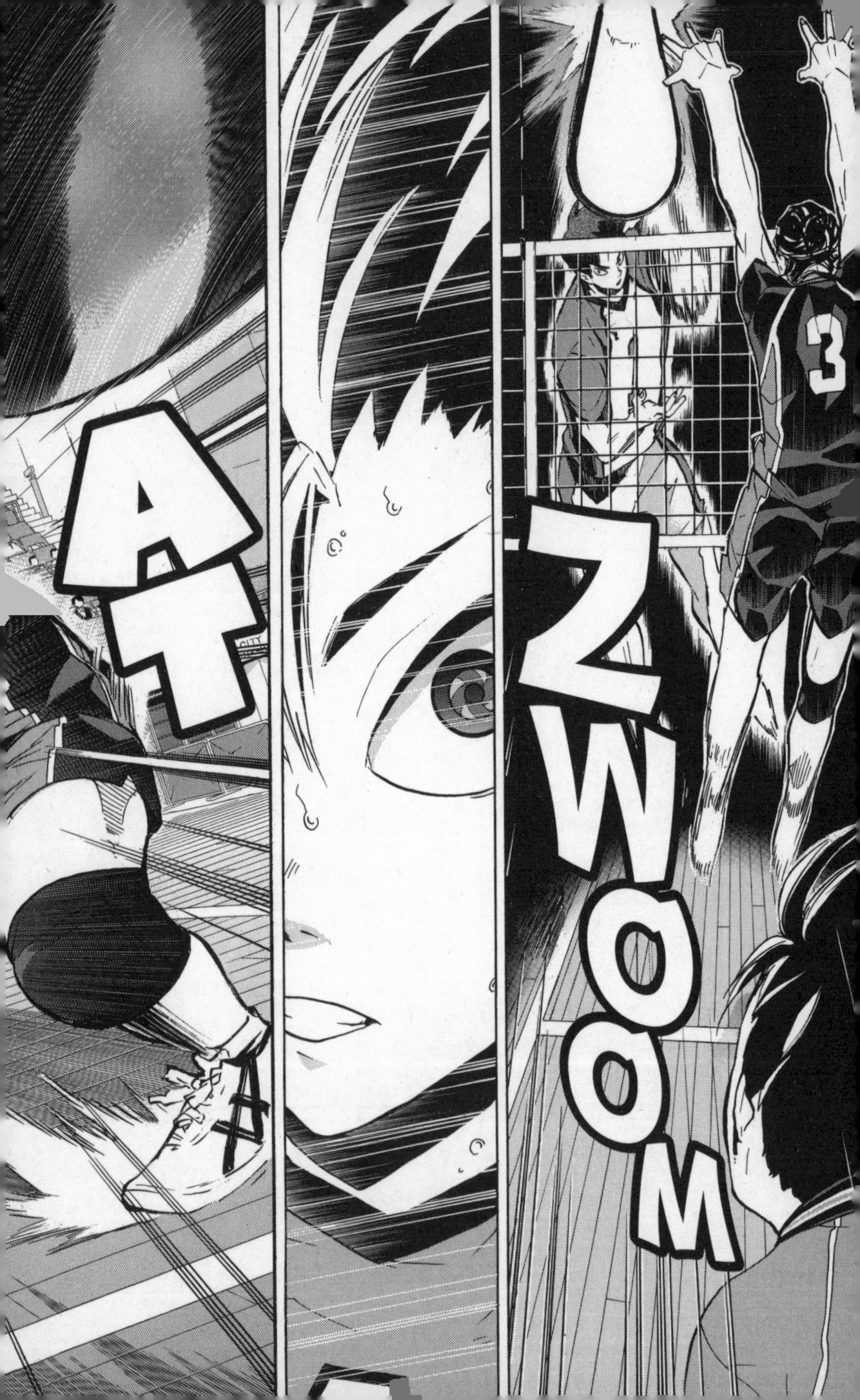
ZWOOM
AT

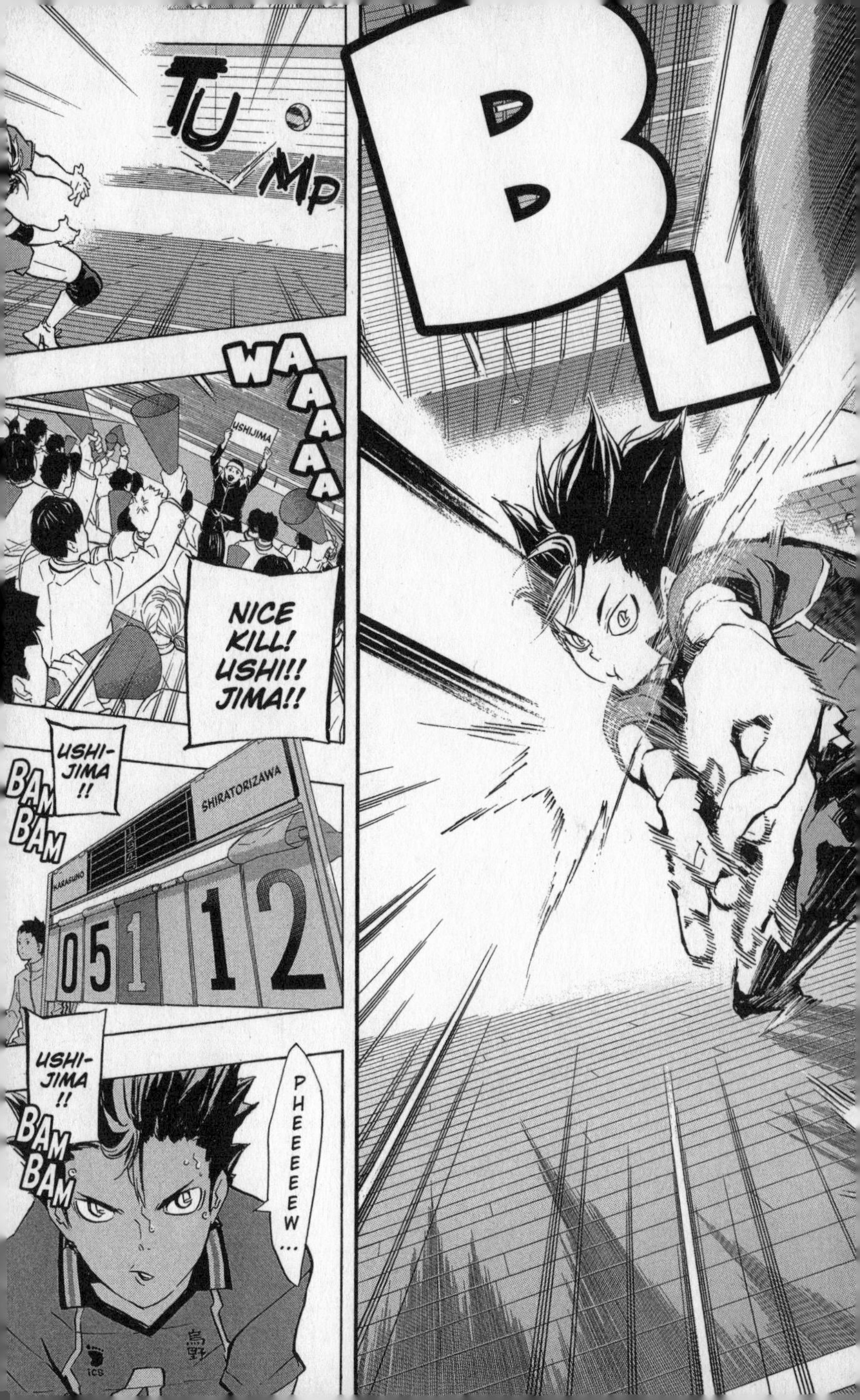
BL
TUMP
WAAAAAA
USHIJIMA
NICE KILL! USHI!! JIMA!!
USHI-JIMA!!
BAM BAM
SHIRATORIZAWA
KARASUNO
05 1 12
PHEEEEEW...
USHI-JIMA!!
BAM BAM

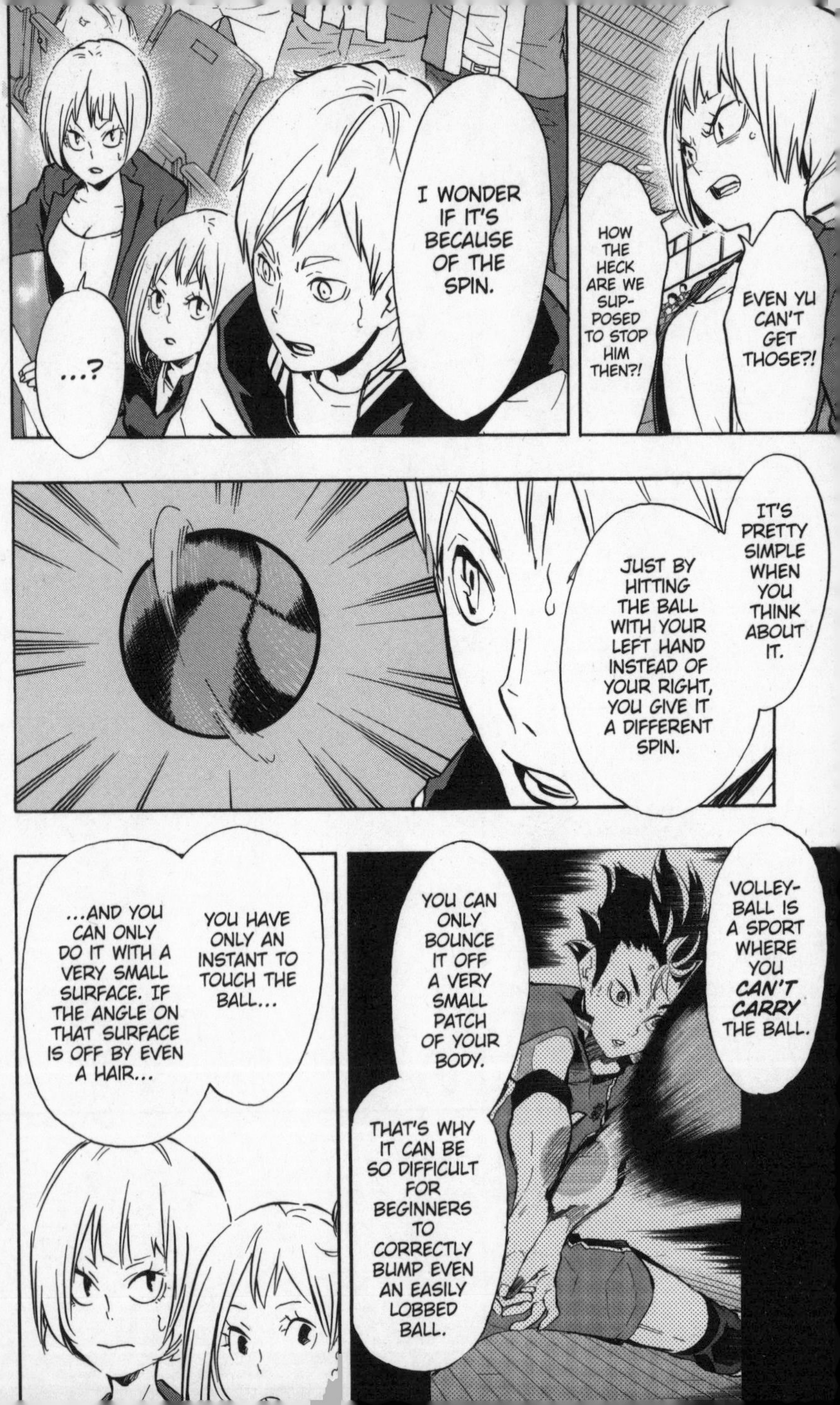
EVEN YU CAN'T GET THOSE?!
HOW THE HECK ARE WE SUP-POSED TO STOP HIM THEN?!
I WONDER IF IT'S BECAUSE OF THE SPIN.
...?
IT'S PRETTY SIMPLE WHEN YOU THINK ABOUT IT.
JUST BY HITTING THE BALL WITH YOUR LEFT HAND INSTEAD OF YOUR RIGHT, YOU GIVE IT A DIFFERENT SPIN.
VOLLEY-BALL IS A SPORT WHERE YOU *CAN'T CARRY* THE BALL.
YOU CAN ONLY BOUNCE IT OFF A VERY SMALL PATCH OF YOUR BODY.
THAT'S WHY IT CAN BE SO DIFFICULT FOR BEGINNERS TO CORRECTLY BUMP EVEN AN EASILY LOBBED BALL.
YOU HAVE ONLY AN INSTANT TO TOUCH THE BALL...
...AND YOU CAN ONLY DO IT WITH A VERY SMALL SURFACE. IF THE ANGLE ON THAT SURFACE IS OFF BY EVEN A HAIR...

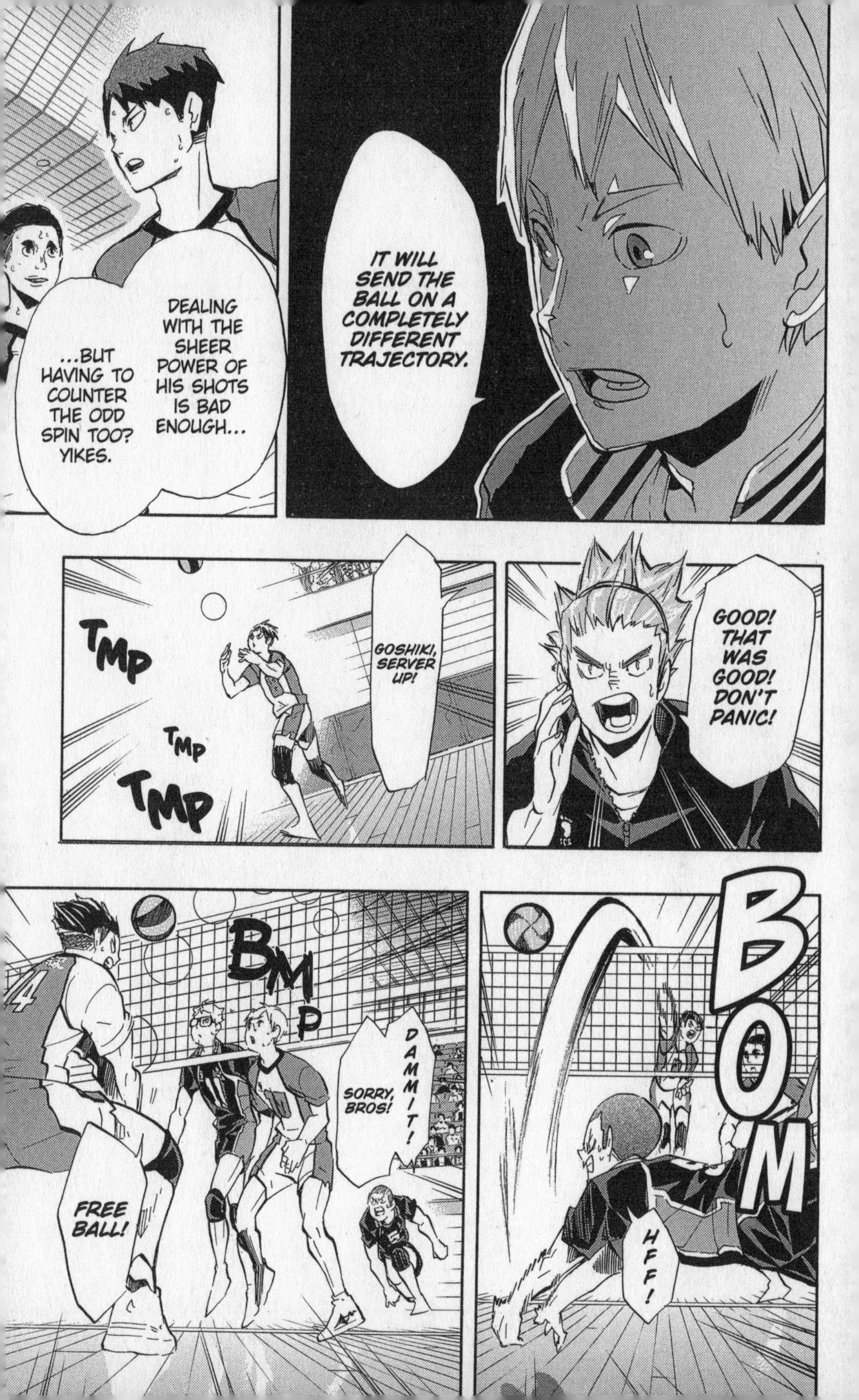
IT WILL SEND THE BALL ON A COMPLETELY DIFFERENT TRAJECTORY.
DEALING WITH THE SHEER POWER OF HIS SHOTS IS BAD ENOUGH...
...BUT HAVING TO COUNTER THE ODD SPIN TOO? YIKES.
GOOD! THAT WAS GOOD! DON'T PANIC!
GOSHIKI, SERVER UP!
TMP
TMP
TMP
BOM
HFF!
DAMMIT!
SORRY, BROS!
BMP
FREE BALL!

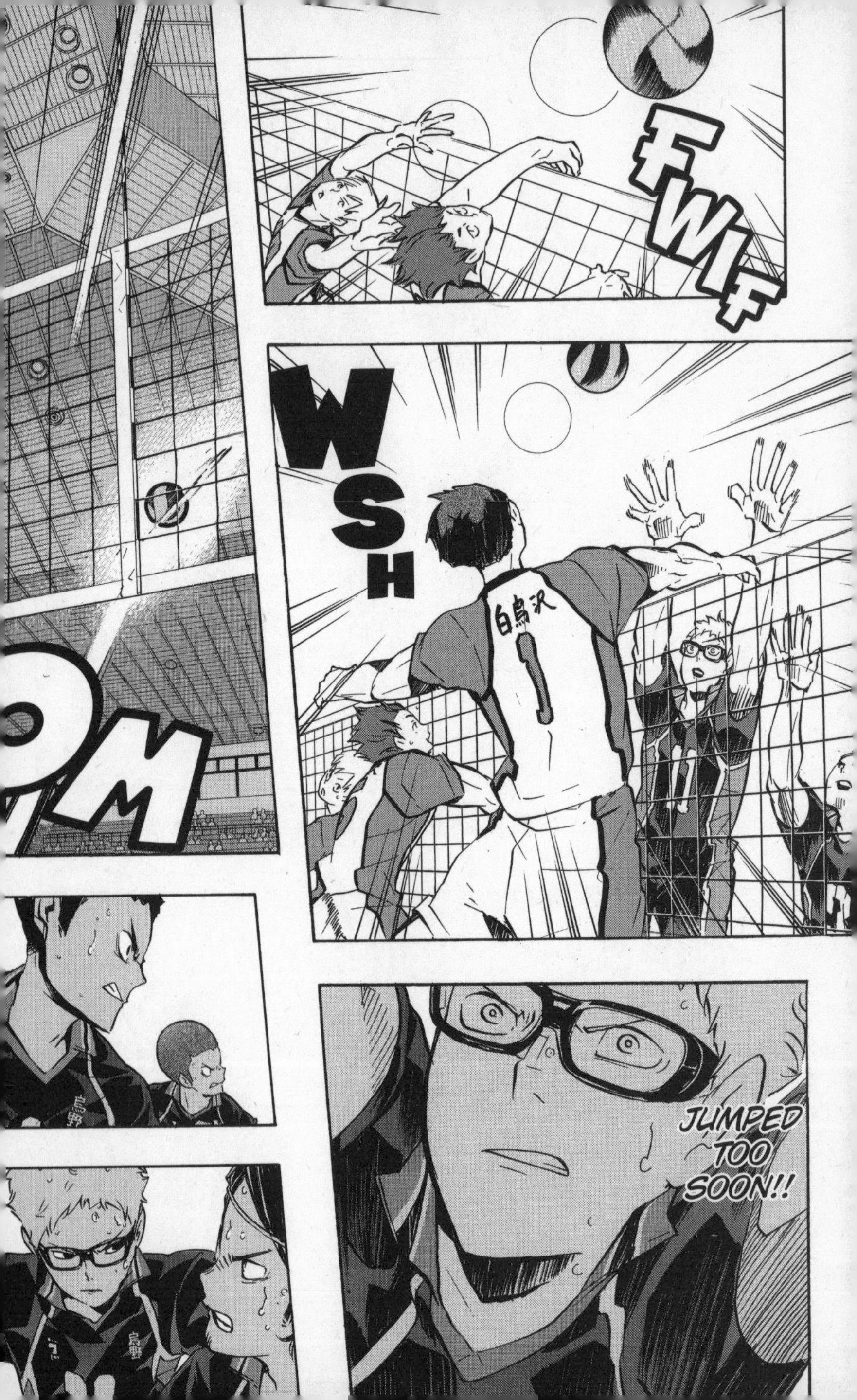
FWIF
WSH
白鳥沢
JUMPED TOO SOON!!

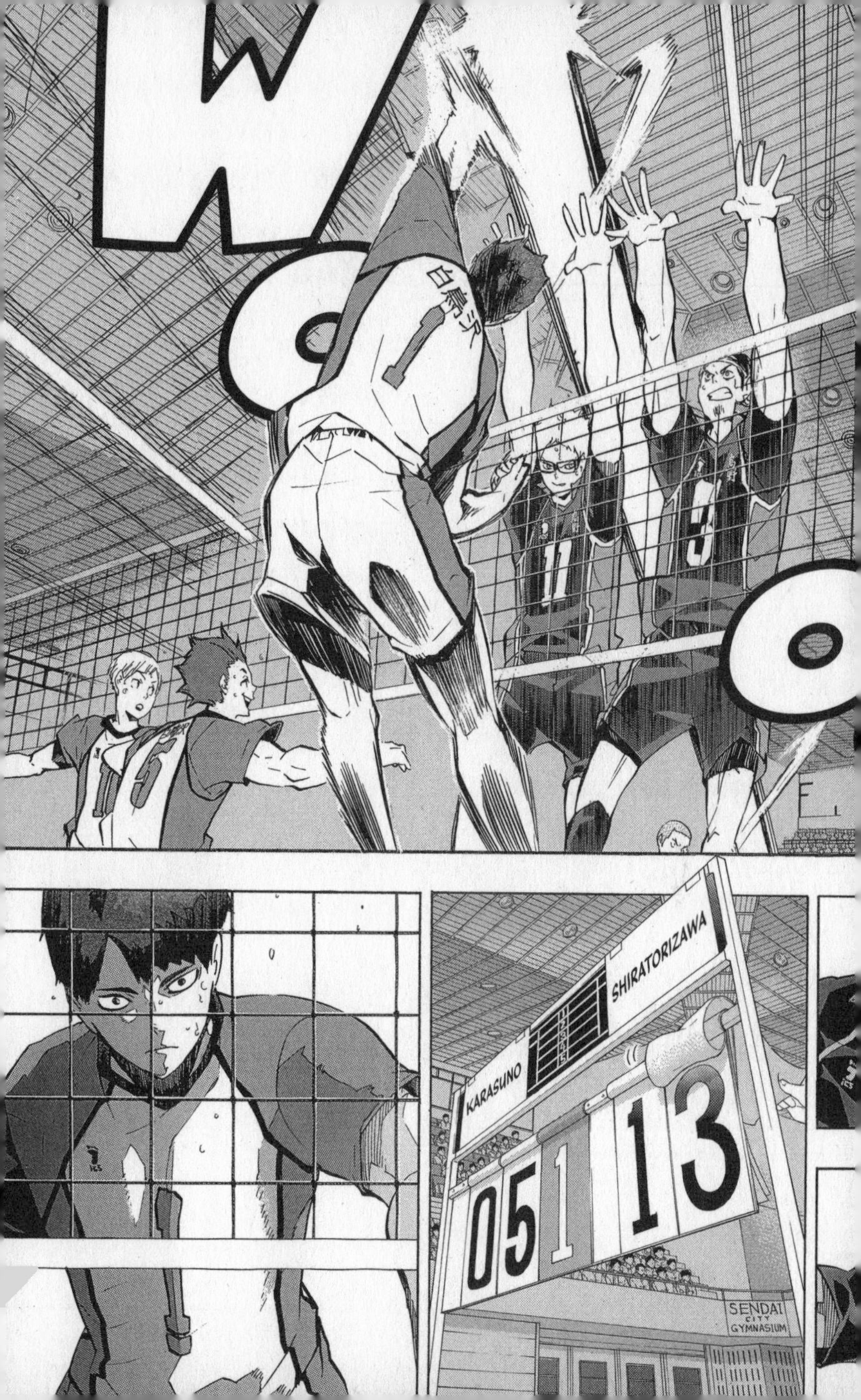
WOO
KARASUNO
SHIRATORIZAWA
05 1 13
SENDAI CITY GYMNASIUM

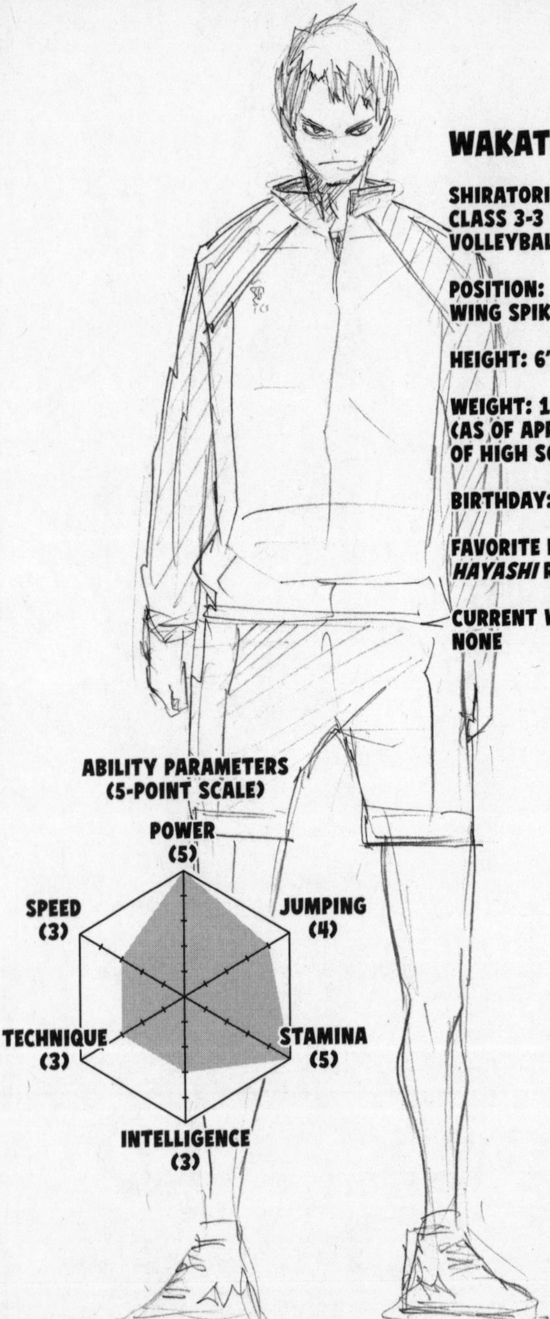
POWER (5)
JUMPING (4)
STAMINA (5)
INTELLIGENCE (3)
TECHNIQUE (3)
SPEED (3)

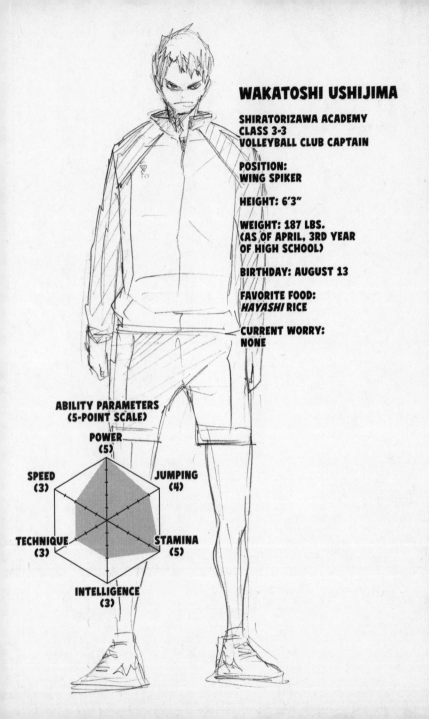

WAKATOSHI USHIJIMA

SHIRATORIZAWA ACADEMY
CLASS 3-3
VOLLEYBALL CLUB CAPTAIN

POSITION:
WING SPIKER

HEIGHT: 6'3"

WEIGHT: 187 LBS.
(AS OF APRIL, 3RD YEAR
OF HIGH SCHOOL)

BIRTHDAY: AUGUST 13

FAVORITE FOOD:
HAYASHI RICE

CURRENT WORRY:
NONE

ABILITY PARAMETERS
(5-POINT SCALE)

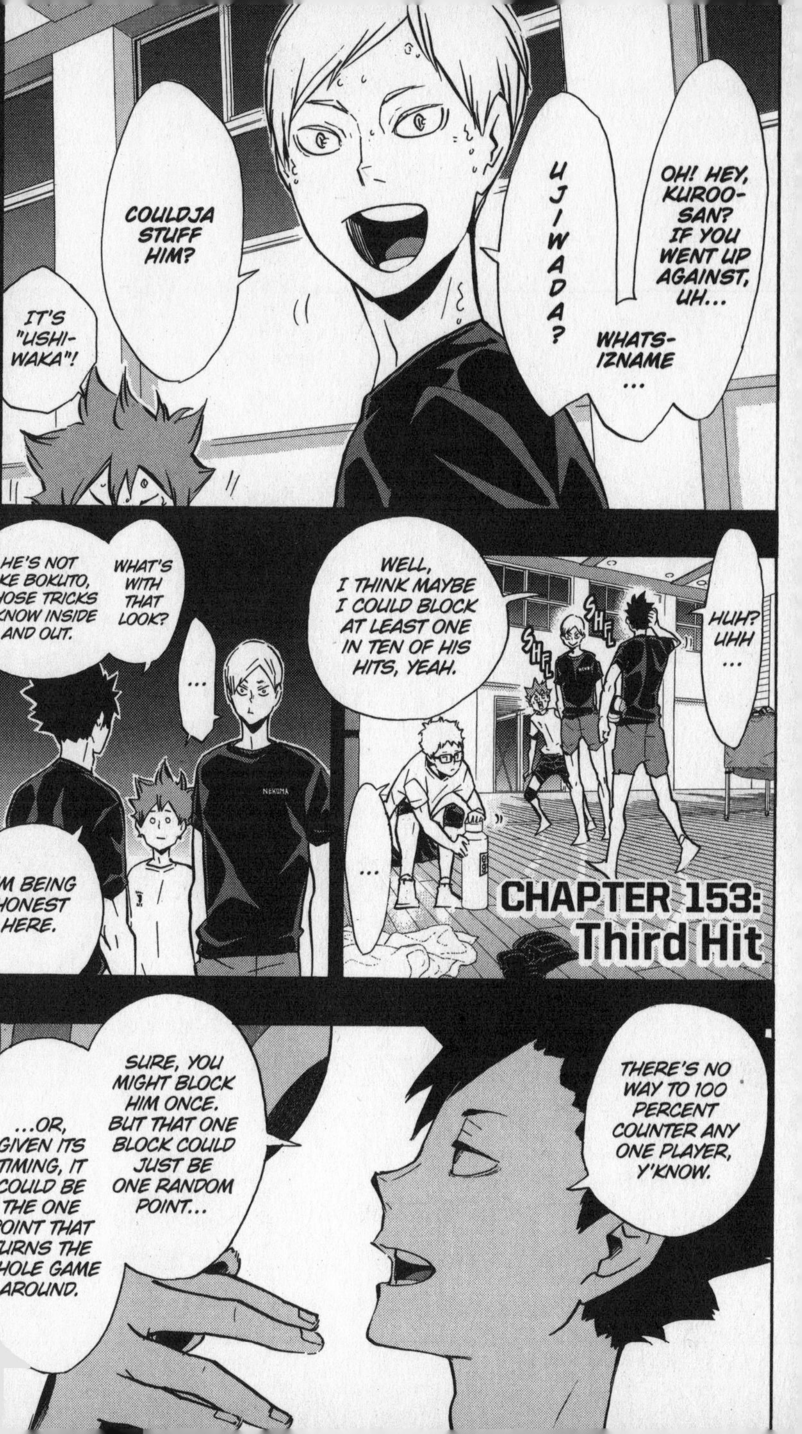
OH! HEY, KUROO-SAN? IF YOU WENT UP AGAINST, UH...
WHATS-IZNAME ...
UJIWADA?
COULDJA STUFF HIM?
IT'S "USHI-WAKA"!
HUH? UHH ...
WELL, I THINK MAYBE I COULD BLOCK AT LEAST ONE IN TEN OF HIS HITS, YEAH.
SHFL
SHFL
...
CHAPTER 153:
Third Hit
WHAT'S WITH THAT LOOK?
HE'S NOT LIKE BOKUTO, WHOSE TRICKS I KNOW INSIDE AND OUT.
...
I'M BEING HONEST HERE.
THERE'S NO WAY TO 100 PERCENT COUNTER ANY ONE PLAYER, Y'KNOW.
SURE, YOU MIGHT BLOCK HIM ONCE. BUT THAT ONE BLOCK COULD JUST BE ONE RANDOM POINT...
...OR, GIVEN ITS TIMING, IT COULD BE THE ONE POINT THAT TURNS THE WHOLE GAME AROUND.

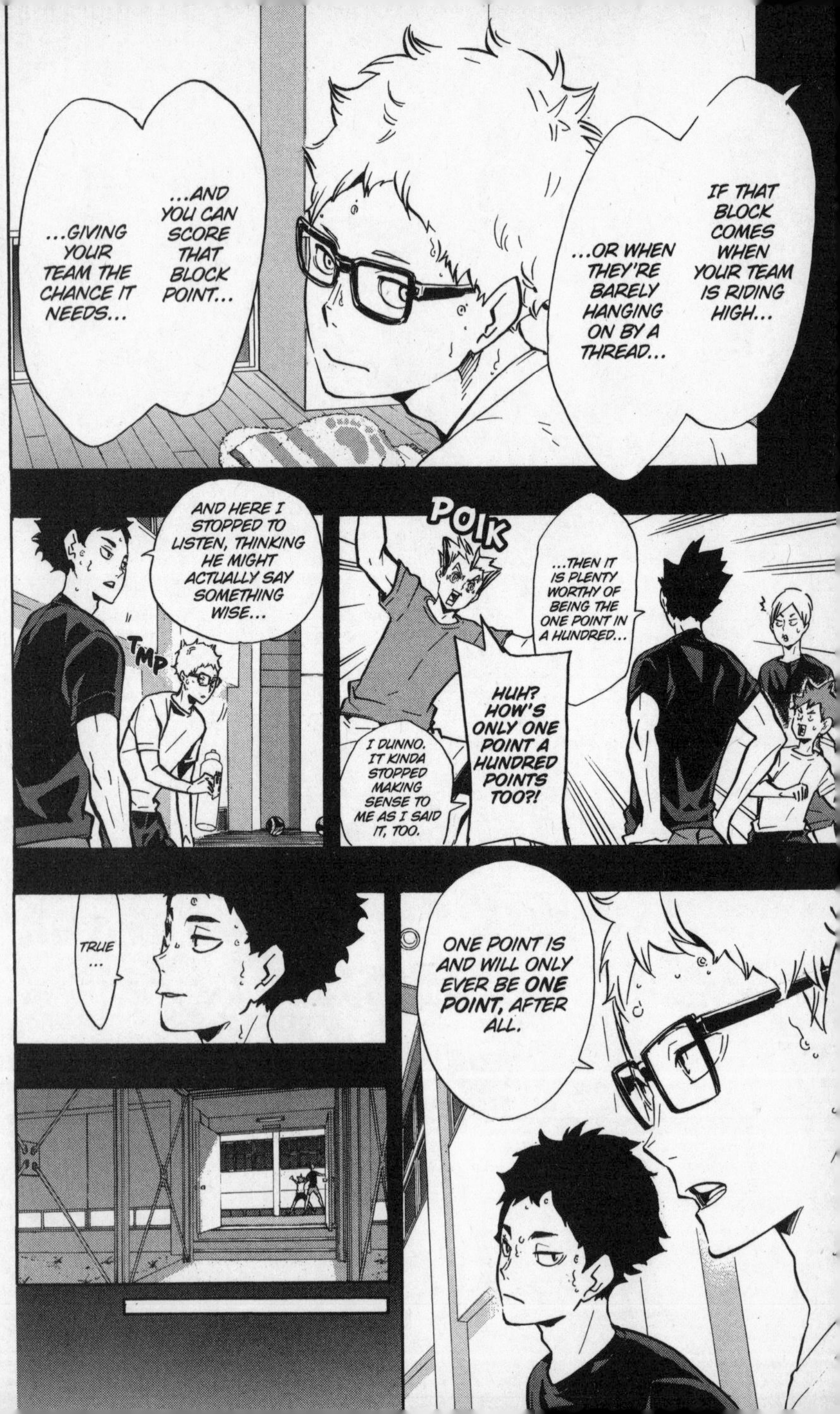
IF THAT BLOCK COMES WHEN YOUR TEAM IS RIDING HIGH...
...OR WHEN THEY'RE BARELY HANGING ON BY A THREAD...
...AND YOU CAN SCORE THAT BLOCK POINT...
...GIVING YOUR TEAM THE CHANCE IT NEEDS...
POIK
...THEN IT IS PLENTY WORTHY OF BEING THE ONE POINT IN A HUNDRED...
HUH? HOW'S ONLY ONE POINT A HUNDRED POINTS TOO?!
I DUNNO. IT KINDA STOPPED MAKING SENSE TO ME AS I SAID IT, TOO.
AND HERE I STOPPED TO LISTEN, THINKING HE MIGHT ACTUALLY SAY SOMETHING WISE...
TMP
ONE POINT IS AND WILL ONLY EVER BE ONE POINT, AFTER ALL.
TRUE...

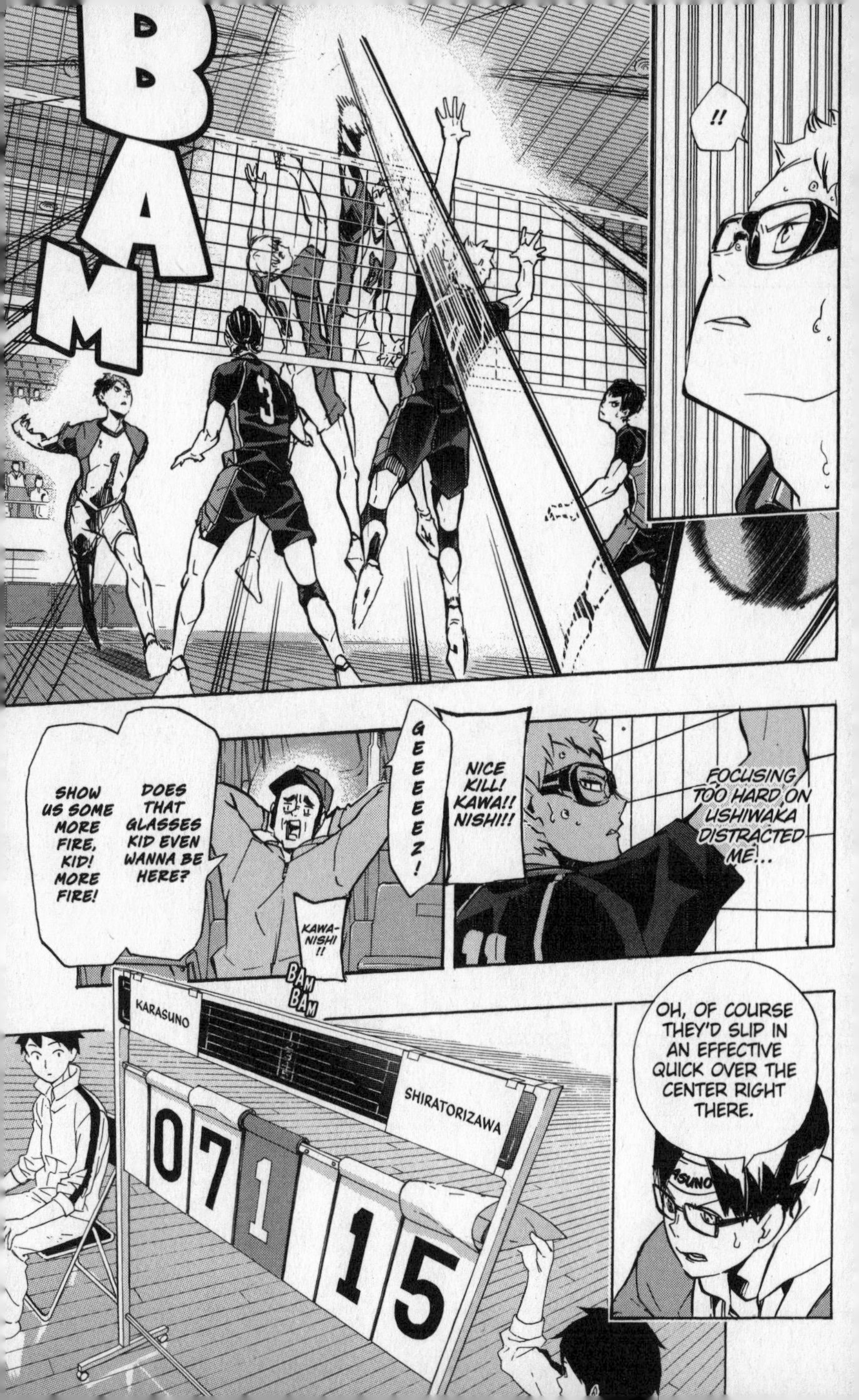
!!
BAM
FOCUSING TOO HARD ON USHIWAKA DISTRACTED ME...
NICE KILL! KAWA!! NISHI!!!
GEEEEEZ!
DOES THAT GLASSES KID EVEN WANNA BE HERE?
SHOW US SOME MORE FIRE, KID! MORE FIRE!
KAWA-NISHI !!
BAM BAM
OH, OF COURSE THEY'D SLIP IN AN EFFECTIVE QUICK OVER THE CENTER RIGHT THERE.
KARASUNO
SHIRATORIZAWA
07
1
15

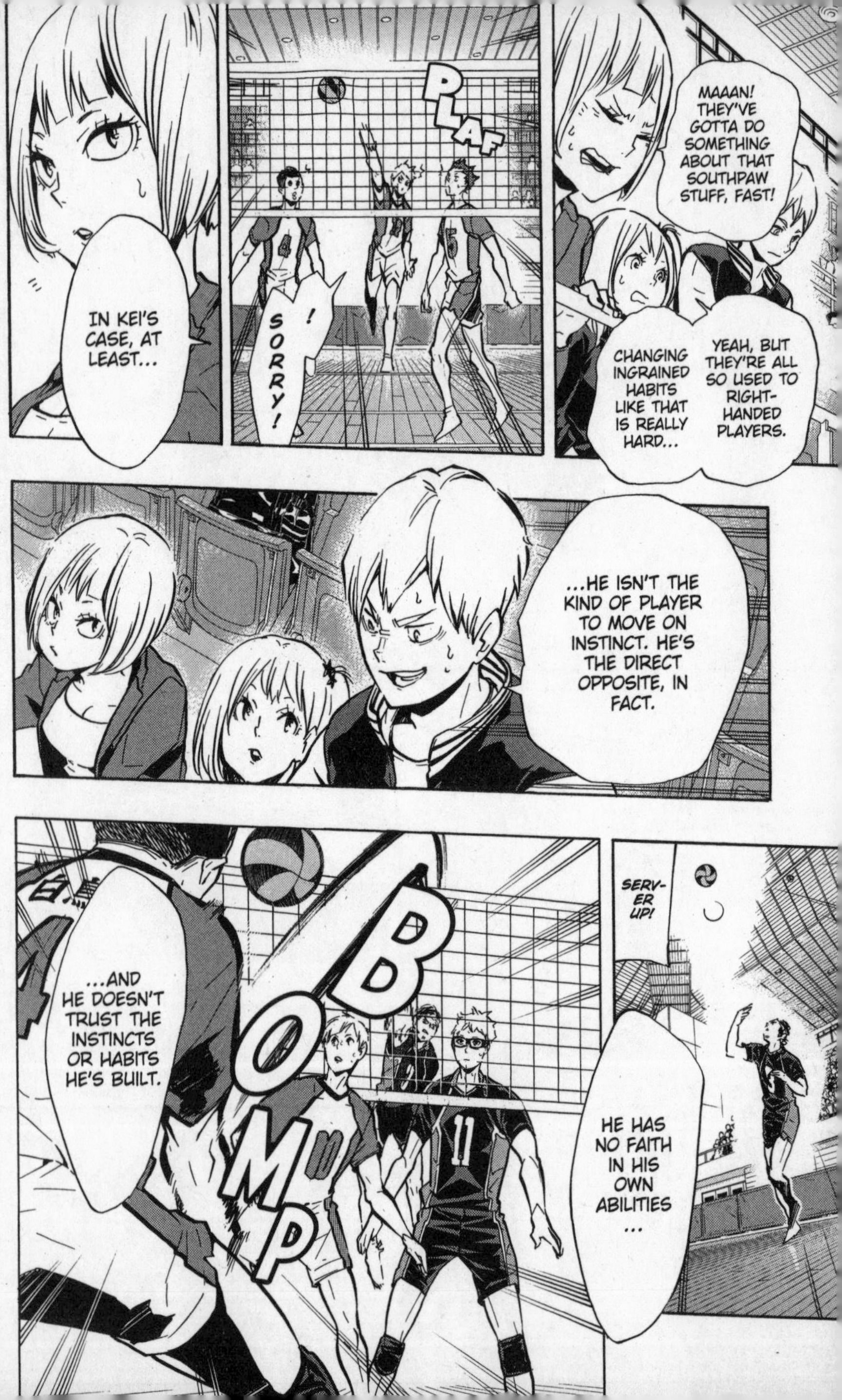
MAAAN! THEY'VE GOTTA DO SOMETHING ABOUT THAT SOUTHPAW STUFF, FAST!
YEAH, BUT THEY'RE ALL SO USED TO RIGHT-HANDED PLAYERS.
CHANGING INGRAINED HABITS LIKE THAT IS REALLY HARD...
PLAF
!
SORRY!
IN KEI'S CASE, AT LEAST...
...HE ISN'T THE KIND OF PLAYER TO MOVE ON INSTINCT. HE'S THE DIRECT OPPOSITE, IN FACT.
SERV-ER UP!
HE HAS NO FAITH IN HIS OWN ABILITIES...
BOMP
...AND HE DOESN'T TRUST THE INSTINCTS OR HABITS HE'S BUILT.

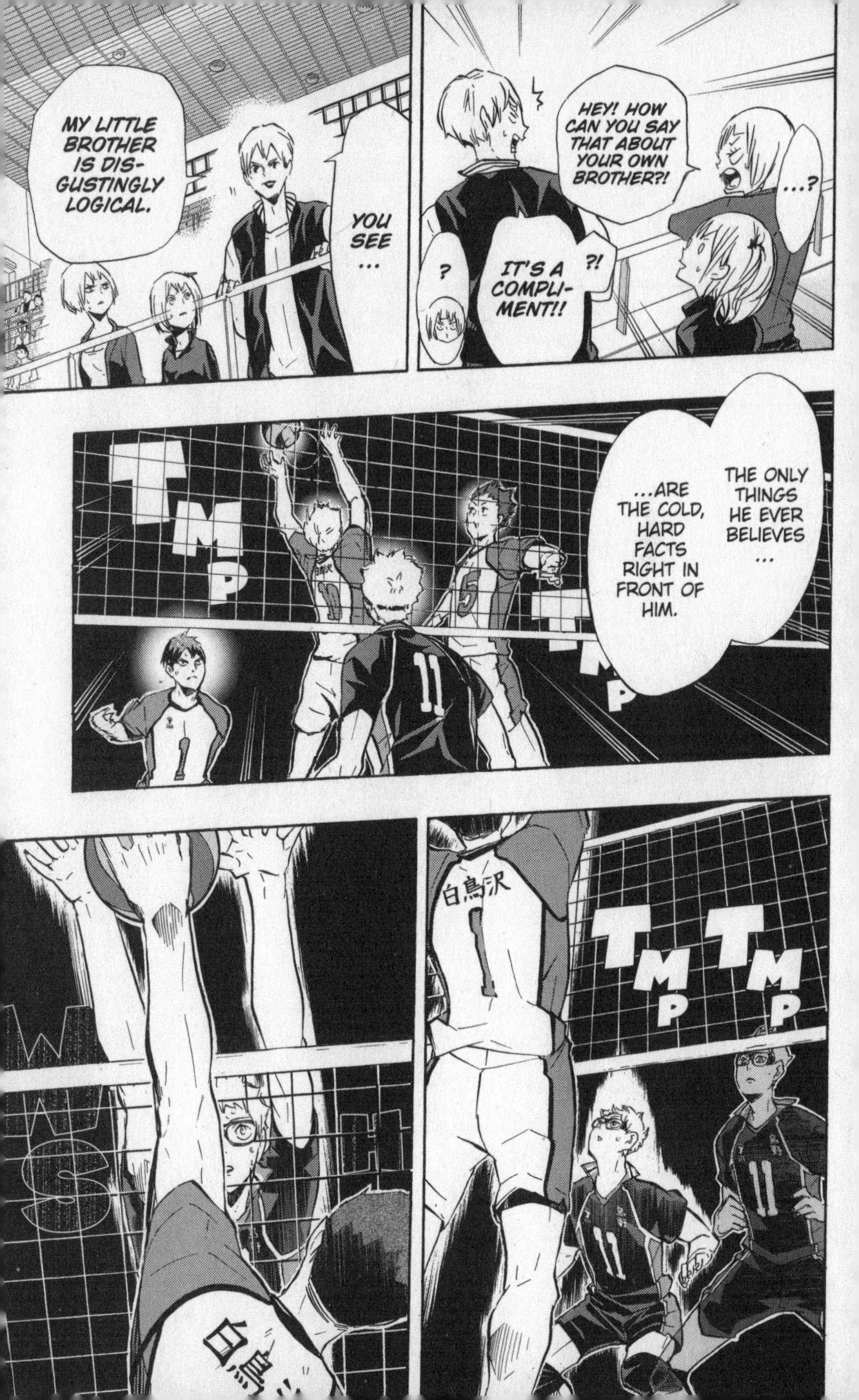
HEY! HOW CAN YOU SAY THAT ABOUT YOUR OWN BROTHER?!
...?
?!
IT'S A COMPLIMENT!!
?
YOU SEE ...
MY LITTLE BROTHER IS DIS-GUSTINGLY LOGICAL.
THE ONLY THINGS HE EVER BELIEVES ...
...ARE THE COLD, HARD FACTS RIGHT IN FRONT OF HIM.
TMP
TMP
TMP
TMP
白鳥沢

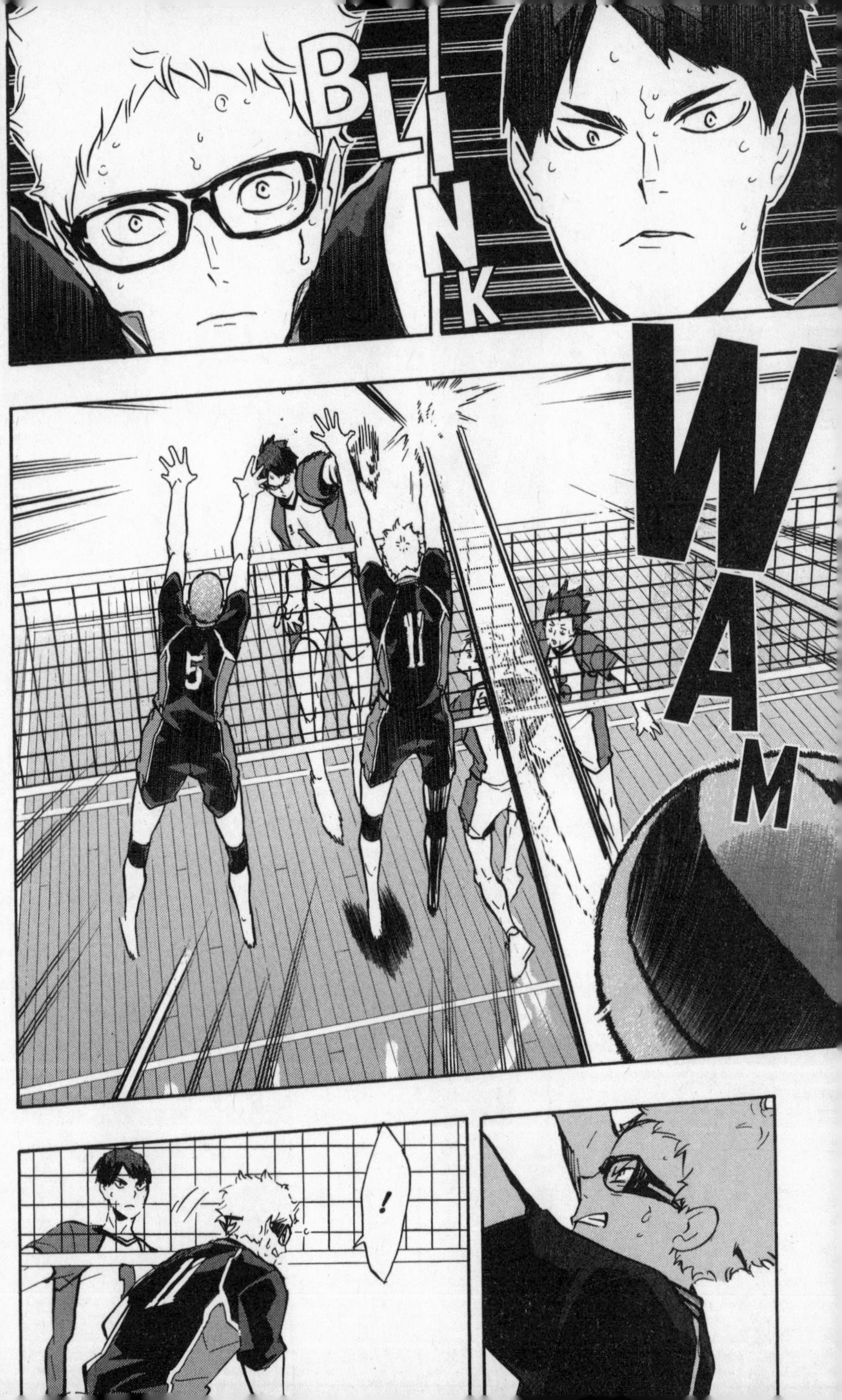
BLINK
WAM
!

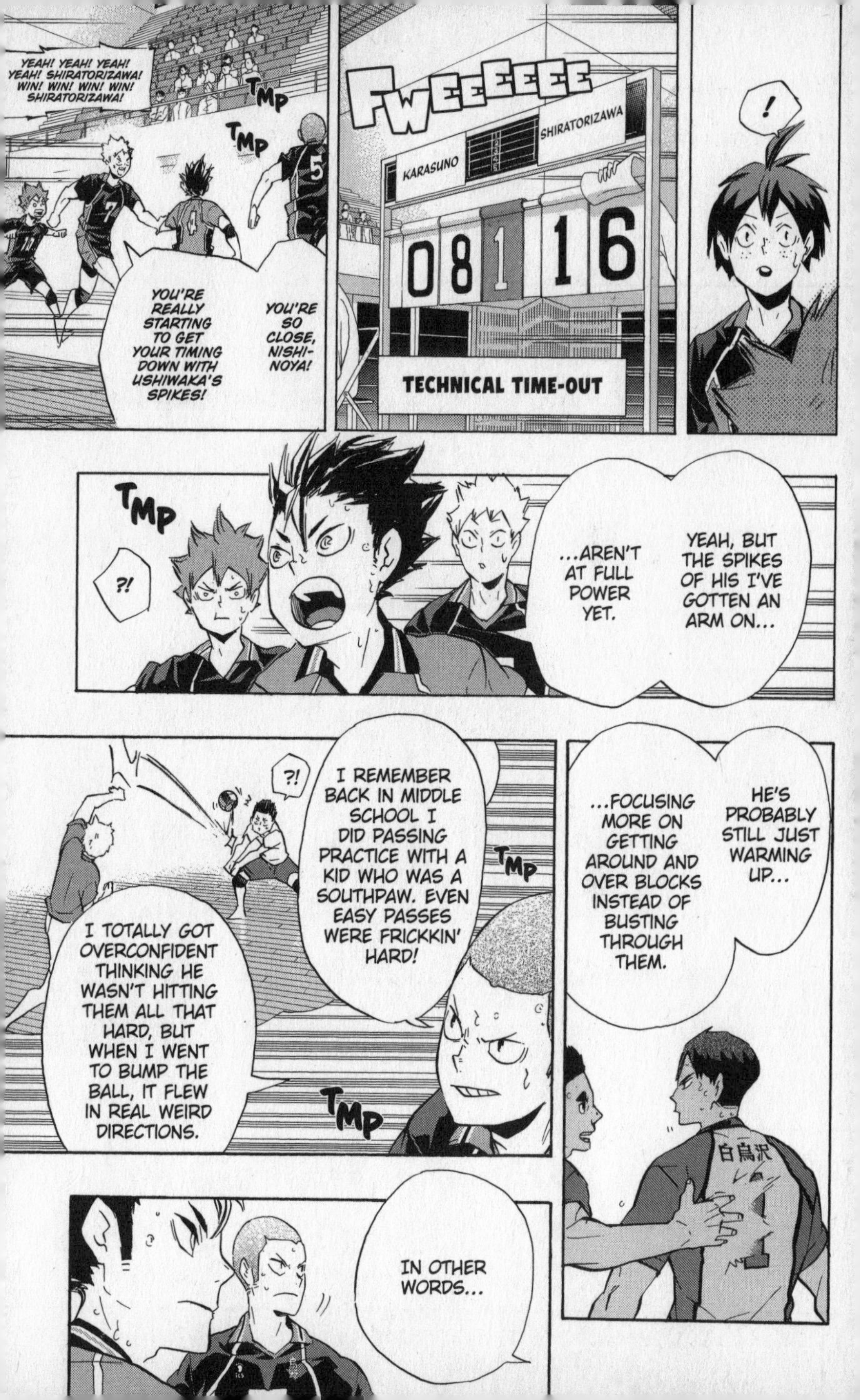
!
FWEEEEEE
SHIRATORIZAWA
KARASUNO
08 1 16
TECHNICAL TIME-OUT
YEAH! YEAH! YEAH! YEAH! SHIRATORIZAWA! WIN! WIN! WIN! WIN! SHIRATORIZAWA!
TMP
TMP
YOU'RE SO CLOSE, NISHI-NOYA!
YOU'RE REALLY STARTING TO GET YOUR TIMING DOWN WITH USHIWAKA'S SPIKES!
YEAH, BUT THE SPIKES OF HIS I'VE GOTTEN AN ARM ON...
...AREN'T AT FULL POWER YET.
?!
TMP
HE'S PROBABLY STILL JUST WARMING UP...
...FOCUSING MORE ON GETTING AROUND AND OVER BLOCKS INSTEAD OF BUSTING THROUGH THEM.
白鳥沢
I REMEMBER BACK IN MIDDLE SCHOOL I DID PASSING PRACTICE WITH A KID WHO WAS A SOUTHPAW. EVEN EASY PASSES WERE FRICKIN' HARD!
?!
TMP
I TOTALLY GOT OVERCONFIDENT THINKING HE WASN'T HITTING THEM ALL THAT HARD, BUT WHEN I WENT TO BUMP THE BALL, IT FLEW IN REAL WEIRD DIRECTIONS.
TMP
IN OTHER WORDS...

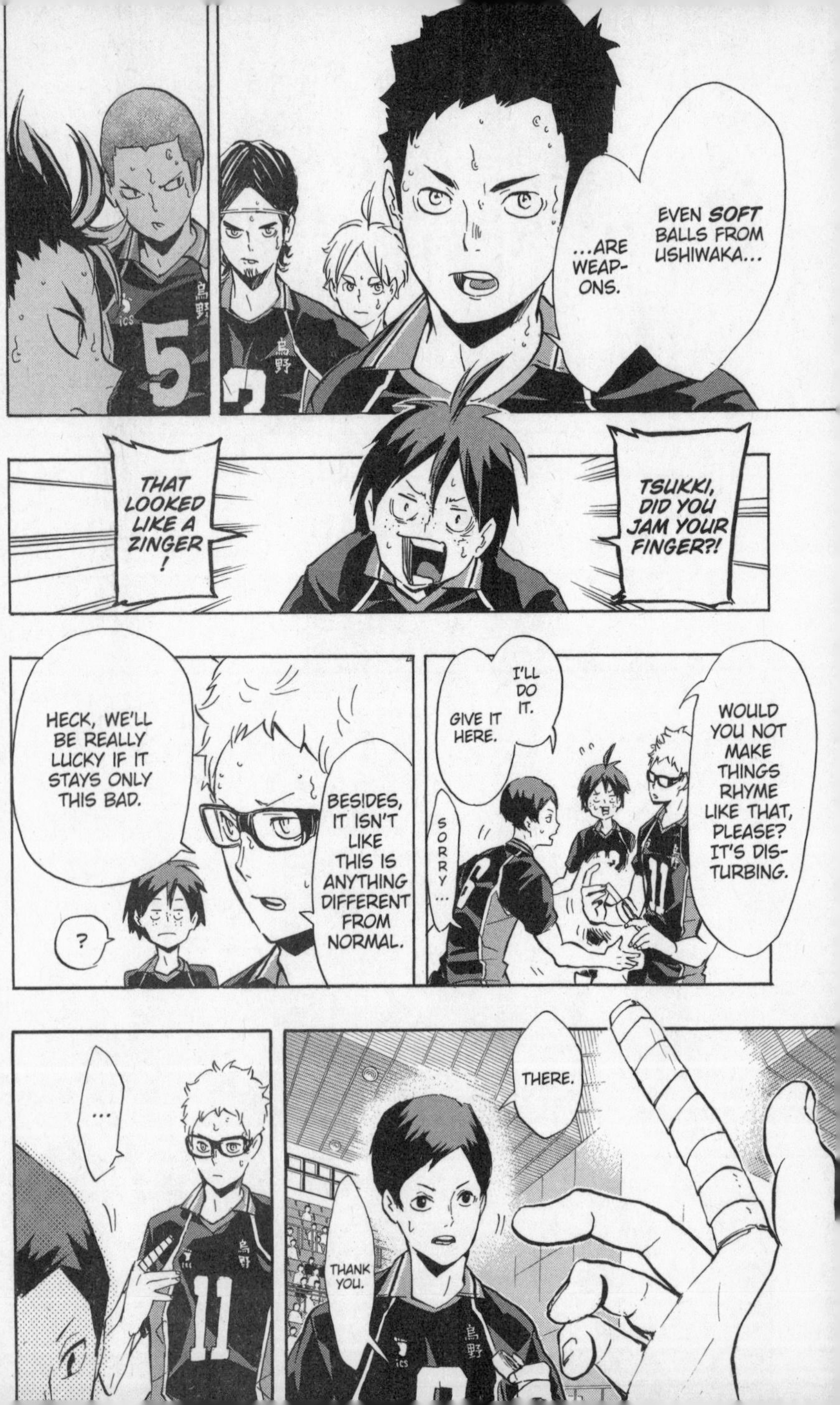
EVEN SOFT BALLS FROM USHIWAKA...
...ARE WEAPONS.
TSUKKI, DID YOU JAM YOUR FINGER?!
THAT LOOKED LIKE A ZINGER!
WOULD YOU NOT MAKE THINGS RHYME LIKE THAT, PLEASE? IT'S DISTURBING.
SORRY...
I'LL DO IT. GIVE IT HERE.
BESIDES, IT ISN'T LIKE THIS IS ANYTHING DIFFERENT FROM NORMAL.
HECK, WE'LL BE REALLY LUCKY IF IT STAYS ONLY THIS BAD.
?
THERE.
THANK YOU.
...

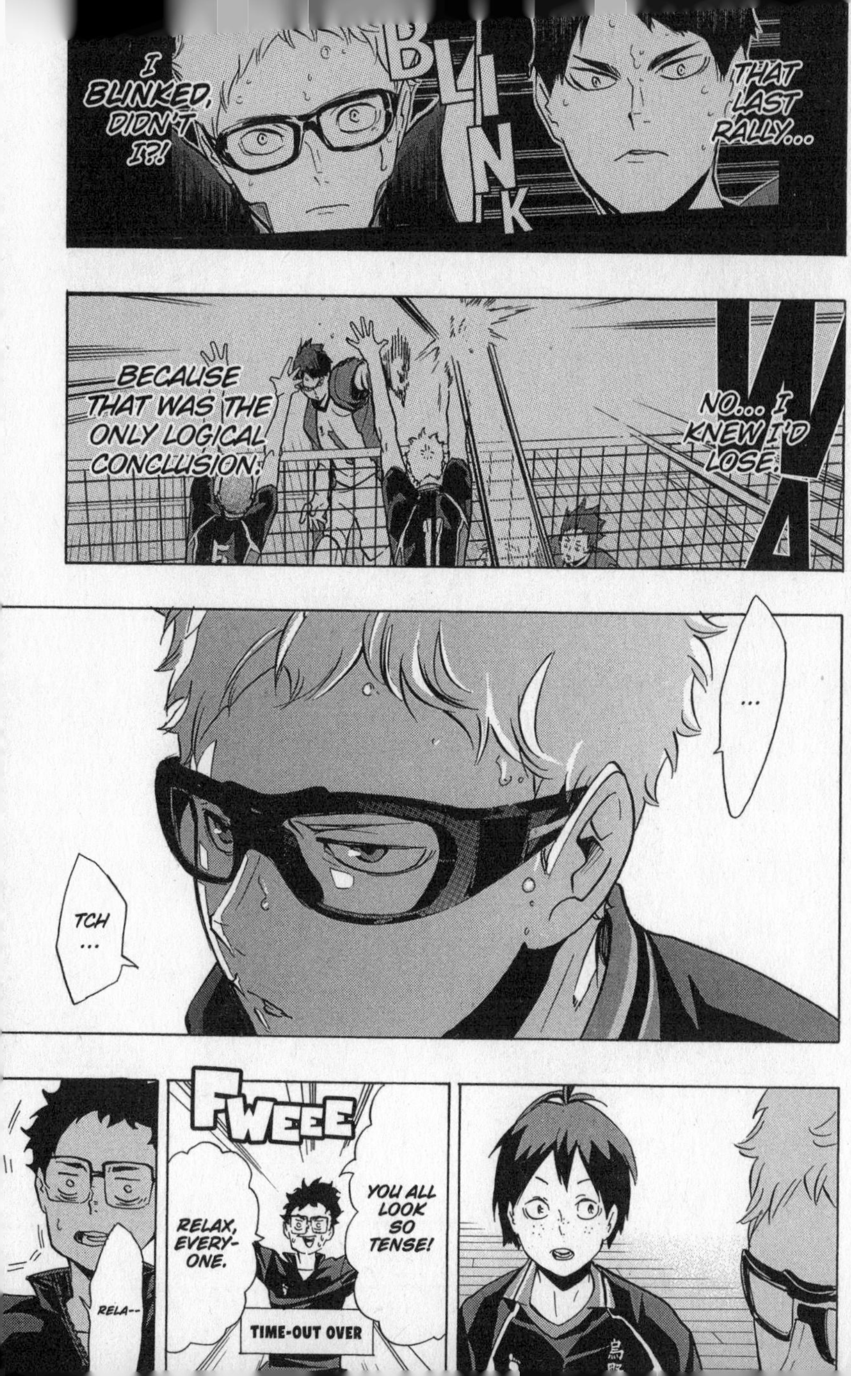
THAT LAST RALLY...
BLINK
I BLINKED, DIDN'T I?!
NO... I KNEW I'D LOSE.
BECAUSE THAT WAS THE ONLY LOGICAL CONCLUSION.
...
TCH...
FWEEE
YOU ALL LOOK SO TENSE!
RELAX, EVERY-ONE.
TIME-OUT OVER
RELA--

BAM
BABAMBAM
BAMBA
BAMBAM

SERVER UP!

TAM

TAM

PFFFFFFF...

OH DEAR ...

AZUMANE	SAWAMURA	HINATA (NOYA)	
TSUKISHIMA	KAGEYAMA	TANAKA	

NET

SHIRABU	TENDO	OHIRA
GOSHIKI	KAWANISHI (YAMAGATA)	USHIJIMA

SERVE

FWEEEEEE

IT'S HIS BRUTE STRENGTH THAT'S THE ISSUE. AS ALWAYS.

HE DOESN'T HAVE OIKAWA'S MONSTER-GRADE ACCURACY OR CONTROL, NO...

LIKE THERE'D BE *TWO* HIGH SCHOOLERS LIKE HIM... UGH, DON'T SCARE ME.

OUT!!

WE WERE LUCKY THAT THE FIRST TIME HIS SERVE CAME AROUND IT WENT OUT.

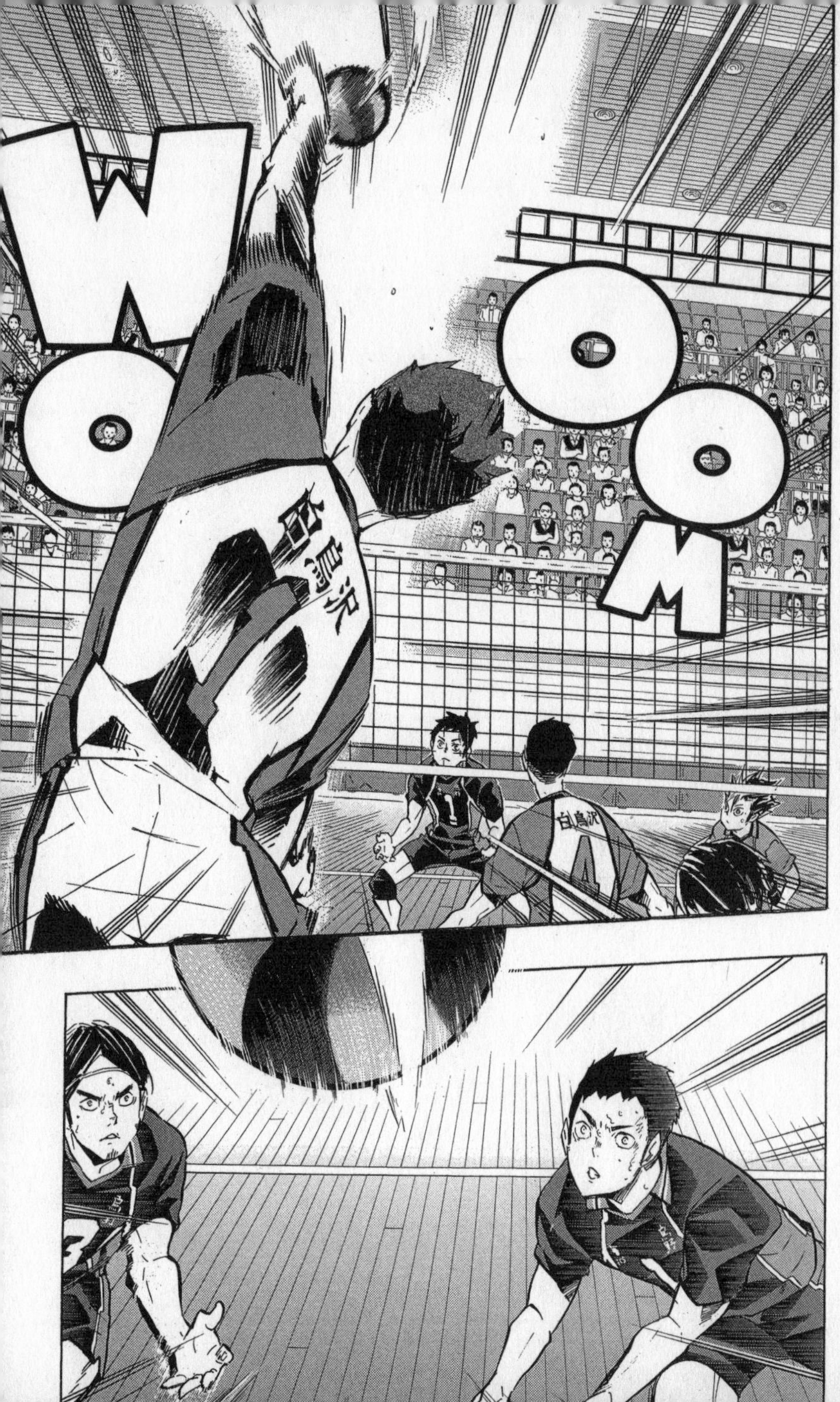
WOOOM

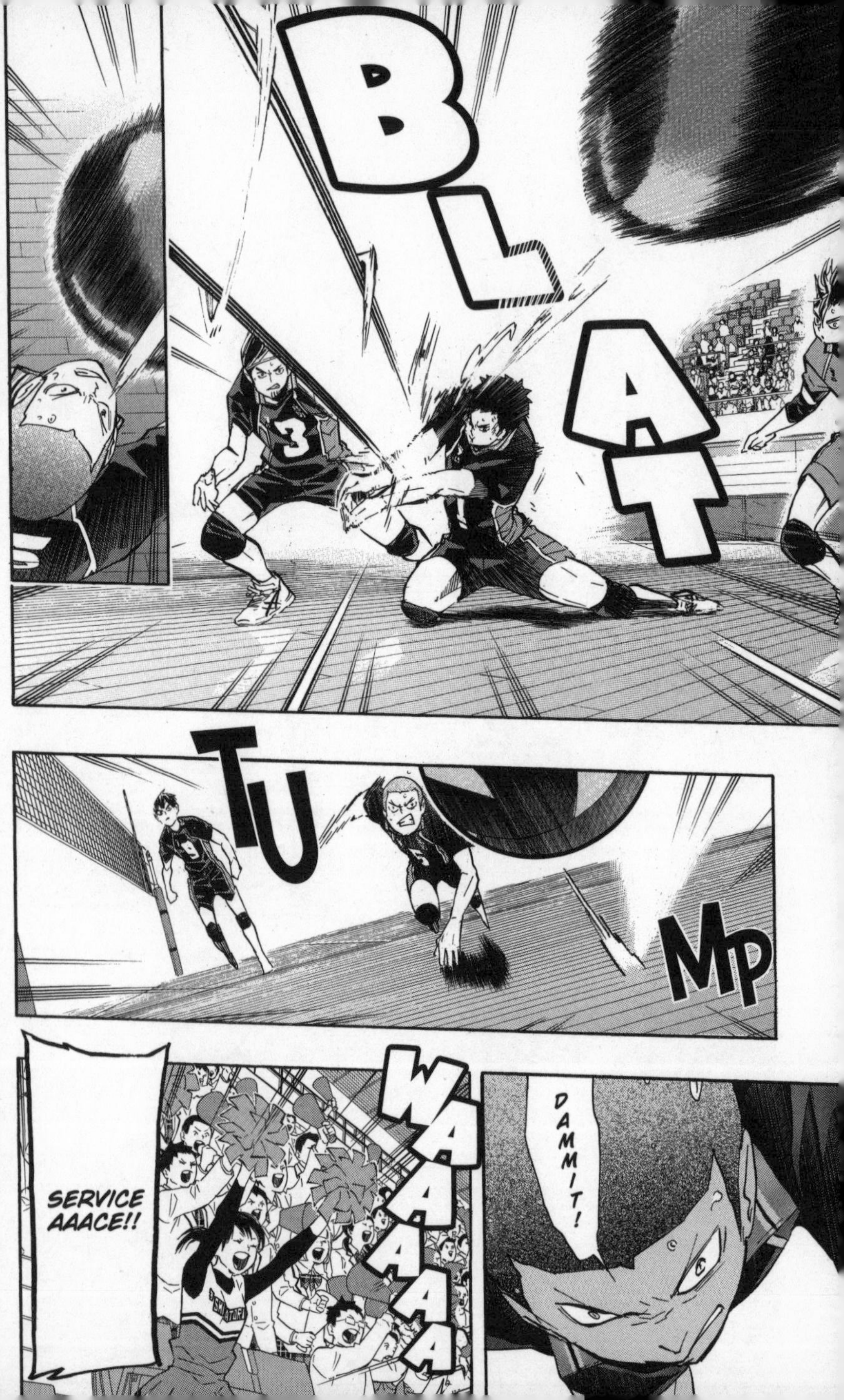
BLAT
TUMP
DAMMIT!
WAAAAAA
SERVICE AAACE!!

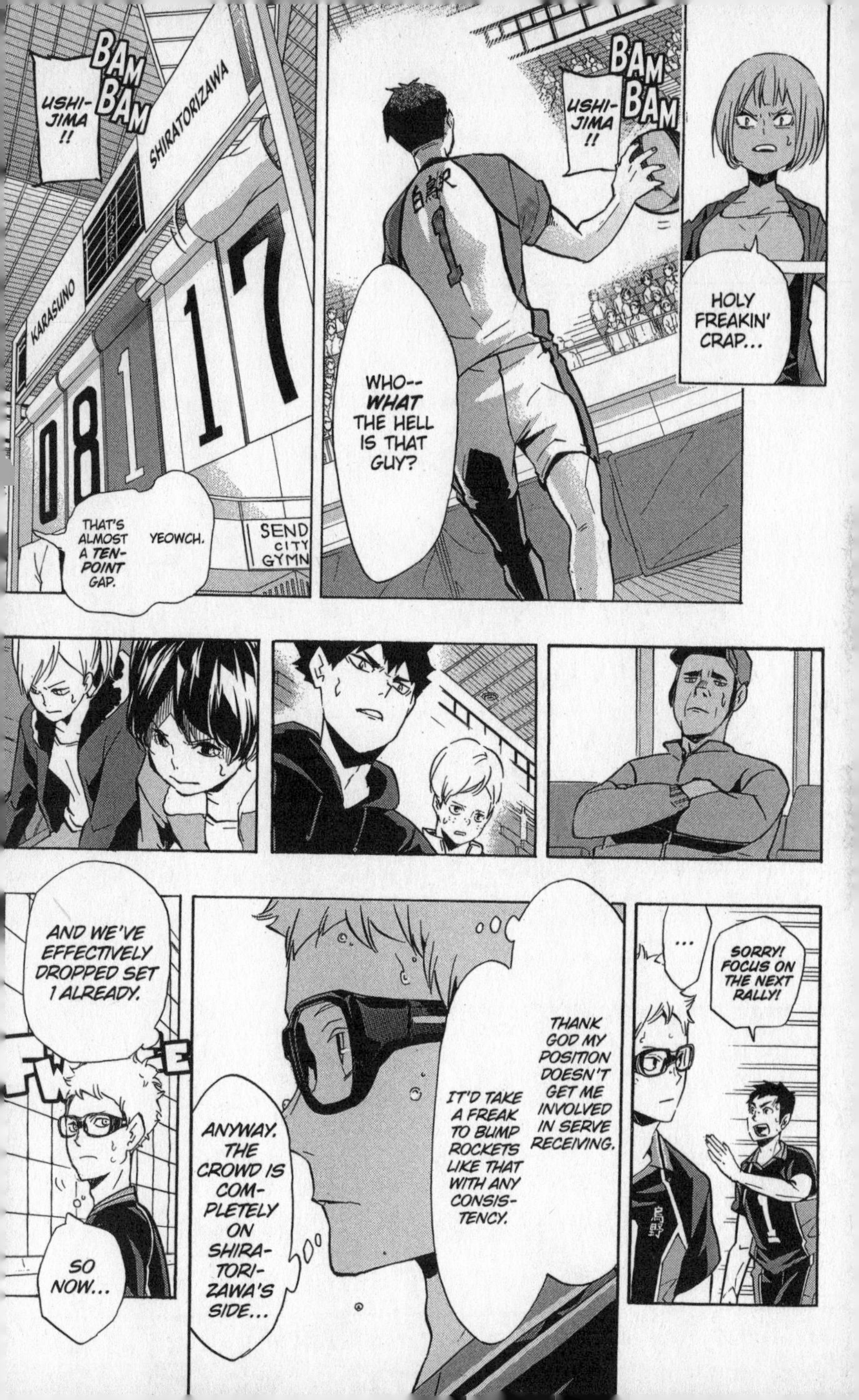
HOLY FREAKIN' CRAP...
BAM BAM
USHI-JIMA !!
WHO-- ***WHAT*** THE HELL IS THAT GUY?
BAM BAM
USHI-JIMA !!
SHIRATORIZAWA
KARASUNO
08 11 17
YEOWCH.
THAT'S ALMOST A *TEN-POINT* GAP.
SEND CITY GYMN
SORRY! FOCUS ON THE NEXT RALLY!
...
THANK GOD MY POSITION DOESN'T GET ME INVOLVED IN SERVE RECEIVING.
IT'D TAKE A FREAK TO BUMP ROCKETS LIKE THAT WITH ANY CONSISTENCY.
ANYWAY. THE CROWD IS COMPLETELY ON SHIRATORIZAWA'S SIDE...
AND WE'VE EFFECTIVELY DROPPED SET 1 ALREADY.
FWEE
SO NOW...

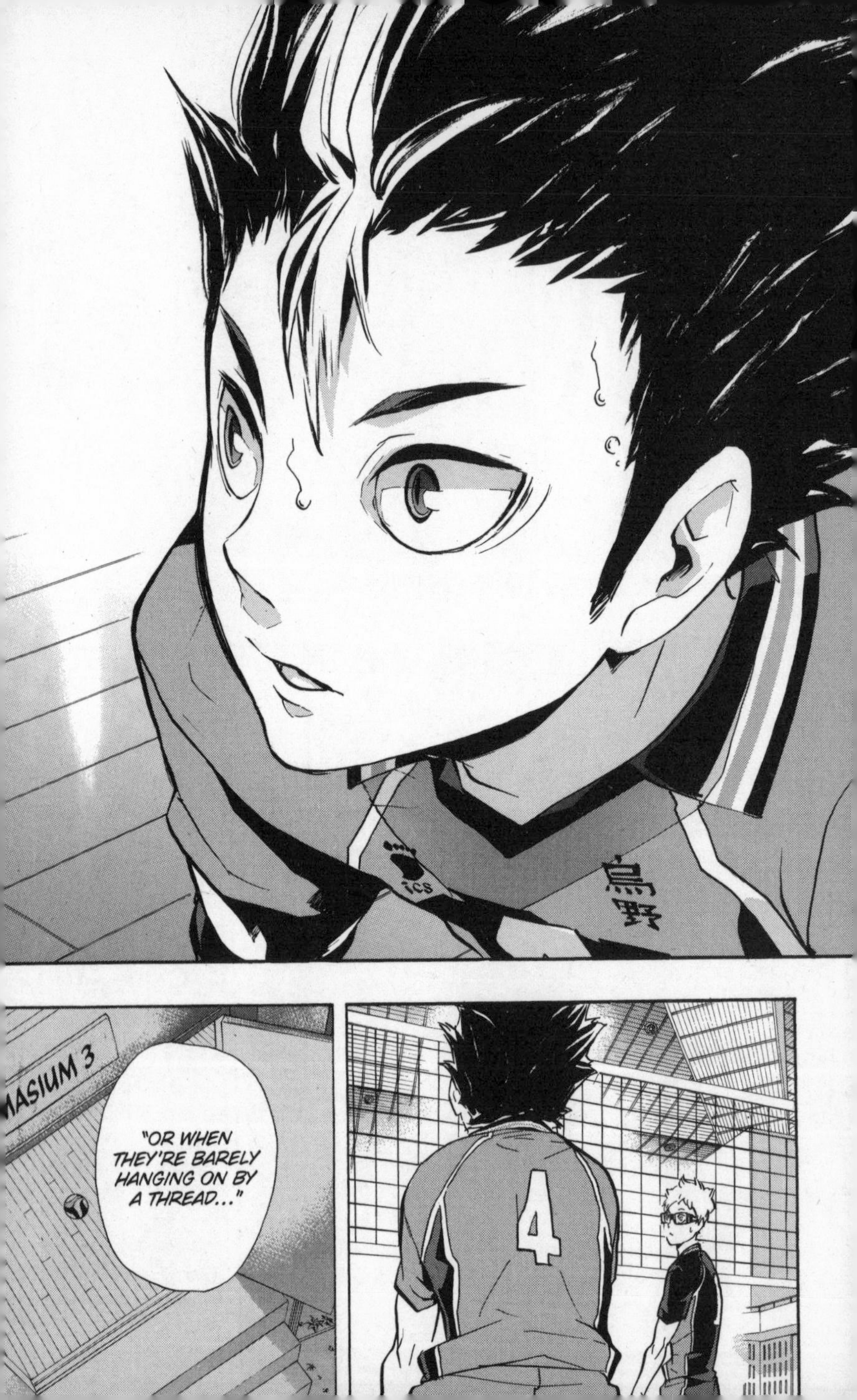
MASIUM 3
"OR WHEN THEY'RE BARELY HANGING ON BY A THREAD..."

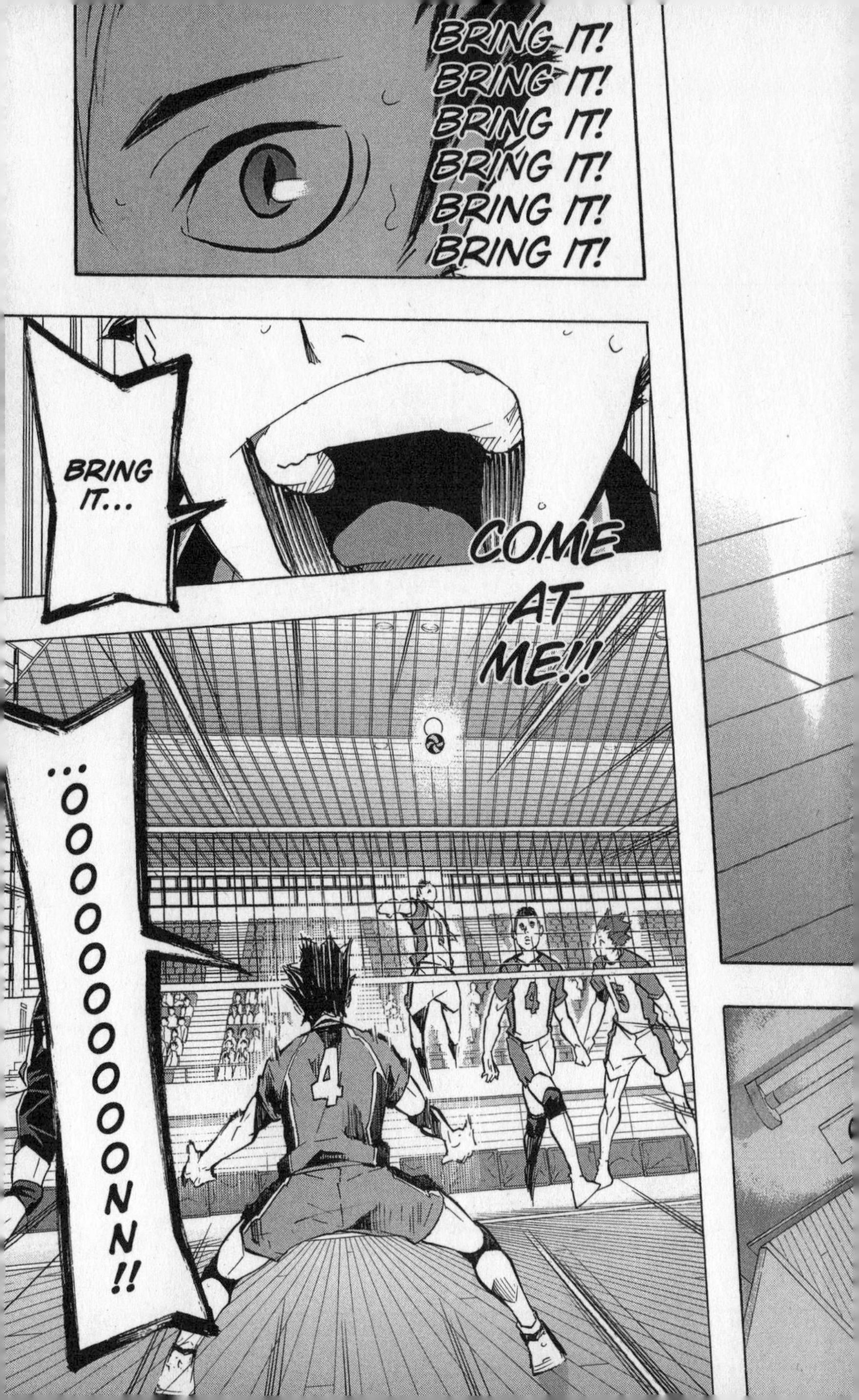
BRING IT! BRING IT! BRING IT! BRING IT! BRING IT! BRING IT!
COME AT ME!!
BRING IT...
...OOOOOOOOOOONN!!

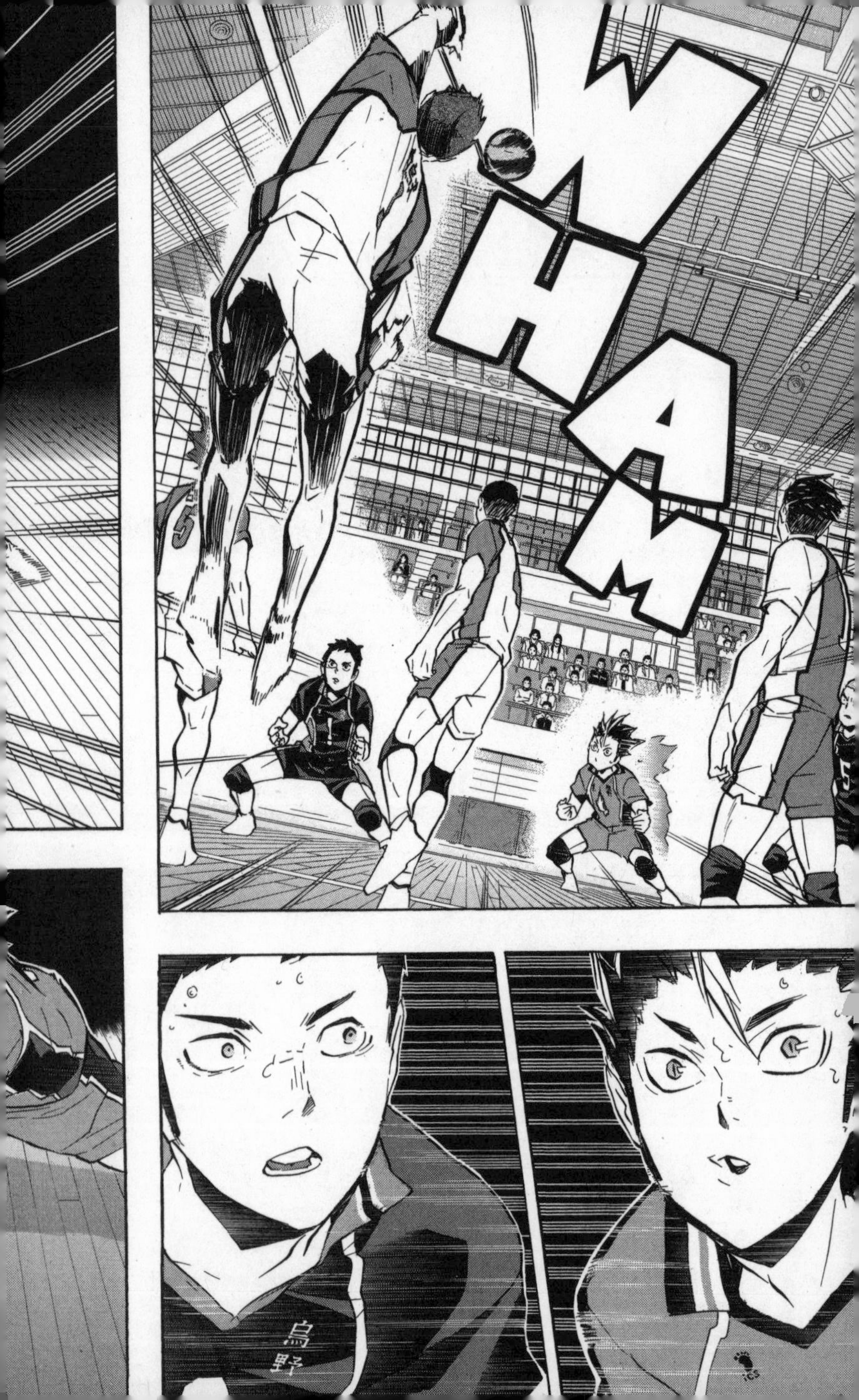
WHAM
烏野

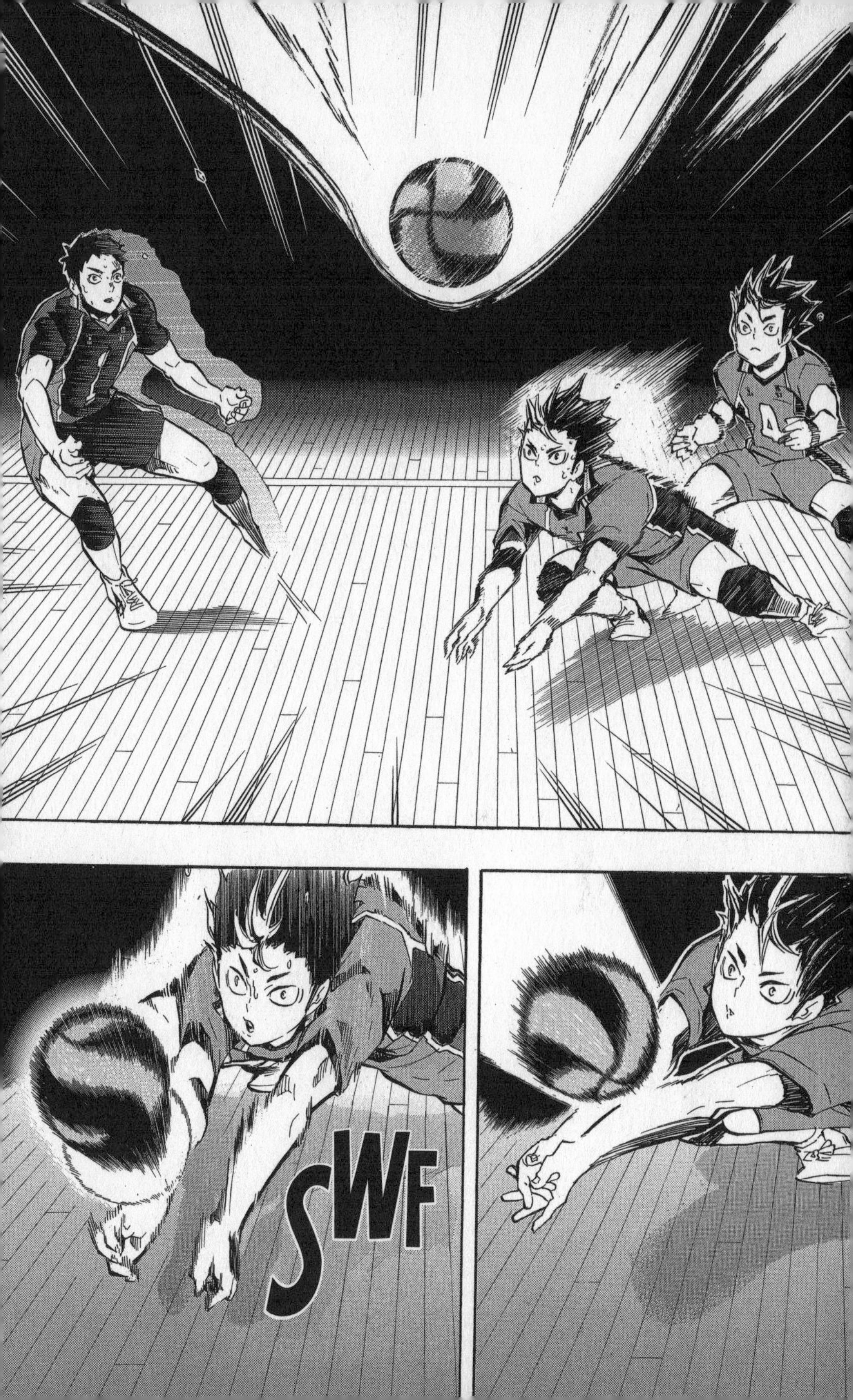
SWF

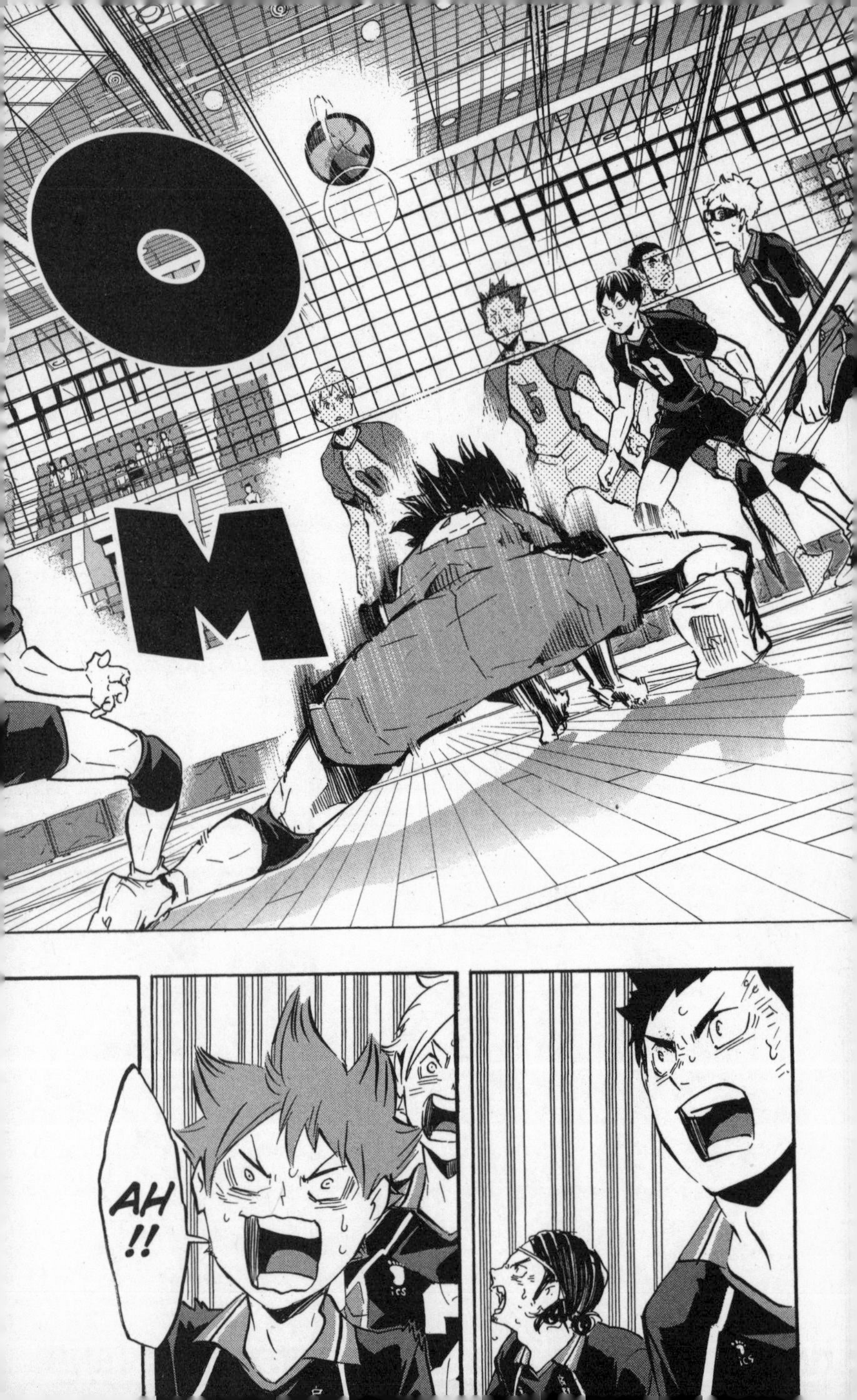

OM
AH !!

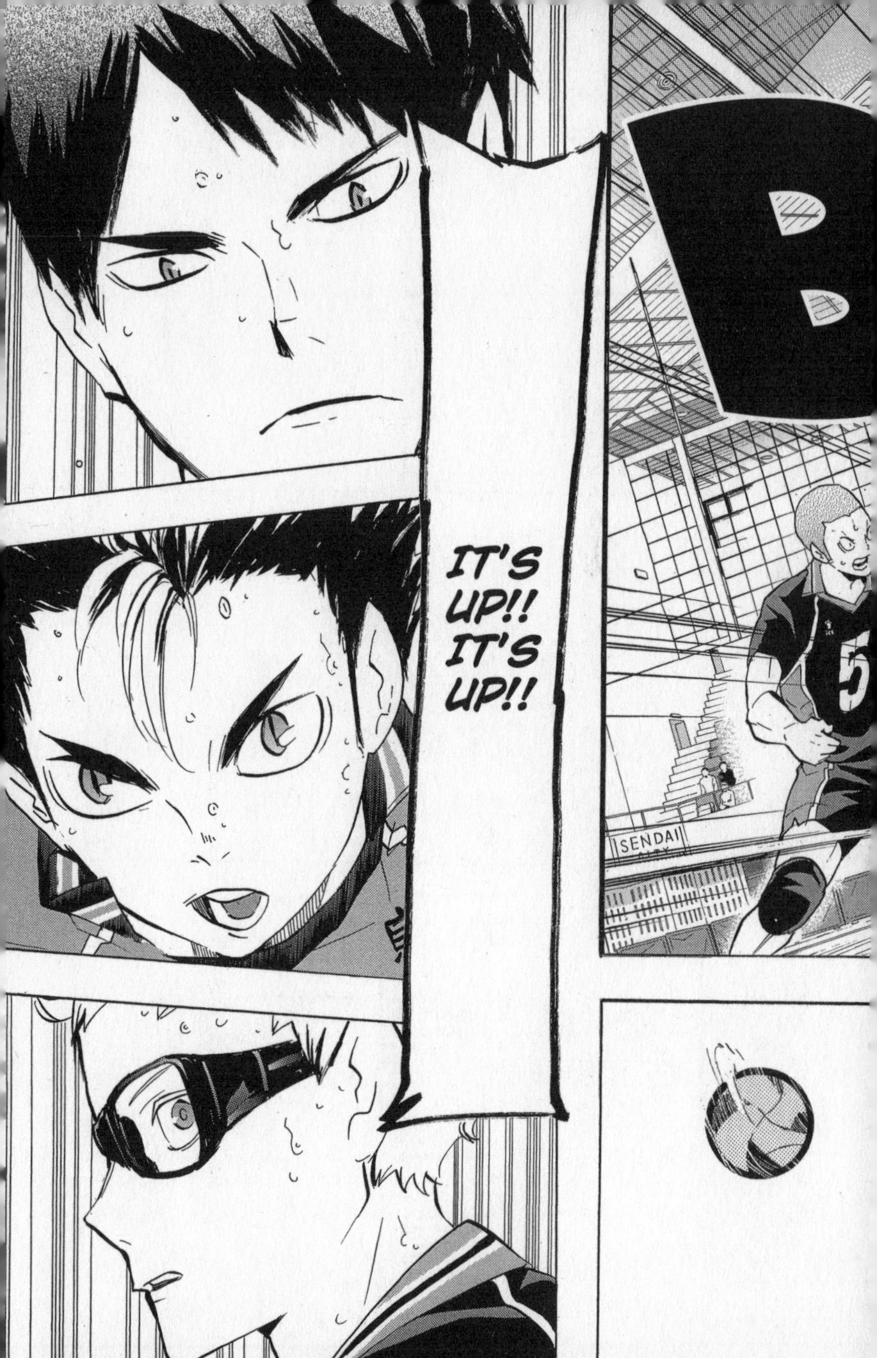
IT'S UP!! IT'S UP!!
SENDAI

HAIKYU!! VOL 17: TALENT AND INSTINCT (END)

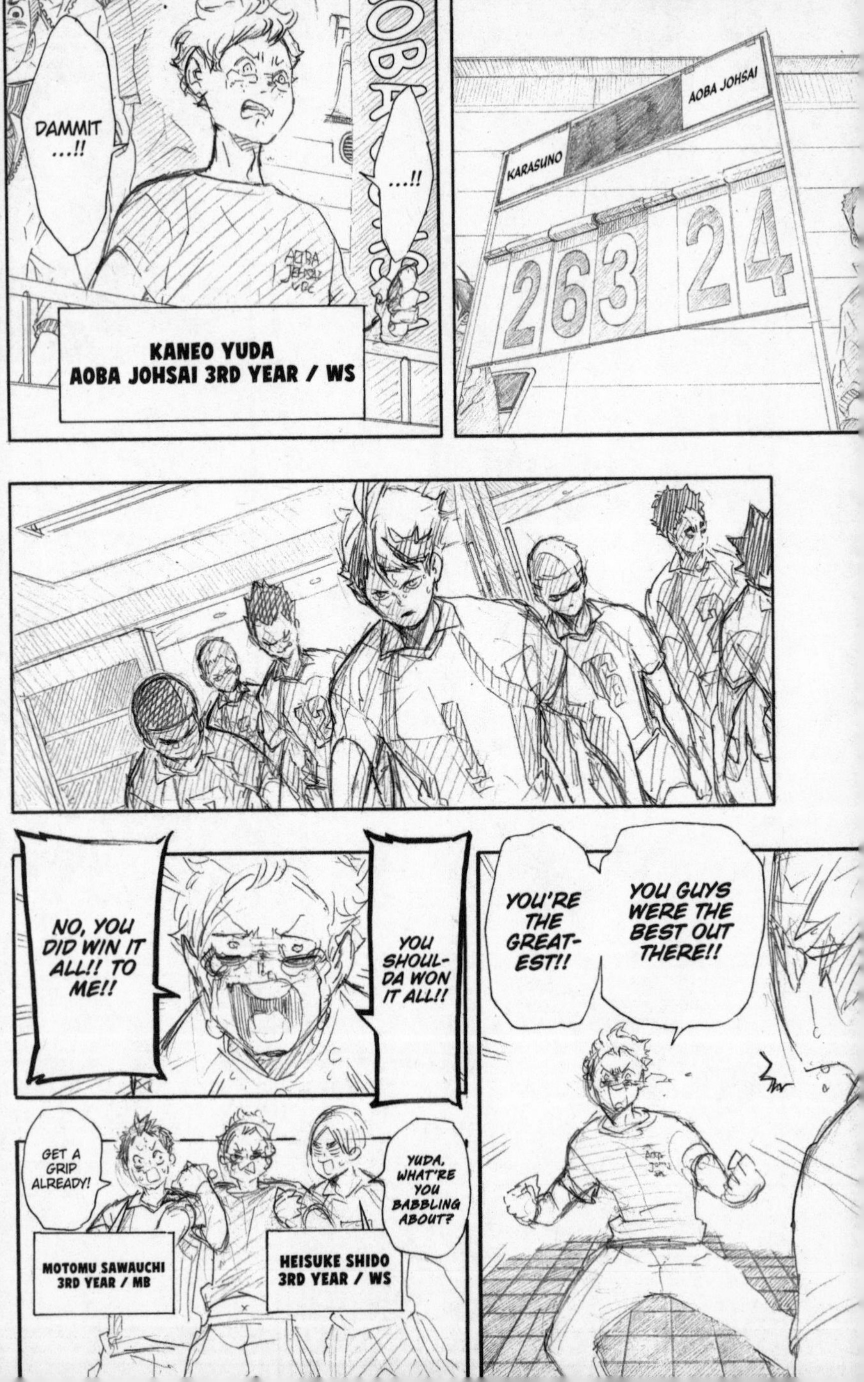
AOBA JOHSAI
KARASUNO
26 3 24
AOBA
...!!
DAMMIT ...!!
KANEO YUDA
AOBA JOHSAI 3RD YEAR / WS
YOU GUYS WERE THE BEST OUT THERE!!
YOU'RE THE GREAT-EST!!
YOU SHOUL-DA WON IT ALL!!
NO, YOU DID WIN IT ALL!! TO ME!!
YUDA, WHAT'RE YOU BABBLING ABOUT?
HEISUKE SHIDO
3RD YEAR / WS
GET A GRIP ALREADY!
MOTOMU SAWAUCHI
3RD YEAR / MB

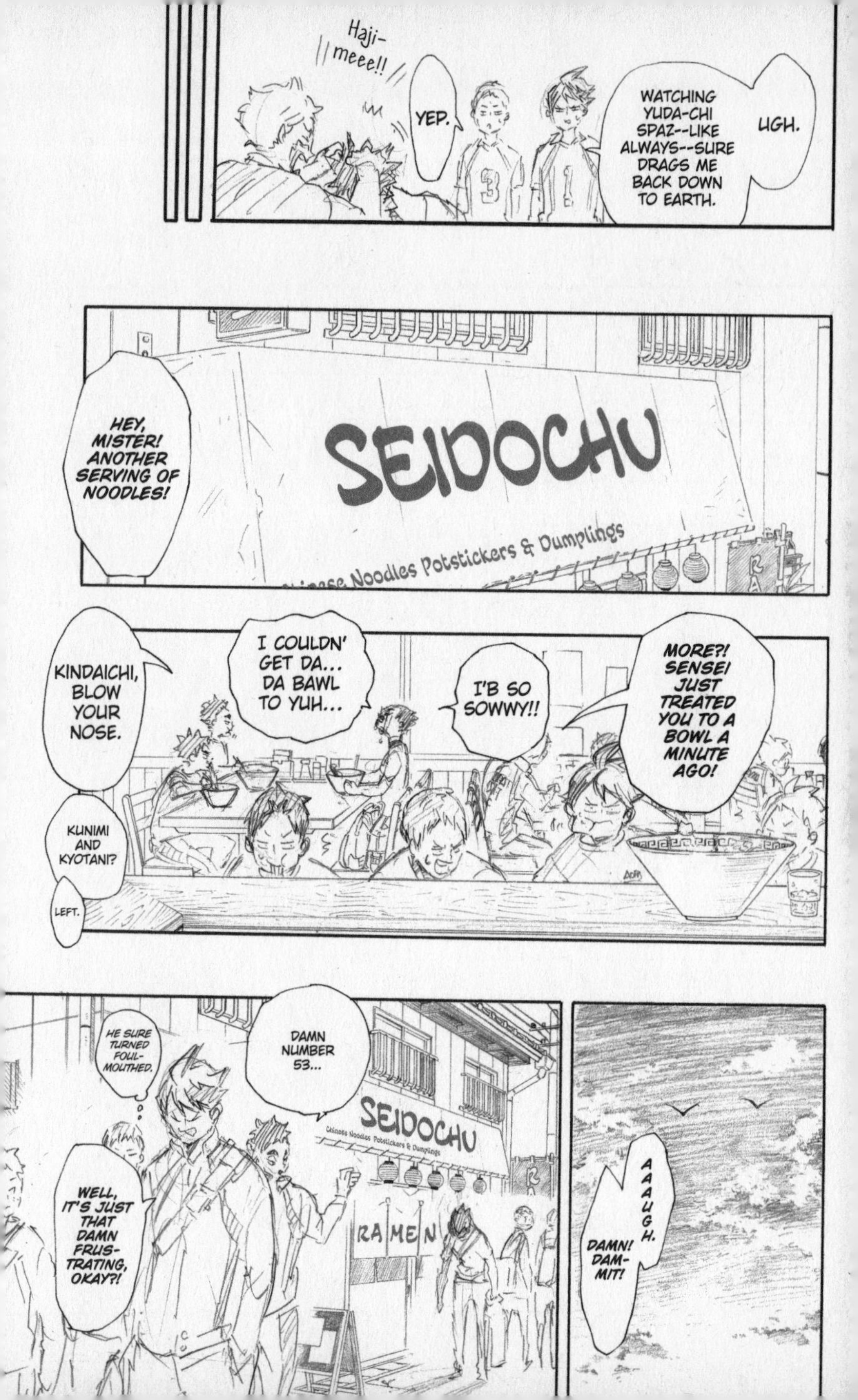
UGH.
WATCHING YUDA-CHI SPAZ--LIKE ALWAYS--SURE DRAGS ME BACK DOWN TO EARTH.
YEP.
Haji-meee!!
SEIDOCHU
Noodles Potstickers & Dumplings
HEY, MISTER! ANOTHER SERVING OF NOODLES!
MORE?! SENSEI JUST TREATED YOU TO A BOWL A MINUTE AGO!
I'B SO SOWWY!!
I COULDN' GET DA... DA BAWL TO YUH...
KINDAICHI, BLOW YOUR NOSE.
KUNIMI AND KYOTANI?
LEFT.
AAAAUGH.
DAMN! DAM-MIT!
DAMN NUMBER 53...
HE SURE TURNED FOUL-MOUTHED.
SEIDOCHU
Chinese Noodles Potstickers & Dumplings
RAMEN
WELL, IT'S JUST THAT DAMN FRUS-TRATING, OKAY?!

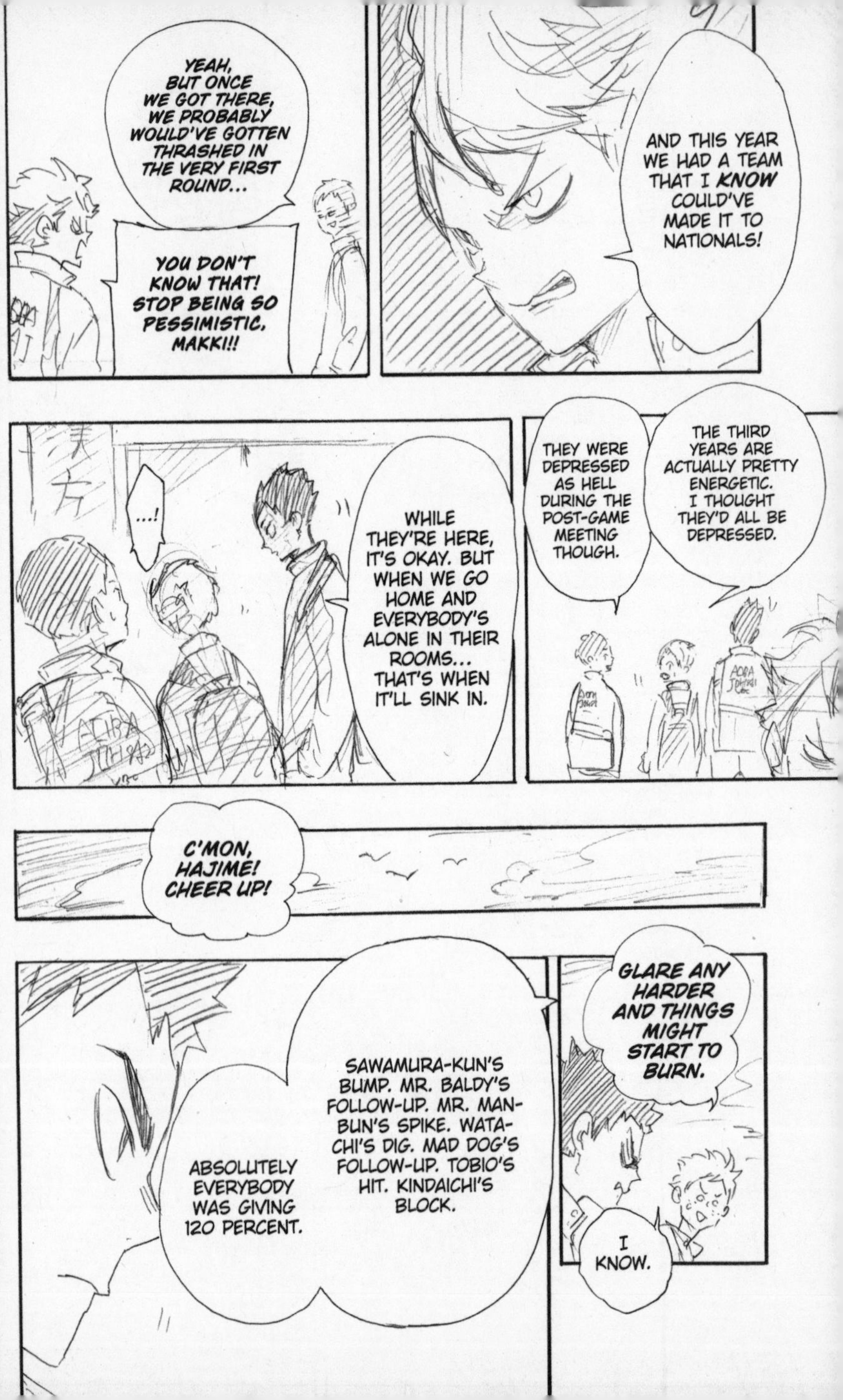
AND THIS YEAR WE HAD A TEAM THAT I *KNOW* COULD'VE MADE IT TO NATIONALS!
YEAH, BUT ONCE WE GOT THERE, WE PROBABLY WOULD'VE GOTTEN THRASHED IN THE VERY FIRST ROUND...
YOU DON'T KNOW THAT! STOP BEING SO PESSIMISTIC, MAKKI!!
THE THIRD YEARS ARE ACTUALLY PRETTY ENERGETIC. I THOUGHT THEY'D ALL BE DEPRESSED.
THEY WERE DEPRESSED AS HELL DURING THE POST-GAME MEETING THOUGH.
WHILE THEY'RE HERE, IT'S OKAY. BUT WHEN WE GO HOME AND EVERYBODY'S ALONE IN THEIR ROOMS... THAT'S WHEN IT'LL SINK IN.
...!
C'MON, HAJIME! CHEER UP!
GLARE ANY HARDER AND THINGS MIGHT START TO BURN.
I KNOW.
SAWAMURA-KUN'S BUMP. MR. BALDY'S FOLLOW-UP. MR. MAN-BUN'S SPIKE. WATA-CHI'S DIG. MAD DOG'S FOLLOW-UP. TOBIO'S HIT. KINDAICHI'S BLOCK.
ABSOLUTELY EVERYBODY WAS GIVING 120 PERCENT.

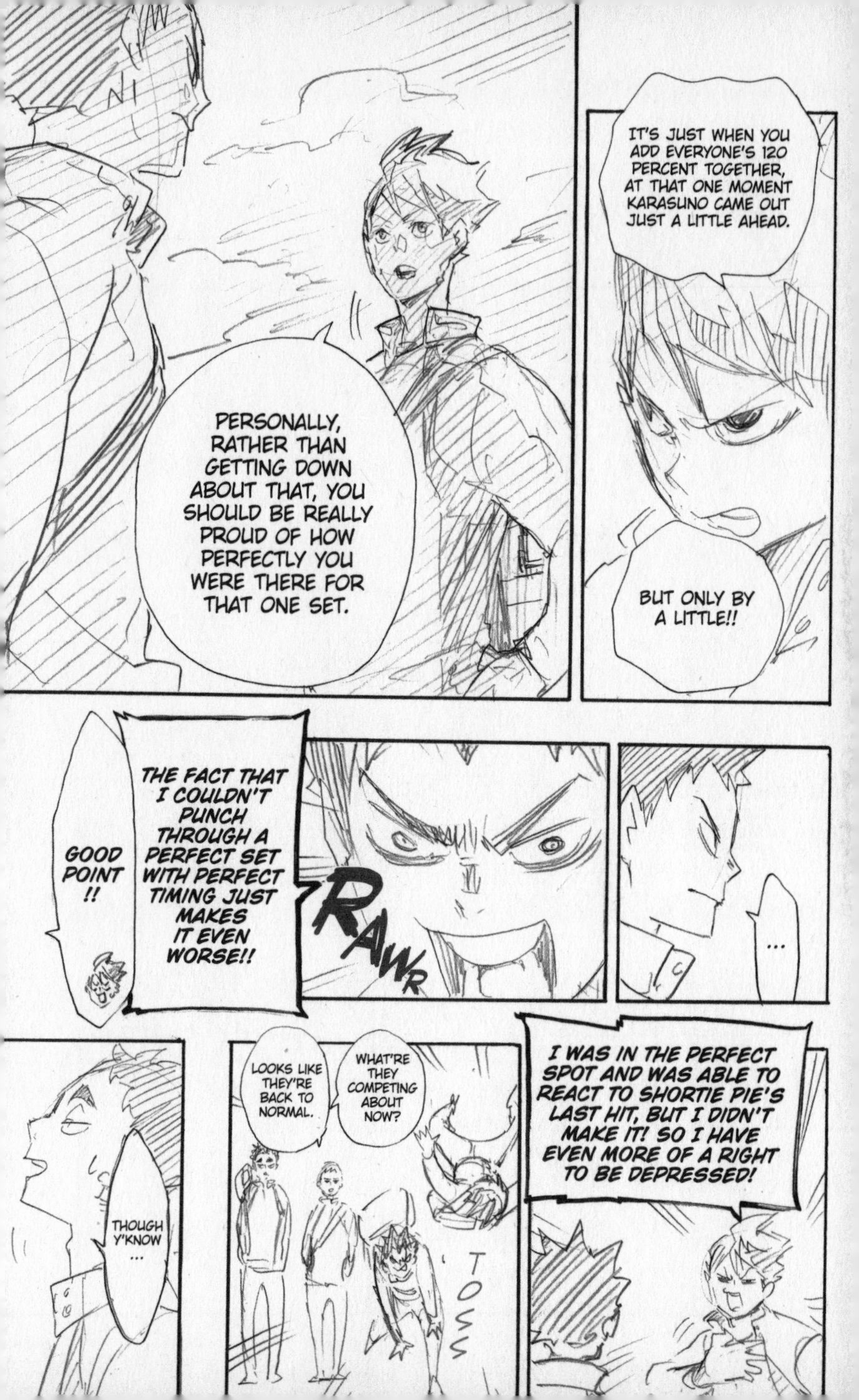
IT'S JUST WHEN YOU ADD EVERYONE'S 120 PERCENT TOGETHER, AT THAT ONE MOMENT KARASUNO CAME OUT JUST A LITTLE AHEAD.
BUT ONLY BY A LITTLE!!
PERSONALLY, RATHER THAN GETTING DOWN ABOUT THAT, YOU SHOULD BE REALLY PROUD OF HOW PERFECTLY YOU WERE THERE FOR THAT ONE SET.
...
RAWR
THE FACT THAT I COULDN'T PUNCH THROUGH A PERFECT SET WITH PERFECT TIMING JUST MAKES IT EVEN WORSE!!
GOOD POINT !!
I WAS IN THE PERFECT SPOT AND WAS ABLE TO REACT TO SHORTIE PIE'S LAST HIT, BUT I DIDN'T MAKE IT! SO I HAVE EVEN MORE OF A RIGHT TO BE DEPRESSED!
WHAT'RE THEY COMPETING ABOUT NOW?
LOOKS LIKE THEY'RE BACK TO NORMAL.
TOSS
THOUGH Y'KNOW ...

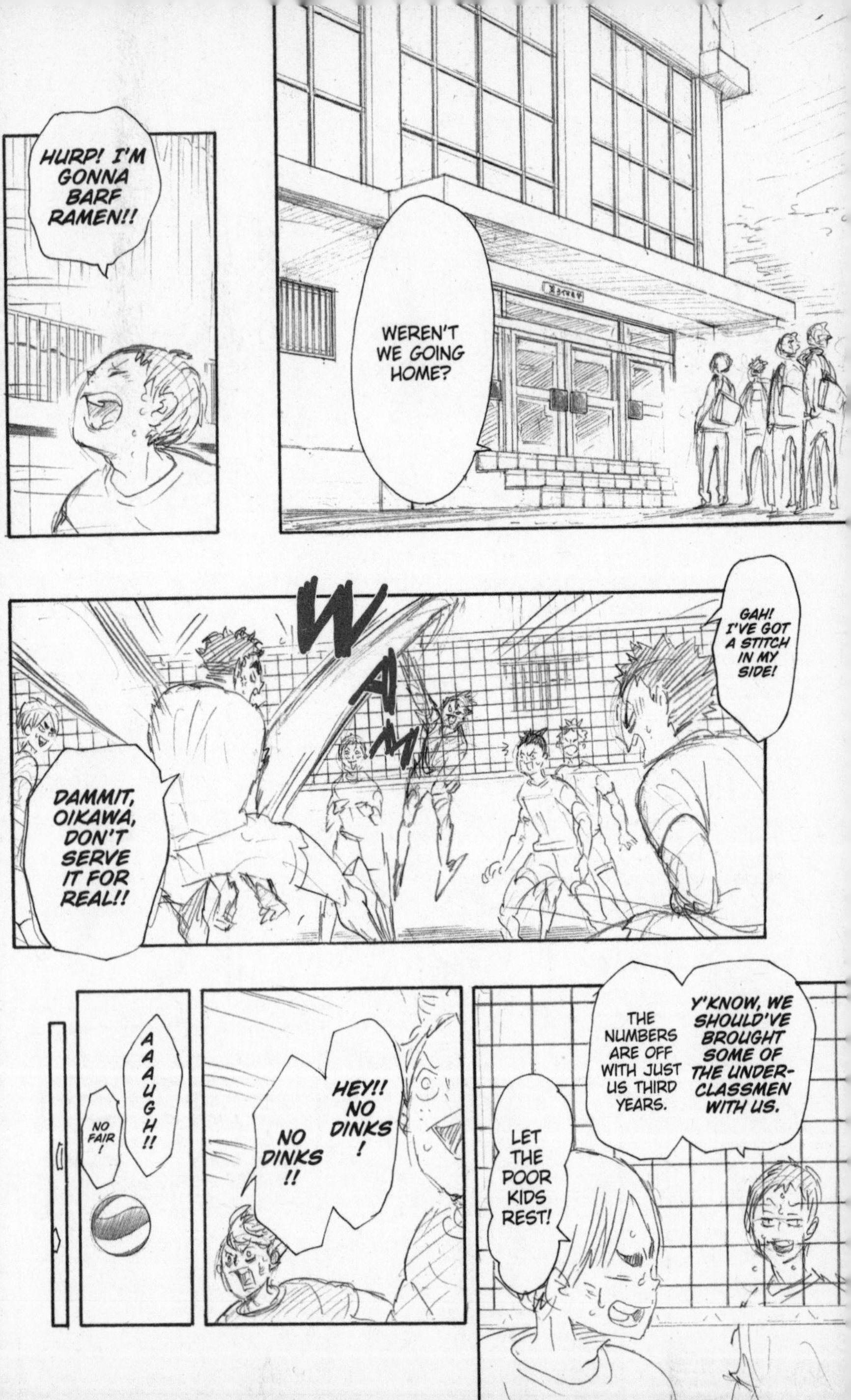
WEREN'T WE GOING HOME?
HURP! I'M GONNA BARF RAMEN!!
GAH! I'VE GOT A STITCH IN MY SIDE!
WAM
DAMMIT, OIKAWA, DON'T SERVE IT FOR REAL!!
Y'KNOW, WE SHOULD'VE BROUGHT SOME OF THE UNDER-CLASSMEN WITH US.
THE NUMBERS ARE OFF WITH JUST US THIRD YEARS.
LET THE POOR KIDS REST!
HEY!! NO DINKS!
NO DINKS!!
AAAAUGH!!
NO FAIR!

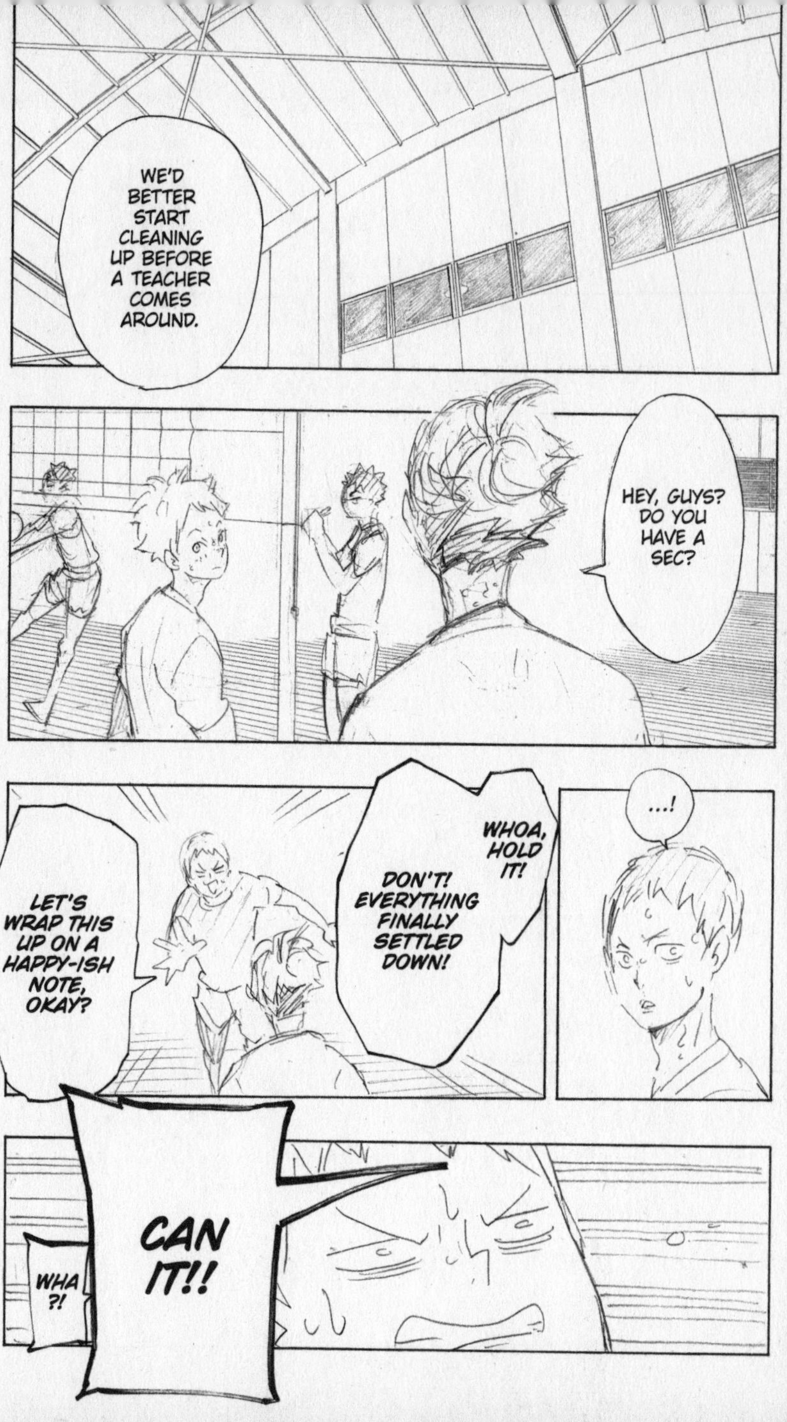
WE'D BETTER START CLEANING UP BEFORE A TEACHER COMES AROUND.
HEY, GUYS? DO YOU HAVE A SEC?
...!
WHOA, HOLD IT!
DON'T! EVERYTHING FINALLY SETTLED DOWN!
LET'S WRAP THIS UP ON A HAPPY-ISH NOTE, OKAY?
CAN IT!!
WHA?!

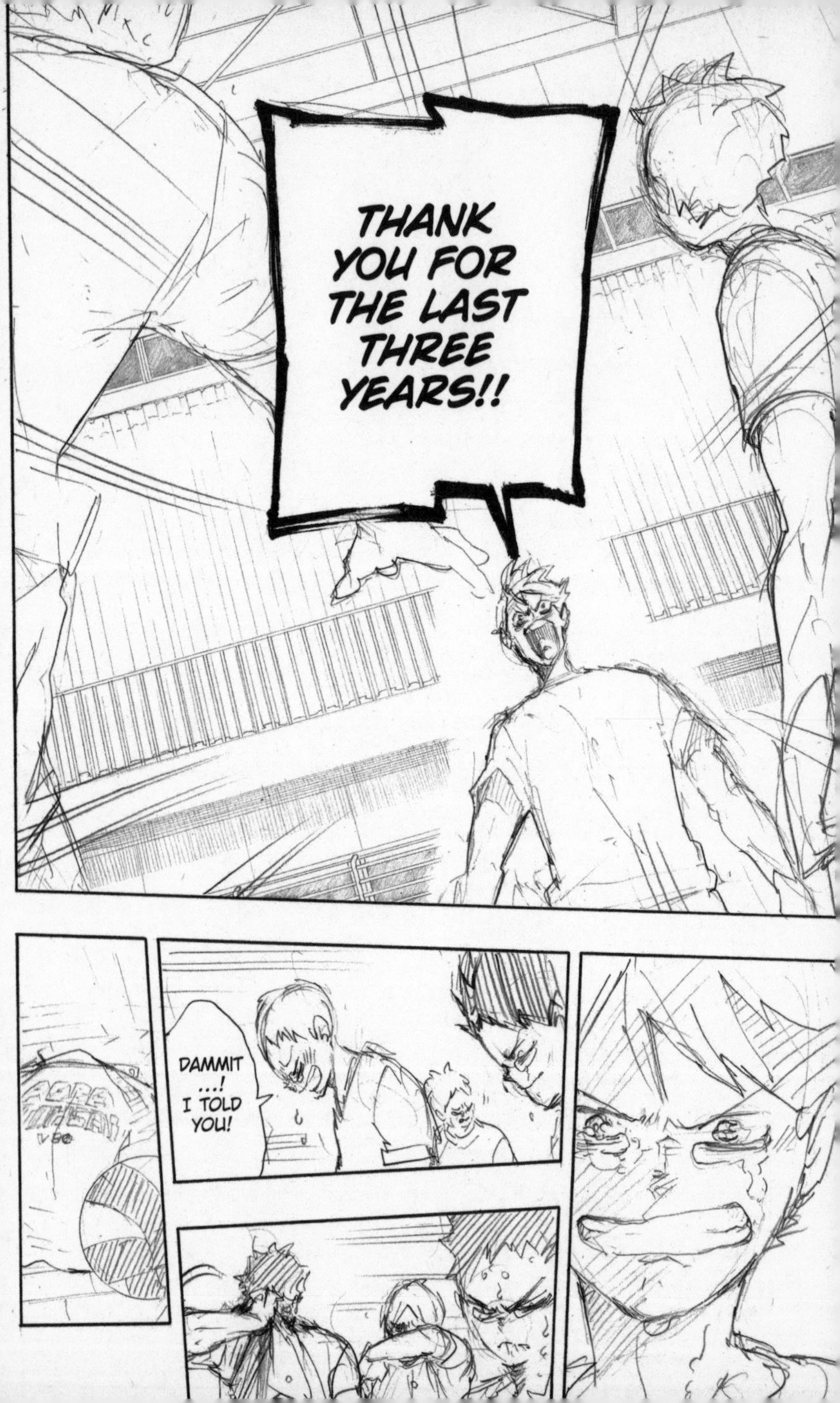
THANK YOU FOR THE LAST THREE YEARS!!
DAMMIT ...! I TOLD YOU!

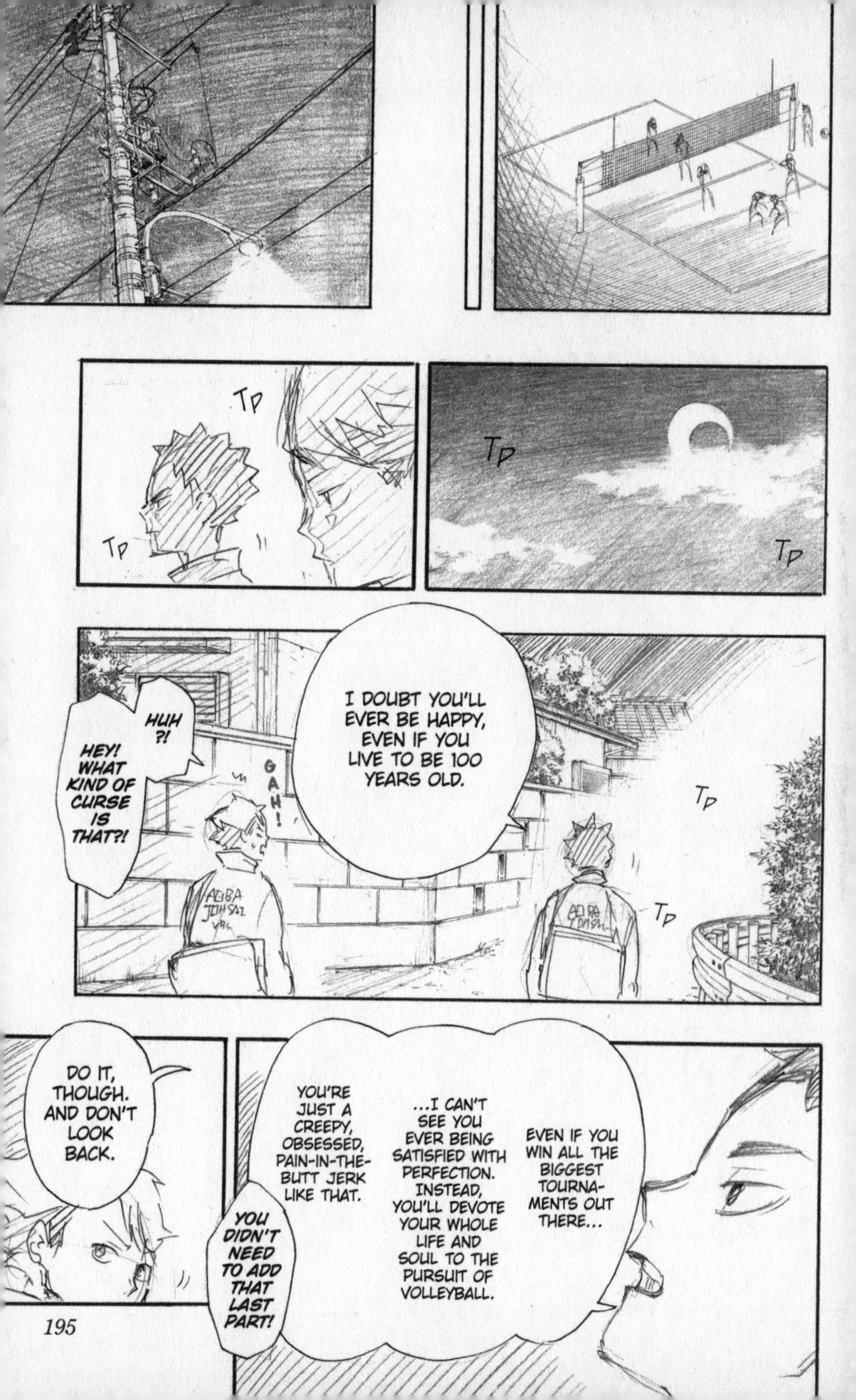
Tp
Tp
Tp
Tp
Tp
Tp
I DOUBT YOU'LL EVER BE HAPPY, EVEN IF YOU LIVE TO BE 100 YEARS OLD.
GAH!
HUH?!
HEY! WHAT KIND OF CURSE IS THAT?!
Tp
EVEN IF YOU WIN ALL THE BIGGEST TOURNAMENTS OUT THERE...
...I CAN'T SEE YOU EVER BEING SATISFIED WITH PERFECTION. INSTEAD, YOU'LL DEVOTE YOUR WHOLE LIFE AND SOUL TO THE PURSUIT OF VOLLEYBALL.
YOU'RE JUST A CREEPY, OBSESSED, PAIN-IN-THE-BUTT JERK LIKE THAT.
YOU DIDN'T NEED TO ADD THAT LAST PART!
DO IT, THOUGH. AND DON'T LOOK BACK.

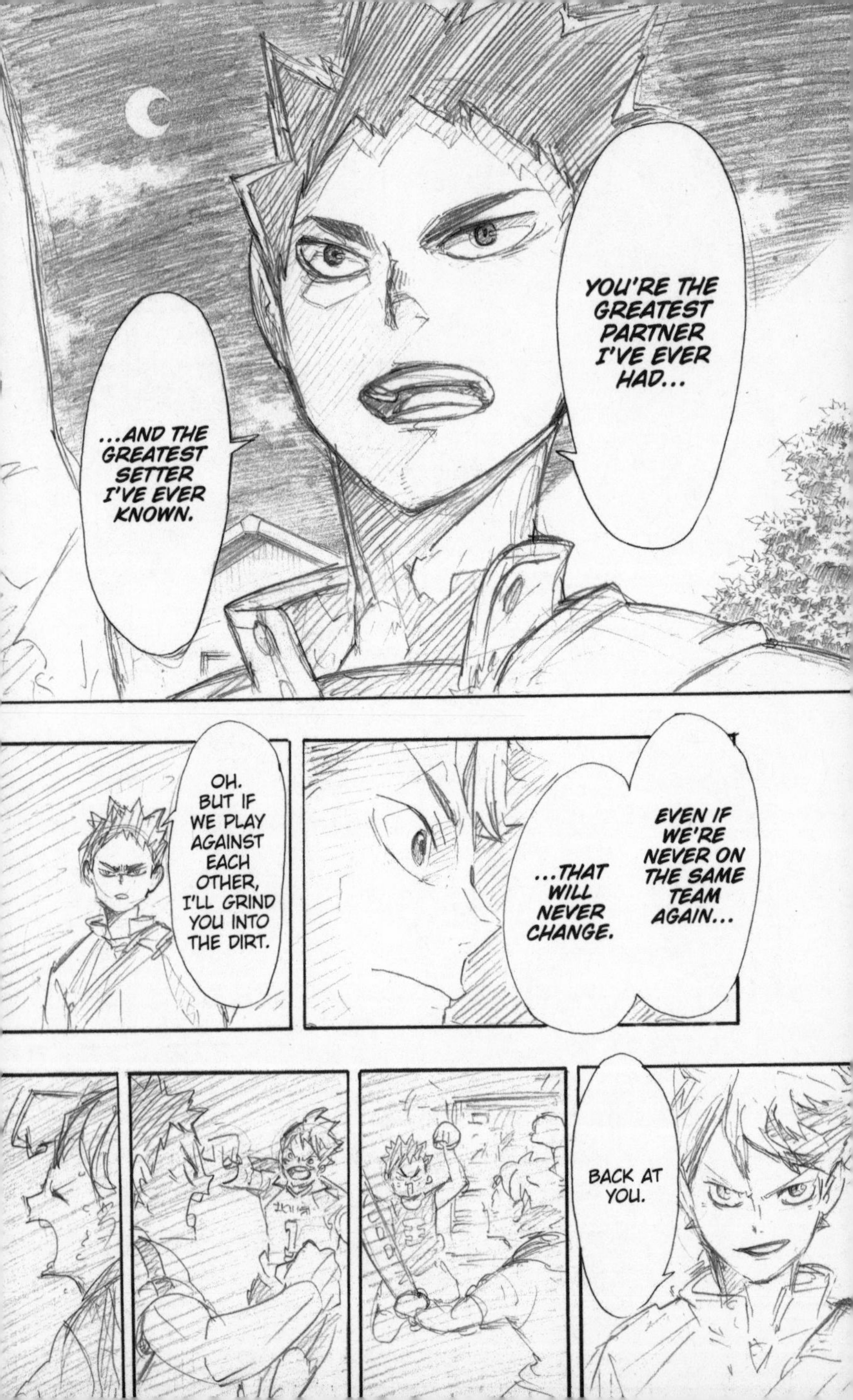
YOU'RE THE GREATEST PARTNER I'VE EVER HAD...
...AND THE GREATEST SETTER I'VE EVER KNOWN.
EVEN IF WE'RE NEVER ON THE SAME TEAM AGAIN...
...THAT WILL NEVER CHANGE.
OH. BUT IF WE PLAY AGAINST EACH OTHER, I'LL GRIND YOU INTO THE DIRT.
BACK AT YOU.

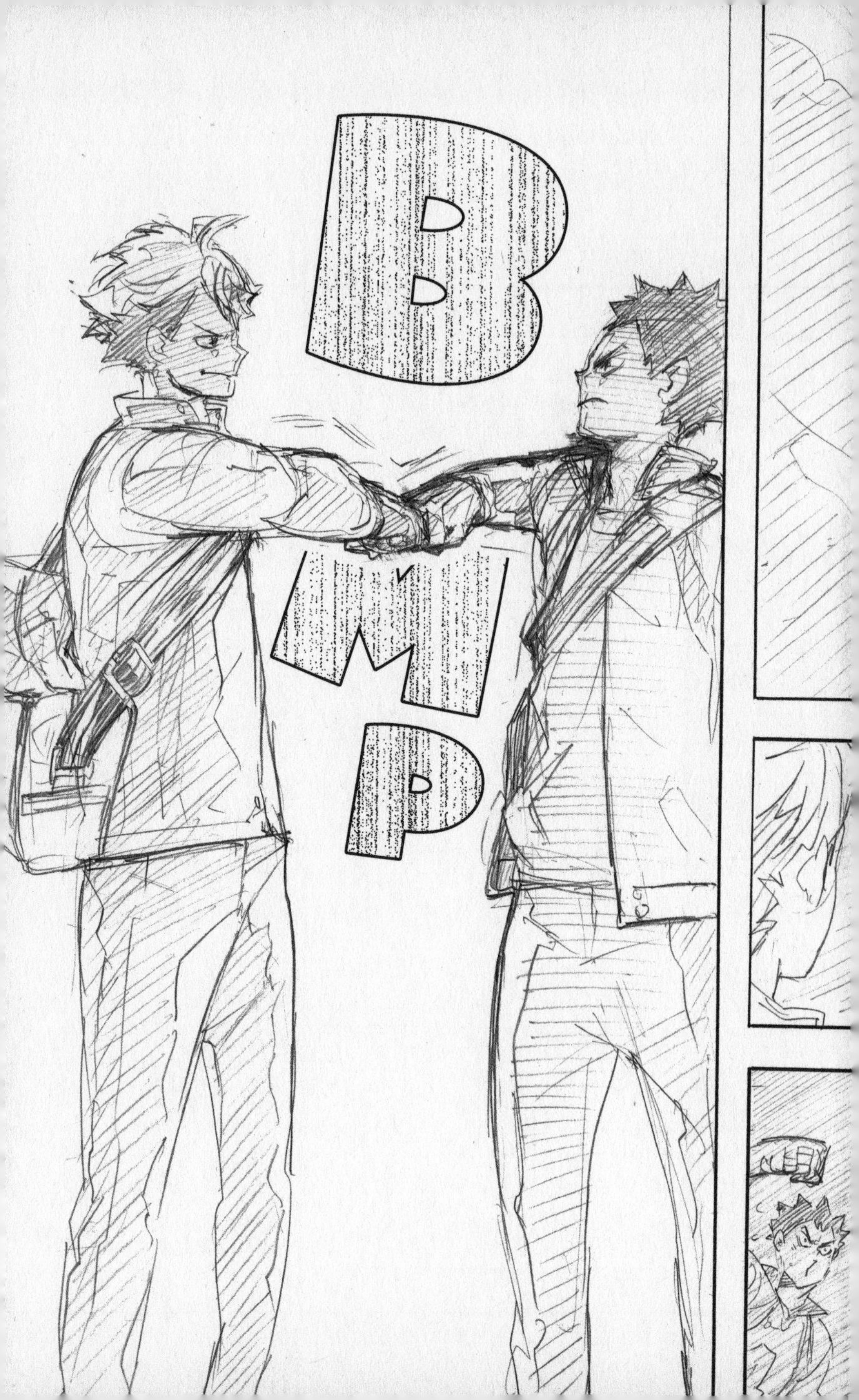
BUMP

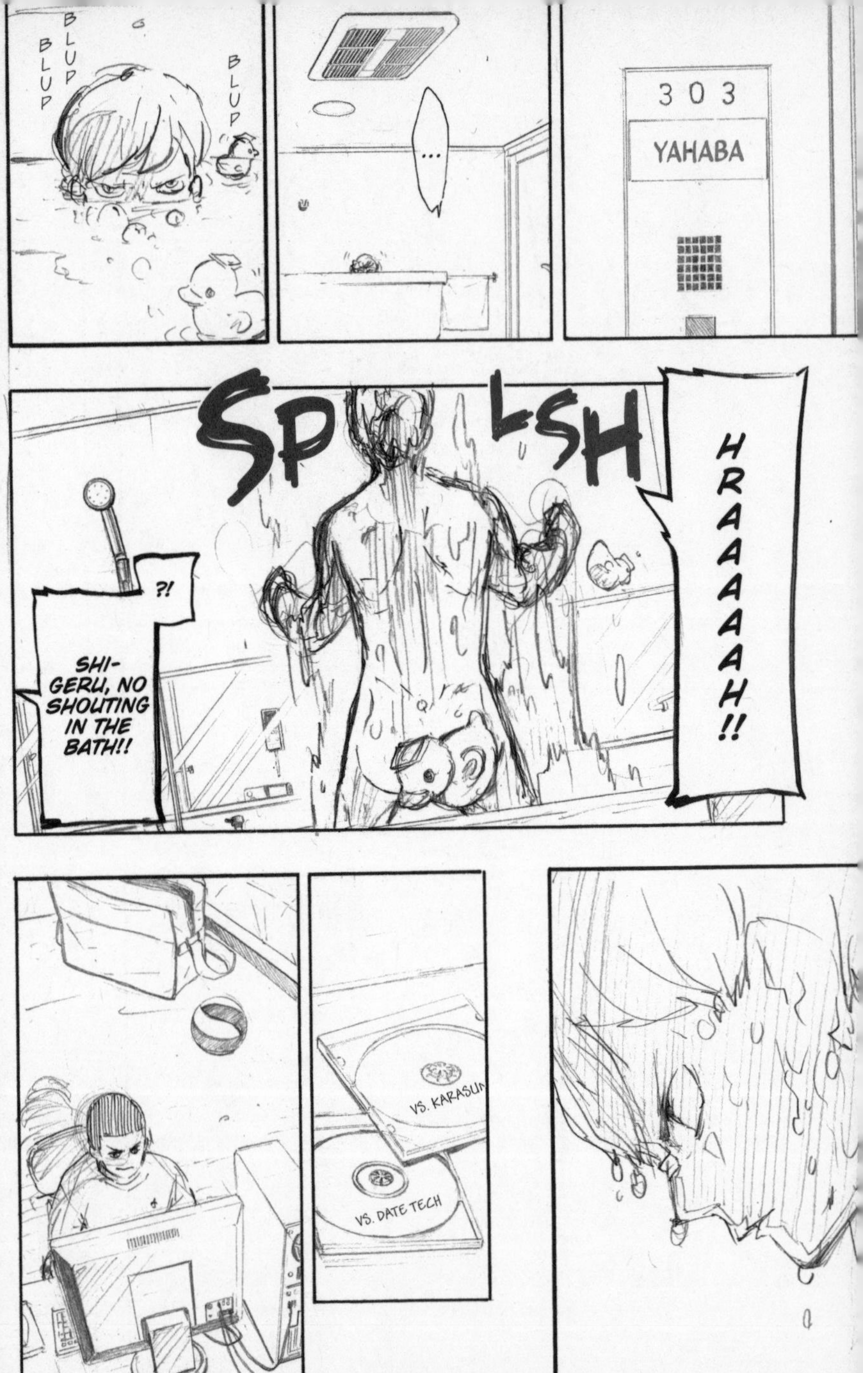
303
YAHABA
...
BLUP BLUP
BLUP
HRAAAAAAH!!
SPLSH
?!
SHI-GERU, NO SHOUTING IN THE BATH!!
VS. KARASUN
VS. DATE TECH

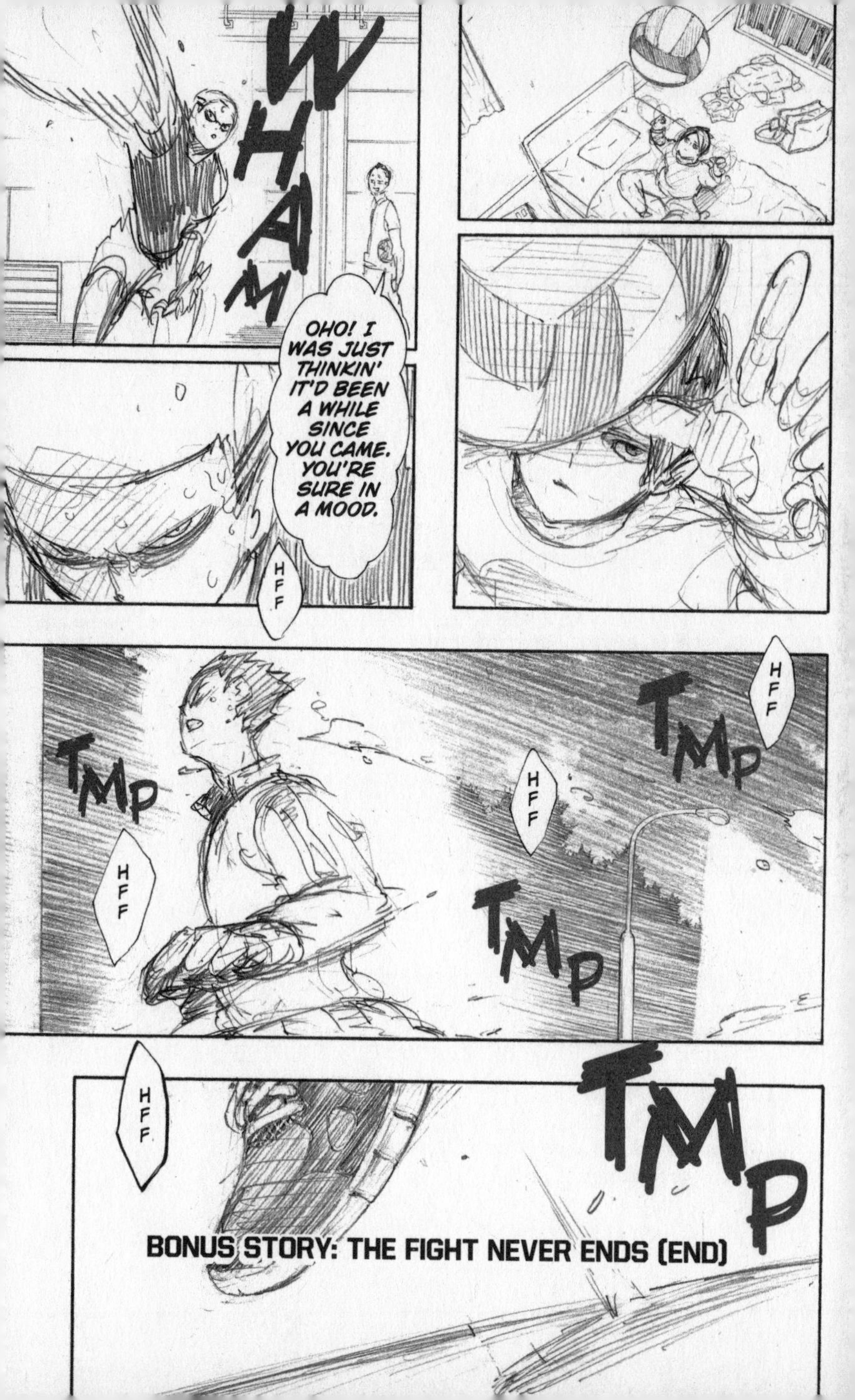
WHAM
OHO! I WAS JUST THINKIN' IT'D BEEN A WHILE SINCE YOU CAME. YOU'RE SURE IN A MOOD.
HFF
HFF
TMP
HFF
TMP
HFF
TMP
TMP
HFF
BONUS STORY: THE FIGHT NEVER ENDS (END)

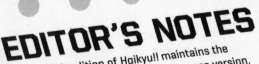

EDITOR'S NOTES

The English edition of Haikyu!! maintains the honorifics used in the original Japanese version. For those of you who are new to these terms, here's a brief explanation to help with your reading experience!

They Hate Losing
Is this a race?
WSH
WSH

When saying someone's name in Japanese, a suffix is often attached to indicate how familiar the speaker is with the person. Some are more polite and respectful, while others are endearing.

1 ***-kun*** is often used for young men or boys, usually someone you are familiar with.

2 ***-chan*** is used for young children and can be used as a term of endearment.

3 ***-san*** is used for someone you respect or are not close to, or to be polite.

4 ***Senpai*** is used for someone who is older than you or in a higher position or grade in school.

5 ***Kohai*** is used for someone who is younger than you or in a lower position or grade in school.

6 ***Sensei*** means teacher.

7 ***Bluecastle*** is a nickname for Aoba Johsai. It is a combination of *Ao* [blue] and *Joh* [castle].

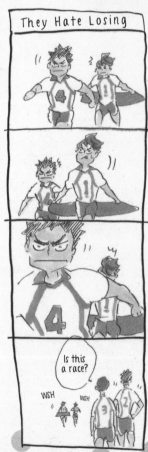

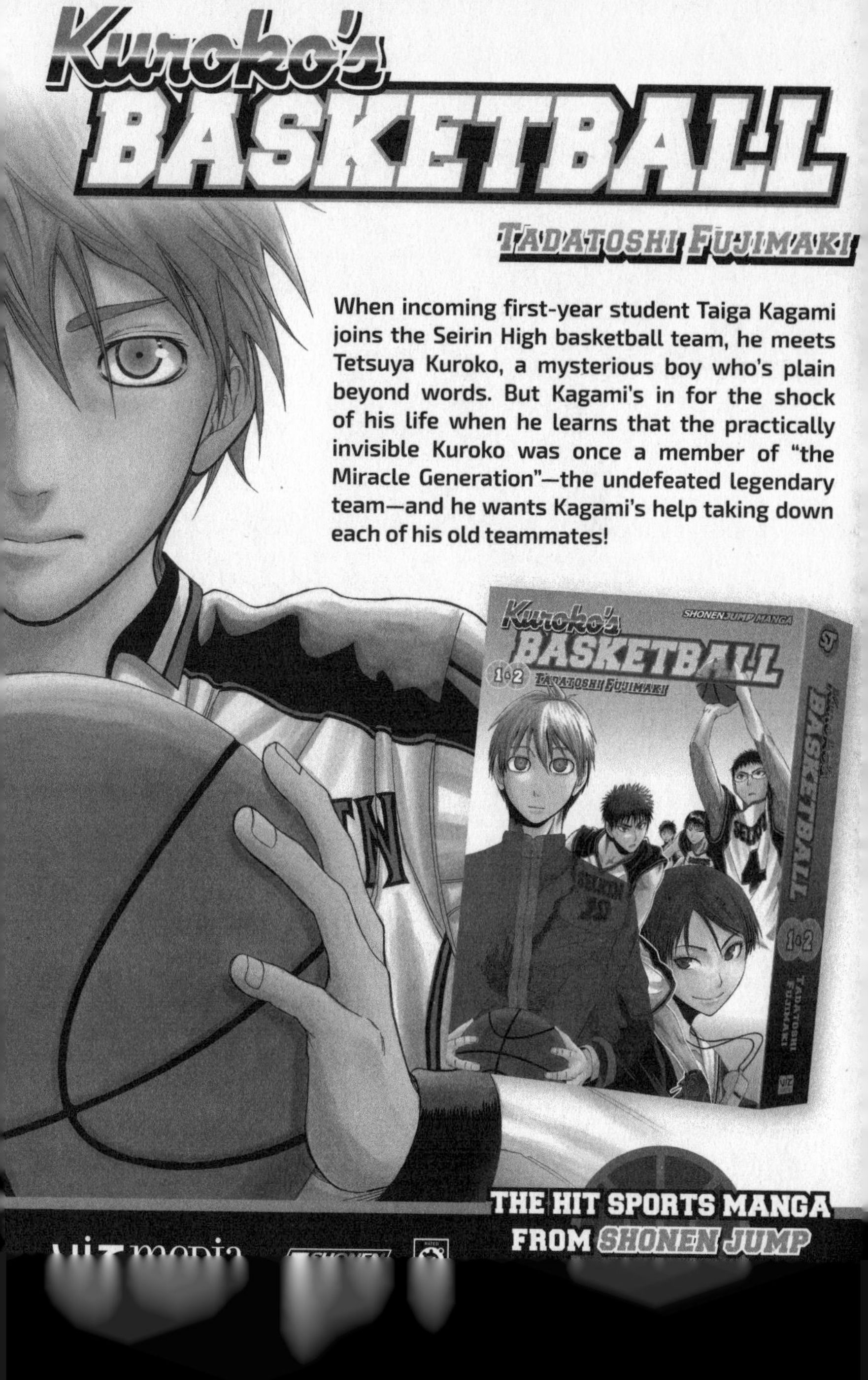
Kuroko's
BASKETBALL
TADATOSHI FUJIMAKI
When incoming first-year student Taiga Kagami joins the Seirin High basketball team, he meets Tetsuya Kuroko, a mysterious boy who's plain beyond words. But Kagami's in for the shock of his life when he learns that the practically invisible Kuroko was once a member of "the Miracle Generation"—the undefeated legendary team—and he wants Kagami's help taking down each of his old teammates!
SHONEN JUMP MANGA
Kuroko's BASKETBALL
1◦2
TADATOSHI FUJIMAKI
THE HIT SPORTS MANGA
FROM SHONEN JUMP

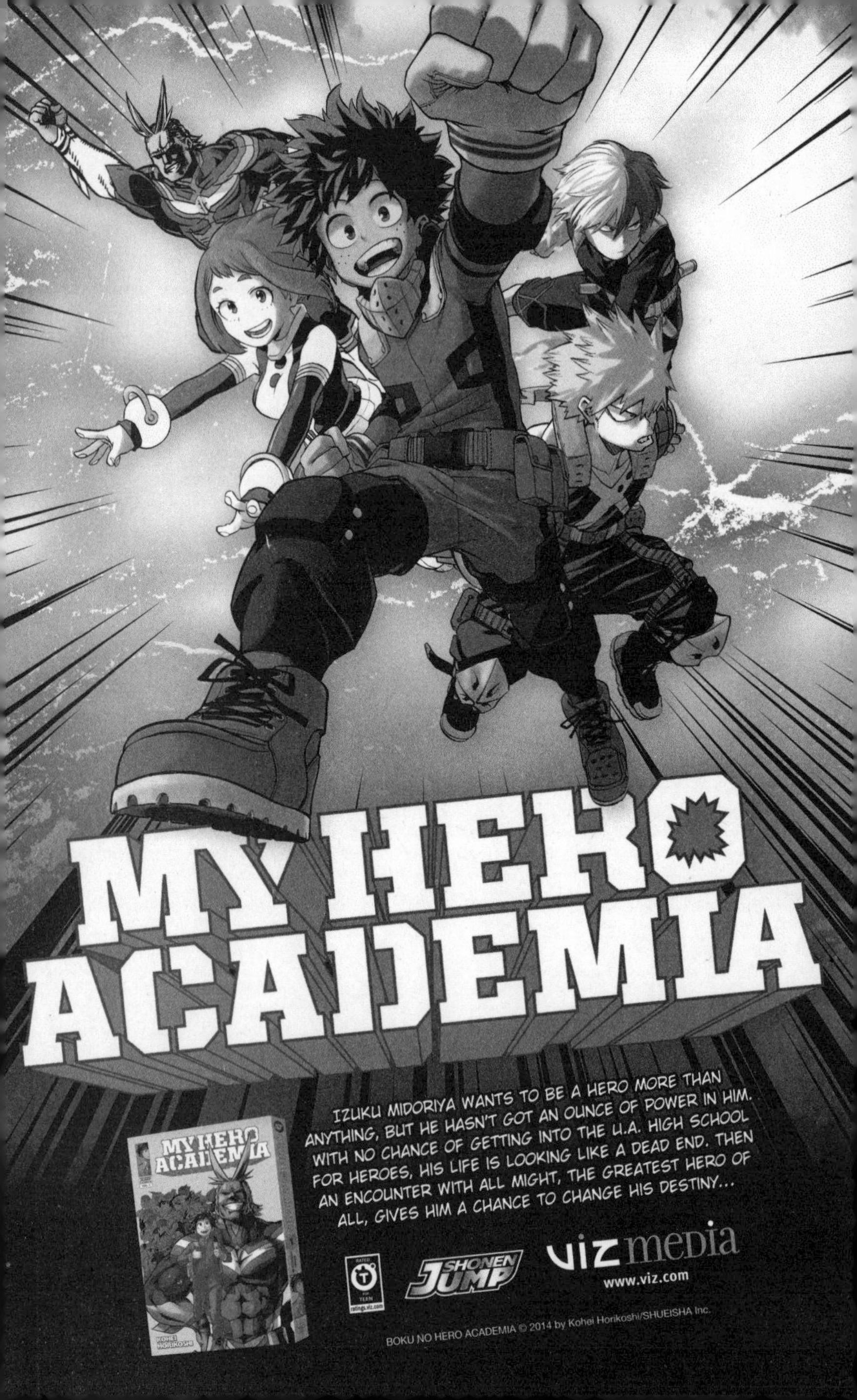
MY HERO ACADEMIA
IZUKU MIDORIYA WANTS TO BE A HERO MORE THAN ANYTHING, BUT HE HASN'T GOT AN OUNCE OF POWER IN HIM. WITH NO CHANCE OF GETTING INTO THE U.A. HIGH SCHOOL FOR HEROES, HIS LIFE IS LOOKING LIKE A DEAD END. THEN AN ENCOUNTER WITH ALL MIGHT, THE GREATEST HERO OF ALL, GIVES HIM A CHANCE TO CHANGE HIS DESTINY...
SHONEN JUMP
viz media
www.viz.com
BOKU NO HERO ACADEMIA © 2014 by Kohei Horikoshi/SHUEISHA Inc.

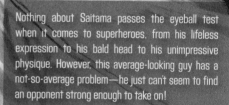

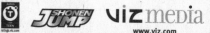

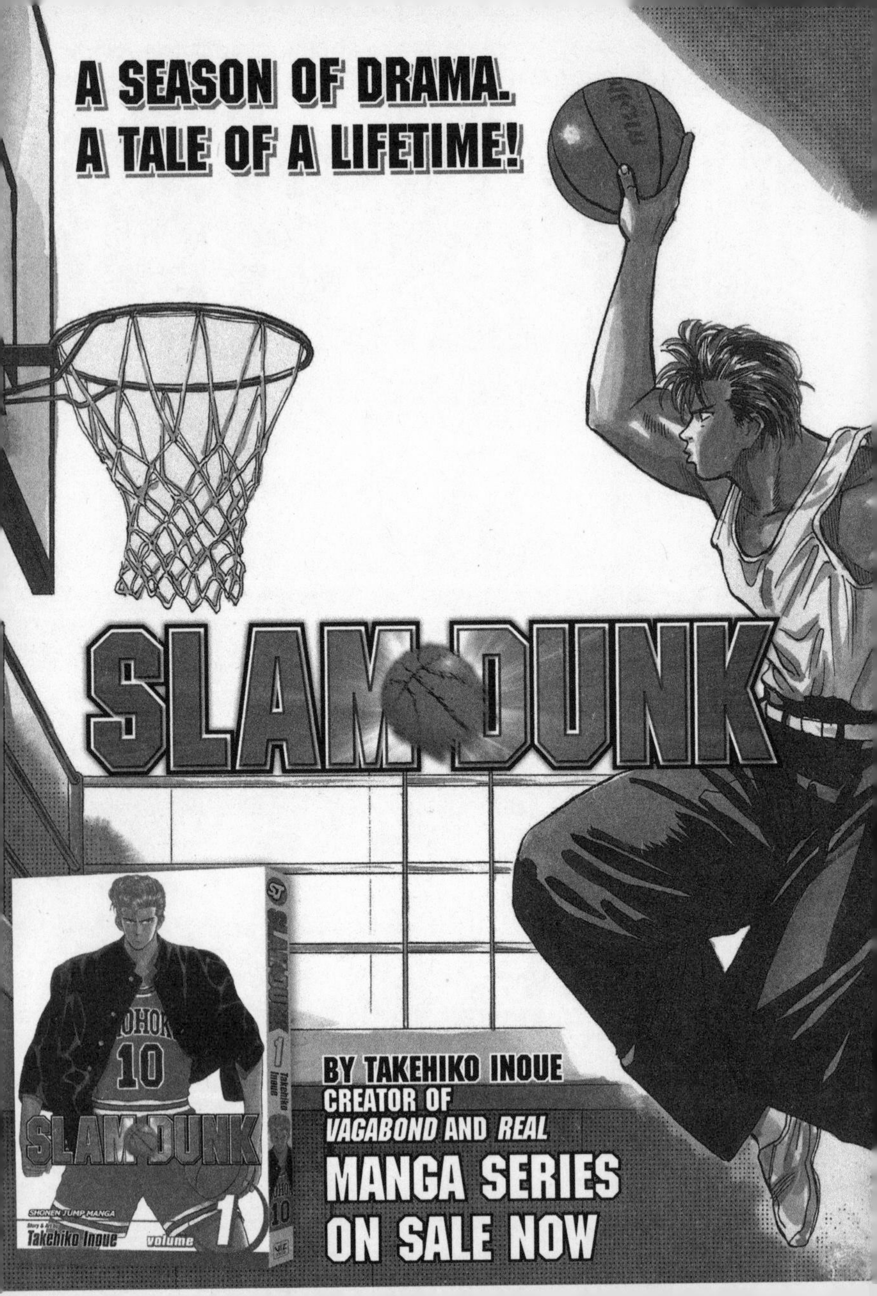
A SEASON OF DRAMA.
A TALE OF A LIFETIME!
SLAM DUNK
BY TAKEHIKO INOUE
CREATOR OF
VAGABOND AND REAL
MANGA SERIES
ON SALE NOW
SLAM DUNK
SHONEN JUMP MANGA
Story & Art by
Takehiko Inoue
volume 1

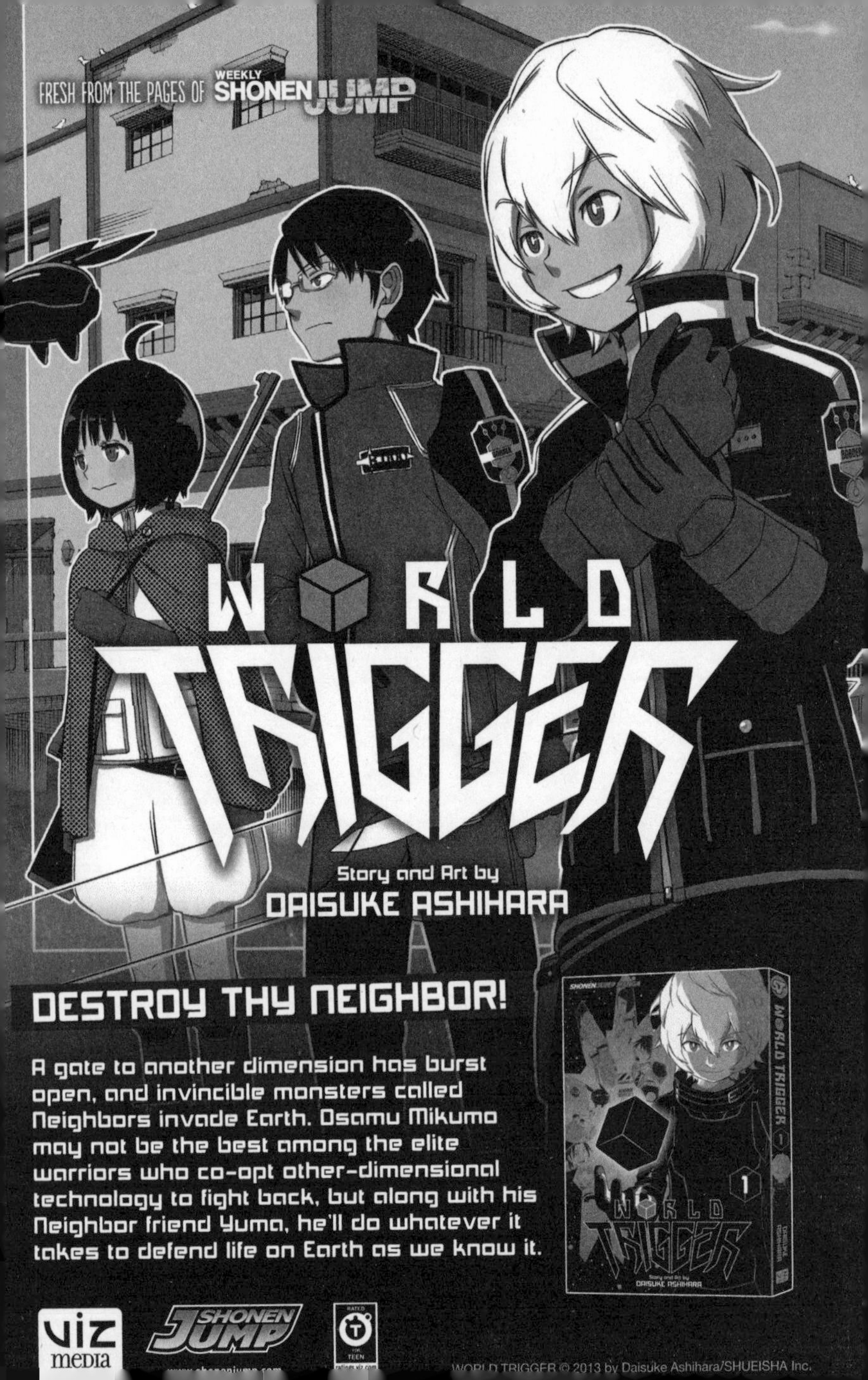
FRESH FROM THE PAGES OF WEEKLY SHONEN JUMP
WORLD TRIGGER
Story and Art by
DAISUKE ASHIHARA
DESTROY THY NEIGHBOR!
A gate to another dimension has burst open, and invincible monsters called Neighbors invade Earth. Osamu Mikumo may not be the best among the elite warriors who co-opt other-dimensional technology to fight back, but along with his Neighbor friend Yuma, he'll do whatever it takes to defend life on Earth as we know it.
SHONEN JUMP
WORLD TRIGGER
1
Story and Art by
DAISUKE ASHIHARA
viz media
SHONEN JUMP
RATED T FOR TEEN
WORLD TRIGGER © 2013 by Daisuke Ashihara/SHUEISHA Inc.

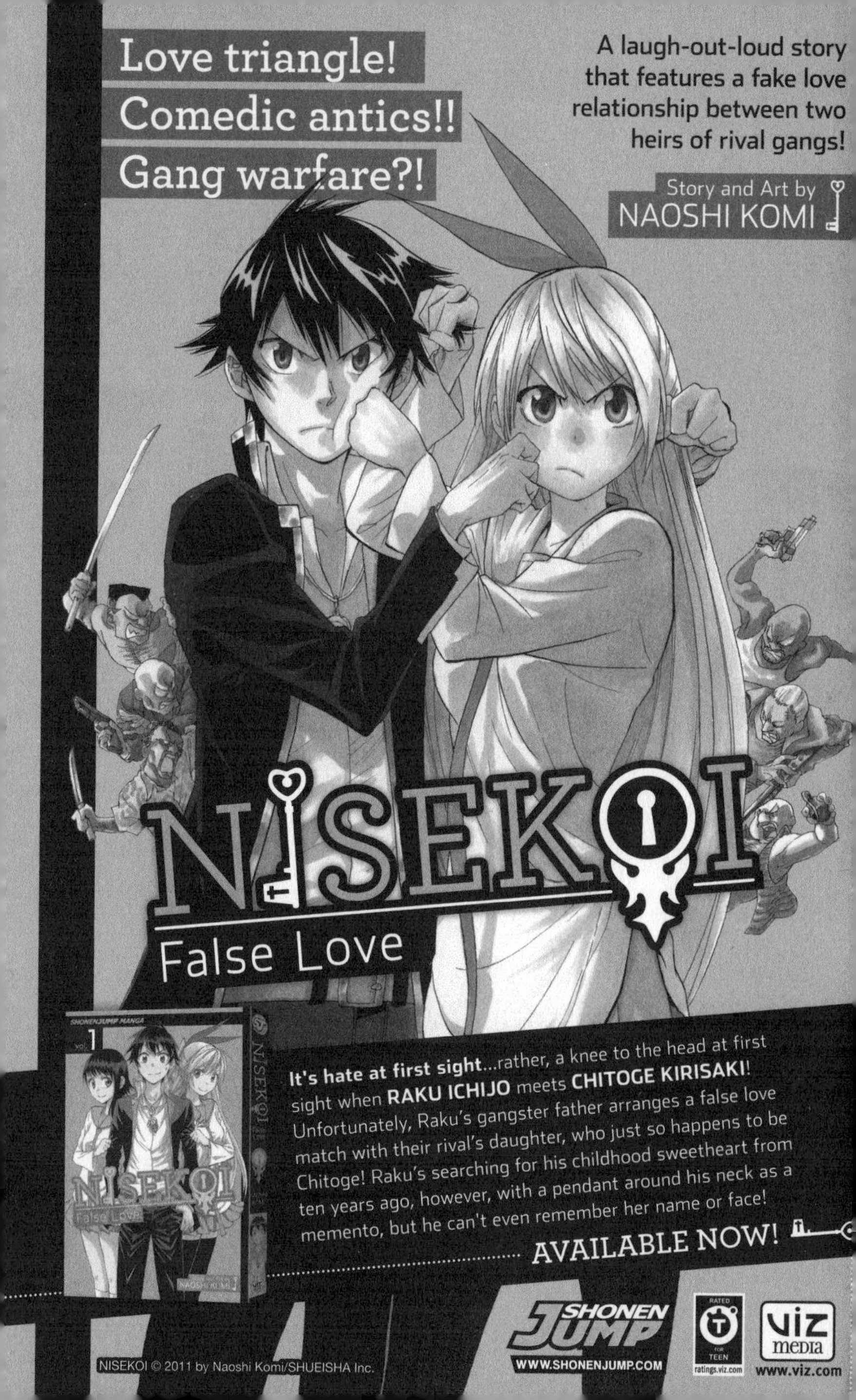

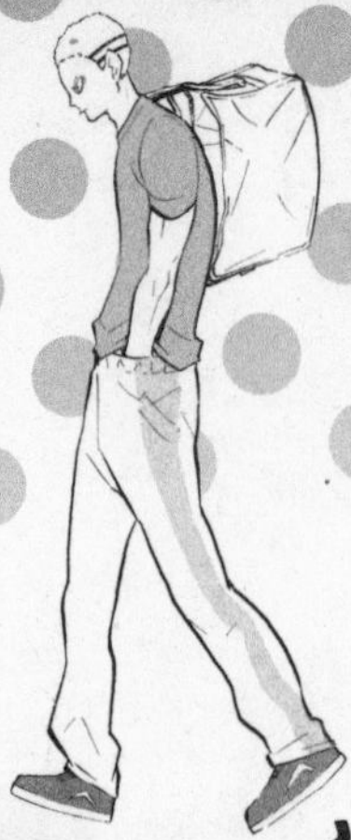

You're Reading the WRONG WAY!

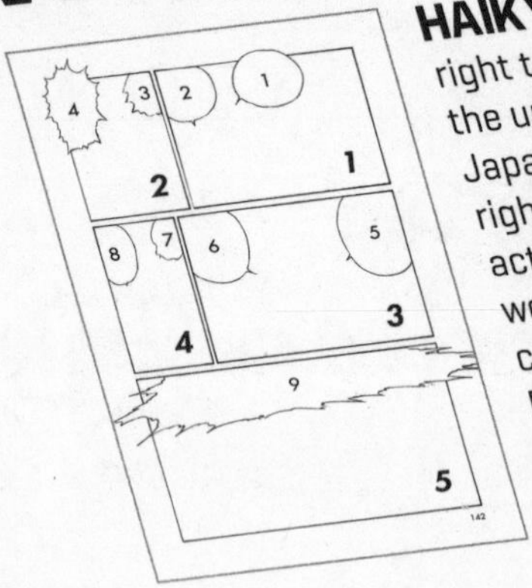

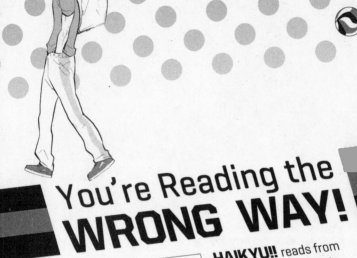

HAIKYU!! reads from right to left, starting in the upper-right corner. Japanese is read from right to left, meaning that action, sound effects and word-balloon order are completely reversed from English order.

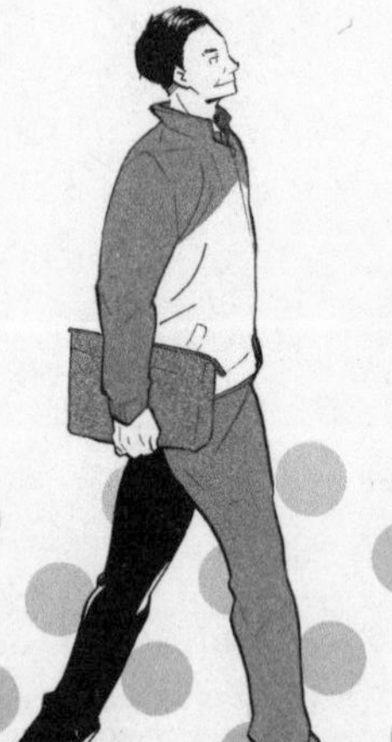